Clashing Views in

Childhood and Society

SEVENTH EDITION

TAKING SIDES

Clashing Views in

Childhood and Society

SEVENTH EDITION

Selected, Edited, and with Introductions by

Diana S. DelCampo
New Mexico State University

and

Robert L. DelCampo
New Mexico State University

**McGraw-Hill
Higher Education**

Boston   Burr Ridge, IL   Dubuque, IA   New York   San Francisco   St. Louis
Bangkok   Bogotá   Caracas   Kuala Lumpur   Lisbon   London   Madrid   Mexico City
Milan   Montreal   New Delhi   Santiago   Seoul   Singapore   Sydney   Taipei   Toronto

McGraw-Hill
Higher Education

TAKING SIDES: CLASHING VIEWS IN CHILDHOOD AND SOCIETY,
SEVENTH EDITION

Published by McGraw-Hill, a business unit of The McGraw-Hill Companies, Inc., 1221 Avenue of the Americas, New York, NY 10020. Copyright © 2008 by The McGraw-Hill Companies, Inc. All rights reserved. Previous edition(s) 1995–2006. No part of this publication may be reproduced or distributed in any form or by any means, or stored in a database or retrieval system, without the prior written consent of The McGraw-Hill Companies, Inc., including, but not limited to, in any network or other electronic storage or transmission, or broadcast for distance learning.

Some ancillaries, including electronic and print components, may not be available to customers outside the United States.

Taking Sides® is a registered trademark of the McGraw-Hill Companies, Inc.
Taking Sides is published by the **Contemporary Learning Series** group within the McGraw-Hill Higher Education division.

 This book is printed on recycled, acid-free paper containing 10% postconsumer waste.

1 2 3 4 5 6 7 8 9 0 DOC/DOC 0 9 8 7

MHID: 0-07-351513-2
ISBN: 978-0-07-351513-7
ISSN: 1094-7558

Managing Editor: *Larry Loeppke*
Production Manager: *Faye Schilling*
Senior Developmental Editor: *Jill Peter*
Editorial Assistant: *Nancy Meissner*
Production Service Assistant: *Rita Hingtgen*
Permissions Coordinator: *Lori Church*
Senior Marketing Manager: *Julie Keck*
Marketing Communications Specialist: *Mary Klein*
Marketing Coordinator: *Alice Link*
Project Manager: *Jane Mohr*
Design Specialist: *Tara McDermott*
Senior Administrative Assistant: *DeAnna Dausener*
Senior Operations Manager: *Pat Koch Krieger*
Cover Graphics: *Maggie Lytle*

Compositor: ICC Macmillan Inc.
Cover Image: Randy Allbritton/Getty Images

Library of Congress Cataloging-in-Publication Data

Main entry under title:
Taking sides: clashing views in childhood and society/selected, edited, and with introductions by Diana S. DelCampo and Robert L. DelCampo.—7th ed.

Includes bibliographical references and index.
1. Children—United States. 2. Child welfare—United States. I. DelCampo, Diana S., *comp.* II. DelCampo, Robert L., *comp.*
305.23

www.mhhe.com

Preface

Children are society's most valuable resource, and however clichéd that idea may be, there can be no doubt about the urgency of the issues confronting children today and the people who care for them and care about them. Each day we are bombarded with media reports on issues affecting children—complex issues related to child care, schooling, violence, morality, gangs, divorce; the list goes on. In this book we look at 17 of those controversial issues and ask you to think about them, perhaps for the first time, perhaps in ways you may not have previously considered.

For the student who likes to memorize facts and learn *the* right answer, the controversies in this book could be most unsettling! However, a good education should include the nurturing of your ability to think critically and to be an active learner. This book endeavors to put you on the path toward further developing these skills. As you read each side of an issue and grapple with the points made by the authors, you will be moved to consider the merits of each position. In the process, you may adopt the point of view of one side, or the other, or formulate an opinion completely your own on the issue. And when you attend class, you will be exposed to your classmates' and instructor's ideas on the issue as well. This may further challenge you to reconsider and defend your position, which is the essence of critical thinking and a primary purpose of this book.

Plan of the book *Taking Sides: Clashing Views in Childhood and Society,* seventh edition, is designed to be used for courses in child development, human development, or parenting. The issues can be studied consecutively or in any order, as each is designed to be independent of the other. We have included 17 issues encompassing 34 selections from a wide variety of sources and authors. Each unit of the book deals with one of four developmental phases of childhood: infancy, early childhood, middle childhood, and adolescence. Within each unit are issues related to aspects of child development at that stage. Each issue has an *introduction,* which provides some background about the controversy, briefly describes the authors, and gives a brief summary of the positions reflected in the issue. Each issue concludes with a *postscript,* which contains some final thoughts on the issue and offers a bibliography of related readings should you want to explore the topic further.

A listing of all the *contributors* to this volume is included at the back of the book to give you additional information on the scholars, practitioners, educators, policymakers, and social critics whose views are debated here.

Changes to this edition The seventh edition of *Taking Sides: Clashing Views in Childhood and Society* includes some important changes from the sixth edition. Two completely new issues have been added, and 4 previous issues have new selections. As a result, there are 10 new readings. The two new issues are

"Should the HPV Vaccination Be Mandatory for Girls in Later Childhood?" (Issue 14) and "Is the Internet a Safe Place for Teens to Explore?" (Issue 17).

Issue 4, "Do Federal Laws Make Transracial Adoptions More Commonplace?" has been renamed and has two new selections. Issue 16, "Is Abstinence-Only Sex Education the Best Way to Teach about Sex?" has a new title and one new source.

Issue 7, "Does Divorce Create Long-Term Negative Effects for Children?" has two new sources. Issue 8, "Is Viewing Television Violence Harmful for Children?" has one new source. Issue 15, "Should Children Who Are at Risk for Abuse Remain with Their Families?" has a new issue number.

In addition to changes in topics and selections, the *Internet References* page that precedes each part opener has been updated. For these pages, several relevant sites on the World Wide Web have been identified and annotated.

A word to the instructor An *Instructor's Resource Guide With Test Questions* (both multiple-choice and essay) is available through the publisher for the instructor using this volume of *Taking Sides*. A general guidebook, *Using Taking Sides in the Classroom*, which discusses methods and techniques for integrating the pro-con approach into any classroom setting, is also available. An online version of *Using Taking Sides in the Classroom* and a correspondence service for Taking Sides adopters can be found at http://www.mhcls.com/usingts.

Taking Sides: Clashing Views in Childhood and Society is only one title in the Taking Sides series. If you are interested in seeing the table of contents for any of the other titles, please visit the Taking Sides Web site at http://www.mhcls.com/takingsides/.

Acknowledgments We would like to thank Libby Pierce and Sharon Lewin for assisting with the seventh edition of the book.

We also want to extend warm thanks to Jill Peter, Senior Developmental Editor, McGraw-Hill Contemporary Learning Series.

We look forward to receiving feedback and comments on this seventh edition of *Taking Sides: Clashing Views in Childhood and Society* from both faculty and students who experience the book. We can be reached via the Internet (ddelcamp@nmsu.edu or rdelcamp@nmsu.edu), or you can write us in care of the Taking Sides series at McGraw-Hill Contemporary Learning Series.

Diana S. DelCampo
New Mexico State University

Robert L. DelCampo
New Mexico State University

Contents In Brief

Contents

Preface   v

Introduction   xv

Kyla Dunn, a former biotech researcher and now a reporter for PBS and CBS, details the six months that she spent with scientists inside the labs of Advanced Cell Technology (ACT), a group openly pursuing human cloning for medical purposes. Dunn outlines what the group hopes to accomplish through cloning, why the group believes that cloning is the best way to accomplish these goals, and the political and monetary trials that ACT faces. Robert A. Weinberg, a member of the Whitehead Institute for Biomedical Research and a biology professor at MIT, offers his concerns about what he calls the "cloning circus." Weinberg discusses the damage that many cloning groups have been doing to serious research and the impending dangers of reproductive cloning.

Ezra E. H. Griffith and Rachel L. Bergeron, formerly professors at Harvard Law School, suggest that there is a cultural preference for race matching in adoptions. As a result, federal statutory attempts to omit race as a factor in child placement decisions have not been effective. Elizabeth Bartholet, the Morris Wasserstein Professor of Law and faculty director of the Child Advocacy Program at the Harvard Law School, and Diane Schetky, clinical professor of psychiatry at the Maine Medical Center, state that the current law is clear and effective in prohibiting adoptions based on race. They suggest that in the future, the need for legislation in this area will diminish even further.

UNIT 2 EARLY CHILDHOOD 103

Columbia University researcher Elizabeth Thompson Gershoff analyzed results from 88 studies and concluded that corporal punishment negatively affected children's behavior. Among the 10 negative outcomes were increased child aggression, decreased quality of the parent-child relationship, and increased risk of abusing a child or spouse in adulthood. Diana Baumrind and Philip A. Cowan, researchers from the University of California-Berkeley, and Robert E. Larzelere, from the Nebraska Medical Center, refuted Gershoff's findings by questioning her definition of corporal punishment and analysis techniques of the 88 studies. They feel mild spankings, when appropriately administered, are useful in shaping children's behavior.

Professor of family social science W. J. Doherty, psychologist Edward F. Kouneski, and Martha F. Erickson, director of the University of Minnesota's Children, Youth and Family Consortium, explore the contextual influences on fathering and conclude that a quality marriage in the optimal context promotes responsible fathering. Professor of human development and family sciences Alexis J. Walker and Lori A. McGraw, 4-H program coordinator at Oregon State University, contend that there is no empirical evidence that children need active fathers in their lives.

Judith Wallerstein, Julia Lewis, and Sandra Blakeslee, authors of a long-term study on children of divorce, contend that children who experienced divorce carried the negative effects of post-divorce life into their adulthood. These children of divorce have difficulty developing trusting and intimate relationships with marriage partners. E. Mavis Hetherington, long-time researcher on children and divorce, and co-author John Kelly assert that children of divorce are mostly happy as adults. Although these children experienced unhappiness, they are able to develop normally and have successfully completed the tasks of young adulthood.

L. Rowell Huesmann, Jessica Moise-Titus, Cheryl-Lynn Podolski, and Leonard D. Eron, from the Research Center for Group Dynamics, Institute for Social Research at the University of Michigan, found that both males and females are more likely to develop violent behavior in adulthood as a result of watching violent TV shows in early childhood. Jib Fowles, a professor of communication at the University of Houston, asserts that although television violence has increased steadily, the violent crime rate has in fact decreased.

can be traced to the increased use of media. The Center for Science in the Public Interest, a consumer advocacy organization on nutrition and health, views the high-calorie, non-nutritious foods found in school vending machines as the culprit in the rise in childhood obesity rates.

Stephen Krashen, professor of education at the University of Southern California, contends that good bilingual education programs provide background knowledge of subject matter and literacy in the child's native language. Then, the program provides English input using English as a second language technique along with sheltered subject matter teaching in English. Krashen argues against assertions that immersion is more successful than bilingual education. Rosalie Pedalino Porter, director for the Institute for Research in English Acquisition and Development (READ), states that bilingual education is a failed endeavor. Porter cites drop-out rates and parental sentiment as evidence as to why bilingual education should be discontinued.

The National Adoption Information Clearinghouse (NAIC) presents facts regarding gay and lesbian adoptive parents. The NAIC gives current information on the background and laws regarding homosexual parenting, and confronts the issues and concerns many people have regarding homosexual adoption, including the idea that children are molested by homosexual parents. Dr. Paul Cameron, of the Family Research Institute, presents his case against allowing homosexuals to become parents—foster parents in particular. He mainly discusses case study information regarding the proclivity for homosexual parents to molest foster children.

Cynthia Dailard, a senior public policy associate for the Alan Guttmacher Institute, suggests that the HPV vaccine be administered to females as a school entry requirement. She believes the vaccine is safe and effective and therefore should be universally administered to young girls. The best way to ensure the vaccine is available to these girls is by enacting state laws or policies requiring children to be vaccinated before school or day care enrollment. Roni Rabin, a columnist for *The New York Times*, objects to making the HPV vaccine mandatory for girls. She agrees that the vaccine is a significant development for the health and safety of our children. However, she does not believe every girl should be required to be vaccinated because the vaccine is costly and can be managed through current, less costly procedures such as Pap smears.

UNIT 4   ADOLESCENCE   327

Lisa Kolb, a public information specialist, asserts that the family preservation model is the best way to help families in crisis. Family preservation keeps all the family members together in the home while helping the family solve its problems. Freelance writer Mary-Lou Weisman argues that orphanages and out-of-home placements are necessary for children whose parents abuse or neglect them. She maintains that society has an obligation to take children away from parents who are doing serious harm to them and that some children have their only real family experience when living in an institutional setting.

Robert Rector, who is a research fellow for the Heritage Foundation, and Melissa G. Pardue and Shannan Martin, policy analysts for the Heritage Foundation, argue that comprehensive sex education approaches are misleading because they do little to promote abstinence. Under the auspices of the Heritage Foundation, a conservative organization based in Washington, D.C., they present the results of a poll they conducted that sought to measure parental support for ideas taught in "abstinence-only" and "comprehensive sex education" programs. Advocates for Youth and the Sexuality Information and Education Council of the United States (SIECUS) promote comprehensive education about sexuality and advocate for the right of individuals to make responsible sexual choices. SIECUS compares abstinence-only sex education to comprehensive sex education and finds shortcomings regarding abstinence-only programs.

Michele Fleming and Debra Rickwood, professors at the University of
Canberra in Australia, contend that parents need to be vigilant about their
teens surfing the Web, but that it is generally a safe place and that the
prevalence of cyberpredators is overstated. Chang-Hoan Cho, assistant
professor at the University of Florida, and Hongsik John Cheon, assistant
professor at Frostburg State University, believe that the Web can be a
dangerous place for teens to explore. They conducted a study that found
that children are exposed to more negative Internet content than parents
expect. Factors that reduced children's exposure to negative Internet
content included parental interaction and family cohesion.

Introduction

Children in Society

Diana S. DelCampo
Robert L. DelCampo

Childhood can be a wondrous time when days are filled with play and new discoveries, nights provide rest and security, and dedicated, loving parents nurture their children and meet their needs. Some children do indeed experience the full joy of childhood; however, regretfully, there are other, more sobering scenarios: There are children who do not have nurturing adults to guide them, who go to bed hungry, and some who do not even have homes. Most typically, childhood experiences fall between these two extremes. So there is a wide variety of experiences that can impact the developing child, and larger social forces are at work as well. Ask yourself as you debate the issues in this book the extent to which society must collectively address and resolve them. This is a vital function of society because children are society's future.

In order to understand and appreciate children in contemporary society, it may be useful to briefly review how society's views of children have changed over time. Most child development texts review the history of adult perceptions of children in western European society. Would it surprise you to know that in ancient times children were sometimes killed as religious sacrifices and buried in the walls of buildings? People believed that this practice would strengthen a building's structure. Up until the fourth century, parents were legally allowed to kill their newborns if the children were not in good health at birth. They were also permitted to do away with a child if they already had too many children, if the child was female, or if the child was illegitimate. In 374 A.D., the Romans outlawed infanticide, hoping that this would end the killing. Since parents could no longer legally kill their children, unwanted infants began to be abandoned. This practice endured for over 1,000 years. It was not until the 1600s that child abandonment was outlawed throughout most of Europe.

During the seventeenth century, foundling homes were established to provide for the needs of unwanted children. During this period, children were considered to be miniature adults. They were dressed like adults and were expected to act as adults would act. By contemporary standards, parents took a rather casual attitude toward their children. This was probably due to the high child mortality rate at the time. Since parents thought it likely that their children would die in infancy or childhood, they did not get as emotionally close to their young children as parents typically do today. It was not until the end of the century that society began to look upon children as different from adults.

Early in the 1700s European societal attitudes about children underwent further change. Children were no longer considered to be miniature adults, and literature written specifically for children began to emerge. By the end of the century, children who went to school were grouped by age, reflecting an awareness of stages of growth. The eighteenth century also marked the rise of the systematic study of children, which centered around the moral development of children and child-rearing problems.

It was not until the beginning of the twentieth century that three distinct age groupings emerged in the study of human development: infancy through age four or five; childhood to late puberty or early adulthood; and adulthood. This time period also marked the beginnings of the distinct field of child study. Early child study emphasized descriptive accounts of individual children and was mainly concerned with aspects of physical growth. As the century progressed, the term *child study* was changed to *research in child development*. Mothering became an important concept in the study of early child development, and the psychological aspects of development began to be examined more rigorously. Today, in the twenty-first century, research in child development focuses on issues related to family systems and the larger social issues that affect child development.

Nature-Nurture Controversy

There are many things that impact individuals as they progress through the human life cycle. People, places, events, illnesses, education, success, failure—have you ever thought about the number of experiences each of us encounters in our lives? If one were to place all of the variables that influence human development into two general categories, those categories would be heredity and environment. As you may know, your genetic blueprint was determined at the moment of conception with chromosomes contributed by your father and mother. In a sense, for many of us, environment is also determined at the moment of conception. A good portion of the major elements of what makes up one's environment is often determined before a person is born. The society in which one will live, one's cultural and ethnic heritage, and one's family and subsequent socioeconomic status, for example, are usually predetermined for a child.

For this edition of *Taking Sides: Clashing Views in Childhood and Society*, we have selected articles that look at children in general and how they affect or are affected by the issues raised, rather than give you, the reader, clinical case examples of issues related to a certain child or children. For the purposes of this book, we make three assumptions: (1) When we discuss a child's environment, we are usually describing elements of the society in which a child is growing, developing, and otherwise being socialized; (2) all child development occurs within this social context; and (3) children cannot help but affect and be affected by the societal forces that surround them. In most university classes, students derive a certain sense of security in receiving definitions of terms that are used frequently in a given class. We offer the following one for *society*, which we have adapted from Richard J. Gelles's 1995 textbook *Contemporary Families*:

> Society is a collection of people who interact within socially structured relationships. The only way that societies can survive their original members

is by replacing them. These "replacements" are the children about whom the issues in this book are concerned.

Determining an appropriate group of societal issues and fitting them into the confines of only one work on children and society is a challenging task. Consider, for example, the diversity of contemporary society. We live in a sea of divergent and unique subcultures and ethnicities. Categorizing and describing the myriad values, customs, and belief systems of these groups could fill many volumes. In America and Canada, for example, there are many ethnic subgroups of citizens who are considered to be of Anglo descent, such as English, Irish, Italians, Polish, Germans, Greeks, Russians, and Scots. There are people of native descent, who are affiliated with scores of different tribes and subtribes. Some Canadian and American citizens trace their heritages to a variety of Asian countries, including China, Japan, Vietnam, Cambodia, Thailand, and the Philippines. Among blacks, there are those who trace their roots to the Caribbean region and those who identify with different regions of Africa.

In light of the above, it may be reasoned that there are really no "typical" children in society! Although there are strong arguments supporting similarities within each of these general groups, there is a wide array of subgroupings and differences in customs and beliefs. As a consequence, when reading a book such as this one, it is important to be mindful of the extent to which differences might exist for those who may be of another race, ethnicity, religion, or socioeconomic status than the target group of children about which a selection focuses. It would also be prudent to consider geographic locale—rural, urban, northeastern, southwestern—when considering the relevance of a given argument to a specific subgroup of children.

Children in Contemporary Society

It is worth understanding children's points of view as they are molded by society. It can be astonishing to take a step back and observe children as they undergo the socialization process in contemporary society. They come into the world totally helpless, unable to feed, care for, or protect themselves. As they grow and develop, children undertake the process of acquiring a sense of identity and learning the rules of the society in which they live. This process of socialization is fostered by many of the subsystems of society that provide prescriptions for behavior in particular areas of life. These subsystems include the family, the peer group, the school system, religion, and the media.

One important consideration is that up to about age five, children are oblivious to most racial, ethnic, religious, or socioeconomic differences. Typically, children can only realize differences in external appearance. One implication of this fact is that children can be much more amenable to learning and embracing a variety of cultural behaviors, attitudes, and even languages when they are young. Only as children move into middle childhood do they begin to recognize and understand other, more subtle differences. It is important to note that although young children may be oblivious to these differences, they are nonetheless impacted by them in the way they are socialized by their parents, families, and the significant others in their lives. This is done through

family rituals, traditions, and outings; religious ceremonies; types of food prepared in the home; location where children live; and things that are found in
the home, such as books, magazines, music, and so on.

Societal influences on children do not stop within the family system. As
children grow, other institutions in society, such as schools, the economy,
politics, and religion, expand their life experiences. Controversy arises as to
how children react to these experiences. Consider, for example, what happens
to children when both parents are employed outside the home. There are factions in our society who adamantly ascribe many of the problems associated
with children to the fact that many parents are overly involved with work at
the expense of time with their children. They contend that one parent (usually
the mother) should stay home with the children, especially when they are
young. Children who care for themselves after school and the quality of after-
school child care are also hotly contested, related issues.

Few readers of this book will be unfamiliar with the attacks on the mass
media for its portrayal of violence in movies, television programming, and
video games targeted at children. Again, researchers, clinicians, teachers, policymakers, and others fall on both sides of what should be done to address this.

As children move toward adolescence and become more independent,
concerns regarding identity, values, morals, and sexual behavior become
issues of controversy. Homosexuality, for example, which often is first evidenced by a person in adolescence, is considered by many to be a learned and
abhorrent form of sexual expression. Others believe that there are people who
are predisposed to homosexuality for reasons that are as yet unclear.

Events in contemporary society have a direct or indirect impact on children, despite attempts to protect them. Violence, inflation, war, poverty,
AIDS, racism, and new technology are just a few of the phenomena that shape
the society in which our children are socialized.

Researching Children

In finding answers to controversial topics, policymakers and the public alike
often look to research literature for clues. The typical college student might
think of researching a topic as going to the library or logging onto the Internet
and looking up information on a subject, reading that information, formulating
a conclusion or opinion about the topic, and writing a paper that conveys the
student's findings. This is not the type of research about which we are referring! The type of research that we refer to here is called empirical research. This
means that there is some question or group of interrelated questions to be
answered about a topic. Data are then collected relative to the topic, and this
typically sheds light on how one goes about answering the question.

Data collection in research on children is undertaken from a variety of
approaches. It could entail things like observing children at play in preschool or
interacting with their parents at home. This is called observing children in a
natural setting. With this method, observers must code behavior in the same
way each and every time it is seen. Most of the information we have today on
physical growth and developmental stages was acquired through observation by

child development pioneers such as Arnold Gessell and Louise Bates Ames. You can imagine how time-consuming this form of study must be.

Another type of data collection is called an experiment. Experimental researchers systematically control how certain things happen in a situation and then observe the results. In this type of research, an experimental group and a control group are chosen. Both groups are examined to determine that they are the same before the experiment begins. The experimental group then receives some kind of treatment, while the control group receives no treatment. Then tests are conducted to see what kind of change, if any, has occurred between the two groups.

Interviewing children with a structured set of questions or giving children a structured questionnaire on a given research topic are other ways of collecting data. Projective techniques, where children might reveal their first thoughts about a picture or word, is also a form of the interview method.

The study of children can be organized in a variety of ways. One is by stages. The parts of this book (infancy, early childhood, middle childhood, and adolescence) are one type of stage organization. Another way to organize research endeavors is by topics. Topics are usually organized within the context of social, emotional, intellectual, physical, creative, and even spiritual aspects of development.

The time frames used to gather data on children also varies. In longitudinal data collection, information is collected from the same subjects over a long period of time. For example, one could examine the effects of preschool education on performance in elementary school by following and testing the same children during the preschool years and all the way through the elementary years. Because this type of research can take years to complete, a shorter method, cross-sectional research, could be used. In the previous example, one group of preschoolers would be compared to a similar group of elementary school children in order to answer the research question.

There are ethical considerations in studying children that some other disciplines may not face. Children should never be manipulated or put in danger in designing an experiment to answer research questions. Similarly, experiments that would not be in a child's best interests should not be conducted. Studies of abuse and neglect, for example, rely on retrospective techniques in which children who have already been abused report what has previously happened to them. No ethical researcher would ever put children at risk in order to observe the effects of abuse on children. Because of these ethical constraints, it can be frustrating for a researcher to fully answer questions raised in a research project. Additionally, it may take years to demonstrate the effectiveness of intervention for a particular social problem. Consequently, research on children and resultant intervention initiatives rarely offer "quick fixes" to the problems of children and society.

Future Directions

The study of children in society can begin to offer solutions to many of the more pressing societal problems. Quality child care, parenting skills education, stress reduction, affordable housing, job training, and humane political policies are a few ideas for solutions to some of the controversies that will be raised in this book.

The imbalance between work and family in the United States has created problems in the economy as well as in the family system. Workers are expected to produce quality goods and services, but they receive little social support in raising their families. Employers must acknowledge the strain that workers feel as they are pulled between work and family responsibilities. Health insurance, family-friendly work policies, flexible work schedules, parental and dependent care leave, exercise facilities, quality child care and sick child care, on-site or nearby one-stop service centers with post offices, grocery stores, and dry cleaners would be ways of providing support for families in the workplace.

Schools contribute to the problems of child-care arrangements by keeping to an antiquated schedule that was first developed to meet the needs of the farm family. Years ago, schools were let out in the early afternoon and all summer so that children could help with the crops, livestock, and other farm-related chores before sunset. However, ours has been a predominantly industrial society for a large part of the twentieth century and into the twenty-first century. As a result, a different type of schedule is required. Many concerned families advocate activities for children after school and schools that are open all year long to match the schedules of workers. The economy has changed and families have changed; why have educational institutions remained static?

The majority of children somehow manage to grow and develop successfully in a variety of family forms, but the stressors on all families are constantly increasing, which may, in turn, decrease the likelihood of continued success. Parents worry that the cost of a college education will be more than they can afford; parents worry about their children and AIDS, violence, and drugs; parents are concerned that in adulthood their children will not be able to live as well as they have lived. Families need emotional support, and parents need opportunities to learn stress management and parenting skills.

Society can promote the optimal growth and development of its children by taking responsibility for them. There is an old saying, "It takes a village to raise a child." Our society can raise its children by establishing policies in schools, workplaces, and other institutions that reflect the importance of nurturing children.

Internet References . . .

Families and Work Institute

This Web site provides resources from the Families and Work Institute, which conducts policy research on issues related to the changing workforce and operates a national clearinghouse on work and family life.

http://www.familiesandwork.org

Human Cloning Foundation

The Human Cloning Foundation is one of the strongest proponents of human cloning. This Web site includes information on essays, books, reviews, and personalities advocating human cloning.

http://www.humancloning.org

The National Parent Information Network (NPIN)

The National Parent Information Network contains resources related to many of the controversial issues faced by parents raising children in contemporary society. In addition to articles and resources, discussion groups are available.

http://npin.org

Zero to Three: National Center for Infants, Toddlers, and Families

Zero to Three: National Center for Infants, Toddlers, and Families is a national organization dedicated solely to infants, toddlers, and their families. It is headed by recognized experts in the field and provides technical assistance to communities, states, and the federal government. The site provides information that the organization gathers and disseminates through its publications.

http://www.zerotothree.org

The Future of Children

The Future of Children is a publication of The Woodrow Wilson School of Public and International Affairs at Princeton University and The Brookings Institution. The Future of Children Web site provides research and analysis that promotes effective policies and programs for children.

http://www.futureofchildren.org

American Academy of Pediatrics (AAP)

The American Academy of Pediatrics (AAP) and its member pediatricians dedicate their efforts and resources to the health, safety, and well-being of infants, children, adolescents, and young adults.

http://www.aap.org

Infancy

*I*nfancy and toddlerhood encompass the time period from birth to age two or three. During this time, the most dramatic growth of a child's life takes place. Traditionally, much of the literature on infancy has dealt with the physical aspects of development; more recently, however, researchers, practitioners, and policymakers have begun to be concerned with the interaction of brain development on later learning and the social and emotional aspects of the infant's development. The issues examined in this section focus on how the family and social institutions influence children's development from the time they are born.

- Is Institutional Child Care Beneficial to Children?

- Does Maternal Employment Have Negative Effects on Children's Development?

- Should Scientists Be Allowed to Clone Children?

- Do Federal Laws Make Transracial Adoptions More Commonplace?

ISSUE 1

Is Institutional Child Care Beneficial to Children?

YES: Greg Parks, from "The High/Scope Perry Preschool Project," *Juvenile Justice Bulletin* (October 2000)

NO: T. Berry Brazelton and Stanley I. Greenspan, from *The Irreducible Needs of Children: What Every Child Must Have to Grow, Learn, and Flourish* (Perseus, 2000)

ISSUE SUMMARY

YES: Greg Parks, an intern program specialist at the Office of Juvenile Justice and Delinquency Prevention, details the results of the Perry Preschool Project. Parks contends that evaluations of the program show significant benefits in adulthood for the children who attended the preschool.

NO: Pediatrician T. Berry Brazelton and Stanley I. Greenspan, clinical professor of psychiatry and pediatrics at George Washington University Medical School, question the practice by many families of placing their children into the institutional settings of child-care centers.

Increasingly, parents are placing their children in some kind of child care during the day so that they are free to work to support the family economically. This is true not only for single parents but also for parents in a two-parent household who must work in order to live even modestly. In the past, the majority of children in child care were cared for in a family setting by a relative or a home day care with a few children. Today, many families have no relatives close by to whom they can turn for help. In addition, mothers used to take as much time as possible after the birth of a baby to stay at home during a large part of the child's infancy. Things have changed; many women return to work within six weeks of giving birth and, when faced with choices for child care, find that they must place their infant in an institutional or chain-type day care facility.

These day care centers usually serve children of varying ages, from infancy to four or five years of age, and often have after-school programs for elementary school children. These centers often have many rooms and are housed in a large building with as many as 20 caregivers. Child-caregivers must meet licensing standards, but because of the low pay and no benefits, the child-care industry is plagued with a high turnover rate. Thus, caregivers might change many times during a child's stay, depending upon the center's pay structure and the administration's philosophy of quality care. These types of centers look somewhat institutional because of their large building size, numerous rooms, and large number of personnel. Many object to the institutional-type child-care centers because they do not have the home-type atmosphere that one usually associates with the care of very young children.

What is a parent to do? Parents must work to support their families, and they must find a safe place to leave their children. Is a large institutional-like setting appropriate for infants and toddlers who need the security of a close, warm environment? Will these young children be harmed by having several caregivers within a week, or is institutional child care the best environment for children? This is the dilemma discussed in the following two selections. T. Berry Brazelton and Stanley I. Greenspan, long respected in the world of child development, voice their concerns about America's youngest children being enrolled in day care at an alarmingly high rate. In contrast, the Perry Preschool Project results, which are detailed by Greg Parks, indicate that child care is beneficial for children. Longitudinal data from the Perry Preschool Project span over 40 years and show the program to have been beneficial for the children who attended the center.

YES

The High/Scope Perry Preschool Project

The Office of Juvenile Justice and Delinquency Prevention (OJJDP) recently published *Costs and Benefits of Early Childhood Intervention* (Greenwood, 1999), a Fact Sheet reviewing the benefits of early childhood intervention in the prevention of later delinquency. Among the most notable and longstanding secondary prevention programs considered was the High/Scope Perry Preschool Project of Ypsilanti, MI.[1] This [selection] examines this successful program model, which demonstrates a potential link between early childhood intervention and delinquency prevention.

The High/Scope Perry Preschool Project is a well-established early childhood intervention that has been in operation for almost 40 years. A review of the program's findings is useful at this time in light of the field's growing knowledge of risk factors associated with juvenile delinquency, including early childhood risk factors that may be diminished by secondary prevention programs targeted at high-risk populations. Juvenile justice research has made great strides in identifying risk factors that may be precursors to delinquency. Although the problem of delinquency increases with the number of risk factors, specific risk factors appear to vary according to a child's stage of development and may be reduced with appropriate preventive measures. These developmental differences for risk factors indicate the need for targeted interventions that address specific age-related factors (Wasserman and Miller, 1998). Given this link between early risk factors and later delinquency, it is important for practitioners to plan intervention programs for high-risk youth early in a youth's life so that he or she can develop a strong foundation for later development.

Background

The High/Scope Perry Preschool Project, which began in 1962, is the focus of an ongoing longitudinal study—conducted by the High/Scope Educational Research Foundation—of 123 high-risk African American children.[2] Participants were of low socioeconomic status, had low IQ scores (between 70 and 85, the range for borderline mental impairment) with no organic deficiencies (i.e., biologically based mental impairment), and were at high risk of failing school. Fifty-eight of these 3- and 4-year-old children were assigned to the

From Greg Parks, "The High/Scope Perry Preschool Project," *Juvenile Justice Bulletin,* a publication of The Office of Juvenile Justice and Delinquency Prevention (October 2000). References omitted.

program group, and 65 of these children were assigned to a control group that did not go through the program. The groups were matched according to age, IQ, socioeconomic status, and gender. There were no differences between the groups with regard to father absence, parent education level, family size, household density, or birth order. Researchers collected followup data annually when the children were between ages 4 and 11 and at ages 14, 15, and 19 and collected age 27 data from 1986 to 1991 (Schweinhart, Barnes, and Weikart, 1993; Schweinhart and Weikart, 1995).[3]

The High/Scope Perry Preschool Project's high-quality educational approach is based on an active learning model that emphasizes participants' intellectual and social development. Children attended the preschool Monday through Friday for 2.5 hours per day over a 2-year period. During that same period, a staff-to-child ratio of one adult for every five or six children enabled teachers to visit each child's family in their home for 1.5 hours each week. In addition, parents participated in monthly small group meetings with other parents, facilitated by program staff.

Although it was initiated as an educational intervention, the High/Scope Perry Preschool Project has demonstrated a number of other positive outcomes, including a significantly lower rate of crime and delinquency and lower incidence of teenage pregnancy and welfare dependency. Overall, the program group has demonstrated significantly higher rates of prosocial behavior, academic achievement, employment, income, and family stability as compared with the control group. The success of this and similar programs demonstrates intervention and delinquency prevention in terms of both social outcome and cost-effectiveness and has a number of useful implications for policy, practice, and ongoing research. This Bulletin reviews the program outcomes, describes the early childhood risk factors that can be targeted with intervention, and explores the relationship between program components and risk factors.

Program Outcomes

Outcomes of the High/Scope Perry Preschool longitudinal study can be divided into three major categories: social responsibility, scholastic success, and socioeconomic success (Schweinhart et al., 1985). Social responsibility variables include delinquency, marital status, and pregnancy. Scholastic success is determined by a number of factors including graduation rate, grade point average, and postsecondary education, whereas socioeconomic success is measured in terms of employment, earnings, and welfare assistance. Cost-benefit is included as an additional outcome because of the long-term savings to society as a result of program success.

Social Responsibility

Delinquency   Data collected from police and court records show that juvenile delinquency was significantly lower for the High/Scope Perry Preschool program group as compared with the control group, including fewer arrests and fewer juvenile court petitions (Schweinhart, Barnes, and Weikart, 1993; Schweinhart and Weikart, 1995). Only 31 percent of the program group had ever been arrested, compared with 51 percent of the control group. In addition to police and court records, data collected from respondents at age 19 were used as an overall indicator of delinquency. When study participants were 19 years old, researchers found significant differences between the program and control groups. The program group had fewer arrests overall than the control group (averages of 1.3 versus 2.3 arrests per person), fewer felony arrests (averages of 0.7 versus 2.0 arrests per person), and fewer juvenile court petitions filed (averages of 0.2 versus 0.4 petitions per person).

Like the criminal record data, a misconduct scale based on teacher-report data and self-report data from the 19-year-old respondents demonstrates a significant difference between the program and control groups, as reflected by the following results for the program group:

- Lower overall scores for total misconduct and serious misconduct at ages 15 and 19.
- Lower incidence of fighting and other violent behavior.
- Lower incidence of property damage.
- Fewer police contacts.

Data collected from respondents at age 27 indicate significant differences between the program group and control group for adult arrests: the control group underwent more than twice as many arrests as the program group (averages of 4.0 versus 1.8 arrests per person). Thirty-six percent of the control group accounted for 98 felony arrests between ages 19 and 27, while 27 percent of the program group accounted for 40 felony arrests during the same period. Thirty-five percent of the control group were considered frequent offenders (defined as five or more arrests), compared with only 7 percent of the program group. In addition, 25 percent of the control group had been arrested for drug-related offenses, versus 7 percent of the program group. The control group also averaged more months on probation (6.6 versus 3.2 months) and had more than twice as many of its members placed on probation or parole for longer than 18 months (20 percent versus 9 percent).

Marital status and pregnancy   Marital status among the males was the same for both groups, with 26 percent married at age 27, although program group males, on average, had been married for a longer period (6.2 versus 3.3 years). Marital status among the females differed significantly, with 40 percent of program group females married, compared with 8 percent of the control group females. Although fewer females in the program group were parents (64 percent versus 75 percent), significantly more of them were married, cohabiting parents (28 percent versus 8 percent). Fifty-seven percent of mothers in the program group gave birth out of wedlock, compared with 83 percent of mothers in the control group. In measures related to family stability, the program group scored significantly higher on a measure of closeness to family and friends (66 percent versus 48 percent) and the ability to maintain persistence at tasks (i.e., work or study hard all day) (47 percent versus 33 percent).

Scholastic Success

Participants in the High/Scope Perry Preschool study were characterized by better academic performance than those in the control group, as measured by higher graduation rates, better grades, higher standardized test scores, and fewer instances of placement in special education classes. In addition, the program group spent more time on homework and demonstrated more positive attitudes toward school at ages 15 and 19. More parents of program group members had positive attitudes regarding their children's educational experiences and were hopeful that their children would obtain college degrees. The program group demonstrated significant academic differences in the following areas:

- **Special education for mental impairment.** Only 15 percent of the program group had been placed in special education programs for mental impairment, compared with 34 percent of the control group.
- **Test scores.** Each year from ages 7 to 14, the mean achievement test scores of the program group were noticeably higher than those of the control group (an average difference of 16 percent). The difference in the final achievement test scores of the two groups at age 14 was particularly significant: the program group's scores were 29 percent higher than those of the control group.
- **Grade point average.** The mean high school grade point average of the program group was higher than that of the control group (2.09 versus 1.68).
- **Graduation from high school.** Seventy-one percent of the program group graduated from high school, compared with 54 percent of the control group. The difference was largely accounted for by graduation rates among females (84 percent and 35 percent, respectively).

Socioeconomic Success

Data collected at ages 19 and 27 indicate that the program group has been more successful socioeconomically than the control group. The data for age 19 reveal that significantly more program group members were employed (50 percent versus 32 percent) and self-reporting (45 percent versus 25 percent). These data also reflect that fewer program group members received welfare assistance (18 percent versus 32 percent). The data for age 27 reveal a continuation of significant economic differences characterized by more economic stability among the program group members, as measured by the following indicators:

- **Public assistance.** Fifteen percent of the program group were receiving public assistance, versus 32 percent of the control group.
- **Monthly earnings.** Twenty-nine percent of the program group had monthly earnings of $2,000 or more, versus 7 percent of the control group (36 percent versus 11 percent, respectively, when comparing only employed members in each group).
- **Household earnings.** When the income of the spouses of the study participants was taken into account, 47 percent of the program group had household income earnings of $3,000 or more per month, versus 17 percent of the control group.

- **Home ownership.** Thirty-six percent of the program group owned a home, versus 13 percent of the control group.
- **Automobile ownership.** Thirty percent of the program group owned a second car, versus 13 percent of the control group.

Cost-Benefit Analysis

A cost-benefit analysis of the High/Scope Perry Preschool study indicates a savings to the public of more than seven times the initial investment per child, with a return of $7.16 for every dollar spent (Barnett, 1983). When adjusted for inflation and a 3-percent discount rate, the investment in early childhood prevention resulted in a taxpayer return of $88,433 per child from the following sources:

- Savings in welfare assistance (prior to welfare reform).
- Savings in special education.
- Savings to the criminal justice system.
- Savings to crime victims.
- Increased tax revenue from higher earnings.

An independent reanalysis is provided in a recent RAND Corporation report (Karoly et al., 1998). This report found that eliminating the largest and least reliable savings category (savings to crime victims) still left a return of more than twice the initial investment. Savings to crime victims make up 65 percent of the total investment return in the earlier analysis (Barnett, 1993). Although victim savings should be considered a significant outcome and societal benefit of early childhood intervention, this factor is also distinct from the other factors that can be estimated based on direct governmental costs and savings. With victim savings factored out of the analysis, the largest savings category is in criminal justice costs (40 percent), followed by increased taxable revenue (26 percent), reduced educational services (25 percent), and reduced welfare costs (9 percent).

Early Childhood Risk Factors for Delinquency

An understanding of early childhood risk factors for delinquency is helpful to interpreting the success of the High/Scope Perry Preschool Project. One factor identified with risk for delinquency is poor language skills. (Stattin and Klackenberg-Larsson, 1993). As a component of overall mental development, language functions as an indicator of later intelligence and is a critical factor in the relationship between intelligence and delinquency. Additional early risk factors include poor attachment to caregivers (Egeland and Farber, 1984; Shaw and Bell, 1993), poor parenting skills (Hawkins et al., 1998; Loeber and Stouthamer-Loeber, 1986), and multiple family stressors (Fergusson and Lynskey, 1996; Shaw et al., 1998). These risk factors may not only directly affect delinquency but may also indirectly influence other factors that interact with delinquency, such as school- and community-related risk factors.

As demonstrated in the Prenatal and Early Childhood Nurse Home Visitation Program supported by OJJDP (Olds, Hill, and Rumsey, 1998), prenatal and early postnatal prevention are shown to reduce risk factors that contribute to the development of antisocial behavior in childhood. Early childhood intervention during the preschool years also offers an opportunity to halt the developmental trajectory toward delinquency and related behavioral disorders. Family support services help develop parenting skills, attachment, and coping mechanisms that have a positive effect on family stressors. A multicomponent approach to enhancing child development promotes protective factors and reduces risk factors by addressing the many systems and influences that affect a child's development.

Program Components and Related Risk Factors for Delinquency

The components of the High/Scope Perry Preschool Project affect a number of the early childhood risk factors associated with later delinquency and other behavioral problems. In addition to directly reinforcing early developmental processes in the educational setting, the program strengthens positive parenting skills.

The High/Scope Educational Research Foundation explains the effectiveness of the High/Scope Perry Preschool model in terms of empowerment, which includes developing skills for success by enabling children to be active and independent learners, helping parents to support the development of their children, and providing teachers with effective training and support (Schweinhart and Weikart, 1995).

Because an ongoing home-school relationship enhances socialization, involving parents early in the educational process is critical to the later success of participants in an early childhood intervention such as High/Scope Perry Preschool (Seitz, 1990). Weekly home visits by teachers and regular parent group meetings promote the strengthening of parent-child relationships and increase parent involvement in the educational process. A more recent OJJDP longitudinal study, the Rochester Youth Development Study (Thornberry et al., 1998), confirmed a significant relationship between parents' involvement in their children's lives and reduced delinquency.

In addition to enhancing parent attachment, parent involvement, and parenting skills, early childhood intervention aimed at both parents and children influences a child's attachment to school and later commitment to school success (Thornberry et al., 1998). Findings from the Rochester study confirm earlier research linking poor school attachment, commitment, and achievement to delinquent behavior and drug use (Krohn et al., 1995; Smith et al., 1995). Another OJJDP study, the Seattle Social Development Project (Hill et al., 1999), found that a lack of success in elementary school was linked to later gang membership. Even in the midst of multiple other factors placing youth at high risk for delinquency, school success (as indicated by higher standardized test scores, school commitment, attachment to teachers, college aspirations, and parent expectations) appears to be a protective factor against delinquency (Smith et al., 1995). Academic achievement outcomes of the High/Scope Perry Preschool study indicate that the program group was more successful than the control group in school-related factors that appear to protect against delinquency.

The positive outcomes of the High/Scope Perry Preschool study are the result of a cumulative effect that begins with increased school readiness (Berrueta-Clement et al., 1987; Zigler, Taussig, and Black, 1992). School readiness results in positive reinforcement from teachers in the early grades followed by enhanced academic performance in subsequent grades and an overall stronger commitment to school. A correlational analysis of the High/Scope Perry Preschool data reveals a strong association between school motivation in the early years and literacy scores at age 19 (Schweinhart, Barnes, and Weikart, 1993). School motivation is also higher correlated with the highest year of schooling completed, which is associated with higher monthly earnings in adulthood and fewer lifetime arrests.

Program and Policy Implications

The outcomes of the High/Scope Perry Preschool study demonstrate the value of prevention and early intervention efforts in promoting protective factors that reduce delinquency. The program was developed for high-risk children who stood to benefit the most from such an intervention. The intervention also affected multiple risk factors and was carried out in multiple domains (i.e., home and school). In an extensive review of early childhood interventions, Yoshikawa (1995) concluded that the combination of an early educational component with family support, as exemplified by the High/Scope Perry Preschool Project, is a determining factor in long-term effects on antisocial behavior. Other combination programs that have demonstrated long-term effects on delinquency include the Yale Child Welfare Project (Seitz and Apfel, 1994), Houston Parent Child Development Center (Johnson and Walker, 1987), and Syracuse Family Development Research Program (Lally, Mangione, and Honig, 1988). Single-component models, such as those that address only educational factors, have not been shown to demonstrate significant results.

In addition to the need to target appropriate populations and address multiple risk factors in multiple domains, program quality is essential to success. The High/Scope Perry Preschool model is based on a high-quality educational approach that assumes a low staff-to-child ratio, an active learning curriculum, and a home visitation component that engages parents in the educational process. Furthermore, teachers are well educated, adequately compensated, and well supported in their tasks.

Head Start, perhaps the largest and best-known early childhood intervention program, has recently made efforts to expand and improve its effectiveness by emphasizing family support, staff training, and performance standards (U.S. Department of Health and Human Services, 1999). The 1994 legislation reauthorizing Head Start incorporated a number of recommendations from the Advisory Committee on Head Start Quality and Expansion (1993), including increased parent involvement, a lower staff-to-child ratio, and increased mental health services.[4] Head Start has increased the emphasis on curriculum and child outcomes as a result of this reauthorization and has formed

Head Start Quality Research Centers to respond to the need for additional research in the area of early childhood intervention. Further research is clearly needed to build on the limited existing knowledge base and assess the effectiveness of programs across various demographic groups, risk factors, and co-occurring factors that are related to delinquency, such as mental health issues and substance abuse (Yoshikawa, 1995).

Although the High/Scope Perry Preschool study's sample size was small in proportion to its eventual influence, its strong experimental design has contributed to its prominence in the field of early childhood education. Subsequent early childhood research that is carefully controlled and longitudinal in design remains limited. The limited research involving similar models that combine educational and family support components, however, supports the positive outcomes of the High/Scope Perry Preschool model. Subsequent independent evaluations of the programs that have implemented the High/Scope model have rated those programs significantly higher than comparison programs, with 58 percent of High/Scope programs versus 40 percent of comparison programs being rated as high quality (Epstein, 1993). In addition, 72 percent of children in High/Scope programs versus 57 percent of children in comparison programs scored high on measures of emotional, social, cognitive, and motor development.

Some targeted, multicomponent early childhood interventions have been demonstrated to exceed their costs in eventual savings and benefit to the public. However, implementing an effective prevention strategy requires a commitment to provide empirically based quality programming and to invest the up-front resources that will result in long-term savings and positive social change in the lives of children and families. The High/Scope Perry Preschool Project provides one such model for early childhood intervention that has proven successful when executed with quality and commitment to long-term results. The complexity of juvenile delinquency requires multiple strategies that address the problem at various stages of development; early childhood intervention is one promising component in the context of a more comprehensive approach, as recommended in OJJDP's *Comprehensive Strategy for Serious, Violent, and Chronic Juvenile Offenders* (Wilson and Howell, 1993). The High/Scope Perry Preschool model is worthy of consideration as an effective early childhood intervention as communities attempt to implement a comprehensive strategy that includes prevention, intervention, and graduated sanctions (Howell, 1995; Wilson and Howell, 1993).

Notes

1. Unlike primary prevention programs, which are directed at the general population, secondary prevention programs target children at risk for school failure or delinquency.

2. The original Perry Preschool no longer exists, but the High/Scope Educational Research Foundation—founded in 1970 by Perry Preschool researcher David Weikart—continues to collect followup data from the participants of the 1962 study. The foundation is an independent organization dedicated to nonprofit research, development, training, and public advocacy. Its principal goals are to promote the learning and development of children worldwide from

infancy through adolescence and to support and train educators and parents as they help children learn. In a High/Scope program, students should learn through active involvement with materials, events, and ideas. The Foundation disseminates the High/Scope Preschool model worldwide.

3. Researchers are currently collecting followup data from the original program participants. Called the High/Scope Perry Preschool Midlife Study, researchers have already interviewed 30 of the 39- to 41-year-old participants. The interview emphasized health and the performance of the program participants' children. The researchers expect to complete the data collection by the end of 2001. This study is funded by the McCormick Tribune Foundation in Chicago, IL.

4. Head Start Act Amendments of 1994. Pub. L. No. 103–252, tit. 1 § 108, Stat. 624 (1994).

when all the mothers were there. After a while, only one mother was left and all the children gravitated to her. I turned to the very talented day-care people there and said, "They really seem to desert you, don't they?" They said, "When there's a mother here, we don't even exist." The children were already differentiating among caregivers. It doesn't even have to be their mother; it just has to be a mother.

SIG: That's not so great. In a number of day-care centers, when the children are mobile, I see a lot of emotionally hungry children. Children come up to any new adult and hang on. Some of that reaching out for any mother is simply reaching out to anyone who will give them some attention. It's a little indiscriminate. We see that in institutions such as orphanages where there is emotional deprivation. A minute here and there of reciprocal interaction, sometimes around feeding or diapering, is not enough to provide the needed security and sense of being cared for.

If we are going to give parents flexible options, we need both to improve day care and to reduce the number of hours per week children spend in day-care situations.

TBB: Again, I think it needs to be a case-by-case decision, weighing this or that, rather than simply telling people what to do. Some parents are better parents if there is an outlet for them. But we do need to provide the child with an optimal secondary caregiver.

SIG: When I talk to college students, I often ask them how they see their lives in terms of having children. As they think about a career and getting married, are they taking into account child-rearing, as well as the demands of a profession? Are they engaged to a neurosurgeon or are they going to be neurosurgeons themselves? Are they planning on having several children? Having two neurosurgeons in the family along with four children may be more difficult and demanding than they can possibly imagine. On the other hand, if two people are getting married and both want careers, and one of them is a writer and the other a psychologist, they may have more control of their time. Each one could work two-thirds time or one could work halftime and they could get child care for the limited remaining hours. But a lot of these potential parents haven't thought this out. They want children and a good career and see no problem. What they're being led to believe now is that full-time day care in the first years of life is as good as if not better than what they can provide: "I'll have a baby, take a two month leave of absence, put the baby in day care, and I'll be a lawyer and my spouse will be a lawyer. We'll work until 8:00 at night. We'll pick up the baby, come home, and play for an hour." In families like this I see children not getting their basic needs for nurturing met.

TBB: When I see a family like that I see a lot of grieving. That kind of treatment of the child is ignoring the child's interests to such an extent that there must be a lot of denial. Something is so painful that these parents have to hide behind defenses.

SIG: But do we support this type of denial or help parents out of it? As new parents make their decisions early on, some parents intuitively plan for the flexibility to be home more; sometimes it's the mom and sometimes it's the dad who stays home. The parents who are more ambivalent and tend to use denial often look around for guidance. But they're getting a lot of misinformation. They're told it doesn't make a difference. If parents-to-be knew more about this need for a continuous, close relationship, they might plan more realistically. They would see how hard it is to have such relationships with two full-time jobs and full-time day care. If parents see the options, they could make choices. If they have a caregiver at home and pick well, they have a greater likelihood, if they can afford it, of having the same caregiver being with them for a number of years. In day care, by design, the caregivers change each year. Turnover is so great, though, that there may be another change or two changes even within one year. There may be three changes of caregivers by the time a baby has had a year of day care. Minimum wages, lack of training, and so on contribute to this. The caregiver in a day-care setting is not like a *meta peleth* in a kibbutz in Israel, who is a stable person in a child's life, with him for four or five years. It doesn't have to be the mother. It could be the father or the grandfather or grandmother. The child needs a caregiver in his or her life who's going to be there for the long haul.

TBB: To improve day care, I see three babies per adult as the absolute maximum for the first year of life. But now the norm is four babies per caregiver. Imagine a mother with triplets and how hard it is for her to care for all three babies at the same time.

SIG: Would you recommend, Berry, that a baby should keep the same caregivers for the first three or four years? One group of caregivers, for example, would follow a group of children who started as infants on up through their toddler years.

TBB: This would work as long as the caregiver really liked each baby, but suppose she didn't like one? Couldn't it be moved to another caregiver's group? Caregivers and babies, like parents, could be evaluated for "goodness of fit" between them. Also, when you go up into the second and third years, and taking care of four children becomes possible, a fourth child will be added to the group of three. The fourth baby wouldn't necessarily get the same caregivers.

SIG: The extra children in the group might come from outside, perhaps from home. To make this work, you'd have to have expanding entry into day care at the second and third years, with each class being larger than the last. More children are in day care by age three than in the first two years of life. Then we have to create incentives for the staff of day-care centers to stay on, giving better wages and training.

TBB: We have to increase wages to a decent level, and we need to improve their status. At present, they are thought of as "baby-sitters" with some scorn.

SIG: That's what we need to correct. We need to get across all that's involved in meaningful care of a child: creating ongoing dialogues, reflecting and accepting a variety of emotions. You can sometimes find people who are warm and nourishing and emotionally responsive, even though they haven't been given a chance to educate themselves. Sometimes you can find young people who want to get experience with children and who are naturally sensitive and flexible.

TBB: Day-care staff need constant refueling. It's a demanding job, taking care of somebody else's children. If parents and day-care personnel could handle their natural, inevitable gatekeeping, parents could become peer "fuelers" of the day-care personnel. The team (of parents and child care worker) could share the child's optimal development.

SIG: We need to see all this from the point of view of prevention. It's a public health issue.

TBB: When Congress was talking about that $22 billion for improving child care, I got a chance to go down to Washington, and told them that if they just turn the money over to the states, it will all get eaten up. You'd do better to give the money to states tied to choices based on the quality child care that we know how to produce, and to let them pick their choices. When it came to laying out choices that will work for the child, they said, "Oh, we have to do some research." I told them there was already plenty of research. What we need now is just the will to put the research into practice. They asked if I could tell them what programs work. I said not by myself, but I certainly could gather a bunch of colleagues who could tell you which ones we guarantee would work.

State governments can eat up revenues for child care at the top, if we're not careful. The one sector that could make a real difference and could afford to, and might be motivated to if we were smart enough, would be big business. If we could get them to set up a center in every business site that would contain preventive health care, child care, after-school care, and elder care, then maybe we could begin to reach a lot of people. I don't think we need to use the schools for this, but Ed Zigler at Yale has a model he calls the "School of the 21st Century," in which all these caregiving situations are gathered into school buildings that are not in use and made into centers for families in their communities. In our Touchpoints model, we are recommending that parent centers be established in every community where parents could receive child care, preventive health care, after-school care, and elder care. Parent resource centers, such as Family Support America, could be established for peer resources. Parents could then begin to feel a sense of community around them.

Our Touchpoints model has been developed at Children's Hospital in Boston to train multidisciplinary representatives from communities that are ready for change in an outreach, relational model. We want to improve preventive health care and child care with several goals. At each visit of parents and child, the provider (child care or medical care) identifies the strengths versus the failures of the parent. The child's development is the language between professional and parent. The parent is valued as the expert in the child's development. In this way, the passion of the parent is fostered. The relationship is transactional versus top-down. Each visit becomes an opportunity for sharing the child's new achievements and encouraging the child's development, both physical and psychological. Twenty-five centers have espoused our ideas, and they are changing communities to become parent-friendly. Our goal is to offer preventive outreach for the present 40 percent of underserved. We do know what to do. Can we do it? . . .

Relationships in Day Care

It is also important to consider now how these same principles can be applied to other contexts where children may find themselves such as family day care, makeshift baby-sitting arrangements, as well as institutional day care settings and care by relatives. These same standards for the nurturing care of children growing up in families apply to these other settings. In other words, a child in family day care or day care center should spend most of her time in facilitated activities or direct one-to-one interactions. However, in observations of day-care settings we found it rare that there were long interactive sequences between the caregivers and the babies.

Since it is so hard for caregivers to have long, nurturing interactions when caring for four or more babies (standard in most institutional day care), and because of the staff turnover that is characteristic of most institutional day-care settings, as well as the tendency to have staff change each year as children move from the infant room to the toddler room to the preschool room, we believe that in the first two years of life full-time day care is a difficult context in which to provide the ongoing, nurturing care by one or a few caregivers that the child requires. Part-time day care, on the other hand, may be quite helpful in giving mothers and fathers a chance to do other things and may not compromise either the security of ongoing nurturing care or the types of experiences we have described. But 35-plus hours a week for infants and toddlers makes it very difficult to have the consistency of caregiver and the depth of nurturance required, or the amount of facilitating interaction with the environment or direct interaction that we believe is healthy for infants and toddlers.

Because some families will need full-time day care in the early years, we must work to improve its quality. This means lower child/caregiver ratios, better training and salaries and maintaining the same caregiver from birth to roughly age 3. Although there is general agreement on the need to improve day care, improvements in the last 25 years have been modest. As we pointed out earlier, studies of the quality of available day care are not optimistic. We may be trying to rationalize a system that simply isn't providing the essentials of what children need. It may therefore be best to reconsider our assumptions. The best way these assumptions can be reconsidered is by each and every family having good and accurate information. With awareness we believe most will make a wise and enlightened choice.

Recommendations

In making the recommendations that follow, we are both mindful of the fact that there are many circumstances where nonparental care may be highly desirable or absolutely necessary. Single parents working to put food on the table, even if able to provide high-quality care themselves, may have no choice but to use out-of-home child care for 40-plus hours a week. Here, the goal would be to find the best care available and to work with the child care providers as a team to provide integrated care for that baby or toddler. There may be families where there is emotional stress in individuals or family stress that makes it highly desirable to have 30-plus hours of care provided by others. On balance this will provide a much stronger support system for this particular baby or toddler. Each circumstance has to be weighed individually, and parents have to make wise and enlightened choices regarding their own particular situation.

Continuous Relationships

- In the first three years, every child needs one or two primary caregivers who remain in a steady, intimate relationship with that child.
- During the infancy, toddler, and preschool years, children should always be in the sight of caregivers. There should be no time, other than when they are sleeping, that they are out of sight of caregivers.
- No more than one-third of infants', toddlers', and preschoolers' time should be spent in fully independent activities. The time that is spent in independent activities should be spent for 10 or 15 minutes here and there rather than a longer period in independent activities.
- The other two-thirds or longer time should be spent between two types of activities: those in which the caregiver facilitates interactions with the environment and direct interaction, such as cuddling, holding, shared pretend play, and funny face games. Infants and toddlers need at least four or more 20-minute or longer periods of direct interactive time. Preschoolers need at least three of these direct, interactive play opportunities. In a two-parent family, both parents should be part of these spontaneous, joyful games.
- During the facilitated time, caregivers are available to comment on, respond to, and help in the child's explorations, though also engaged in other activities, such as cooking or putting clothes in the washing machine. Some of this time a small child could be accompanying parents to the supermarket or being a junior chef. During the school years, when we consider available time, we are considering time minus schooltime, after-school activities, and peer playtime. Here, too, we recommend that of the available time two-thirds be spent with the caregiver being available for facilitating or directly interacting. The "facilitating" time could be spent helping a child with homework, hobbies, or other activities. The times of direct involvement, which should include at least two 20-minute periods (each parent should participate where possible) might mean imaginative play, games or other activities in which the child can take the lead.
- We recommend that working parents both be available for at least two-thirds of the evening hours, from 5:30 or 6:00 to 9:00, and that, if possible, in addition, one of the parents be available in the late afternoon when the children are home, often playing with peers or siblings, or involved in after-school activities. Also, the parents should be available enough so that they or the children don't have to be measuring each moment of time and the guidelines outlined above can be taken for granted.

Parental Leave

We recommend a leave of most of the first year of life for one parent.

Day Care

- We do not recommend full-time day care, 30 or more hours of care by nonparents, for infants and toddlers if the parents are able to provide high-quality care themselves and if the parents have reasonable options. We also recommend improving day care considerably by lowering ratios, improving training and wages, and, for children in full-time day care, having the same caregiver remain with the infant she cares for for three to four years. Those families that require day care will then have options for higher-quality day care than is now the case.
- In the first three years, a primary caregiver should be assigned to each child and should remain the same from year to year.
- For the first year there should be no more than three babies to one adult.
- For the second year, there should be no more than four toddlers to one adult.
- For the third and fourth years, there should be no more than five to eight children to one adult.

Group or Institutional Settings

- Various types of institutional arrangements, including children in group situations, need to follow the same guidelines outlined earlier for the family. Ongoing nurturing care with one or a few constant primary caregivers should include direct or "facilitated" interactions for at least two-thirds of the available time. In-service training, growing financial incentives with experience and training, and support structure to facilitate nurturing attitudes are all important components of satisfying this requirement for ongoing nurturing care in group or institutional settings.

POSTSCRIPT

Is Institutional Child Care Beneficial to Children?

The quality of child care appears to be one of the most important issues in the debate over whether or not to send young children to child-care centers. Low adult-child ratios, competent and caring caregivers, and clean and nurturing environments are what contribute to quality child care. Is this type of setting preferable over being at home with a parent who does not want to be there and who does nothing to stimulate a child intellectually or emotionally? Consider another alternative—poor quality child care, with multiple caregivers who have no training and no desire to work with young children in a dirty, nonstimulating environment. Contrast this scenario with a child's being at home with a parent who loves the child and provides educational materials and one-on-one interaction most of the day. These are the extremes to the question of how and where to best care for young children.

Another factor that confounds this argument is how much time and what quality of time parents who use day care spend with their children when they are at home. Mediocre out-of-home care can be mitigated by a stimulating home environment when children and parents are together. On the other hand, a poor, nonnurturing home environment, which could be devastating for a child's development, can be supplemented positively by a quality child-care experience.

An April 2001 release of the results from a longitudinal study by the National Institute of Child Health and Human Development, a federal agency that has been studying children in child-care settings for 10 years, made headlines and caused a furor in the child-care industry. Some conclusions of the study, many say, were taken out of context and sensationalized by the press. It was reported that children who attended day care were found to be more aggressive than their stay-at-home counterparts. In actuality, the level of aggression for day care children was still within the normal range of behavior. These kinds of misinterpretations and partial facts create confusion for parents who are just trying to do the best they can for their children. American society asks parents to work to support their families but then asks them to stay home to take care of their children. This dichotomy of thinking and expectations makes it difficult to feel good about any choice made related to child care.

ISSUE 2

Does Maternal Employment Have Negative Effects on Children's Development?

YES: Wen-Jui Han, Jane Waldfogel, and Jeanne Brooks-Gunn, from "The Effects of Early Maternal Employment on Later Cognitive and Behavioral Outcomes," *Journal of Marriage and Family* (February 2001)

NO: Thomas M. Vander Ven, Francis T. Cullen, Mark A. Carrozza, and John Paul Wright, from "Home Alone: The Impact of Maternal Employment on Delinquency," *Social Problems* (May 2001)

ISSUE SUMMARY

YES: University professors and researchers Wen-Jui Han, Jane Waldfogel, and Jeanne Brooks-Gunn from Columbia University conclude that maternal employment in the first year of a child's life has a significant negative effect on verbal ability at age 3 or 4 and lowered math achievement when children were 7 to 8. When ethnicity was controlled for, these negative effects were found for white children, but not for African-American children.

NO: University professors and researchers Thomas M. Vander Ven, Francis T. Cullen, Mark A. Carrozza, and John Paul Wright found that mother's employment in the first year of the baby's life had no effect on child delinquency when the child got older.

The numbers of women who combine work and motherhood have risen steadily from 1975 to the present. Fifty-six percent of married mothers with a child under age 1 are employed, and 59 percent of unmarried mothers with a child under 1 are employed. The percentages of women entering the labor force increases as their children get older. Sixty-two percent of married mothers with a child aged 2 are working, and 75 percent of unmarried moms with a child aged 2 are working.

As more women moved into the workforce in the 1960s, research on maternal employment's effects on children became a popular topic of study. For the past 20 years, maternal employment has evolved from being studied as a single factor affecting children's development to being studied as a more complex issue. It was once thought that maternal employment had a direct single influence on children. Now researchers agree that maternal employment is more than a question of whether or not the mother works. The issue needs to be studied within the context of the family, the society, and cultural norms. Study on maternal employment's effects must simultaneously answer these questions. What quality of child care does the child receive? How does the mother feel about working? What societal and family support do the mother and child receive?

Researchers are divided on what variables to study, as well as what methods to use in studying maternal employment effects. For example, some researchers combine several social classes to study the interactive effects of working mothers with child-care arrangements, whereas others examine only one social class and how it intersects with the mother's personality traits and type of work and family environment.

The effects of maternal employment on children are determined by many factors such as mother's work satisfaction and morale, amount and control over work, and mother's perception of quality versus quantity time with her children. Depending on which studies one reads, how the data were collected, and which combination of variables was studied, different conclusions are reported. For example, some studies show that working moms spend more quality time with their children than non-working moms, while other studies show exactly the opposite results.

Research on maternal employment continues to become more refined, yet the question still remains: Should moms stay home with their babies? Often women will drop out of the workforce for at least the first few years to stay home and care for their children in order to make a connection. The concept that mother-child attachment in the first few years is critical to the child's later development has been established from years of significant research. Conversely, other research suggests that quality child-care providers may be able to meet the same attachment needs that mothers previously met. In addition, research shows that being exposed to a variety of quality caregivers, including other family members, fosters positive personality characteristics and independence in the child later on.

In the following selections, Wen-Jui Han, Jane Waldfogel, and Jeanne Brooks-Gunn argue that maternal employment has negative effects on children. They found that mothers' working was associated with their children's lower scores on verbal ability and lower math achievement scores. Thomas M. Vander Ven, Francis T. Cullen, Mark A. Carrozza, and John Paul Wright assert that maternal employment does not affect children's development. They found that maternal employment during the child's first year of life had no relationship to subsequent child delinquency.

YES

Wen-Jui Han, Jane Waldfogel, and Jeanne Brooks-Gunn

The Effects of Early Maternal Employment on Later Cognitive and Behavioral Outcomes

Recent trends in labor force participation have given new urgency to understanding the effects of early maternal employment—employment begun in the child's 1st year of life—on child outcomes. Women with infants have had the fastest growth in labor force participation of any group in the United States. With welfare reform, even more mothers will be working in the labor market before their child's first birthday. These trends are of potential concern given prior research that has found negative effects of early maternal employment on outcomes for children.

Several studies have used data from the 1986 wave of the National Longitudinal Survey of Youth (NLSY) to investigate the effects of maternal employment in the 1st year on children's cognitive and behavioral outcomes as assessed at ages 3 or 4. In this article, we revisit these same children 2 and 4 years later, when they are aged 5 and 6 and aged 7 and 8, to see whether the effects that earlier studies found at ages 3 and 4 would persist. We also wanted to better understand what might cause these effects and how they might be moderated.

With one exception, all the NLSY studies to date have analyzed children at young ages or at one point in time. In a recent study, Harvey analyzed all the children in the NLSY born in 1980 or later. Her study is exceptional in that it assesses some outcomes as late as age 12 and at several different points in time. Unlike our study, however, Harvey's was not longitudinal in design. In our study, we follow one group of children from ages 3 and 4, to ages 5 and 6, and to ages 7 and 8. We are thus able to show whether the effects that many studies have found at a point in time persist over time or whether they attenuate. Another point of difference between our study and Harvey's is that she analyzes White, African American, and Hispanic children together. If there are important differences in the effects of early maternal employment across racial and ethnic groups, as some prior research has found and as we have found here, then analyzing children separately is likely to yield more accurate estimates.

Research on maternal employment and child outcomes has been conducted within several theoretical frameworks. The first is attachment theory,

From *Journal of Marriage and Family,* vol. 63 (February 2001), pp. 336–354. Copyright © 2001 by National Council on Family Relations. Reprinted by permission. References omitted.

which posits that children whose mothers are absent during critical periods of early child development are less likely to develop secure attachments with their mothers. Attachment theory had in mind extended round-the-clock separations due to hospitalizations, illness, incarceration, and so on, and debate continues about whether maternal employment in the 1st year of life constitutes a comparable absence. Early studies conducted in the 1970s and 1980s, for the most part with small samples of primarily middle-class White children, found some evidence that maternal employment in the 1st year is associated with insecure attachment, but the effects were small. The most recent research, with a larger and more heterogeneous sample, does not find similar negative results. This discrepancy in findings may reflect in large part the differential selection of mothers into employment in the 1990s as compared with earlier decades when it was less common for mothers of infants to work.

Security of attachment to the mother is not the only child outcome of interest in the debate about maternal employment. Studies informed by child developmental psychology have paid particular attention to socioemotional adjustment (primarily behavior problems) and cognitive outcomes (primarily receptive verbal ability or early achievement test scores). Research on such outcomes has focused on large samples of children, with the bulk of studies analyzing data from the NLSY. These studies have found that maternal employment in the 1st year of life has a different effect on later emotional adjustment than does employment begun thereafter. There is also evidence that employment begun in the 1st year of life may have negative effects on cognitive development for some groups, whereas employment after the 1st year of life seems to have positive effects.

The few studies that have been able to control for child-care quality when examining maternal employment effects find that it plays an important mediating role, as does the type of care. High-quality care, if available to some low-income children, may make a bigger difference in their development than it does in high-income families. It may also matter how many hours the mother works.

Child and family characteristics also can mediate the effects of early maternal employment. The child's age when the mother begins work is obviously a critical mediating factor, but so, too, are factors such as the child's characteristics, family background, and current living situation. Moreover, the effects of early maternal employment may be moderated by family characteristics. For instance, family income is an important variable in its own right; mothers in low-income families may experience greater financial strain and hardship, which are in turn negatively associated with parental psychological functioning and parenting behavior. These effects may be more pronounced in low-income families where mothers are working than in families where they are not. In addition, low-income families may be less able to purchase high-quality and stable child care than more affluent families. Therefore, one might expect greater negative effects of maternal employment in low-income than in middle- or high-income families. Nonetheless, if children from high-income families have more to lose when they are separated from their mothers because their mothers are more nurturing or more cognitively skilled, then we might instead expect high-income children to be more vulnerable to the effects of early maternal employment.

Taken together, previous empirical findings and theory generate a rich set of hypotheses as to the likely effects of maternal employment in the 1st year on children's later cognitive and behavioral outcomes, the causes of these effects, and the potential buffers of them. We list the major hypotheses below and indicate which ones we will and will not test in this article. The premise of all these hypotheses is that all development is contextualized; any effects of early maternal employment are likely to vary as a function of context.

> Hypothesis 1: Children of mothers who work in the 1st year of life will have poorer long-term cognitive and behavioral outcomes because the time they would have spent with a cognitively stimulating and nurturing mother is spent instead with a substitute caregiver who is less cognitively stimulating and nurturing (because she or he has lower cognitive skills than the mother, because she or he is less motivated to stimulate and nurture the child, or because she or he is less able to give the child one-on-one attention).

We will test this hypothesis by estimating the effect of 1st-year maternal employment on later child cognitive and behavioral outcomes. We will also test several extensions of this hypothesis.

1. If there are racial or ethnic differences in mother-child interactions in the 1st year and/or in substitute caregiving arrangements in the 1st year, then the effects of maternal employment on child outcomes may differ by racial or ethnic group. We will test this by analyzing non-Hispanic White and African American families separately.
2. If children are more sensitive to maternal absences due to employment early in the 1st year of life than later, then effects of employment should be largest when it occurs earlier in the 1st year. We will test this by examining the quarter of the 1st year in which employment was initiated.
3. If the effects of employment are cumulative, the effects should be largest when mothers work longer hours. We will test this by comparing effects of full-time and part-time employment.
4. If boys are generally more vulnerable in the 1st year of life, then the effects of maternal absence in the 1st year should be larger for boys than for girls. We will test this by comparing the effects of 1st-year employment for boys and girls.
5. If the effects of 1st-year employment are due to the loss of the mothers' cognitive stimulation, then the effects should be more pronounced for children whose mothers have higher cognitive ability themselves. We will test this by comparing the effects of 1st-year maternal employment for children whose mothers have differing levels of cognitive ability (as measured by the AFQT).
6. It is unclear a priori how the effects of early maternal employment might vary by family income. If the effects of 1st-year employment are due to the absence of the mother, then the effects might be most pronounced for children from higher income families in which the

mothers might be more stimulating. If the effects of 1st-year employment are due to the low quality of the care in which the child is placed, however, and if income is correlated with quality of child care, the effects might be most pronounced for children from lower income families. We will test these competing hypotheses by comparing the effects of early maternal employment for children from families of differing income levels.

7. If the effects of 1st-year employment are due to the low quality of care in which children are placed, then the effects should be most pronounced for children in the lowest quality care. We cannot test this directly because we lack data on child-care quality. Instead, we will control for child-care type, which may be correlated with quality.

Hypothesis 2: Children of mothers who work in the 1st year of life will have poorer long-term cognitive and behavioral outcomes because during the time the mother is with the child, she is tired and stressed and therefore is less nurturing and stimulating.

We will test this hypothesis by comparing families of different income levels because working mothers in low-income families may face more strain and hardship than those in higher income families. We also would like to test this hypothesis by controlling for the home environment in the 1st year of life, but we have no measures of this (we only have measures of the concurrent home environment starting at age 3).

Hypothesis 3: Children of mothers who work in the 1st year of life may have poorer long-term cognitive or behavioral outcomes because of other omitted factors that are correlated with mothers' employment (e.g., single parenthood, fathers not working, mothers entering and exiting the labor force).

We test this hypothesis by controlling for an extensive set of child and family characteristics, including single parenthood and by comparing the effects of 1st-year maternal employment in families where fathers do or do not work and in families where mothers work continuously compared with families where mothers transition in and out of the labor market.

There are several other hypotheses that we are not able to test with the data at hand. These include hypotheses that focus on child-care characteristics, such as stability and quality; job characteristics, such as low wages, poor working conditions, low satisfaction, and nonstandard working hours; and maternal mental health and role strain.

Implicit in each of our hypotheses is the idea that the effects of early maternal employment on cognitive or behavioral outcomes might be sustained. That is, we might see effects persisting to the latest year when we observe our sample, at ages 7 and 8. This possible persistence of effects raises the question of whether these effects might be moderated by subsequent experiences. Although a full examination of moderating effects is beyond the scope of this study, we do control for subsequent maternal employment, years spent living in a single-mother family, and whether the family was ever poor.

We also explicitly examine whether the quality of the home environment starting at age 3 has a moderating effect, given prior evidence on the importance of home environment for child development.

Data and Method

Data

Our main samples are composed of all the White and African American children in the NLSY whom we can follow, with no missing data on any outcome variables, from ages 3 and 4 in 1986 to ages 7 and 8 in 1990. Because there are missing data on PIAT scores for some children and because a number of children (the children of the disadvantaged White oversample) were dropped in 1990, the resulting samples are quite small ($n = 244$ for Whites, $n = 218$ for African Americans). Following Baydar and Brooks-Gunn (1991), we do not analyze Hispanic children because the tests, which were mainly administered in English, may not be reliable for them.

Our sample of children is not a random sample of all children born in 1982 and 1983. Rather, it represents children born in those years to the young women in the NLSY, who ranged in age from 17 to 26 at the time of their child's birth. Consequently, our sample consists of children of relatively young mothers, who will tend to have lower educational levels and lower incomes.

We also conducted supplementary analyses of a somewhat larger sample, the non-Hispanic White children whom we can follow with no missing data from age 3 and 4 in 1986 to age 5 and 6 in 1988; the main difference is that this sample includes children from the White disadvantaged oversample that was dropped in 1990. The results from this larger sample are consistent for the most part with the results for our main sample.

Measures

Maternal employment. We use the detailed maternal employment information in the NLSY to establish the employment status of a mother during each year of her child's life. The following six measures were constructed: employed during the 1st year of life (coded as 1 if the mother worked any hours at all during the child's 1st year); employed during the 2nd or 3rd year; employed after age 3 up to the year before assessment; currently working; quarter of the 1st year that maternal employment began; and full-time–part-time work in the 1st year, with full-time defined as working 21 or more hours per week. The usual cut-off point of 35 hours for full-time was not used because we assume that very young children are more sensitive to the quantity of time a mother spends with them than are school-aged children. In addition, scholars have found that mothers working more than 20 hours are associated with poorer cognitive outcomes for children.

Parental presence and work status. Six categories were constructed to represent all possible combinations of the mother's working status and father's presence and working status in the 1st year of a child's life: working mother and no father (7.0%), working mother and nonworking father (2.5%), working mother and working father (43.9%), nonworking mother and no father (7.8%), nonworking mother and nonworking father (0.8%), and nonworking mother and working father (38.0%).

Home environment. The Home Observation for Measurement of the Environment-Short Form was used. This scale, which was scored by either maternal report or interviewer observation, measures the degree to which the child's home environment provided emotional support and cognitive simulation. The earliest information is from 1986 when the children were aged 3 to 4. We use information from the 1986, 1988, and 1990 HOME scores to investigate the effects of contemporary HOME environment on children's achievements. The mean scores for Whites and Blacks were 103 (with *SD* of 13) and 92 (with *SD* of 14), respectively.

Child care. Child-care arrangements during the first 3 years of a child's life were asked of the mothers retrospectively at the time of the 1986 survey. We categorize the primary child-care arrangement during the 1st year of the child's life as follows: parental care (care by mother or father); relative care (care by sibling, grandparent, or other relative); nonrelative care (care by someone other than a relative, whether in home or not); or center care (day-care center, group care center, nursery school, or preschool). As noted earlier, an important limitation of the NLSY data on child care is the absence of information pertaining to the quality of child care. Thus, our child-care results must be interpreted with caution.

Sociodemographic variables. Children and families' sociodemographic characteristics have substantial effects on children's cognitive ability, as evidenced by previous studies. Thus, we also controlled for gender, having older siblings, ever having lived in poverty, and years living in a single-parent family. To compare families at various income levels, three dummy variables were constructed to represent poverty (income-to-needs ratio ≤ 1), low income (income-to-needs ratio > 1 and ≤ 2), and middle income and higher (income-to-needs ratio > 2) in the 1st year of life. Mother's cognitive ability, as measured by the Armed Forces Qualification Test (AFQT; Bock & Mislevy, 1981) score, was included to not only capture the effect of mother's intelligence on a child's cognitive outcomes, but also to control for its possible effect on selection into the labor force.

Child's achievement and receptive vocabulary outcomes. The Peabody Picture Vocabulary Test-Revised was used to measure children's verbal ability at ages 3 and 4, and the Peabody Individual Achievement Test. Math and Reading Recognition are used to measure math and verbal achievement respectively for children at ages 5 and 6 and at ages 7 and 8. Thus, we are using different tests to compare children's cognitive outcomes at different points in time. Because the PPVT-R correlates significantly with other measures of verbal intelligence and with measures of reading and math achievement, however, these variables should allow us to assess the influence of maternal employment on the cognitive development of a child over time while still using tests that are appropriate to the age of the child. The PPVT-R test assesses vocabulary knowledge in children aged 3 years and older. The PIAT-Math measures achievement in mathematics and the PIAT-Reading Recognition assesses the attained reading knowledge of children aged 5 years or older. (We do not use PIAT-Reading Comprehension because many 5- to 6-year-olds have missing values, as their scores were lower than the national PIAT sample. The mean of PPVT-R score for Whites is 96.55 (*SD* 16.40), and it is 73.66 (*SD* 18.47) for Blacks. The mean of PIAT-Math score for Whites is about 102 (*SD* 12), and it is about 95 (*SD* of 12) for Blacks. The mean of PIAT-Reading Recognition for Whites is about 106 (*SD* 13), and it is about 101 (*SD* 11) for Blacks.

Behavioral problems.   The Behavioral Problems Index measures six dimensions of behavior problems (antisocial behavior, anxiousness/depression, headstrongness, hyperactivity, immaturity, and dependency). We use the total BPI score, as well as two subscales (internalizing and externalizing problems). This measure was collected only for children aged four or older. The two subscales used in the analysis have Cronbach's alpha of .70 and .84.

Empirical Strategy

Our statistical procedure is multiple regression, estimated using ordinary least squares. We regress the child's PPVT-R score at ages 3 or 4 and the PIAT-Math and Reading Recognition scores at ages 5 or 6 and at ages 7 or 8 on a set of demographic and socioeconomic family background variables, together with alternative sets of variables describing the mother's employment behavior over the child's early lifetime. We examine not only the impact of early maternal employment per se, but also the impact of the timing and the extent of early maternal employment. We also examine some moderating effects. We then turn to similar models where we estimate the effects of early maternal employment on the BPI and its two subscales.

Empirical Results

Does Early Maternal Employment Affect Cognitive Outcomes, and Do These Effects Vary by Race or Ethnicity?

. . . Consistent with previous studies, maternal employment in the 1st year of life has a significant negative effect on the PPVT-R score at age 3 or 4, reducing the score by 7 points at those ages. The results for the White children at age 5 to 6 and age 7 to 8 indicate that the negative effects of 1st-year maternal employment persist over time. Looking at the PIAT results, having a mother who worked in the 1st year lowers math achievement by 5 points at age 7 to 8 and lowers reading recognition by about 5 points at both age 5 to 6 and age 7 to 8. Subsequent maternal employment, in contrast, is mainly positive; in particular, having a mother who worked in the 2nd or 3rd year largely offsets the effects of 1st-year employment for reading at age 5 to 6 and age 7 to 8.

The results for African Americans ... are quite different, with no significant effects of maternal employment on cognitive outcomes in any of the models. We also found no significant effects for African Americans in any of the other models that we ran, providing some support for the notion that there are important racial or ethnic differences at work here. Therefore, the rest of our analyses are reported for White children only.

Do the Effects of Early Maternal Employment Vary by When the Employment Began?

The existence of negative effects of 1st-year maternal employment for some children raises the question of whether these effects are more pronounced if they occur during earlier periods within the 1st year. ... With everything else held constant, timing within the 1st year may matter. The results for PPVT-R at age 3 to 4 suggest that starting employment before the 4th quarter of the year could lower a child's PPVT-R score by 7 points, whereas starting employment in the 4th quarter has no significant effect. The results for other outcomes at other ages further indicate that the strong negative effect for White children of the mother entering the labor force before the 4th quarter persists over time.

Do the Effects of Early Maternal Employment Vary by the Mothers' Hours?

We also examined whether the effects of maternal employment varied by women's full-time versus part-time working status in the 1st year. The results ... suggest that the effects of working part-time in the 1st year are not significantly different than the effects of working full-time. The analysis was also reestimated using mother's continuous working hours; the results are not significant.

Do the Effects of Early Maternal Employment Vary by the Child's Gender?

We also examined whether the effects of maternal employment varied by the child's gender. ... We found no significant differences in the effects of maternal employment on cognitive outcomes by gender.

Do the Effects of Early Maternal Employment Vary by Mothers' Cognitive Ability?

To further test the hypothesis that it is the absence of a cognitively stimulating mother that leads to lower outcomes for children whose mothers work in the 1st year and that children of the more highly skilled mothers would be more affected, we use data on mothers' AFQT scores to divide our sample into quartiles of cognitive ability. We use AFQT rather than educational attainment because these scores are strongly associated with children's cognitive scores and are likely to be a better measure of these relatively young mothers' cognitive ability than their educational attainment at the time of the birth.

. . . The results of the F tests . . . indicate that 1st-year maternal employment has statistically significant negative effects in one of five models for children of mothers in the top quartile of AFQT scores, in three of five models for children of mothers in the 2nd quartile, and in two of five for children of mothers in the 3rd quartile; there are no significant effects for children of mothers in the lowest quartile. This pattern of results is consistent with the hypothesis above in that we find some significant effects of early maternal employment for children whose mothers are moderately to highly skilled but no significant effects for children whose mothers are very low skilled (with a mean AFQT of 41).

Do the Effects of Early Maternal Employment on Cognitive Outcomes Vary by Family Income?

As we saw earlier, children from low-income families may be more affected by early maternal employment if their mothers are more stressed or if they are placed in poorer quality child care. At the same time, children from high-income families might be more affected if they have more to lose from the absence of their mother. We tested whether the effects of early maternal employment vary by family income. . . . The F tests . . . indicate that 1st-year maternal employment has statistically significant negative effects in all five models for children of low-income families, compared with three of five models for middle-income families and two of five for high-income families. Thus, maternal employment has the most significant effects on cognitive outcomes for children in low-income families, as we would expect if income is correlated with child-care quality and if low child-care quality is part of the reason for the adverse effects of early maternal employment, or if mothers who work in low-income families experience greater financial strain and hardship.

Do the Effects of Early Maternal Employment Vary by Child-Care Type?

Given these results, it would be of particular interest to control for child-care quality. As noted earlier, however, we cannot do so with the NLSY. The best we can do is to control for the type of child care the child attended during the 1st year. . . . We find that relative care, nonrelative care, and center care have positive effects on PPVT-R at age 3 to 4 compared with the reference category, parental care, which might suggest that quality child care can compensate to some extent for early maternal employment.

Do Other Factors Such as Fathers' Employment Status, Single Motherhood, or Mothers' Subsequent Employment Patterns Account for the Effects of Early Maternal Employment?

Bearing in mind that these children were born in 1982 or 1983, a time when maternal employment was less typical than it is today and when the United States was undergoing a recession, . . . we tested the hypothesis that mothers' employment might be associated with fathers' employment status and that this might affect child outcomes. . . . [C]hildren from two-parent families whose mothers worked in the 1st year have lower cognitive scores than the reference group (children in two-parent families whose mothers did not work in the 1st year and whose fathers did). . . . [T]he negative effects of 1st-year maternal employment are largest for children whose fathers were present but not working, however, suggesting that there is a connection between mothers' and fathers' work in the 1st year and outcomes for children. . . . [We] compared children in single-mother families where the mother did or did not work in the 1st year. We find no significant differences between these groups (both have lower PPVT-R scores than the reference group at age 3 to 4 and lower PIAT-Math scores at age 7 to 8).

[We] examined the impact of mothers' subsequent employment status by categorizing women according to their employment across the first 3 years of the child's life. The results show that only for those women who worked in the 1st year and then left the labor force is there a significant long-term negative effect of that 1st-year employment; for those who worked in the 1st year and continued working, the effect of 1st-year employment, although still negative, is not significant after the 1st year. . . . [A]lthough White children might have higher cognitive scores at ages 3 to 4 if their mothers delayed entry into the labor force into the 2nd or 3rd year, this difference is no longer significant by the time they are age 5 to 6 and 7 to 8. This result lends some support to the hypothesis that factors other than 1st-year maternal employment (e.g., entry and exits) may account for some of the effects of maternal employment.

Does Contemporary Home Environment Moderate the Effects of Early Maternal Employment?

To test for the moderating effect of the quality of home environment, we added the contemporary HOME score to the model. In results not shown, although the home environment does have a significant positive effect on children's cognitive outcomes, no significant result was found for the interaction between HOME score and early maternal employment, and the addition of HOME scores did not reduce the effect of early maternal employment.

Does Early Maternal Employment Affect Behavioral Outcomes?

In analyses using the total BPI score . . . we find no statistically significant effects of maternal employment on White children's behavioral problems, but timing seems to matter when they are 7 to 8 years old. Specifically, entering the labor force before the 4th quarter of the 1st year has a significant effect on children's behavioral outcomes (the higher the score, the more problems).

. . . [We] compare the difference between internalizing and externalizing problems. The results indicate that 1st-year maternal employment, and entering the labor force early in the 1st year, have a significant effect only on externalizing problems, with effects at age 4 and again at ages 7 to 8.

In results not shown, we interacted gender with maternal employment but found no significant differences in these behavioral problem models; when we interacted family income with early maternal employment, we found that children in high-income families exhibit more externalizing problems at age 4 if their mothers worked in the 1st year.

Discussion and Conclusions

The empirical results in this study indicate that early maternal employment has a significant negative effect on White children's cognitive outcomes at age 3 or 4 and that these effects persist to age 7 or 8 in some instances but not in others. We found no significant effects of early maternal employment on cognitive outcomes for African American children, suggesting that the effects of early maternal employment do vary by racial and ethnic group. We can only speculate as to the reason for this difference, but one possibility is that it reflects the fact that employment of mothers of young children has been traditionally more common in African American families and therefore may be seen as more normative; that is, the context in which early maternal employment occurs may differ for different groups.

Given the small size of our sample, our results are somewhat tentative, but we found evidence that the effects we find among White children may be more pronounced for some children than others. Specifically, we found that the effects may be more pronounced for children whose mothers start work early in their 1st year of life. But we found no significant differences between children whose mothers worked full-time or part-time in the 1st year. We also found no significant differences in the effects of early maternal employment for boys and girls.

With regard to the mother's level of cognitive ability, we found some significant effects of early maternal employment on cognitive outcomes for children of mothers who had moderate to high AFQT scores. We found no significant effects for children of mothers who had very low AFQT scores (in the bottom quartile), however; these children have lower cognitive scores, as expected, but this was the case whether or not their mothers worked. This pattern of results lends some support to the hypothesis that it is the loss of a cognitively stimulating mother that accounts for some of the ill effects of early maternal employment on cognitive outcomes for children.

Comparing children from poverty, low-income, and moderate- and high-income families, we found the most significant effects of early maternal employment for the children from poverty-income families. These stronger effects may be due to the low quality of the child care they attend, to turbulence in their child-care arrangements, to the strain and hardship their mothers experience when they are working, or to a combination of these factors. We were not able to assess the impact of child-care quality because of the limitations of the NLSY data.

We found no support for the hypothesis that the effects of early maternal employment might be due to the correlation between employment and single motherhood. We did find, however, that controlling for fathers' employment status and for mothers' subsequent employment status did make a difference.

Children whose mothers worked in the 1st year and whose fathers were present but did not work, and children whose mothers worked in the 1st year and then dropped out of the labor market, fared worse in terms of their long-run cognitive outcomes than did other children whose mothers worked in the 1st year of life.

Turning to moderating effects, we found that the effects of early maternal employment may be buffered for children whose families provide a nurturing and stimulating home environment. Whether they might also be buffered for children whose child-care settings are nurturing and stimulating is an important question but one that we are not able to address with the data at hand.

We also found some negative effects of 1st-year maternal employment on behavioral problems for White children, mainly at ages 7 to 8. The effects seem to be concentrated in the area of externalizing problems. We found no significant effects of 1st-year maternal employment on behavioral outcomes for African American children, again suggesting important racial and ethnic differences.

The question remains: Why are there negative effects of 1st-year maternal employment, and why do these effects persist over time for some children but not others? This study included an extensive set of controls. Nonetheless, we were still unable to control for some characteristics that might help explain the persistent effects for some children of maternal employment in the 1st year. For instance, information on the quality of child care, as well as the quality of time mothers spend with their infants, would be helpful, given previous findings on the positive effects of high-quality child care on children's cognitive outcomes.

The significant negative effects of early maternal employment found for some children in this study were not found in Harvey's recent work. The differences between these two sets of results primarily reflect the different approaches used in these two studies. The samples were different: Harvey used a larger sample but did not follow the same children over time, whereas we followed a longitudinal sample that was of necessity smaller. Most important, our study analyzed non-Hispanic White and African American children separately, whereas her study pooled Whites, African Americans, and Hispanics together. When we pooled the three racial and ethnic groups (results not shown), we, too, found much weaker links between 1st-year maternal employment and later outcomes.

The generalizability of our results is limited in that we examined children of relatively young mothers. Analyses of a more representative sample of children should be undertaken. Despite these limitations, however, our study makes a unique contribution by assessing the effects of early maternal employment on children's cognitive and behavioral outcomes over time. Our findings that 1st-year maternal employment has negative effects on cognitive outcomes for White children and that these effects persist in some instances to ages 7 and 8 merit further research, as does the suggestion that there may be some longrun effects on behavioral problems for White children as well. The negative effects we found are fairly small. Nonetheless, if for some children these effects occur in addition to those associated with other risk factors, such as poverty or a non-employed father, the cumulative effects may be of concern.

Proponents of family leave legislation have argued that such laws will improve maternal and child health. Our results suggest that giving parents the right to longer periods of parental leave might improve some children's cognitive and behavioral outcomes as well. In this regard, research on the impact on child outcomes of the recently adopted U.S. Family and Medical Leave Act, and of the more generous family leave legislation in place in other countries, would be welcome. Nonetheless, we are mindful that there is a good deal of variation in preferences and outcomes among families and that the effects of early maternal employment will depend on many contextual factors. Therefore, we also recommend more research on child-care quality and policy initiatives designed to raise the quality of child care provided to infants.

completed the Child Self-Administered Supplement (CSAS) in 1992 and in 1994. This self-report booklet collects information on a wide range of variables including child-parent interaction, peer relationships, and involvement in various delinquent activities.

Additionally, the children of the NLSY mothers were studied every other year beginning in 1986, so data on various developmental outcomes are available from early childhood up through early and middle adolescence for this sample. To study the effects of both early and current maternal employment on delinquency, we follow this sample from 1994 back to 1986 when study children were between the ages of 2 and 5 years old. We selected 1986 as the study year for early employment effects because it was the first year that NLSY researchers collected extensive data on parent-child interaction and family relations. We take advantage of the longitudinal nature of the NLSY data by controlling for 1994 employment when examining the effects of 1986 employment on 1994 delinquency. By controlling for current employment, it will lend support to any assertions that the effect of early employment is independent of the effect of current employment.

The NLSY data, while presenting great possibilities for research, have their shortcomings. One limitation of these data, for example, is that over 27 percent of the children who were between the ages of 10 and 14 in 1994 were born to mothers who were less than twenty years old when they gave birth to their children. As a result, many of these mothers are less-educated and are more likely to be members of a minority group than one would find in a representative sample where maternal age is normally distributed. Because early childbearers are more prone to having children with developmental deficits, such as low cognitive ability, and are at a greater risk for criminality, these children should be considered to be a high-risk group.

While other researchers use weighted data to correct for the large number of lower socioeconomic and minority women in the sample, we perform our analysis on the unweighted sample. The NLSY guide to Child Data strongly cautions against using weighted data across years because "analyzing data from persons interviewed in multiple years creates problems since the yearly weights are not appropriate to such a universe." Using the weighted data in regression equations that represent longitudinal effects, then, may result in substantial miscalculations of standard errors. Guo argued that bias can be reduced in the unweighted sample by controlling for those characteristics that are overrepresented, such as race, maternal education, and an assessment of mother's cognitive ability. Controls for each of these variables are included in each of our analytical models. As a check on our results, we also performed our main analyses using weighted data. The relationships between variables did not differ substantially when using the unweighted rather than the weighted sample. All reported results, hereafter, reflect the unweighted analysis.

. . . Correlation matrix analysis and tolerance tests did not detect the presence of multicollinearity between any two independent measures. Mean replacement was used to address missing values. The main analysis was also estimated without mean replacement. No substantial differences were found.

Dependent Variable: Delinquency

The 1994 CSAS includes nine highly correlated items that assess involvement in deviant and delinquent acts. Five of the items measure relatively minor to moderate acts of youth deviance: breaking parents' curfew, dishonesty (i.e., lying to a parent), school problems (i.e., parent came to school because of child behavior), truancy, and staying out all night. The other four items involve more serious acts of lawbreaking: alcohol abuse, vandalism (i.e., damaged school property on purpose), store theft, and violence (i.e., hurt someone badly enough to need bandages or a doctor). These nine items are summed to create our scale measuring youth deviance and delinquency (alpha = .78).

The respondents were asked to report on their involvement in each of these behaviors over the last twelve months. If the children reported that they had no involvement in any given act, that variable received a score of 0. If the respondent was involved in that activity over the past year, the variable received a score of 1. Measuring delinquent involvement in this way is common in the delinquency literature. We should note, however, that we also conducted our analyses using the same delinquency scale but with involvement measured by the number of times the respondent committed each act (i.e., the frequency score). The results of this investigation did not differ from results produced by the main analysis.

This measure of delinquency is skewed towards non-offending. Nearly 25 percent of the adolescent sample reported no involvement in any of the nine items used to create the scale. Furthermore, over 75 percent of the sample reported involvement in no more than three of the nine items used to construct the index. This variable is transformed into a new measure equal to the natural logarithm of the delinquency variable in order to increase the explainable variance in delinquency.

Independent Variables

Maternal employment status. A continuous measure of hours usually worked is used in this analysis. In past studies, investigators assigned missing values to work-hour variables for non-employed mothers, who were then excluded from the analysis. Thus, these studies focused on the effects of paid maternal employment among a sub-group of working mothers only. Other studies include non-employed mothers but as a dummy category that is used in equations with other dummy variables capturing increasing levels of time commitment to paid employment (e.g., part-time, full-time, over-time). Measuring maternal work hours via a series of dummy variables is arguably a good strategy for organizing information and for detecting non-linear effects. As Harvey points out, however, this method is problematic because the dummy categories are formed from continuous variables so there are infinite ways one could create categories and arbitrary boundaries between categories are often created. Moreover, using continuous variables does not prevent the detection of nonlinear effects. Based on this rationale, we use a continuous measure of hours worked in our primary analysis.

In order to compare non-working mothers to working mothers on various pathway and delinquency variables, we assign non-working mothers mean values for work hours. As suggested by Menaghan, et al., we run models where dummy variables are employed to capture employment status (i.e., welfare, coercive, technical, and bureaucratic work controls) while substituting mean values for the continuous variable measuring work-role conditions (i.e., hours worked) for non-working mothers. Regression estimates for the continuous hours variable will reflect the effects for working mothers, and coefficients for the occupational class dummy variables will "reflect the contrast between that group and the reference category, evaluated at average conditions on the continuous variables."

One might argue that assigning the mean hours worked to non-employed mothers blurs the analysis since the main objective here is to examine the impact of real differences (e.g., the effects of zero hours of employment vs. the effects of forty hours of employment) in maternal work commitment. To bolster confidence in our measure of work hours, we conducted separate analyses where non-working mothers were assigned zeros for work hours. No substantive differences in the results were found. Furthermore, consistent with Parcel and Menaghan's usual strategy, we also measure work hours with a series of dummy variables capturing part-time, full-time, and overtime work schedules in a separate analysis. Again, our results did not differ from results produced using the continuous measure of work hours. In all analyses, non-working mothers (those who neither worked nor received welfare in the previous year) serve as the reference category.

To identify welfare-reliant mothers, we use a dummy variable, which is coded as 1 if the respondent reported that she did not work during the survey week and if the respondent answered affirmatively to the question, "Did you or your spouse receive income from AFDC in the past calendar year?" In this way, we distinguish between those who draw income primarily from welfare and those who may draw welfare but participate in the workforce as well.

Current employment is measured in 1992. We used the 1992 work variables and controls in the current effects model because the delinquency items ask respondents to report on delinquency involvement over the previous 12 months. Therefore, to approximate the temporal order of our conceptual model, we chose to measure employment status in the year preceding the reported delinquency.

Finally, we construct measures of father's employment to examine the relative effects of father's work as compared to mother's work. Father's work is measured as the paid employment of spouses who are co-residing with the family—biological fathers and stepfathers are counted equally. We assign them work hours values and occupational class classifications drawn from maternal reports in the NLSY data.

Occupational class.   We measure occupational class in two ways. First, following Parcel and Menaghan, we construct a 19-item-based occupational complexity scale by matching occupational titles reported by NLSY respondents to job descriptions reported in the Dictionary of Occupational Titles. As stated above, we estimate models using this measure of job complexity along with dummy variables for part-time, full-time and overtime hours. Our primary strategy, however, involves the use of a series of dummy variables capturing workplace controls, as outlined below, along with a continuous measure of work hours. We should note that our results did not differ when substituting the job complexity measure for our workplace control dummy variables.

Our primary measure of workplace conditions is developed based on the work of Mark Colvin. Drawing from Kohn and Edwards, Colvin links the workplace controls experienced by parents to the patterns and styles of control parents exert upon children. Unskilled, non-unionized employees (Fraction I workers) are subjected to "simple control" in the workplace, which is coercive and alienating. Simple control involves exacting worker compliance through the threat of job termination. This type of control is then reproduced in the home through erratic, harsh, and punitive parenting. Children who are raised under these conditions may be likely to form an alienated bond with authority, which frees them to behave in anti-social and delinquent ways.

Skilled laborers and craftspersons (Fraction II workers), who often belong to labor unions, experience greater job security and are controlled via "technical control"—the machine-paced atmosphere of manufacturing and industrial workplaces where workers are motivated to produce by wage increases and job security. Workers who are controlled by "technical control" will be more likely to control their children through extending and suspending rewards and punishments, which results in the formation of calculative bonds to authority in children. Such children are less likely to be involved in serious delinquency than the children of Fraction I workers.

Fraction III workers are those skilled workers, technicians, salaried professionals, and supervisory staff who experience greater self-direction, job complexity, and job security in the workplace. Fraction III workers are controlled in a bureaucratic fashion which relies on the power of normative pressure to control workers. These workers are heavily invested in the rules of the organization due to their favored status and, as a result, tend to be self-regulating employees. Due to high levels of autonomy in the workplace, Fraction III workers are positively bonded to authority, which they reproduce in their children through a steady and consistent style of parenting. Children of Fraction III workers are least likely to deviate from rules and laws due to their strong, normative bond with authority.

Colvin and Pauly's class fraction scheme provides a simple and parsimonious method for linking general job conditions to family life and to delinquency. For that reason, we measure working conditions by assigning each NLSY mother an occupational class value. First, using occupational codes in the NLSY data, we make an initial assessment about class fraction membership based on the presumed skill-level, autonomy, and job stability of each occupation. Fraction I workers are those unskilled, non-union workers found in agricultural labor, small-manufacturing firms, retail and food services, household domestic work, low-level clerical jobs (e.g., stock clerk) and sales (e.g., shoe sales, retail). All NLSY workers whose occupational titles fit the above description were placed in Fraction I. Those assigned to Fraction II include skilled blue-collar workers (e.g., welders, plumbers, steelworkers, auto assemblers), skilled clerical workers (e.g., secretaries), craftsworkers, and low-level supervisors (e.g., foreman). Fraction III status was assigned to professionals, technicians, managers, government workers, and proprietors.

Family income.   Total family income is included in all models. By employing a family income measure, we are able to assess the impact of mother's employment experiences while controlling for the total standard of living of each family included in the analysis. Controlling for family income helps to isolate the independent effects of occupational variables in the analysis.

Child care.   Following Parcel and Menaghan, we measure child care with a series of dummy variables. Dummy variables representing professional daycare settings, childcare provided by a relative (including fathers), and childcare provided by a non-relative are included.

Pathway Variables

The NLSY was designed primarily to study labor market experiences across the life course. Because it was not constructed as a criminological data set, some of our measures, although reasonable, are not ideal. Further, although scales are available to measure some variables, for other constructs we used one-item measures. In these instances, the results should be viewed with appropriate caution. All pathway variables are measured in 1986 for the early models and 1992 for the current models. All scales are constructed using a simple summing of the component items.

Supervision.   Criminologists commonly operationalize parental supervision as the degree to which parents know the whereabouts of children when they are away from home and who they are with when away from home. We employ a similar measure of supervision found in the CSAS. The one-item measure is a four-point scale reflecting the child's report on how often "your mother knows who you are with when not at home."

Attachment.   Attachment is often measured by items that relate to a child's feelings of closeness, love, or admiration for a parent. It is difficult to measure attachment among young children because they are unable to answer standard survey questions. The NLSY data, however, contain mother-reported items related to the insecure behaviors exhibited by children. Mothers were asked if their 2 to 5 year-olds were difficult to soothe or calm, anxious and or worried when left alone, prone to crying when left alone, or tended to need help with most things. Attachment in young children is often studied via mother-reported assessments of child behavior. Our insecure attachment index has a reliability of .61. To measure attachment in adolescence, we use a one-item question drawn from the CSAS that asks, "How close do you feel to your mother?"

Maternal support.   In the present analysis, we measure maternal support at two intervals—in 1986 when study children were in their pre-school years and in 1992 in early adolescence. Past researchers using the NLSY data captured expressive maternal support, from mother to children, with a warmth and responsiveness scale. Our warmth and responsiveness scale is an adaptation of the measure used by Menaghan, et al. This five-item index is drawn from interviewer observations of the warmth and responsiveness shown by mothers toward children. Interviewers observed whether or not mothers: spoke simultaneously to their child twice or more, responded verbally to child's speech (excluding scolding), answered child's questions or requests verbally, caressed, kissed, or hugged the child at least once, or conveyed positive feelings about the child. The reliability of the warmth and responsiveness scale is .79.

To examine maternal support in adolescence, we use a five-item index drawn from interviewer observations of maternal treatment of children in the home. This index is similar to the warmth and responsiveness scale used for pre-school children, but the items are tailored for school-age children. The items include whether mothers: encouraged the child to talk, answered child's questions, spoke with child, introduced the child to the interviewer by name, or used a loving voice toward child. The reliability of this scale is .76.

Spanking.   Punitive parenting, such as corporal punishment, is associated with negative behavioral outcomes in children. Some scholars argue that the causal relationship between physical discipline and child behavior has yet to be untangled. Child misbehavior and physical punishment, that is, are likely to be related reciprocally. Other researchers claim that early physical discipline is independently related to misbehavior later on. We measure early maternal spanking with an item that asks mothers to report the number of times they spanked their child during the last week. This NLSY item was used by previous researchers interested in the maternal characteristics associated with spanking.

Delinquent peer association.   Delinquent peer association is generally captured through survey questions tapping into the number of delinquent friends possessed by the respondent. Johnson, Marcos, and Bahr argue that the differential association process should not be seen simply in terms of the kinds of people one associates with, but should also consider the *situational pressures* that go along with associating with certain types. The process, then, is best evaluated by gaining measures on the amount of pressure to be delinquent exerted by one's friends. The CSAS asked youth to report whether they felt pressure from friends to try cigarettes, drugs, alcohol, skip school, or commit crime or do something violent. We combine these items into a scale ranging from 0 to 5, with 5 being the highest degree of delinquent pressure. The reliability of this scale is .79.

School attachment.   Following Wiatrowski, Griswold, and Roberts', we focus on level of satisfaction with school as the measure of school attachment. The response item—drawn from the CSAS—asks respondents to report their satisfaction with their school. The responses range from 1, meaning very dissatisfied, to 4, meaning very satisfied.

Maternal Resources

AFQT.   Mother's cognitive skills are estimated by her score on the Armed Forces Qualification Test, administered to all respondents in 1980. An AFQT score can be seen as an individual difference which is likely to influence a mother's life chances and those of her children similarly.

Maternal education.   Mother's educational attainment is measured as the highest grade completed by mothers as of 1992. When examining the effects of early maternal employment, education is equal to the highest grade completed as of 1986.

Structural and Family Background Factors

In all models we control for race, sex, and age of study children. Age is an interval measure and race and sex are dummy variables. Race is coded 1 = Black or Hispanic and 0 = White. In separate equations, the Black and Hispanic children were isolated from one another to examine any differences between these groups and between these groups and the white sub-group. No differences were found. Sex is coded 0 = male and 1 = female. Family structure is a measure of the presence of mother's spouse in the home. An "intact" family is a home where the mother is married and presently co-residing with her partner. Thus, biological fathers, stepfathers, and adoptive fathers are all counted equally. Intact Family is coded 0 = no marital partner in the home and 1 = marital partner present.

Neighborhood Disorder

There is a strong relationship between certain neighborhood traits, such as poverty and joblessness, and crime. Those who have unstable, low-paying, or coercively controlled jobs are more likely to live in an economically and socially impoverished community where informal controls on behavior are low. The children of sub-employed or welfare-reliant mothers may be doubly at-risk because of the effects of economic strain and because poverty constrains families to live in socially disorganized settings. Researchers interested in the negative effects of community breakdown focus on the rates of joblessness, poverty, and family breakdown in neighborhoods. Because the NLSY lacks data on the rates of these problems at the community level, we construct a measure of neighborhood disorder from maternal responses to items related to community disorder. Our scale is drawn from responses to questions about whether the neighborhood had a "problem" with crime and violence, lack of parental supervision, and abandoned or run-down buildings (alpha = .85).

Statistical Analysis

The analysis of the data is conducted through the use of ordinary least squares regression (OLS). Our strategy is to examine 1) the direct effects of maternal employment hours and of maternal employment conditions on delinquency and 2) the indirect effects of maternal work on delinquency through the delinquency pathway variables. In this model, non-employed, welfare-reliant, and employed mothers are all included. Because working conditions are captured via a series of dummy variables reflecting the three working class fractions, nonemployed mothers and welfare-reliant mothers are treated as occupational class categories.

The analytic strategy follows a three-equation process. In the first equation, we examine the direct effect of maternal employment on the delinquency pathways. In this equation, each pathway is regressed against the employment/non-employment variables while controlling for maternal resources and child characteristics (age, sex, and race).

The second equation involves regressing the delinquency index against the employment/non-employment variables with mother and child control measures. The results of this equation demonstrate the direct effects of employment on delinquency without taking the delinquency pathways into consideration.

In the third, and final, equation, the delinquency index is regressed against maternal employment and the delinquency pathways. This equation produces estimates for the direct effects of all preceding variables on delinquency. Furthermore, by using this strategy, the third equation produces estimates of the direct effect of maternal employment on delinquency, while controlling for the delinquency pathways.

As a complement to this main strategy, we also perform an Analysis of Moment Structures (AMOS) analysis on the main model. Structural modeling allows us to assess the total, direct, and indirect effects of maternal employment on delinquency and will serve as confirmatory evidence for the findings based on the OLS strategy.

Findings

The Impact of Early Maternal Employment on Early Pathways to Delinquency

. . . [The] results of regression models that examine the effects of early maternal employment status on insecure attachment, maternal warmth and responsiveness, and spanking, controlling for maternal resources, child characteristics, and child care arrangements [show] . . . few significant effects. Child's age is inversely related to insecure attachment, warmth and responsiveness, and mother's use of spanking. Increasing AFQT score is associated with less insecure attachment and increasing warmth and responsiveness. Finally, higher family income is related to less maternal use of spanking. None of the early employment variables are related to the early delinquency risks.

The Impact of Early Maternal Employment on Delinquency

. . . [A] multiple regression equation . . . that examines the impact of early maternal employment status, with controls for mother and child background effects and child care arrangements, on the 1994 delinquency index. Current family income and current hours employed are also controlled to estimate the independent effects of early work.

. . . [C]hild's sex and child's age are both significant predictors of delinquency; females are less involved in delinquency than males, and increasing age is associated with greater involvement in delinquency. As the data show, none of the early employment variables, including welfare reliance, are significant predictors of delinquency in 1994. It should be noted, however, that a near significant effect of coercive maternal work on later delinquency appeared. When mothers were employed under coercive conditions in 1986, their children had greater involvement in delinquency in 1994. This relationship was significant at the .07 level of probability. Finally, current family income is inversely related to delinquency.

The impact of father's early and current employment status and work hours on delinquency was also examined. With professional fathers as the reference category, the effects of father's work were assessed. Controls for maternal resources, child characteristics, family income, and maternal work were included in the model. No significant effects on delinquency for either the early or current measures of paternal work were detected. Furthermore, the inclusion of paternal work measures did not change the relationships between mother's work and delinquency.

Early Maternal Employment, Early Pathways, and Delinquency

. . . [The] effects of early work, maternal resources, child characteristics, child care, and delinquency pathways on delinquency . . . [show] both child's sex and age remain significantly associated with delinquency. Introducing the pathway variables—spanking, warmth and responsiveness, and insecure attachment—does not diminish the influence of sex and age. Again, we should note that coercive maternal work during the child's early school years remains related to greater delinquency in 1994 at the .07 level. Current family income remains a significant predictor of delinquency.

Furthermore, none of the early pathway variables exhibited a significant influence on delinquent involvement. The addition of these variables did not contribute any additional explained variation over the model that consisted only of maternal resources, child characteristics, and maternal employment. In this sample, spanking, maternal warmth and responsiveness, and insecure attachment cannot be considered "pathways" to delinquency.

Current Maternal Employment and the Pathways to Delinquency

. . . [The] effects of current maternal work on five "pathways" to delinquency—supervision, delinquent peers, warmth and responsiveness, mother-child attachment, and school attachment . . . [show] older children are supervised less by mothers. . . . [Being] female is associated with greater maternal supervision, less delinquent peer association, higher attachment to mothers, and greater school attachment. Greater maternal AFQT and higher family income are linked to more warmth and responsiveness in parenting, while welfare reliance had the opposite effect. Increasing AFQT is also related to a closer mother-child bond in adolescence. Increasing family income positively influences school attachment.

Paid employment appears to share a complex relationship with maternal supervision. Employment hours are positively, but very weakly, related to supervision. This suggests that greater maternal involvement in the paid workforce results in a higher level of maternal supervision of children. On the other hand, being employed in a bureaucratically controlled setting reduces maternal supervision. Compared to non-employed mothers, female professionals are less involved in the supervision of their children. Finally, children living in a disorganized neighborhood are prone to more delinquent peer association.

The Impact of Current Maternal Employment and Delinquency

. . . [Only] child's age and child's sex are associated with delinquent involvement. According to the data, being older and being male are associated with greater involvement in delinquency. Consistent with the early employment model, none of the current employment categories exerts influence on delinquency.

The Impact of Current Maternal Employment and Delinquency

Pathways on delinquency. . . . [The] influence of mother's current employment status, delinquency pathways, and control variables on delinquency . . . shows three delinquency pathways exert direct influence on delinquency. Greater maternal supervision, lesser delinquent peer influence, and greater school attachment are associated with less delinquent involvement. That is, controlling for maternal resources, child characteristics, and mother's work, those children who are supervised more closely, those who have relatively fewer delinquent peer associations, and those more attached to school are less involved in delinquent activities. These pathways exert the most powerful influence on delinquency in the analysis.

The above analysis suggests that maternal employment had no direct effect on delinquency, but did have an indirect impact through its influence on maternal supervision. Specifically, maternal work hours are related to higher supervision, which reduces delinquency. On the other hand, working under bureaucratic controls was related to lower supervision and, thus higher delinquency. These indirect effects, though small in size, are worth noting. These findings were confirmed by an AMOS structural modeling analysis of the main model: the small effects of maternal hours and bureaucratic workplace controls on delinquency were accounted for entirely by their impact on supervision.

Discussion

Are the children of working mothers more likely to be delinquent than other children? According to past studies and to the results of our analysis, the answer is a qualified "No." The present study demonstrates that regardless of how this issue is examined, having a working mother has only a small and indirect effect on delinquency. This general pattern holds whether we considered maternal employment in a child's pre-school years or maternal work in adolescence. Furthermore, with the lone exception of maternal supervision, maternal employment has little influence on several known pathways to delinquency.

Like Parcel and Menaghan and more recent findings by Harvey, our research suggests that the widespread concern over the fates of working women and their children is largely unsupported. Rather than being a social problem whose untoward effects can be demonstrated empirically, the maternal employment-delinquency connection is better understood as a socially constructed problem. As a perceived social problem, the dark side of maternal employment has a long history in America. Fueled by scientific data on the link between early family processes and delinquency and by cherished popular beliefs in the sanctity of the "first relationship"—the coupling of mother and child—for decades politicians and social commentators have pointed to modern trends in female labor participation to explain social problems such as crime. But if the unprecedented entrance of mothers into the paid workforce is related to delinquency, it must be because working mothers fail their children by depriving them of the support and discipline they need. The current study adds to the growing literature that casts doubt on these assumptions.

Our findings suggest other notable conclusions. First, it is maternal and family resources, rather than the characteristics of maternal work, that most influence some well-known pathways to delinquency in our study. Maternal AFQT score, a measure of intellectual resources, affects both parental support and mother-child bonds in early childhood and in adolescence: mothers who draw from greater cognitive resources are more supportive in parenting and raise more securely attached children.

Although the AFQT measures an individual's intellectual capacity, it reflects the subject's developed abilities rather than a biologically assigned aptitude. The AFQT score varies with family of origin, geographic region, and years of schooling, which implies that, like maternal education, an AFQT score reflects relative social advantage or disadvantage. Our findings should be interpreted as further evidence that social disadvantage is reproduced partly through its effect on parent-child relations. Consistent with this theme, our analysis found that an important family resource, family income, exerts a positive influence on warm and responsive parenting in adolescence, while welfare reliance has the opposite effect. This relationship is consistent with past research that identified economic hardship as a strain on family functioning.

The most powerful predictors of delinquency in our analysis are maternal supervision, delinquent peer association, and school attachment. Adolescents who are supervised more closely, those who have fewer delinquent peers, and those who are more attached to school show less involvement in delinquency. This result supports a large body of research that identifies these factors as important to the production of antisocial behavioral patterns. We reiterate, here, our discovery that maternal employment had relatively little negative impact on these important pathways to delinquency.

In one instance, however, workplace controls had a small indirect effect on delinquency. Specifically, bureaucratic work controls were negatively related to maternal supervision and, thus, had a slightly positive effect on delinquency. One interpretation of this result is that professional mothers may invest more time in their careers than the average mother does which may diminish their ability to monitor children. On the other hand, the negative effect of bureaucratic controls on supervision may not reflect a difference in time spent with children so much as a difference in parenting style. The freedom and autonomy experienced by the professional parent may translate into a parenting style characterized by less overt supervision and greater attempts to equip children with internal normative controls.

Conversely, we found that maternal work hours were indirectly related to lower involvement in delinquency, through their positive effect on supervision. Again, although the effect is small, maternal work hours is actually related to greater supervision in our sample. This may be due to the stabilizing influence of steady employment on family life. As Wilson has argued, a job "constitutes a framework for daily behavior and patterns of interaction because it imposes disciplines and regularities" upon a parent.

Furthermore, while no maternal employment variable is related to delinquent peer association, neighborhood disorder is. This finding is consistent with social disorganization theory: the breakdown of informal neighborhood controls leaves children at a greater risk for being socialized in intimate delinquent peer groups. It is instructive that our analysis points to community breakdown, as it operates through delinquent peer influence, as a cause of delinquency rather than family breakdown related to the absence of a working mother.

Finally, if improving family life is a goal of crime control policy, it would make good sense to aim at addressing the structural factors that limit maternal and family resources and that contribute to community disorder. Our study suggests that policy debates should avoid ideological attacks on working mothers, which portray them as leaving their children "home alone," and concentrate instead on the economic and educational inequalities that weaken families and neighborhoods.

POSTSCRIPT

Does Maternal Employment Have Negative Effects on Children's Development?

Selections in this issue provide an understanding of how some researchers argue the effects of maternal employment. One selection shows a negative effect on cognitive development in children whose mothers join the workforce. The second study opposes the first by asserting that maternal employment has very little effect over children's behavioral outcomes, particularly the development of delinquency. Each selection's authors used valid methods and yet found opposite results. What is the answer to how maternal employment in a child's first year of life affects their children's subsequent development?

It is difficult to control for all characteristics that may affect the outcome of studies on maternal employment. Researchers suggest that more studies be conducted on a larger population so that they might generalize the results for the population as a whole. It is also suggested that the research methods include a larger diversity of ethnic groups and social classes to gain a better understanding of how maternal employment affects a child's development and behavioral outcomes.

Researchers agree that maternal employment's effects on children need to examine the interaction of multiple variables, such as child care quality, control over work situation, and family and societal support systems. They do not agree on which sets of variables combine to give an accurate picture of how a mother's employment affects children's development.

Attitudes toward maternal employment have changed somewhat because of societal changes. It has become more socially acceptable today for moms to work. As more women obtain high-profile jobs in politics and corporations, more workplace assistance programs have been developed. These include on-site child care, flexible work hours, and allowing moms to work from home via computer technology. The realization that it is an economic necessity for single moms as well as both parents in a dual-parent household to work has created more of an acceptance for working mothers. Many families need two incomes to make ends meet.

Time-saving appliances such as self-cleaning ovens, dishwashers, and microwave ovens have given working moms more time to spend with their children. Obtaining food for dinner from the growing number of restaurants offering drive-through or pick-up service has also relieved working moms from the hassle of running home from work to make dinner. Of course, these time-saving means are only available to those who can afford them. Women with lower wages still struggle to balance work and family time. Welfare reform created a predicament for those who believed mothers should stay at home with their infants. With no governmental monetary support, how does a single mom stay at home with her children and still make a living for her family?

Young children want to be with their parents and need their parents to care for them. In an ideal world, most people want babies to be cared for by someone who loves them. In all but extreme abuse cases, this is generally the mom or dad. In our society, those who want to stay home and care for their children should have the opportunity to do so. Yet, the economic environment prevents this from happening. Perhaps another way to look at the issue of maternal employment's effects on children's development is to develop ways to allow moms who want to stay home to raise their children to do so, as well as to give social support to those moms who want to work outside the home.

Related Readings

Barnett, Rosalind Chait. (2004). Women and work: Where are we, where did we come from, and where are we going? *The Journal of Social Issues, 60,* 667–674.

Galinsky, Ellen. (2000). Ask the children: The breakthrough study that reveals how to succeed at work and parenting. Quill Publishers.

Hoogstra, L. (2005). The design of the 500 family study. In *Being together, working apart: Dual-career families and the work-life balance,* edited by B. Schneider and L. Waite. Cambridge University Press.

Schneider, B., & Waite, L. J. (2005). Why study working families? In *Being together, working apart: Dual-career families and the work-life balance,* edited by B. Schneider and L. Waite. Cambridge University Press.

Tiedje, Linda Beth. (2004). Processes of change in work/home incompatibilities: Employed mothers 1986–1999. *The Journal of Social Issues, 60,* 787–800.

Williams, Joan C., & Cooper, Holly Cohen. (2004). The public policy of motherhood. *The Journal of Social Issues, 60,* 849–865.

ISSUE 3

Should Scientists Be Allowed to Clone Children?

YES: **Kyla Dunn**, from "Cloning Trevor," *The Atlantic Monthly* (June 2002)

NO: **Robert A. Weinberg**, from "Of Clones and Clowns," *The Atlantic Monthly* (June 2002)

ISSUE SUMMARY

YES: Kyla Dunn, a former biotech researcher and now a reporter for PBS and CBS, details the six months that she spent with scientists inside the labs of Advanced Cell Technology (ACT), a group openly pursuing human cloning for medical purposes. Dunn outlines what the group hopes to accomplish through cloning, why the group believes that cloning is the best way to accomplish these goals, and the political and monetary trials that ACT faces.

NO: Robert A. Weinberg, a member of the Whitehead Institute for Biomedical Research and a biology professor at MIT, offers his concerns about what he calls the "cloning circus." Weinberg discusses the damage that many cloning groups have been doing to serious research and the impending dangers of reproductive cloning.

With several cloning groups, such as the Raelians, claiming to have cloned humans, society's debate over cloning is becoming even more heated. On one side there are conservative politicians, clergymen, scientists, and many members of the American public who believe that cloning is ethically wrong. On the other side are other scientists who have invested their professional lives toward cloning research and people suffering from degenerative diseases whose lives may be saved through therapeutic cloning.

Is cloning morally and ethically wrong? Is there a difference between therapeutic and reproductive cloning? Could cloning possibly be the key to curing many diseases? Is the utilization of embryonic stem cells the only way to proceed with this science, or can adult stem cells be used? These are just a few of the myriad questions being asked about cloning. While some of the questions have definitive answers, the ethical debate over cloning does not have an easy or definite answer.

As you read the following selections, try to suspend the personal attitudes about cloning that you may have developed. Try to learn about the process of cloning, what it truly is intended to do, and what it could possibly accomplish. In addition, consider what could be the consequences of allowing cloning to occur.

In the following selections, Kyla Dunn gives us an inside look into the cloning labs of ACT and the circumstances of a boy whose life could possibly be saved by cloning. The scientists at ACT are trying to make medical break-throughs that may cure many diseases. However, they must also deal with the pressure of finding adequate funding to continue their work. In addition, they live with the knowledge that on any day, governments around the world might ban their efforts all together. Robert A. Weinberg contends that many cloning groups have made a "circus" out of the scientific research community. He heightens awareness of the problems with animal clones and the far-reaching consequences that these problems may have on human clones.

Can governments worldwide effectively stop the rapidly evolving tech-nology and science of cloning? If human cloning were to be banned world-wide, would scientists throughout the world truly desist in their endeavors? Or, is the "cloning genie out of the bottle" with no possible way to return to the type of science that was practiced before cloning became possible?

YES

Kyla Dunn

Cloning Trevor

At 9:00 in the evening on January 29, just as President George W. Bush was about to begin his first State of the Union address, I gathered with three anxious scientists in a small, windowless laboratory in Worcester, Massachusetts. We were at Advanced Cell Technology—a privately owned biotechnology company that briefly made international headlines last fall by publishing the first scientific account of cloned human embryos. The significance of the achievement was debatable: the company's most successful embryo had reached only six cells before it stopped dividing (one other had reached four cells, another had reached two)—a fact that led to a widespread dismissal, in the media and the scientific community, of ACT's "breakthrough." The work was largely judged to be preliminary, inconsequential, and certainly not worthy of headlines. Many people in political and religious circles, however, had a decidedly different view. They deemed ACT's work an ethical transgression of the highest order and professed shock, indignation, and horror. . . .

Skin cell to embryo—it's one of the most remarkable quick-change scenarios modern biology has to offer. It's also one of the most controversial. Since the announcement, in 1997, of the cloning of Dolly the sheep, attempts to use human cells for cloning have provoked heated debate in the United States, separating those who have faith in the promise of the new technology from those who envision its dark side and unintended consequences.

Crucial to the debate is the fact that human cloning research falls into two distinct categories: reproductive cloning, a widely frowned-on effort that aims to produce a fully formed child; and therapeutic cloning, a scientifically reputable procedure that takes place entirely at the microscopic level and is designed to advance medical therapies and cure human ailments. The two start out the same way—with a new embryo in a petri dish. But the scientists I was observing in the lab had no intention of creating a person. Instead they were embarking on an experiment that, if successful, would be a first step toward creating radical new cures for patients like the donor of the skin cell—Trevor Ross (not his real name), a two-year-old boy afflicted with a rare and devastating genetic disease.

The mood in the lab was tense in part because of the uncertain outcome of the experiment. But it was also tense because of concern over what President Bush might say about cloning in his address to the nation. A radio in one corner of the room was tuned to the broadcast as the scientists began their work, and they were listening carefully: in perhaps no other field of science are researchers as mindful of which way the political winds are blowing. The ACT scientists had good reason to be concerned—what they were doing that night might soon be made illegal.

On July 31 of last year, by a 100-vote margin, the U.S. House of Representatives passed the Human Cloning Prohibition Act of 2001, which would impose a ban on the creation of cloned human embryos for any purpose, whether reproductive or therapeutic. Both forms of cloning would be punishable by up to ten years in prison and a million-dollar fine. The House passed the measure over the objections of a long list of biomedical organizations (including the Association of American Medical Colleges and the American Society for Cell Biology) and patients' advocacy groups. . . .

Politics and religion, it seemed, were trumping science. Therapeutic-cloning research was already ineligible for federal funding in the United States. In 1995 Congress had passed legislation barring the use of federal funds for any experiment in which a human embryo is either created or destroyed, thus making official a de facto ban that had been in existence since 1975. . . . As a result, the burden of moving many areas of important medical research forward has fallen on the private sector, a situation that by many accounts has severely hobbled research into treatments for infertility—and even disorders such as childhood cancer and birth defects. These research areas, like therapeutic-cloning research, demand the kind of long-term study and financial commitment that only the federal government can provide. This past summer human therapeutic cloning already fell squarely under the federal-funding ban, yet Congress was now going further, considering making that research illegal. . . .

Last fall, with the prospect of a Senate vote looming, I decided to take a considered look at cloning research. The time seemed right: it was a unique moment in what could be the development of a major new medical technology, an odd period of legislative limbo in which the first halting steps were being taken toward creating cloned human embryos just as such efforts were in imminent danger of being outlawed. . . .

Progress Measured in Eggs

"That's Trevor's cells," Jose Cibelli told me in the ACT cloning lab on January 23. Cibelli is the vice-president of research at ACT, and the scientist in charge of its therapeutic-cloning attempts. He's a gentle, compact man with dark hair, a trim moustache and goatee, and a vaguely worried expression. A native of Argentina, he speaks quietly and with a thick accent. . . .

The cells had come from a round plug of Trevor's skin, three millimeters across, and had arrived at ACT just five days before. The Rosses' dermatologist had chosen a crease between Trevor's buttock and thigh, where a scar would not be likely to show, and had punched down with a circular razor blade—past the dead cells of the epidermis and into the dermis, where fibroblasts grow and thrive. . . .

Cibelli now had fibroblasts for potential therapeutic-cloning experiments stored away at ACT from five patients: one with a spinal-cord injury, one with diabetes, two with healthy but aging bodies, and Trevor. But skin cells are the easy part—they're plentiful, hardy, easy to obtain and work with. Eggs are much trickier, and Cibelli had thus started measuring the likelihood of progress not in years but in eggs. "When do I think we'll get this to work?" he asked me rhetorically. "About two hundred eggs from now."

"We've gotten a handful of eggs so far," he had earlier explained. "It's a whole different game when you're talking about animal embryology versus human embryology." In the cow-cloning lab next door, for example, ACT receives 1,400 eggs on a typical day. But whereas cow eggs are available in abundance from slaughterhouses, human eggs must be obtained from young women who have undergone two weeks of hormone injections, regular visits to a doctor, and a nontrivial surgical procedure. All told, it costs ACT about $22,000 to take an egg-donation procedure from start to finish. "And the number is so small," Cibelli added. "I mean, you get ten eggs! Instead of working with a hundred embryos, I'm working with one." From July to October of last year, ACT collected a total of seventy-one eggs from seven donors—of which only nineteen were designated for cloning. That didn't leave much room for error, or much chance to tinker with conditions that might improve the chances of success. . . .

At five days of development a human embryo is smaller than a grain of sand. It's a perfectly round ball with a fluid-filled core. The internal architecture of the ball, however, is somewhat lopsided. Huddled against one wall of its interior is a group of cells known as the inner cell mass. The outside of the ball is destined to become the placenta and associated membranes; the inner cell mass is what forms a baby. But after only five days of development no cell's fate has yet been determined—it's impossible to tell which cells will become blood or muscle, skin or brain, gut or liver. All that is present is the simple raw material from which the more than 200 cell types in a human body will eventually be built.

If the inner cell mass of an embryo is removed at this early stage, it can yield cells known as human embryonic stem cells—which retain the ability to form any cell or tissue in the body. In a sense they are immortal, in that they can divide indefinitely in the lab, producing large quantities of cells. With the right coaxing those cells can theoretically be converted into an unlimited supply of tissue for transplant: new heart muscle for heart-attack survivors; insulin-secreting cells for diabetics; neurons to treat those suffering from spinal-cord injuries, the effects of stroke, or Parkinson's disease. Tissue engineers hope someday to build even more complex structures from these stem cells: new blood vessels for bypass surgery, new liver tissue, even new kidneys—all from what began as a loose collection of cells in a lab dish. They dream of a future in which all kinds of organs and tissues can be custom made to replace those ravaged by disease, injury, or a lifetime of hard use. . . .

A Radical Hope

Adrienne and Ben Ross (all names of the family members have been changed) first came to ACT late last October, ten months after their son, Trevor, and two of his cousins had received a diagnosis of X-linked adrenoleukodystrophy

(ALD), a relatively rare and underdiagnosed genetic disorder that can abruptly ravage the white matter of the brain, with devastating and often fatal results.

. . . Boys with ALD who are lucky enough to escape childhood cerebral onset are almost certain to suffer a degeneration of the spinal cord in adulthood, which can lead to such symptoms as muscle spasms in the legs, loss of bladder control, and general weakness and stiffness. Although symptoms in adults can vary a great deal in severity, a third of adults with the disease also develop brain involvement and are reduced to a vegetative state or die within three to four years of onset. . . .

Currently, the best treatment for childhood cerebral onset of ALD is a bone-marrow or umbilical-cord-blood transplant from a healthy, well-matched donor. . . . Compatible transplant donors are extraordinarily hard to find, however—and even when suitable donors are found, the transplants don't always take. Sometimes transplants don't work because a patient's immune system rejects the transplanted cells as foreign. In other cases mature immune cells in the transplanted material actually reject and attack their new host, a life-threatening condition known as graft-versus-host disease. . . .

The Rosses had sought out ACT with the radical hope that therapeutic cloning might someday allow doctors to create a transplant that would carry no risk of rejection. The work of a bone-marrow transplant is actually done by hematopoietic stem cells—cells in the marrow that restock our blood and immune systems throughout life, serving as a reservoir of new components as old ones wear out. HSCs are also the cells that have rescued patients with ALD. What the Rosses were exploring with ACT was the idea of coaxing human embryonic stem cells, taken from cloned embryos, into forming HSCs that might someday save Trevor. . . .

❧⟨◎⟩❧

What therapeutic cloning should allow scientists to do, [Michael] West explained, is provide a pure population of genetically modified cells. Use one modified cell for cloning, and the entire cloned embryo will then carry that modification. So will embryonic stem cells derived from it, and any therapeutic tissues they produce. Alternatively, scientists could do the modification in embryonic stem cells after cloning, and then grow a limitless supply of tissue from one properly modified cell. "We can give the patient cells that all have the same precise targeted modification," West said. "One hundred percent. We won't do that with gene therapy in our lifetime."

A therapy for Trevor isn't the only thing at stake. The stem cells derived from cloned embryos bearing an ALD mutation could be powerful research tools. In fact, scientists consider creating cloned embryos that match patients with a genetic predisposition to disease to be one of the most important therapeutic applications of the technology, because, for one thing, it would allow diseased tissues of all kinds to be created and studied in the lab. But such work is rarely discussed in the political debate about cloning.

As she listened to West spin out optimistic future scenarios, Adrienne began to wonder if they would be able to proceed—or if using Trevor's cells for cloning would be pushing the bounds of the law as well as of science. "Can you clarify for me?" she asked, interrupting West. "On the cloning side, if you're not using federal funds, can you do what you want?"

It's understandable that she would wonder. The House's anti-cloning legislation was designed to make everything Mike West and the Rosses were discussing that day illegal. If the Senate were to pass the bill, not only could ACT's scientists be prosecuted for attempting therapeutic cloning for Trevor but Adrienne and Ben could be prosecuted for participating in such an attempt. One provision of the legislation would make it illegal even to "import" a life-saving medical therapy developed elsewhere in the world through cloning.

Adrienne's question was a sore point for West. "Yeah, we're free to do what we want," he answered simply.

"But now they're looking to try to ban that?" Adrienne asked.

West hesitated. "Well, I don't know," he said. "The Senate at some point will take this up, and my honest, best read is, I don't believe the Senate will pass it." Still, he admitted, anything could happen. "We could lose," he said, "and that would be tragic." . . .

A Public-Relations Disaster

A few weeks later ACT took a risk that could have put the company out of business—and, worse, could have closed the door on the budding field of therapeutic-cloning research. On November 9 the company e-mailed a hastily written scientific paper to *e-biomed: The Journal of Regenerative Medicine,* an online publication known for its quick turn-around time. The paper announced dryly that in ACT's lab "three somatic cell-derived embryos developed beyond the pronuclear stage." Robert Lanza, ACT's vice-president of medical and scientific development, called before the report came out to give me a translation. "The news is going to be that we have the world's first cloned human embryos," he said. "I just want to give you a heads-up—because when we make this announcement, it might bump the war [on terrorism] off the front page."

On almost every level the announcement was premature. ACT's original goal had been to publish in a prestigious journal like *Science* or *Nature,* when the company had what it is really after: human embryonic stem cells derived from a cloned embryo. ACT had nothing like that—it had managed only to sustain a cloned embryo to the six-cell stage of development.

At first, ACT's scientists say, they were uncertain whether they should publish such preliminary data. But given that they were working in an ethically fraught area of science, they decided to be as open as possible about their progress.

After Lanza called me about the imminent publication of ACT's cloning paper, I traveled to his house, on an island in a pond in central Massachusetts, to discuss the announcement. . . . He, West, and Cibelli form ACT's core triumvirate. As we sat at his kitchen table, Lanza told me that rumors in the scientific community were starting to make him nervous. Apparently the mavericks of the cloning world—those trying to produce a baby—were possibly on the verge of getting some preliminary results. "If they should come out and make some sort of an announcement first," Lanza said, "it could do severe damage. Because when it breaks, if their goal is reproductive cloning, all of the research will be banned. It will be killed—and it won't matter what we say, because no one's going to listen anymore." Last year, in fact, the outrage surrounding the mavericks' activities had directly contributed to the passage of the House anti-cloning bill.

But ACT itself also bore responsibility. On July 12, just weeks prior to the bill's passage, *The Washington Post* had broken the news that ACT was trying to create cloned human embryos as a source of stem cells—making it the only group in the country to acknowledge such plans publicly. The uproar that followed was still fresh in congressional minds at the time of the vote. Congressman Bart Stupak, of Michigan, one of the bill's co-sponsors, alluded on the day of the vote not only to the renegades but also to ACT. "The need for action is clear," he told his colleagues. "Research firms have announced their intentions to clone embryos for research purposes and then discard what is not needed."

A week before the publication of ACT's paper in *The Journal of Regenerative Medicine,* I called Thomas Okarma, the current chief executive officer of Geron, to get his views on ACT and its reputation. Despite his commitment to stem-cell and therapeutic-cloning research, Okarma was harshly critical of ACT. "They've done more harm to the field than good, I'm afraid," he told me. The most glaring example, he said, was ACT's announcement, just after Mike West joined the company, in the fall of 1998, that it was attempting to fuse human skin cells with cow eggs whose nuclear DNA had been removed. The motivation was sound: ACT was essentially hoping to do therapeutic cloning without the difficulty and expense of using human eggs—reviving experiments Jose Cibelli had started as a graduate student, in 1996, with his own cells. But, in the interest of "transparency" West released details to *The New York Times* and *48 Hours,* and two days after the news broke, President Bill Clinton, "deeply troubled" by the work, asked the head of his National Bioethics Advisory Commission to investigate. By an unfortunate coincidence, one week before the *48 Hours* broadcast, scientists had announced that they had derived human embryonic stem cells for the first time—news that made ACT's announcement seem like me-too publicity.

The cow-human embryos turned out to be "just plain duds," according to West, and ACT has never generated enough data for a significant scientific paper. (Members of the scientific community had predicted this outcome, although researchers in China have recently claimed success using rabbit eggs.) But the damage was done, because the public entirely misinterpreted the experiments. "Religious fundamentalists who, you know, are against reproductive and therapeutic cloning anyway, are using this example," Okarma told me. "'My God,' they say, 'these people are going to make chimeric creatures—mixing cows and humans.' It creates a fantasied negative scenario that casts an umbra on all of us working in the field, and makes it harder for the field to advance. And it's well documented in the scientific literature that fusing cells from two such distantly related species will not work." Okarma was not alone in dismissing ACT: the company's "publication by press release" was widely attacked by other scientists as irresponsible and insubstantial.

He added, "It's not in the same category as the Raëlians"—a religious group, inspired by "revelations" from extraterrestrials, that is working on reproductive cloning—"because there are certainly legitimate scientists at ACT trying to do this work, okay? But from the perspective of the regulatory bodies, they are in the same spaceship." . . .

"An Incredible Gift to Mankind"

. . . The most frequent refrain among political opponents of therapeutic cloning, and of human embryonic-stem-cell research in general, is that adult stem cells are a better choice for the development of medical therapies. Like cells from cloned embryos, adult stem cells are a perfect genetic match for a patient. Unlike embryonic cells, however, they can be found in the tissues of the patient's own body—a fact that prompted Senator [Sam] Brownback [of Kansas], after ACT's announcement, to insist on CNN that adult-stem-cell research is "a much better route to go." Opponents of therapeutic cloning wonder why there's a need to work with embryonic cells at all, since adult stem cells aren't rejected by the immune system, can produce a wide variety of body tissues, and do not require destroying embryos.

A report released by the NIH last July provided some answers, pointing out most adult stem cells are rare, may be difficult or dangerous to harvest from patients, and have a limited capacity to divide in the laboratory, which means that they can't yet be grown in large enough quantities to be of therapeutic value. What's more, adult stem cells have not been found for all types of tissue. . . .

"When there's this ethics debate about adult versus embryonic stem cells and cloning," Mike West told me, "I don't think what's properly weighed in the balance is the amazing breakthrough that this is. I mean, the idea that you can take a person of any age—a hundred and twenty years old—and take a skin cell from them and give them back their own cells that are young! Cells of any kind, with any kind of genetic modification! That's such an incredible gift to mankind! For the U.S. Congress to spend two hours and debate this and say, 'Oh, we'll make all this illegal,' to me is unbelievable. They don't understand." He shook his head. "We've never been able to do anything like this before."

Malcolm Moore's [a specialist in blood-cell development at the Memorial Sloan-Kettering Institute, in Manhattan] main concern is that Congress will shut the door on this research before its full benefits are known—if they indeed exist. "Basically," he told me, "my plea is, don't close down an avenue of research that might be of value in the future in the treatment of human disease. Time, science, and medical practice will be the ultimate proofs of whether these strategies are going to benefit mankind."

Bob Lanza put things more enthusiastically. "I'd stake my life on it," he said. "If this research is allowed to proceed, by the time we grow old, this will be a routine thing." He pounded the table we were sitting at, for emphasis. "You'll just go and get a skin cell removed at the doctor's office, and they'll give you back a new organ or some new tissue—a new liver, a new kidney—and you'll be fixed. And it's not science fiction. This is very, very real."

Breaching the Zona Pellucida

. . . If and when Trevor's skin cell fused with the empty egg, what exactly was going to be created? "You are creating people," Sam Brownback has insisted. "You're creating humans." Opponents of therapeutic cloning believe that embryos deserve governmental protection before they have even divided from one cell into two (although not even the world's major religions agree on when a human life begins).

Positions like Senator Brownback's frustrate Mike West. "I'm just very disappointed," he said to me. "I'm sad, because even the critics admit that millions of human beings and their fate in the hospital may be contingent on this research." As a young man, West was an evangelical Christian and a creationist. He protested outside abortion clinics. But swayed by the scientific evidence for evolution, he eventually abandoned the biblical view of creation. Science now dictates his view of the earliest human embryos as well. "You can be as pro-life as you can get," he told me, "but you can't say that making and destroying a pre-implantation embryo is the destruction of a human. Because it isn't. If it was a human life, I wouldn't touch it. Absolutely not." He went on, "A human individual does not begin at conception. It begins at primitive-streak formation."

The "primitive streak" appears after fourteen days of embryonic development in utero. It's like an arrow drawn on the embryo, one that delineates head and tail, front and back. Until then how many individuals, if any, that tiny ball of tissue will produce is entirely unclear. During the first two weeks of development one embryo can still split into two, a process that produces identical twins. Remarkably, two embryos can also fuse into one, eventually resulting in a single person whose body is a patchwork of two genotypes (with each eye a different color, perhaps, or mottled, two-tone skin). Not until the appearance of the primitive streak are the beginnings of a human individual sketched out. At that point, according to West, "There is no brain, no sensation, no pain, no memory, nothing of that. But it is an individualized human in a very early stage, and I advocate we don't touch that. But before then—they're wrong. It is just cells, it is a kind of raw material for life: the cellular life out of which human life arises."

West's line of thinking is fully consistent with the conclusions laid out by the NIH Human Embryo Research Panel in 1994. "If the President and members of Congress really understood what these little balls of cells were," West went on, "they would have a completely different view."

Adrienne Ross has a blunter assessment. "To me," she told me, "it's like, how dare they tell me that I cannot save my son's life? It's as simple as that.

YES

Ezra E. H. Griffith and
Rachel L. Bergeron

Cultural Stereotypes Die Hard:
The Case of Transracial Adoption

The adoption of black children by white families, commonly referred to as transracial adoption in the lay and professional literature, is the subject of a debate that has persisted in American society for a long time. On one side of the divide are those who believe that black children are best raised by black families. On the other are the supporters of the idea that race-matching in adoption does not necessarily serve the best interests of the child and that it promotes racial discrimination.

Coming as it does in the midst of myriad other discussions in this country about black-white interactions, transracial adoption has occupied an important place in any debate about adoption policy. But in addition, as can be seen in language utilized by the Fifth Circuit Court in a 1977 case, there is a long-held belief that since family members resemble one another, it follows that members of constructed families should also look like each other so as to facilitate successful adoption outcomes. . . .

In utilizing this language, the court acknowledged that transracial adoption ran counter to the cultural beliefs that many people held about the construction of families. Still, the court concluded that while the difficulties attending transracial adoption justified the consideration of race as a relevant factor in adoption proceedings, race could not be the sole factor considered. With a bow to both sides in the transracial adoption debate, the argument could only continue.

As the debate marches on, mental health professionals are being asked to provide expert opinions about whether it would be preferable for a particular black child to be raised by a black family or by a family or adult of a different ethnic or racial group. There are, of course, different scenarios that may lead to the unfolding of these adoption disputes. For example, the question may arise when a black child is put up for adoption after having spent a number of months or years in an out-of-home placement. The lengthy wait of black children for an adoptive black family may understandably increase the likelihood of a transracial adoption. In another situation, the death of a biracial child's parents, one of whom was white and the other black, may lead to competition between the white and black grandparents for the right to raise the child. In a third possible context, the divorce of an interracial couple may result in a legal

From *The Journal of the American Academy of Psychiatry and the Law*, vol. 34, no. 3, 2006, pp. 303–314. Copyright © by American Academy of Psychiatry and the Law. Reprinted by permission.

struggle for custody of the biracial child, with race trumpeted at least as an important factor if not the crucial factor to be considered in the decision about who should raise the child. . . .

We have already alluded to two significant factors that have played a role in the evolution of adoption policy concerning black children, particularly with respect to the question of whether race-neutral approaches make sense and whether transracial adoption is good practice. One factor has been judicial decision-making. In a relatively recent review, Hollinger reminded us that, in general, racial classifications are invalidated unless they can survive the "strict scrutiny" test, which requires meeting a compelling governmental interest. Hollinger suggested that the "best-interest-of-the-child" standard commonly used in adoption practice would serve a substantial governmental interest. Such argumentation would allow the consideration of race as one element in an adoption evaluation. Following this reasoning, while race-neutral adoption may be a lofty objective, the specific needs of a particular child could legally allow the consideration of race.

The second factor to influence the evolution of adoption policy in this arena has been the academic research on transracial adoption. This work has cumulatively demonstrated that black children can thrive and develop strong racial identities when nurtured in families with white parents. Transracially adopted children also do well on standard measures of self-esteem, cognitive development, and educational achievement. However, neither judicial decision-making nor scholarly research has settled the debate on transracial adoption policy.

In this article, we focus on a third factor that emerged as another mechanism meant to deal with transracial adoptions and the influential race-matching principle. These statutory efforts started with the Multiethnic Placement Act, which Hollinger stated "was enacted in 1994 amid spirited and sometimes contentious debate about transracial adoption and same-race placement policies." We will point out that even though the statutory attempts were meant to eliminate race as a controlling factor in the adoption process, their implementation has left room for ambiguity regarding the role that race should play in adoption proceedings. Consequently, even though the statutes were intended to eliminate adoption delays and denials because of race-matching, they may have allowed the continued existence of a cultural stereotype—that black children belong with black families—and may have facilitated its continued existence. This article is therefore principally about statutory attempts in the past decade to influence public policy concerning transracial adoption. Secondarily, we shall comment on potential implications of these developments for the practice of adoption evaluations. . . .

Brief Review of Race-Matching in Adoption

Feelings about who should raise a black child have run high in the United States for a long time. These feelings come from different groups for different reasons. Kennedy presented a number of historical cases to illustrate this. Among the cases he described, Kennedy told the early 1900s story of a white girl who was found residing with a black family. The authorities concluded that the child had been kidnapped and rescued her. They then placed her with a white family. When it was learned later that the child was black, she was returned to the black family because it was not proper for the black child to be living with a white family. This case, along with others described by Kennedy, is part of the fabric of American racism and racial separatist practices. Kennedy also pointed to the practice during slavery of considering "the human products of interracial sexual unions" as unambiguously black and the mandate that they be reared within the black slave community as an attempt to undermine any possibility of interracial parenting.

Whites have not been the only ones to support the stance of race-matching—the belief that black or white children belong with their own group. In 1972, the National Association of Black Social Workers (NABSW) stated unambiguously that white families should never be allowed to adopt black children. The NABSW opposed transracial adoption for two main reasons: the Association claimed that transracial adoption prevents black children from forming a strong racial identity, and it prevents them from developing survival skills necessary to deal with a racist society.

Since its 1972 statement, the NABSW has remained steadfast in its opposition to transracial adoption. In testimony before the Senate Committee on Labor and Human Resources in 1985, the President of the NABSW reiterated the Association's position and stated that the NABSW viewed the placement of black children in white homes as a hostile act against the black community, considering it a blatant form of race and cultural genocide.

In 1991, the NABSW reaffirmed its position that black children should not be placed with white parents under any circumstances, stating that even the most loving and skilled white parent could not avoid doing irreparable harm to an African-American child. In its 1994 position paper on the preservation of African-American families, the NABSW indicated that, in placement decisions regarding a black child, priority should be given to adoption by biological relatives and then to black families. Transracial adoption "should only be considered after documented evidence of unsuccessful same race placements has been reviewed and supported by appropriate representatives of the African American community." . . .

Race-matching has been and remains an influential and controversial concept regarding how best to construct adoptive families. Matching, in general, has been a classic principle of adoption practice, governing non-relative adoptions for much of the 20th century. Its goal was to create families in which the adoptive parents looked as though they could be the adopted child's biological parents. Matching potential adoptive parents and children on as many physical, emotional, and cultural characteristics as possible was seen as a way of insuring against adoptive failure. It was not uncommon for potential adoptive parents to be denied the possibility of adoption if their hair and eye color did not match those of a child in need of adoption. Differences among family members in constructed families were seen as threats to the integration of an adopted child and the child's identification with the adoptive parents. Race, along with religion, was considered the most important characteristic to be matched, and it continued to be important even as the matching concept regarding other characteristics began to shift. . . .

Matching, of course, continued to influence child placement decisions outside of adoption agencies, as evidenced by the comments of the Drummond court. Following that court's decision, the general rule has been that trial courts may consider race as a factor in adoption proceedings as long as race is not the sole determinant.

Statutory Attempts at Remedies

. . . The Black Social Workers had a quick and striking effect on transracial adoption policy. Following the appearance of the paper, adoption agencies, both public and private, either implemented race-matching approaches or used the NABSW position to justify already existing race-matching policies. As a result, the number of transracial adoptions were estimated to drop significantly—39 percent within one year of the publication of the NABSW statement. Although robust data were lacking, it was thought that the number and length of stay of black children in out-of-home placements increased as social workers and other foster care and adoption professionals, believing that same-race placements were in the best interest of the child, searched for same-race foster and adoptive parents. Agencies and their workers had considerable discretion in deciding the role race played in placement decisions. States, while generally requiring that foster care and adoption decisions be made in the best interest of the child, varied in their directions regarding the extent to which race, culture, and ethnicity should be taken into account in making the best-interest determination.

While race-matching policies were not the sole determinant of increasing numbers of black children in institutions and out-of-home placements, there was growing concern that such policies, with their focus on same-race placement and their exclusion of consideration of loving, permanent interracial homes, kept black children from being adopted. Because he was concerned that race had become the determining factor in adoption placements and that children were languishing in foster care homes and institutions, Senator Howard Metzenbaum introduced legislation to prohibit the use of race as the sole determinant of placement. Senator Metzenbaum believed that same-race adoption was the preferable option for a child, but he also believed that transracial placement was far preferable to a child's remaining in foster care when an appropriate same-race placement was not available.

Multiethnic Placement Act

Congress passed the Howard Metzenbaum Multiethnic Placement Act (MEPA) and President Clinton signed it into law on October 20, 1994. MEPA's main goals were to decrease the length of time children had to wait to be adopted; to prevent discrimination based on race in the placement of children into adoptive or foster homes; and to recruit culturally diverse and minority adoptive and foster families who could meet the needs of children needing placement. In passing MEPA, Congress was concerned that many children, especially those from minority groups, were spending lengthy periods in foster care awaiting adoption placements. Congress found, within the parameters of available data, that nearly 500,000 children were in foster care in the United States; tens of thousands of these children were waiting for adoption; two years and eight months was the median length of time children waited to be adopted; and minority children often waited twice as long as other children to be adopted.

Under MEPA, an agency or entity receiving federal funds could not use race as the sole factor in denying any person the opportunity to become an adoptive or foster parent. Furthermore, an agency could not use race as a single factor to delay or deny the placement of a child in an adoptive or foster care family or to otherwise discriminate in making a placement decision. However, an agency could consider a child's racial, cultural, and ethnic background as one of several factors—not the sole factor—used to determine the best interests of the child. . . .

So, under MEPA, agencies could consider a child's race, ethnicity, or culture as one of a number of factors used to determine the best interests of the child, as long as it was not the sole factor considered, and they could consider the ability of prospective parents to meet the needs of a child of a given race, ethnicity, or culture.

Following the passage of MEPA, the Department of Health and Human Services (DHHS), Office of Civil Rights, provided policy guidance to assist agencies receiving federal financial assistance in complying with MEPA. The guidance permitted agencies receiving federal assistance to consider race, culture, or ethnicity as factors in making placement decisions to the extent allowed by MEPA, the U.S. Constitution and Title VI of the Civil Rights Act of 1964.

Under the Equal Protection Clause of the Fourteenth Amendment, laws or practices drawing distinctions on the basis of race are inherently suspect and subject to strict scrutiny analysis. To pass such analysis, classifications or practices based on race have to be narrowly tailored to meet a compelling state interest. The Supreme Court has not specifically addressed the question of transracial adoption. It has considered race as a factor in a child placement decision in the context of a custody dispute between two white biological parents when the mother, who had custody of the child, began living with a black man, whom she later married. The Court found the goal of granting custody on the basis of the best interests of the child to be "indisputably a substantial government interest for purposes of the Equal Protection Clause." The DHHS guidance on the use of race, color or national origin as factors in adoption and foster care placements addressed the relevant constitutional issues and indicated that the only compelling state interest in the context of child placement decisions is protecting the best interests of the child who is to be placed. So, under MEPA, consideration of race or ethnicity was permitted as long as it was narrowly tailored to advance a specific child's best interests. Agencies receiving federal funds could consider race and ethnicity when making placement decisions only if the agency made a narrowly tailored, individualized determination that the facts and circumstances of a particular case required the contemplation of race or ethnicity to advance the best interests of the child in need of placement. Agencies could not assume that race, ethnicity, or culture was at issue in every case and make general policies that applied to all children. The guidance also specifically prohibited policies that established periods during which same-race searches were conducted, created placement preference hierarchies based on race, ethnicity, or culture, required social workers to justify transracial placement decisions or resulted in delayed placements to find a family of a particular race, ethnicity, or culture.

The DHHS policy guidance did address MEPA's permissible consideration of the racial, cultural, or ethnic background of a child and the capacity of the prospective foster or adoptive parents to meet the needs of a child of this background as one of a number of factors in the best-interest-of-the-child determination. The guidance allowed agencies to assess the ability of a specific potential adoptive family to meet a specific child's needs related to his or her racial, ethnic, or cultural background, as long as the assessment was done in the context of an individualized assessment. . . .

However, agencies were not allowed to make decisions based on general assumptions regarding the needs of children of a specific race, ethnicity, or culture or about the ability of prospective parents of a specific race, ethnicity, or culture to care or nurture the identity of a child of a different race, ethnicity, or culture.

To increase the pool of potential foster or adoptive parents, MEPA also required states to develop plans for the recruitment of potential foster and adoptive families that reflected the ethnic and racial diversity of the children needing placement. The recruitment efforts had to be focused on providing all eligible children with the opportunity for placement and on providing all qualified members of the community with an opportunity to become an adoptive or foster parent. As a result, while MEPA sought in a reasonable way to recruit a broad racial and cultural spectrum of adoptive families, the law was at the same time underlining the idea that there was something special about a black child's being raised by a black family.

Those who objected to the permissive consideration of race in MEPA asserted that it allowed agencies to continue to delay adoptions of minority children based on race concerns. They also argued that race-matching policies could and did continue under MEPA. Social workers could, for example, use race as a factor to support a finding that a transracial adoption was not in a given child's best interest. Supporters of MEPA reached their own conclusion that it did not accomplish its goal of speeding up the adoption process and moving greater numbers of minority children into foster care or adoption placements and that the permissive consideration of race allowed agencies legitimately to continue race-matching to deny or delay the placement of minority children with white adoptive parents. Senator Metzenbaum himself agreed with this conclusion about MEPA and worked for its repeal. As we shall see later, the arguments and counterarguments about the effectiveness of MEPA were being made in the absence of robust data.

The Interethnic Adoption Provisions

MEPA was repealed when on August 20, 1996, President Clinton signed the Small Business Job Protection Act of 1996. Section 1808 of the Act was entitled

"Removal of Barriers to Interethnic Adoption" (The Interethnic Adoption Provisions; IEP). MEPA's permissible consideration provision was removed and its language changed. (The words in brackets were part of MEPA and do not appear in the IEP.) . . .

Under the IEP, states were still required to "provide for the diligent recruitment of potential foster and adoptive families that reflect the ethnic and racial diversity of children in the State for whom foster and adoptive homes are needed."

Failure to comply with MEPA was a violation of Title VI of the Civil Rights Act of 1964; failure to comply with the IEP is also a violation of Title VI. Under MEPA, an agency receiving federal assistance that discriminated in its child placement decisions on the basis of race and failed to comply with the Act could forfeit its federal assistance and an aggrieved individual had the right to bring an action seeking equitable relief in federal court or could file a complaint with the Office of Civil Rights. The IEP added enforcement provisions that specified graduated fiscal sanctions to be imposed by DHHS against states found to be in violation of the law and gave any individual aggrieved by a violation the right to bring an action against the state or other entity in federal court.

The Department of Health and Human Services issued two documents to provide practical guidance for complying with the IEP: a memorandum and a document in question-and-answer format. According to the guidance, Congress, in passing the IEP, clarified its intent to eliminate delays in adoption or foster care placements when they were in any way avoidable. Race and ethnicity could not be used as the basis for any denial of placement nor used as a reason to delay a foster care or adoptive placement. The repeal of MEPA's "permissible consideration" provision was seen as confirming that strict scrutiny was the appropriate standard for consideration of race or ethnicity in adoption and foster care placements. DHHS argued that it had never taken the position that MEPA's permissible consideration language allowed agencies to take race into account routinely in making placement decisions because such a view would be inconsistent with a strict scrutiny standard. It reaffirmed that any decision to consider race as a necessary element in a placement decision has to be based on concerns arising out of the circumstances of the particular situation. . . .

The guidance again made clear that the best interest of the child is the standard to be used in making placement decisions. So, according to the guidance, the IEP prohibits the routine practice of taking race and ethnicity into consideration ("Public agencies may not routinely consider race, national origin, and ethnicity in making placement decisions"), but it allows for the consideration of race, national origin, and ethnicity in certain specific situations ("Any consideration of these factors must be done on an individualized basis where special circumstances indicate that their consideration is warranted"). Once again, such language seems to suggest that, in certain contexts, the adoptive child may well benefit from placement in a same-race family.

The DHHS guidance seemed to frame the possibility for adoption agencies to continue the practice of race-matching. For example, while warning that assessment of a prospective parent's ability to serve as a foster or adoptive parent must not act as a racial or ethnic screen and indicating that considerations of race must not be routine in the assessment function, the guidance conceded that an important aspect of good social work is an individualized assessment of a prospective parent's ability to be an adoptive or foster parent. Thus, it allows for discussions with prospective adoptive or foster care parents about their feelings, preferences, and capacities regarding caring for a child of a particular race or ethnicity. . . .

Discussion

In considering the best interests of a child who is being placed for adoption, DHHS is suggesting that there could be special circumstances uniquely individualized to the child that require consideration of ethnicity and race of the potential adoptive parents. Presumably this should not be done routinely and should not be seen as serving as a proxy for a consistent and mundane contemplation of ethnicity or race in the adoption context. Undoubtedly, what constitutes special circumstances in the practices of any given adoption agency is likely to be a matter of interpretation. While agencies can readily assert what their routine practices are, much may turn on how vigorously supervised are the claims that special circumstances exist with respect to a particular black child that dictate consideration of ethnicity and race in that child's case. As a practical result, while it appears no one is now allowed to claim that every black child needs a black family, it may still be reasonable and practicable to claim that a black child requires adoption by a black family, as dictated by consideration of the best interests of that child. For example, Kennedy has raised the possibility that an older child might say he or she wanted to be adopted only by a black family. Such a context could indeed make it difficult for the child's wish to be refused outright, without any consideration whatsoever.

Such reasoning is articulated starting from the point of view of the child. Giving consideration to the interests of the potential adoptive parent is another matter. In other words, what should we consider about the adoptive parent's interest in raising black children and the parent's ability to do so? The opinions about this matter remain divided. Kennedy and Bartholet have proposed that prospective adoptive parents be allowed to state a preference for adopting a child from a particular ethnic group. This is, in their view, permissible race-matching that ultimately serves the best interests of the child. After all, what would be the use of forcing a family to adopt a child they really did not want? In addition, both authors also have argued that state intervention in such racial selectivity in the formation of families would be akin to imposing race-based rules on the creation of married couples. However, Banks has opposed this accommodationist stance, where in practice adoption agencies would simply show prospective adoptive parents only the class of ethnic children the adoptive parent was interested in adopting. Banks thought this merely perpetuated the status quo, as white adoptive parents had little interest in black children. This would result in black children's continuing to languish in out-of-home placements, and their time spent awaiting adoption would remain prolonged.

Kennedy and Bartholet were permissive in their attitude toward the racial selectivity of prospective adoptive parents, respecting parents' choice to construct families as they wish.

There has been and continues to be strong support for the belief that black children belong with black adoptive parents. It is not only the NABSW, which has called for the repeal of the IEP, that has taken this position. For example, in a 1998 letter to the Secretary of the Department of Health and Human Services, a former executive director of the Child Welfare League of America strongly disagreed with the DHHS's interpretation of MEPA/IEP, stating that prohibiting any consideration of race in adoptive and foster care placement decisions contradicts best-practice standards in child welfare. . . .

The CWLA, in its most recent *Standards of Excellence for Adoption Services* (2000), reiterated its belief that race is to be considered in all adoptions and that placement with parents of the same race is the first choice for any child. Other placements should be considered only after a vigorous search for parents of the same race has failed. . . .

In its most recent policy statement on foster care and adoption (2003), the National Association of Social Workers also reiterated its position that consideration of race should play a central role in placement decisions. . . .

Others have espoused the view that inracial adoption is the preferred option for a black child because black families inherently possess the competence to raise children with strong black identities and the ability to cope with racism. While questions of cultural competence to raise a black child often arise about prospective white adoptive parents, no such questions are posed about prospective black adoptive parents. The competence of black families to raise black children is regularly referred to as though black families are culturally identical or homogeneous and all are equally competent to raise black children and equip them to live in our society. We may all think about black cultural competence as though it is a one-dimensional concept. Indeed, we may all be referring simply to stereotypical indicators of what we think it means to be black. We may be referring to our own personal preferences for the stereotypic activities of black people: involvement in a black church; participation in a community center where black-focused programs are operating; viewing movies with a clearly black theme; reading literature authored by blacks. What is rarely considered is that some black families are drawn to rap music, others to jazz greats, and still others to traditional classical music. Indeed, some families obviously manage to exhibit an interest in all these genres of music. With respect, therefore, to even these stereotyped indicators of what it means to be black, black families vary in the degree of their attachment to the indicators. This is to say that blacks differ in their level of commitment to the salience of black-oriented culture in their individual and family lives. As a result, there is considerable cultural heterogeneity among black families. Such variability may well lead to differences in black families' ways of coping with racism.

To date, the statutory attempts to deal with transracial adoptions have not been considered as spectacularly successful, especially in the case of MEPA. Nevertheless, efforts have been made to limit the routine consideration of race and ethnicity in adoption, with the result that black children may be remaining for shorter periods in undesirable out-of-home placements. (National data are not yet able to demonstrate clear trends.) However, DHHS guidance still permits consideration of race and ethnicity in specific cases, with the apparent concession that some black children may need a black family for the realization of the child's best interests.

The burden is on forensic psychiatrists and other mental health professionals who perform adoption evaluations to point out cogently and logically two points: first, whether race is a factor that is relevant in the adoption evaluation; and second, whether there is something unique or particular about that adoption context that requires race to be considered. It will require special argumentation for the evaluator to claim that a particular black child could benefit more from placement with a black family than with a non-black family. As stated earlier, the evidence is clear that black children can do well in transracial placements. The pointed objective, therefore, in future evaluations will be to show that a particular black child has such unique and special needs that he or she deserves particular consideration for placement in a black family. It will be interesting to see whether our forensic colleagues, in striving for objectivity, will consider the factor of race in their evaluations only when something unique about that particular adoption context cries out for race to be considered so that the best-interest-of-the-child standard can be met. It seems clear that forensic professionals must be careful not to state that they routinely consider race in their adoption evaluations unless they intend to argue clinically that race is always relevant. And even then, they should be cautious about not articulating a general preference for inracial over transracial adoptions.

Despite federal statutory attempts to remove race as a controlling factor in adoption and foster care placement decisions, the debate over transracial adoption is not over. Indeed, strains of the debate are evidenced in the statutes and their implementation guidelines and the argument continues among our mental health colleagues. . . .

**Elizabeth Bartholet and
Diane H. Schetky**

 **NO**

Commentary: Cultural Stereotypes Can and Do Die: It's Time to Move on with Transracial Adoption

Ezra Griffith and Rachel Bergeron write in their article, "Cultural Stereotypes Die Hard: The Case of Transracial Adoption," that the controversy that has long surrounded transracial adoption is ongoing and that the law is significantly ambiguous. Accordingly, they say that psychiatrists and other mental health professionals are faced with a challenge in deciding on the role that race should play in adoption evaluations for purposes of foster and adoptive placement decisions.

I agree that the controversy is ongoing, but think that the law is much clearer than Griffith and Bergeron indicate and that it provides adequate guidance as to the very limited role that race is allowed to play. However, because of the ongoing controversy, many players in the child welfare system are committed to law resistance and law evasion. The challenge for mental health professionals is to decide how to respond to conflicting pressures and whether to use their professional skills to assist in good faith implementation of the law or in efforts to undermine the law. The challenge is a real one, because those committed to undermining the law do so in the name of the ever popular best-interests-of-the-child principle, arguing that best practices require consideration of race in placement decisions. However, in my view the choice should be clear, not simply because the law exists, but because the law takes the right position— right both for children and for the larger society.

Griffith and Bergeron acknowledge that, after a period in which race-matching was common and court-made law allowed at least some regular use of race in the placement process, the U.S. Congress passed laws governing these matters: the 1994 Multiethnic Placement Act and the 1996 amendments to that Act (here referred to collectively as MEPA and, when it is important to distinguish between the original 1994 Act and the amended Act, referred to as MEPA I and MEPA II, respectively). However they say that these laws "may still leave the door open to continued race-matching. . . ." They go on to say:

> [E]ven though the statutory attempts were meant to eliminate race as a controlling factor in the adoption process, their implementation has left room

From *The Journal of the American Academy of Psychiatry and the Law*, vol. 34, no. 3, November 3, 2006, pp. 315–320. Copyright © 2006 by American Academy of Psychiatry and the Law. Reprinted by permission.

for ambiguity regarding the role that race should play in adoption proceedings. Consequently, even though the statutes were intended to eliminate adoption delays and denials because of race-matching, they may have allowed the continued existence of a cultural stereotype—that black children belong with black families—and may have facilitated its continued existence.

Griffith and Bergeron accurately describe how MEPA I allowed the use of race as one factor in placement, so long as it was not used categorically to determine placement or to delay or deny placement:

> An agency . . . may consider the cultural, ethnic, or racial background of the child and the capacity of the prospective foster or adoptive parents to meet the needs of a child of this background as one of a number of factors used to determine the best interests of a child.

And they describe how MEPA II removed that section of the law, and made related amendments designed to limit the use of race. They note that the U.S. Department of Health and Human Services (DHHS), the MEPA enforcement agency, interprets the law to require strict scrutiny as the standard by which to judge use of race in placements and quote one of the guidance memoranda issued by DHHS. . . .

But they conclude that the DHHS guidance "seemed to frame the possibility for adoption agencies to continue the practice of race-matching," and "allows for discussions with prospective adoptive or foster care parents about their feelings, preferences, and capacities regarding caring for a child of a particular race or ethnicity." They go on to cite the positions of the National Association of Black Social Workers, the Child Welfare League of America, the National Association of Social Workers, and some others, all arguing for a systematic preference for race-matching.

While Griffith and Bergeron raise some questions about the wisdom of assumptions made by race-matching proponents that all blacks will be culturally competent to raise black children in a way that no whites will be, they conclude with a message that seems to emphasize the difficulty of the challenge faced by mental health professionals in deciding just how much weight to give race in their placement evaluations. They state that MEPA has not been considered "spectacularly successful," and that DHHS guidance permits some consideration of race in specific cases. . . .

In their final two paragraphs Griffith and Bergeron cite the Adoption and Race Work Group, assembled by the Stuart Foundation, as evidence of the ongoing debate within the mental health community, noting its conclusion that "race should not be ignored when making placement decisions and that children's best interests are served—all else being equal—when they are placed with families of the same racial, ethnic, and cultural background as their own."

There are several problems with the message that this article by Griffith and Bergeron sends to their colleagues. First, the law is much clearer than they indicate. MEPA II did, as they point out, eliminate the provision in MEPA I that had allowed race as a permissible consideration. MEPA II also eliminated related language indicating that some use of race might be permissible—language in MEPA I forbidding agencies to "categorically deny" placement, or delay or deny placement "solely" on the basis of race—and substituted language that tracked the language of other civil rights statutes, simply prohibiting discrimination. As I discuss elsewhere:

> The intent to remove race as a factor in placement decisions could hardly have been made more clear. The legislative history showed that the race-as-permissible-factor provision was removed precisely because it had been identified as deeply problematic. The simple antidiscrimination language substituted had been consistently interpreted in the context of other civil rights laws as forbidding *any* consideration of race as a factor in decision-making, with the increasingly limited exception accorded formal affirmative action plans.

While it is true that DHHS issued a 1997 Guidance Memorandum allowing consideration of race in some circumstances, that Guidance makes clear that race cannot be used in the normal course but only in exceedingly rare situations. . . .

Moreover, when the Guidance states that use of race in placement is governed by the strict scrutiny standard, it invokes a standard known in the legal world as condemning as unconstitutional under the Federal Constitution almost all race-conscious policies.

MEPA's prohibition of racial matching is controversial within the child welfare world, with some arguing for its repeal and others for "interpretations" that would allow for race-matching in blatant disregard for the clear meaning of the law. The positions taken by the Child Welfare League of America, the National Association of Social Workers, and the National Association of Black Social Workers, cited by Griffith and Bergeron, illustrate these organizations' disagreement with the law. The Report issued by the Stuart Foundation's Adoption and Race Work Group, relied on by Griffith and Bergeron in their concluding paragraphs, illustrates the commitment by many who disagree with the law to evade its restrictions. As I wrote when asked for my comments on this Group's preliminary draft report, which became the final report with no significant changes in tone or substance:

> From start to finish [the Report] reads like a justification for the present race-matching system, and an argument for continuing to implement essential features of that system in a way designed to satisfy the letter but not the spirit of [MEPA]. . . .
>
> The general thrust of the Report in terms of policy direction, together with its specific Recommendations, read to me like the advice prepared by clever lawyers whose goal it is to help the client avoid the clear spirit of the law. The general idea seems to be to tell those in a position to make and implement policy, that this is a bad law, based on a misunderstanding of the needs of black children, but that since it is less than crystal clear, it will be possible to retool and reshape current policies and practices so that they look quite different but accomplish much the same thing.

The fact that there is ongoing controversy about and resistance to this law matters. Law is not self-enforcing. It relies on people, nonprofit organizations, and government entities to demand enforcement.

However, just as controversy affects law, so law also affects controversy. The fact that federal law now states that race-matching is equivalent to race discrimination matters in a nation that has committed itself in significant ways to the proposition that race discrimination is wrong. Moreover this particular law mandates powerful penalties, specifying an automatic reduction of a set percentage of the federal funds provided to each state for foster and adoption purposes, for any finding of violation. This changes the risk assessment enterprise for typically risk-averse bureaucrats. Acting illegally can get you into trouble, especially if millions of dollars of financial penalties are at stake. While in the years after MEPA's passage I was one of the most vocal critics of the absence of MEPA enforcement activity, as the years went by I began to get the sense in my travels around the country speaking on these issues that social work practice was adjusting, albeit slowly, to MEPA's demands.

The dramatic new development is on the enforcement front. The U.S. Department of Health and Human Services (DHHS), designated as the enforcement agency for MEPA, has finally moved beyond the tough-sounding words that it issued providing interpretive guidance, to take action—action in the form of decisions finding states in violation of the law and imposing the financial penalties mandated by MEPA for such violations. Griffith and Bergeron make no mention of this development, but it seems likely to have a major impact on child welfare agencies nationwide and accordingly seems likely to change the context in which mental health professionals will work in making placement evaluations and the pressures on them with respect to the race factor. The first such enforcement decision involved Hamilton County, Ohio. In 2003, after a four-and-one-half-year investigation, DHHS's Office for Civil Rights (OCR) issued a Letter of Findings, concluding that Hamilton County and Ohio had violated MEPA as well as Title VI of the 1964 Civil Rights Act (42 U.S.C. Sec. 2000(d)), and DHHS's Administration for Children and Families (ACF) issued a Penalty Letter imposing a $1.8 million penalty. In its extensive Letter of Findings, DHHS confirmed that under MEPA as well as Title VI, strict scrutiny is the standard, and child welfare workers have extremely little discretion to consider race in the placement process. DHHS found that MEPA prohibits any regular consideration of race in the normal course, any regular consideration of race in the context of a transracial placement, and any differential consideration of transracial as compared with same-race placements. Moreover, the Letter stated that MEPA prohibits the variety of policies and practices used to assess transracial placements with a view toward the prospective parents' apparent ability to appropriately nurture the racial heritage of other-race children. More specifically, DHHS found illegal administrative rules requiring that: (1) home-studies of prospective adoptive parents seeking "transracial/transcultural" placements include a determination of whether a prospective parent is able to "value, respect, appreciate and educate a child regarding a child's racial, ethnic and cultural heritage, background and language and . . . to integrate the child's culture into normal daily living patterns"; (2) assessments be made of the racial composition of the neighborhood in which prospective families live; and (3) prospective parents prepare a plan for meeting a child's "transracial/transcultural needs." DHHS stated that, in enacting MEPA II, Congress "removed the bases for arguments that MEPA permitted the routine consideration of race, color, or national origin in foster or adoptive placement, and that MEPA prohibited only delays or denials that were categorical in nature." In the consideration of particular Hamilton County cases, DHHS regularly faulted child welfare workers for demanding that home-studies reflect a child's cultural needs, asking for additional information on racial issues, and inquiring into and relying on prospective parents' statements about their racial attitudes (e.g., intention to raise the child in a "color-blind" manner), the degree of contact they had with the African-American community, the level of racial integration in their neighborhood or school system, their plans to address a child's cultural heritage, their level of realism about dealing with a transracial placement, the adequacy of their training in areas like hair care, their unrealistic expectations about racial tolerance, their apparent ability to parent a child of another race, their willingness to relocate to a more integrated community, their apparent ability to provide a child with an understanding of his heritage, and their readiness for transracial placement.

In rejecting one of Ohio's defenses, based on allegedly inadequate advice on the operation of MEPA, DHHS found that the guidance issued in the form of various memoranda from 1995 through 1998 was fully adequate in clarifying the prohibition against any special requirements related to transracial placements.

The subsequent DHHS decision imposing the $1.8 million penalty took issue additionally with Ohio's apparent attempt to circumvent the law by a new administrative rule providing that an agency determination that race should be considered would trigger a referral for an opinion from an outside licensed professional (psychiatrist, clinical psychologist, social worker, or professional clinical counselor). The professional was to be required to provide an "individual assessment of this child that describes the child's special or distinctive needs based on his/her race, color, or national origin and whether it is in the child's best interest to take these needs into account in placing this child for foster care or adoption." DHHS faulted the process for signaling to the professional that the agency thinks race should be a factor, for the professional's lack of training regarding the legal limitations on considering race and for asking the professional whether race should be considered, while failing to require any finding by the professional: "that there is a compelling need to consider race; that such consideration is strictly required to serve the best interests of the child; and that no race-neutral alternatives exist." DHHS also noted that Ohio had indicated its desire for state approval to obtain opinions from professionals known to be opposed to transracial adoptions. DHHS concluded that the rule was "readily susceptible to being used to foster illegal discrimination."

In 2005, DHHS made a second enforcement decision, involving South Carolina, with OCR issuing a Letter of Findings concluding that the state's Department of Social Services had violated both MEPA and Title VI, and ACF issuing a Penalty Letter imposing a penalty of $107,481. In its Letter of Findings in this case, DHHS again emphasized that strict scrutiny is the standard and that the law forbids any regular consideration of race, allowing its consideration only on rare occasions and even then only to the degree it can be demonstrated to be absolutely necessary. DHHS found illegal South Carolina's practice of treating prospective parent racial preferences with greater deference than other preferences: "By treating race differently from all other parental preferences . . . [the agency] establishes its own system based on racial preference. . . ." DHHS also found illegal the agency's practice of deferring to birth parents' racial preferences, stating that the law requires agencies to make placement decisions "independent of the biological parent's race, color or national origin preference." Furthermore, DHHS found illegal the agency's practice of treating transracial adoptions with greater scrutiny, faulting, for example, the inquiries into prospective parents' ability to adopt transracially, and ability to nurture a child of a different race, as well as inquiries into the racial makeup of such parents' friends, neighborhoods, and available schools. And finally, DHHS found to be illegal various other ways in which the agency took race into consideration, including use of race as a "tie-breaking" factor, matching for skin tone, and use of young children's racial preferences—"the routine deference to and wide range of reasons given for . . . following the same-race preferences of young children undermines any claim that these placement decisions are truly individualized." In addition, DHHS made findings of violations in several individual cases, including that of a black couple interested in adopting a Hispanic child, in which the agency was faulted for inquiry into the couple's ability to meet the child's cultural needs. DHHS specified that any acceptable corrective action plan by the state would have to include, *inter alia*, support and encouragement for parents interested in adopting transracially, the creation of progressive disciplinary action, including termination, for staff continuing to use race improperly, the development of whistle-blower protection for staff who reported the use of race by others, and monitoring and reporting requirements designed to ensure future compliance with the law. The ACF Penalty Letter noted that, having reviewed and concurred in the OCR's Letter of Findings, it was imposing the penalty mandated by MEPA.

While these are the only cases in which Letters of Findings and Penalty Letters have been issued, DHHS's OCR has engaged in compliance efforts in several other cases, resulting in agreements by various state agencies to modify their practices in accord with OCR's demands. In addition DHHS's ACF has through various policy statements reenforced its commitment to rigorous enforcement of MEPA.

DHHS's recent enforcement action constitutes a shot across the bow for all state agencies involved in foster and adoptive placement throughout the nation. The opinions in the two cases in which financial penalties were imposed are as clear as they can be that, at the highest ranks, DHHS believes that MEPA and the various MEPA-related guidance memoranda that DHHS has issued mean that race cannot lawfully be taken into account in any routine way in placement decisions, that it is only in the exceptional cases that race can be considered, and even then that authorities will have to be very careful to demonstrate that compelling necessity demands such consideration, consistent with the strict scrutiny standard.

While DHHS guidance had in my view made all this clear previously, the fact that OCR has now taken enforcement action finding MEPA violations, with ACF imposing financial penalties, raises the stakes in a way that agency directors and agency workers will not be able to ignore. Penalties for MEPA violations are mandated under the law, and they are very severe, reducing by set percentages the federal funds on which states are absolutely dependent to run their child welfare systems. A 1997 DHHS Guidance Memorandum noted that in some states MEPA's penalties could range up to more than $3.6 million in a given quarter and could increase to the $7 to $10 million range for continued noncompliance. State agencies act at their peril in ignoring this law. So, too, do agency workers, since their supervisors are not likely to be pleased with action that puts the state's child welfare budget at risk.

Some will no doubt continue to resist and evade the law, but I predict that such conduct will diminish over time as the law becomes more established in people's minds as simply part of the nation's basic civil rights commitment. While some have called for MEPA's repeal there has been no significant move in this direction.

My hope is that mental health professionals will join ranks with those interested in following the law in good faith, rather than with those interested in evading its mandate. I say this not simply because MEPA is the law, but because I believe it is a good law, one that serves the interests both of children and of the larger society. Griffith and Bergeron note that black children "can" do well in white families, but I believe the social science evidence provides much stronger support for MEPA than that. By now, there is a significant body of studies on transracial adoptees, many of which are good, controlled studies, comparing them to same-race adoptees. My review of these studies and that of others besides me, reveals no evidence that any harm comes to children by virtue of their placement across color lines. By contrast, there is much evidence that harm comes to children in foster or institutional care when they are delayed in adoptive placement or denied adoption altogether, and there is much evidence that race-matching policies result in such delay and denial. In addition, there is evidence that even when child welfare systems purport to use race as only one factor in decision-making, rather than as a categorical factor justifying delay and/or denial of adoptive placement, race ends up being used in ways that result in just such delay and denial. This latter was, of course, the main reason Congress amended MEPA I to eliminate race as a permissible consideration—Senator Metzenbaum, the law's sponsor, became convinced that MEPA I was not succeeding in eliminating the categorical use of race because its permission to use race as one factor was being abused, something that many of us who supported MEPA II had thought was inevitable, based on experience.

So, it seems to me clear that MEPA serves the interests of children, by helping black children in particular to find placements in loving homes of whatever color as promptly as possible. MEPA also seems to me to serve the interests of the larger society, by combating in a small but significant way the notion that race should divide people. Race-matching is the direct descendant of white supremacy and of black separatism. For the state to promote the formation of same-race families and discourage the formation of interracial families, as it does when it endorses race-matching, is wrong in my view for the same reasons that barriers to interracial marriage were wrong. The U.S. Supreme Court struck down those marriage barriers in 1967 in *Loving v. Virginia.* Congress took an important step in passing MEPA II to bring our nation's child welfare policies in line with the rest of our civil rights regimen. This law makes the statement that while race, of course, does matter in myriad ways in our society, it does not and should not define people's capacity to love each other.

                               ·◈·

Commentary: Transracial Adoption— Changing Trends and Attitudes

. . . The increase in transracial adoptions of African-American children in the United States arose in response to the paucity of white babies available for adoption and pressures on public agencies to free children in foster care for adoption. The majority of single teenage mothers now choose to keep their babies. There is increased use of kinship care or adoption, and heightened use of birth control, all of which result in fewer newborn babies being available for adoption. In my state of Maine, the rate of teenage pregnancies has plummeted and is now one of the lowest in the nation. The option of seeking infants from abroad is fraught with uncertainty—concerns about health problems and attachment disorders, delays, expenses, and policies regarding adoptions by foreigners that keep shifting in many nations. Yet another attraction for parents considering adopting African-American babies is the shorter waiting period.

In many parts of the United States and other countries, communities have become more accepting of racially mixed families. In as much as African-American children tend to stay longer in out-of-home care than do white children, freeing them for adoption by white families became a means of alleviating this situation. In the 1990s, public agencies were under a mandate to hasten the exit of children from foster care into permanent care and the Adoption and Safe Families Act of 1995 offered incentives to states that increased adoption of children in foster care. This, combined with the Multiethnic Placement Act, resulted in a dramatic decrease in the number of children in foster care and those awaiting adoption. As of 2001, 14 percent of all adoptions were transracial, although most of them were international adoptions.

As noted by Griffith and Bergeron, the pendulum of statutes regarding transracial adoptions has been swinging like the chapper of a ringing bell. The common thread that runs throughout these debates and dialogues is the concept of adhering to the child's best interests. This guidepost dates back to a 1925 decision by judge Cardozo who first coined the term best interests. Goldstein *et al.* would later elaborate on this concept in their book, *Beyond the Best Interests of the Child,* in which they applied psychoanalytic concepts to the resolution of custody disputes. The best-interest standard has held up well over time and continues to be used by courts in determining child custody determinations. Most states further delineate a list of factors to be considered in making custody recommendations to the court.

Caseworkers and forensic mental health professionals have always had to be mindful of their potential biases in making custody recommendations. Such

problem seems to be in the differing points of view as to how to best achieve these goals.

Suggested Readings

Kennedy, R. (2003). *Interracial intimacies: Sex, marriage, identity and adoption.* Pantheon Books.

Lee, Richard M. (2003). The transracial adoption paradox: History, research and counseling implications of cultural socialization. *The Counseling Psychologist, 31*(6): 711–744.

The National Association of Black Social Workers: Position Statement on Trans-racial Adoptions. September 1972. http://uoregon.edu/~adoption/archive/NabswTRA.htm.

Vonk, E. (2001). Cultural competence for transracial adoptive parents. *Social Work, 46*:246–255.

Zamostny, Kathy P., O'Brien, Karen M., Baden, Amanda L., & O'Leary-Wiley, Mary. (2003). *The Consulting Psychologist, 31*(6), 651–678.

Zitter, J. M. (2004). Race as a factor in adoption proceedings. *American Law Review 4th, 34*:167, 2004.

Internet References . . .

Kids Count

This Kids Count section of the Annie E. Casey Foundation Web site posts data on national and state indicators of child well-being, referred to as state report cards. The Annie E. Casey Foundation is an organization that is dedicated to building a better future for disadvantaged children in the United States.

http://www.aecf.org/kidscount/

Children's Defense Fund

The Children's Defense Fund site includes data from every state on issues related to child care.

http://www.cdfactioncouncil.org

National Network for Child Care (NNCC)

This Web site from the National Network for Child Care (NNCC) provides resources for raising children. Included are links to sites designed especially for children, as well as sites that offer activities for children, nutrition information, and information on parent involvement issues.

http://www.nncc.org

Educational Resources Information Center (ERIC)

This Educational Resources Information Center (ERIC) Web site, sponsored by the U.S. Department of Education, leads to numerous documents related to elementary and early childhood education as well as to other curriculum topics and issues.

http://www.ed.gov

Just in Time Parenting Information

The Just in Time Parenting Information Web site includes newsletters that are designed to provide information relating to a child's specific age. These newsletters were developed by the Cooperative Extension Service in several different states. The timely information helps parents to understand how their children are developing.

http://www.parentinginfo.org

Early Childhood

*T*he period of early childhood is sometimes referred to as the preschool years. It generally encompasses ages two or three through four or five. This is a time when children become much more adept at taking part in physical activities, satisfying curiosities, and learning from experience. Preschoolers play more frequently with other children, become increasingly skilled in daily tasks, and are much more responsive to people and things in their environment. Many children begin school during their preschool years, an experience that gives them their first extended contacts with a social institution other than the family. Changing attitudes about discipline, family size, divorce, and the mass media all have implications for a child's development. This section examines some of the choices families make in rearing their preschool children.

- Is Spanking Detrimental to Children?

- Are Fathers Really Necessary?

- Does Divorce Create Long-Term Negative Effects for Children?

- Is Viewing Television Violence Harmful for Children?

ISSUE 5

Is Spanking Detrimental to Children?

YES: Elizabeth Thompson Gershoff, from "Corporal Punishment by Parents and Associated Child Behaviors and Experiences: A Meta-Analytic and Theoretical Review," *Psychological Bulletin* (vol. 128, no. 4, 2002)

NO: Diana Baumrind, Philip A. Cowan, and Robert E. Larzelere, from "Ordinary Physical Punishment: Is It Harmful? Comment on Gershoff (2002)," *Psychological Bulletin* (vol. 128, no. 4, 2002)

ISSUE SUMMARY

YES: Columbia University researcher Elizabeth Thompson Gershoff analyzed results from 88 studies and concluded that corporal punishment negatively affected children's behavior. Among the 10 negative outcomes were increased child aggression, decreased quality of the parent-child relationship, and increased risk of abusing a child or spouse in adulthood.

NO: Diana Baumrind and Philip A. Cowan, researchers from the University of California–Berkeley, and Robert E. Larzelere, from the Nebraska Medical Center, refuted Gershoff's findings by questioning her definition of corporal punishment and analysis techniques of the 88 studies. They feel mild spankings, when appropriately administered, are useful in shaping children's behavior.

The topic of spanking, also known as corporal punishment, provokes highly emotional responses from family practitioners, parents, researchers, and children. There seems to be no one who is neutral about the subject, especially children. It would be interesting to ask children about their feeling toward spanking. Were you spanked as a child? What was used to spank you? Bare hand? hairbrush? ruler? switch? The list could go on and on. Do you think the spankings negatively affected you, or did they teach you how to act appropriately? The following quotes are often used in relationship to spanking: "Spare the rod and spoil the child. I was spanked and I turned out OK. Kids need to be spanked to show them who's boss."

If you were not spanked, what was used to correct your misbehavior? Was the misbehavior explained? Was your correct behavior rewarded and your misbehavior punished? What about children who were not spanked or corrected in any way? Are they considered spoiled or out of control? Perhaps verbal abuse or a slap to the face was used to correct your behavior, or maybe you were ignored altogether. These techniques are considered similar to spanking in that they can become abusive or neglectful.

Ninety-four percent of American parents report spanking their children by the time their children are 3 years old. Although spanking is a popular form of discipline in the United States, several countries have outlawed spanking and the physical punishment of children: Austria, Croatia, Cyprus, Germany, Israel, Italy, Latvia, Norway, Denmark, Sweden, and Finland. Proponents of spanking point out that these countries' rates of child abuse have not declined as a result of banning spanking.

Spanking is associated with family violence and child abuse. These are the stories often found in the media about parents injuring or even killing their children as a result of physical punishment. While the media exploits these situations and makes the public feel outraged that children are treated this way, one must remember these are extreme cases. Most families feel they use spanking judiciously and do not consider it abusive.

Ultimately, spanking is used as a teaching tool and a way to solve problems. Parents see children misbehave, look for a way to gain the children's attention immediately, and spank them. Parents believe that by inflicting pain, they are changing children's behavior and solving the problem of misbehavior. Opponents of spanking ask the question of how children will change misbehavior if they are not taught what *to do* versus what *not to do*. In addition, the message is sent that I am bigger than you so I can solve this problem by hitting you.

In the following selections, Elizabeth Thompson Gershoff argues that spanking harms children by decreasing moral internalization, increasing aggression as a child and adult, increasing child delinquency and antisocial behavior, decreasing the quality of the parent-child interaction, decreasing the quality of mental health in childhood and adulthood, increasing the risk of being physically abused in adulthood, and increasing the risk of abusing a child or spouse in adulthood. Diana Baumrind, Philip A. Cowan, and Robert E. Larzelere refute Gershoff's claims by showing flaws in her definition of corporal punishment and her method of analyzing the 88 studies she used for her research study. They feel that Gershoff did not address the real issue of whether or not mild spanking is harmful.

YES

Elizabeth Thompson Gershoff

Corporal Punishment by Parents and Associated Child Behaviors and Experiences: A Meta-Analytic and Theoretical Review

Corporal punishment has been an integral part of how parents discipline their children throughout the history of the United States and has been a focus of psychological research for decades. Although a growing number of countries have adopted policies or laws that prohibit parents from using corporal punishment as a means of discipline (Austria, Croatia, Cyprus, Denmark, Finland, Germany, Israel, Italy, Latvia, Norway, and Sweden), both support for and use of corporal punishment remain strong in the United States, with 94% of American parents spanking their children by the time they are 3 or 4 years old.

Psychologists and other professionals are divided on the question of whether the benefits of corporal punishment might outweigh any potential hazards; some have concluded that corporal punishment is both effective and desirable, whereas others have concluded that corporal punishment is ineffective at best and harmful at worst. This controversy over corporal punishment has inspired a series of recent debates among psychological, sociological, and legal scholars about what corporal punishment does and does not do for children.

Despite this controversy and the hundreds of scientific studies invoked on either side of the debate, understanding of the child behaviors and experiences associated with parental corporal punishment has been limited to narrative reviews and "vote count" summaries of the number of positive and negative effects that accrue from corporal punishment. Crucial questions remain unanswered, such as what range of child behaviors and experiences are empirically associated with parental corporal punishment, as well as why, how, and for whom corporal punishment might have such effects. This article provides preliminary answers to these questions by synthesizing the current empirical evidence of, and theoretical explanations for, associations between parental corporal punishment and 11 child behaviors and experiences. . . .

From *Psychological Bulletin*, vol. 128, no. 4, 2002, pp. 539–544. Copyright © 2002 by American Psychological Association. Reprinted by permission. References omitted.

Meta-Analyses of Parental Corporal Punishment and Associated Child Behaviors and Experiences

The first step in understanding whether and how parental corporal punishment affects children is to establish to what degree corporal punishment is associated with the child constructs of interest. Toward this end, I present in this section the results of separate meta-analyses of the associations between parental corporal punishment and 11 frequently identified child constructs. Despite the inability of meta-analyses to yield definitive causal conclusions, they do constitute an effective means of establishing whether the associations of interest are present and thus pave the way for further research into causal mechanisms. To underscore the inability of meta-analyses to support causal conclusions, I refer to child "behaviors and experiences" or "constructs" associated with parental corporal punishment rather than to child "outcomes" in the context of the meta-analyses.

Distinguishing Corporal Punishment from Physical Abuse

Before examining the associations between corporal punishment and child constructs, it is important to establish what is meant by the term *corporal punishment*. Regarding legal definitions, 48 states and the District of Columbia specify what constitutes corporal punishment in their legal statutes defining child abuse; 29 states assert that corporal punishment encompasses the use of "reasonable" force with some adding qualifiers that it must also be "appropriate" (AL, AK, AZ, CA, CO), "moderate" (AR, DE, SC, SD), or "necessary" (MT, NH, NY, OR, TX, WI). Three states see the need to clarify that corporal punishment is limited to "nondeadly force" (AK, NY, TX). The present article adopts the definition of corporal punishment offered by Straus. "Corporal punishment is the use of physical force with the intention of causing a child to experience pain but not injury for the purposes of correction or control of the child's behavior."

A frequent criticism of research on corporal punishment is that nonabusive corporal punishment is often confounded with harmful and abusive behaviors, thus preventing conclusions about the effects of everyday spanking. This apparent confound has arisen because the majority of child abuse researchers view corporal punishment and potentially abusive techniques as points on a continuum of physical acts toward children. However, a consensus on where to draw the line between acceptable corporal punishment and dangerous physical abuse is noticeably absent in the United States. State laws defining what constitutes physical abuse often specifically include corporal punishment. Davidson reviewed the state definitions of *child maltreatment* and found that 12 states (DC, FL, IL, MT, NE, NJ, NY, ND, OH, RI, SC, WV) included the phrase "excessive corporal punishment" in their definitions of child maltreatment; an additional 11 states qualified corporal punishment as constituting abuse when characterized as "cruel" (CT, CO, NE, NM, OH, SD), "unlawful" (CA), "excessive or unreasonable" (WY), "severe" (NJ), "cruel and inhuman" (KS), or "extreme" (ME).

For the purposes of this article, I consider physical abuse to be a potential outcome of corporal punishment. Herein, corporal punishment will be operationally distinguished from physical abuse according to the definition of physical abuse provided by the National Clearinghouse on Child Abuse and Neglect Information, namely:

> Physical abuse is characterized by the infliction of physical injury as a result of punching, beating, kicking, biting, burning, shaking or otherwise harming a child. The parent or caretaker may not have intended to hurt the child, rather the injury may have resulted from over-discipline or physical punishment. (What Are the Main Types of Maltreatment? section, para. 2)

Behaviors that do not result in significant physical injury (e.g., spank, slap) are considered corporal punishment, whereas behaviors that risk injury (e.g., punching, kicking, burning) are considered physical abuse. The studies included in the meta-analyses discussed below explicitly targeted parental corporal punishment, rather than parental physical abuse, as potential predictors of child behaviors and experiences. As I describe in detail below, studies that included potentially abusive techniques in their definitions of corporal punishment were excluded from the analyses.

Methodological Concerns in the Measurement of Corporal Punishment

It is important to acknowledge at the outset that the majority of studies examining links between parental corporal punishment and child behaviors and experiences measure both constructs at the same point in time, thus preventing any conclusions about causality. As I discuss below, even measuring parental corporal punishment at one time point and a child behavior at a future time point may not be sufficient to infer causal direction. True detection of causality may require controlling for the child's rate of the behavior of interest at the first time point as well to account for autocontingency of behavior over time. With these points in mind, the meta-analyses described here do not afford causal conclusions but allow understanding only of whether corporal punishment and child constructs are associated.

In addition, because corporal punishment is used primarily with children younger than 5 years of age, because corporal punishment is used rarely by parents (1–2 times per month), and because assigning parents to spank or no-spank experimental conditions is untenable, researchers must rely on parent reports of corporal punishment rather than on observations. Although some methods of having parents report their use of corporal punishment, such as nightly phone calls or detailed daily discipline diaries, do have high validity, the majority of information on corporal punishment comes from parents' or adolescent and adult children's recollections of frequency of corporal punishment.

Child Behaviors and Experiences Associated with Parental Corporal Punishment

The goal of most research on parenting is to identify which practices promote positive and adaptive behaviors in children. However, in the study of parents' use of corporal punishment, much research has been biased toward finding negative child outcomes associated with corporal punishment. The meta-analyses below specifically include a balance of potentially desirable child constructs (immediate compliance, moral internalization, quality of relationship with parent, and mental health) as well as undesirable child constructs (aggression, criminal and antisocial behavior, abuse of own child or spouse, and victim of abuse by own parent). Discussion of why corporal punishment should be associated with such behaviors and experiences is presented briefly here; the hypothesized processes linking the experience of corporal punishment with these constructs are detailed in the process–context model in the second section of the article.

Immediate Compliance

The primary goal most parents have in administering corporal punishment is to stop children from misbehaving immediately. Laboratory research on learning has confirmed that corporal punishment is indeed effective in securing short-term compliance. Although there are many studies that purport to examine relations between corporal punishment and compliance, most of these studies do not involve observations of whether children comply immediately after corporal punishment is administered. Rather, such studies ask parents how often they typically use corporal punishment and correlate this frequency with parents' reports of how compliant their children are to all forms of discipline. To assess corporal punishment's effect on short- and long-term compliance separately, the subsequent meta-analysis of immediate compliance only includes studies that measured children's compliance to corporal punishment. Compliance that occurs at a point in time removed from an instance of corporal punishment is considered evidence of internalization.

Moral Internalization

Although immediate compliance may be a salient goal when parents initiate discipline, promoting the development of children's internal controls is more important to long-term socialization than immediate compliance. *Moral internalization* is defined by Grusec and Goodnow as "taking over the values and attitudes of society as one's own so that socially acceptable behavior is motivated not by anticipation of external consequences but by intrinsic or internal factors," and it is thought to underlie the development of children's social and emotional competence. Children's internalization of morals is thought to be enhanced by parental discipline strategies that use minimal parental power, promote choice and autonomy, and provide explanations for desirable behaviors. Attribution theorists emphasize that power-assertive methods such as corporal punishment promote children's external attributions for their behavior and minimize their attributions to internal motivations. Additionally, corporal punishment may not facilitate moral internalization because it does not teach children the reasons for behaving correctly, does not involve communication of the effects of children's behaviors on others, and may teach children the desirability of not getting caught.

Aggression

The association between corporal punishment and children's aggression is one of the most studied and debated findings in the child-rearing literature. Over the years, several reviews of the literature have concluded that corporal punishment is associated with increases in children's aggressive behaviors. Corporal punishment has been hypothesized to predict increases in children's aggression because it models aggression; promotes hostile attributions, which predict violent behavior; and initiates coercive cycles of aversive behaviors between parent and child. Early experiences with corporal punishment may model and legitimize many types of violence throughout an individual's life, particularly violence in romantic relationships. Indeed, in one longitudinal study, parents' use of corporal punishment in childhood was the strongest predictor of adolescents' aggression 8 years later, whereas permissive parenting was not a significant predictor. It was my expectation that corporal punishment would be associated in the meta-analyses with aggression in childhood as well as in adulthood.

Although aggression is often combined with antisocial behavior to constitute what are typically referred to as externalizing behavior problems, antisocial behaviors such as stealing are nonviolent and may be related to corporal punishment in different ways than aggression. In the present meta-analyses, the extent to which children engage in delinquent or illegal behaviors are separated from the extent of their aggressive behaviors.

Delinquent, Criminal, and Antisocial Behavior

Across decades of research, corporal punishment has been implicated in the etiology of criminal and antisocial behaviors by both children and adults. Attribution theory posits that associations between corporal punishment and child delinquent or antisocial behavior result from an inability of corporal punishment to facilitate children's internalization of morals and values. Social control theory suggests that parental corporal punishment erodes the parent–child relationship and in turn decreases children's motivation to internalize parents' values and those of the society, which in turn results in low self-control. These same processes may explain the relation between corporal punishment and adult criminality. In Glueck and Glueck's longitudinal study of delinquency, whether boys experienced a harsh parental disciplinary style predicted their arrest rates at ages 17 through 45. J. McCord also found in her longitudinal study that the extent to which parents were aggressively punitive predicted their children's criminal behavior as adults. The connection between criminal and antisocial behavior in childhood and adulthood is examined here in separate meta-analyses.

Quality of the Parent–Child Relationship

The potential for parental corporal punishment to disrupt the parent–child relationship is thought to be a main disadvantage of its use. The painful nature of corporal punishment can evoke feelings of fear, anxiety, and anger in children; if these emotions are generalized to the parent, they can interfere with a positive parent–child relationship by inciting children to be fearful of and to avoid the parent. If corporal punishment does lead children to avoid their parents, such avoidance may in turn erode bonds of trust and closeness between parents and children.

Mental Health

Although little theoretical work has been done to identify the processes by which corporal punishment would lead to mental health problems, harsh punishment (including corporal punishment) has been associated significantly with adolescents' depressive symptomatology and distress, even after controlling for age, gender, family socioeconomic status (SES), and history of physical abuse. Coercive techniques have been associated with decreases in children's feelings of confidence and assertiveness and with increases in feelings of humiliation and helplessness. If corporal punishment does have indelible effects on children's mental health, an association between corporal punishment and adult mental health also might be expected. In the meta-analyses I present below, the constructs of child mental health and adult mental health are analyzed separately and include varied indices of poor mental health, including depression, alcoholism, suicidal tendency, and low self-esteem.

Adult Abuse of Own Child or Spouse

If corporal punishment is associated with a general aggressive tendency in adulthood, this aggression also may manifest in relationships with family members, particularly with a child or spouse. The same processes hypothesized to account for an association between corporal punishment and general aggression also are expected to account for a tendency toward violence against family members. Specifically, if parental corporal punishment leads individuals to view aggression or violence as legitimate, make external attributions for their behavior, and attribute hostile intent to the behaviors of others, they may be more likely to resort to aggression and violence during conflicts with their children and spouses. A tendency toward intergenerational transmission of aggression in close relationships is evident in a strong tendency for parents who were corporally punished to continue the practice with their own children. Similarly, experience with both average (e.g., spanking) and extreme (e.g., kicking, biting, burning, and beating up) forms of corporal punishment by parents are associated with increases in an individual's likelihood of acting violently with an adult romantic partner.

Becoming a Victim of Physical Abuse

As stated above, child abuse researchers tend to see corporal punishment and physical abuse on a continuum, such that if corporal punishment is administered too severely or too frequently, the outcome can be physical abuse. The notion of a corporal punishment–physical abuse continuum is corroborated in part by physically abusive parents themselves: Parents who had abused their children revealed that as many as two thirds of their abusive incidents began as attempts to change children's behavior or to "teach them a lesson." Unfortunately, use of severe and potentially abusive physical techniques may be more common than has been realized. In a recent study, 16% of incidents reported by mothers and 21% of those reported by fathers were rated by independent coders as severe (e.g., use of spoons, sticks, or belts). The potential for the widely used practice of corporal punishment to be associated with a risk for injury to children behooves further research into this connection.

Method

Sample of Studies

I used three main sources to identify all articles that examined the associations between parental corporal punishment and child behaviors and experiences and were available through June 2001. The first source was the reference lists of relevant reviews, namely by Becker, Larzelere, Steinmetz, and Straus. Second, I conducted a computer-based literature search of *Psychological Abstracts* PsycINFO, *Educational Resources Information Center, Social Sciences Index*, and *Dissertation Abstracts International*. Key words used to identify relevant articles were *corporal punishment, physical punishment*, and *spank*. The third and final search involved the "ancestry approach" applied to the reference sections of all retrieved articles, book chapters, and dissertations. In the interest of being exhaustive, qualification for inclusion was not restricted to peer-reviewed journals; I made every attempt to include all relevant and accessible journal articles, book chapters, and dissertations so as to avoid publication biases.

The abstracts and often the full text of over 300 relevant works, including 63 dissertations, were studied for inclusion in the present meta-analyses. Half of these works did not include data, as they were instead focused on the debate about corporal punishment ($n = 69$), the prevalence of corporal punishment in the United States or abroad ($n = 42$), the antecedents to parents' use of corporal punishment ($n = 40$), attitudes about corporal punishment ($n = 21$), or other issues such as the history of corporal punishment and theories about how it affects children ($n = 27$). Of the 189 studies that did present data on potential effects of corporal punishment, 101 were excluded according to the following criteria: (a) 27% combined corporal punishment with abusive techniques or only examined abusive behaviors; (b) 22% predicted dependent variables that have not been considered consistently in the literature on corporal punishment (e.g., intelligence); (c) 22% did not provide sufficient statistics for calculation of an effect size (e.g., only included betas from regression with other variables); (d) 17% combined corporal punishment with other types of discipline (e.g., corporal punishment was grouped with verbal punishment); and (e) 12% did not study corporal punishment administered by parents, used exceptional populations, or were unavailable through interlibrary loan.

A sample of 88 studies, including 8 dissertations, met the above criteria and were included in the analyses. (Multiple articles from the same study were represented in the analyses by the effect size from only one article.) Of the studies included, 67 provided an effect size for a single metaanalysis, 15 provided effect sizes for two meta-analyses, 4 provided three effects sizes, and 2 provided four effect sizes, for a total of 117 effect sizes across the 11 analyses conducted. The total number of participants was 36,309 (studies contributing more than one effect size only counted once), with an average of 413 participants per study and a range of 14 to 4,529 participants per study. The earliest study was from 1938; 5% of the studies were from 1950–1959, 10% from 1960–1969, 10% from 1970–1979, 25% from 1980–1989, 47% from 1990–1999, and 2% from 2000. The range of studies incorporated in the meta-analyses included 26 nonsignificant effect sizes. . . .

Results

Meta-Analyses

. . . All of the composite effect sizes were significant (none of the confidence intervals include zero) and thus parental corporal punishment was associated significantly with each of the 11 child behaviors and experiences. According to J. Cohen's criteria for judging effect sizes, three of the composite mean weighted effect sizes are small (-0.09, 0.13, -0.33), four are small to medium (0.36, 0.42, 0.42, -0.49), two are medium (0.57, -0.58), one is medium to large (0.69), and one is large (1.13, immediate compliance).

Ten of the 11 meta-analyses indicate parental corporal punishment is associated with the following undesirable behaviors and experiences: decreased moral internalization, increased child aggression, increased child delinquent and antisocial behavior, decreased quality of relationship between parent and child, decreased child mental health, increased risk of being a victim of physical abuse, increased adult aggression, increased adult criminal and antisocial behavior, decreased adult mental health, and increased risk of abusing own child or spouse. Corporal punishment was associated with only one desirable behavior, namely, increased immediate compliance. . . .

Diana Baumrind, Philip A. Cowan,
and Robert E. Larzelere

 **NO**

Ordinary Physical Punishment: Is It Harmful? Comment on Gershoff (2002)

In . . . her comprehensive article, Gershoff (2002) used meta-analyses of 88 studies to provide what she offered as a conclusive answer to the question of whether corporal punishment (CP) is significantly associated with 11 frequently identified aspects of children's behavior. She found that except for an association with immediate compliance to parental demands, CP is associated with negative or undesirable behaviors (e.g., aggression, lower levels of moral internalization and mental health). . . .

Measurement Issues: Corporal Punishment, Spanking, and Abuse

Disputes about the potential impact of corporal punishment are occurring in the social context of a vigorous debate about the impact of spanking. There is an international movement by lay organizations such as EPOCH-Worldwide to criminalize corporal punishment or to discourage its use. The advocates of a blanket injunction against spanking have cited associations between physical punishment and detrimental child outcomes, such as those presented in Gershoff's meta-analyses, to support their position. Such direct application of correlational research to social policy decisions presupposes a causal link between physical punishment and the detrimental child behaviors with which it is associated. Before we deal with the issues of causal inference, it is necessary to examine what Gershoff meant by *corporal punishment* to be clear about how it is being defined and measured.

There is a sense in which participants in the current debate about the effects of corporal punishment are talking past each other. One issue to which some attention has been given is the need to make a distinction between legal abuse and corporal punishment. A second issue, which has not been given the attention it deserves, is the distinction between harsh and punitive but not legally designated abusive punishment and the more moderate application of normative spanking within the context of a generally supportive parent–child relationship. Although Gershoff cited Baumrind and

From *Psychological Bulletin*, vol. 128, no. 4, 2002, pp. 580–584, 586. Copyright © 2002 by American Psychological Association. Reprinted by permission. References and notes omitted.

Larzelere as concluding "that corporal punishment is both effective and desirable," it would be more correct to say they concluded only that a blanket injunction against disciplinary spanking is not warranted by the data.

An important scientific consensus conference on corporal punishment defined *spanking* as that subset of the broader category of corporal punishment that is "a) physically non-injurious; b) intended to modify behavior; and c) administered with an opened hand to the extremities or buttocks." Conferees, including Baumrind and Larzelere, agreed that the important debate was not about overly severe forms of corporal punishment but only about parental spanking, which inflicts a minor, temporary level of physical pain, if that. Conferees agreed that abusive corporal punishment should be criminalized and corporal punishment that exceeds mild to moderate spanking or is used with children younger than 18 months or after puberty should be strongly discouraged. Conferees also agreed that a mild spank as a "back-up" to other disciplinary tactics (e.g., reasoning, time-out) could increase the effectiveness of these alternative disciplinary tactics in preschoolers with behavior problems. There was agreement that by itself spanking cannot accomplish the longer term objective of parents—to promote children's competence, moral character, and mental health—and that frequent or severe punishment of any kind signals the presence of a problem in the family dynamics. The issue that was and remains controversial is whether mild to moderate disciplinary spanking (in the years between 18 months and puberty) has been shown to be harmful.

Gershoff's meta-analyses, however, do not address that issue because her conceptual and operational definitions of *corporal punishment* included punishment that was often too severe and was thus a proxy for the harsh, punitive discipline that is acknowledged by all experts to be detrimental to children's well-being and ethically unacceptable. In the fifth moderator variable in the note to her Table 3 (indexing how researchers operationalized corporal punishment), Gershoff included "severity" as Category 2 and "frequency and severity" as Category 3, indicating that severity (as well as frequency) contributed to the CP measure in those studies so categorized. But her other categories, such as "frequency" (Category 1), did not exclude overly severe forms of CP when the specific question asked of the respondent was about their frequency. This meant that slapping in the face or beating with a stick or hitting, pushing, grabbing, or shoving were not coded as severe when the studies asked about their frequency.

Straus claimed that the physical abuse or Severe Violence items in the Conflict Tactics Scale can be used "to partial out physical abuse in a statistical analysis or to remove abused children from the sample in order to avoid confounding corporal punishment with physical abuse." Although Straus's own studies rarely did that, he clearly agreed with us that it is proper to do so. However, Gershoff indicated in her Table 1 that 16% of the 88 studies in her review operationalized CP as "hit with an object," which Straus included in his index of abuse or Severe Violence on the Conflicts Tactics Scale. Thus, some of Gershoff's CP measures included behaviors that are part of Straus's abuse construct.

To determine the influence of overly severe CP on the results of Gershoff's meta-analyses, Larzelere coded the severity of CP for 64 primary studies, including 52 of the 54 studies in the aggression composite (i.e., studies measuring aggression or antisocial behavior in children or aggression, criminal behavior, or physical abuse in adults). Baumrind also coded 41% of the studies for reliability, which yielded good interrater agreement ($k = .91$) for severe versus not overly severe CP. Almost two thirds (65.4%) of the 52 aggression composite studies used overly severe CP. Variables were categorized as overly severe if there was direct evidence of severity, such as a CP measure based only on hitting with a belt or stick (30.8% of the 52 studies in Gershoff's aggression composite); if severity was part of the definition of the highest CP score (28.8%); or if severity was inferred from the label, such as *punitive discipline* (5.8%). That left only 34.6% of the 52 effect sizes in the aggression composite for which the CP measure was not influenced directly by overly severe CP.

This problem of overly severe (and overly broad) CP can best be illustrated with quotes from Gershoff's primary studies. The following descriptions were used to describe at least part of their definition of CP: "slapped on face, head, and ears" and "shook"; "severity of punishment for aggression to parents"; "throwing something at the child" and "severe, strict, often physical" as contrasted with "nonrestrictive, mostly positive guidance," usage of "switch, belt, razor strap, paddle, buggy whip, boxing ears"; and "hit with belt, stick." In all of these five studies, an effect size could have been based on a CP measure that did not include such overly severe components of CP. For example, Mahoney et al. presented separate data for six tactics included in the revised Conflict Tactics Scale's CP measure. The corresponding effect sizes (d) ranged from 0.08 for "spanked bottom with bare hand" to 0.58 for "slapped on face, head, and ears."

In other studies, effect sizes could only be based on CP measures contaminated by overly severe components. Examples include "slaps in the face" and "beating with a stick, a belt, etc."; "slap him in the face" and "wash out his mouth with soap"; "How often were you beaten by your mother (father)?"; "kicked, bit, or hit you with a fist," causing "bruises or cuts," and six more violent items; "rough handling, shaking"; "mom (dad) was a violent or physically abusive person"; and "severe punishment, parents very angry or hostile, beatings, . . . 'Punished him so he wouldn't forget it.'"

In at least one other primary study in the meta-analyses, a large majority of those who were physically punished were also physically abused. In Lester's study of inmate records, 49% of those who had attempted suicide had been physically punished by their fathers, but almost as many (44%) had been physically abused. Therefore, it would appear that only 5% of the inmates were physically punished without being abused.

We thus conclude that the meta-analyses included studies of overly severe CP to a far greater extent than a casual reading of the selection criteria would indicate. To address the current debate about mild to moderate spanking, Gershoff would have had to exclude CP that is excessive, extreme, or cruel. But Gershoff only excluded CP that "knowingly would cause severe injury to the child," although (according to Gershoff) corporal punishment constitutes abuse in definitions of 22 states not merely when it is intended to result in "significant" physical injury but when it is "excessive," "cruel," "extreme," or "severe."

Beyond the question of measurement of CP, there is an important question of meaning. In her review, Gershoff stated that many studies ask parents about their use of CP but do not define what the researchers mean and do not ascertain what the participants mean. The question is whether it makes sense to aggregate all these studies in a meta-analysis when the definition of the key variable measuring CP is so varied and ambiguous.

Threats to the Validity of the Meta-Analyses

With the exception of the links between CP and immediate compliance or physical abuse, Gershoff disavowed causal implications of the meta-analyses she presented. However, it is primarily within a causal context that meta-analysis is judged to be superior to a conventional review for theory development and application to social policy. The very term *effect size* implies a causal relationship. If, for example, an equally plausible argument can be made that child aggression is a contributing cause of CP as can be made that CP is a contributing cause of child aggression, then it is arbitrary to treat CP as though it is the independent variable and child aggression as the dependent variable, and certainly without first establishing temporal order. Yet antispanking advocates frequently draw causal implications from the associations between CP and child behaviors. For example, on the basis of similar associations, Straus projected that a reduction in CP would "result in fewer people who are alienated, depressed or suicidal, and in fewer violent marriages" and "include lower crime rates . . . and less money spent on controlling or treating crime and mental illness."

Methodologists in epidemiology and behavioral science have emphasized the importance of empirically establishing the causal status of a correlate by first showing that it is a risk factor and then that it is a causal risk factor. A *risk factor* (causal or not) must be shown to precede the outcome and to be associated with an increase in the outcome compared with its population baserate. An experimental or prospective longitudinal design is a prerequisite for establishing a temporal sequence by showing that the outcome has not occurred prior to, or simultaneously with, the presumed risk factor. Although, as Greenland stated, "No meta-analysis can compensate for the inherent limits of non-experimental data for making inferences about causal effects," non-experimental studies differ greatly in their research quality and thus in their relevance to a causal argument.

We next consider threats to the validity first of the primary studies in Gershoff's analyses and then of the synthesis itself that may have systematically inflated the effect size estimates or compromised the generalizability of the results.

Threats to the Validity of the Primary Studies

Although experimental studies are the gold standard in separating causal from noncausal explanations, correlational studies can contribute to a causal explanation to the extent that they meet certain criteria, the most important of which are temporality and control of third variables that could plausibly account for an association. Other threats include the use of retrospective reports or shared method variance in assessing parenting behavior and children's outcomes.

Establishing temporal sequences between risks and outcomes. A cross-sectional design cannot show that an association is a risk factor because it cannot establish temporal order. Fifty-eight percent of all the effect size estimates in Gershoff's meta-analyses came from cross-sectional analyses, and only 17% came from either experimental or prospective longitudinal studies. Thus, most of the primary studies did not provide adequate information for identifying a risk factor, much less a causal risk factor. A *causal risk factor* for an outcome is a risk factor believed to be a generative cause of that outcome—that is, to have produced that outcome. Experimental designs or systematic attempts to rule out plausible confounds in quasi-experimental and prospective longitudinal designs are necessary to establish a risk factor as causal.

Prospective longitudinal studies, unlike cross-sectional studies, can establish temporality and have more potential for controlling third variables adequately. They can provide evidence of causal direction from parents' use of CP to subsequent child behaviors by controlling for baseline child behaviors that provoke punishment and for the autocorrelation of behavior over time. We should note that Gershoff cited a paper by Cowan, Powell, and Cowan to the effect that correlational and follow-back studies are not sufficient to establish causality. Although they have some design advantages that we have highlighted in this section, it is still important to note that longitudinal models are necessary but not sufficient to establish the order of events. Parenting behavior assessed at Time 1 may predict child behavior at Time 2, but it is also possible that the parent may be reacting to child behavior that occurred before the study began.

Controlling for third variables. In their seminal discussion of the use of meta-analytic synthesis for theory development, Miller and Pollock stated "Assessing evidence that a relationship exists and that it is nonartifactual is a first step in assessing its validity." In correlational studies this requires controlling for plausible third variables. For a relationship not to be spurious, it must persist in the form of a nonzero partial correlation between the supposed independent variable and the dependent variable with plausible third variables held constant (for example, baseline child misbehavior or parental rejection). Quasi-experimental studies are designed to exclude spurious variables from the group of causal influences affecting the results being observed. However, Gershoff used DSTAT, whose manual explicitly prohibits basing effect sizes on coefficients from multiple regression. If only the zero-order correlations can be used to calculate effect size, the methodological advantage of most quasi-experimental studies is lost, which makes the meta-analytic conclusions less relevant for determining whether CP is a causal risk factor for the detrimental child outcomes with which it is associated.

The use of retrospective recall. As Gershoff pointed out, reliance on retrospective recall in all but three of the studies linking CP in childhood to adult aggression, criminality, mental health, and physical abuse is a severe method-ological inadequacy of those studies. Typically, retrospective recall is biased by the current status of the reporter. For example, adult reporters asked to report on their own depression and their parents' disciplinary practices may try to explain their current mental state by their parents' mistreatment.

Shared method variance. Problems associated with the fact that raters are not independent and thus that information about parenting and child out-comes is filtered through the same source constitute a critical limitation of half of the primary studies in the review. Shared method variance results in spuriously high correlations among constructs. The largest proportion of independent data sources occurred in compliance studies (four of five), whereas the smallest proportion of independent data sources were in adult-hood studies of abuse (one of five) and aggression (one of four). The bias introduced by shared method variance is well illustrated in the analyses by Yarrow et al. They grouped their results in tables to demonstrate how a "con-taminated design" artifactually increases an association. Mothers' reports on "severity of punishment for aggression to parents" correlated at .40 with their reports on the child's aggression toward adults in the home (which the authors refer to as the *contaminated design*), compared with a .13 correlation with teacher-reported aggression. Gershoff chose to base her effect size on the correlation of .40 from the contaminated design rather than the .13 correla-tion in the uncontaminated design.

Threats to the Validity of the Synthesis

In addition to the problems caused by an overinclusive definition of CP, which could inflate effect sizes, Gershoff also based effect size estimates partly on cross-sectional correlations when longitudinal correlations were available. An alternative strategy would have been to base effect sizes on the most valid associ-ations available in a study or the ones most relevant to the debate about mild or moderate corporal punishment. Gershoff did not state the rules she used to include or exclude effect sizes when several options were available in a study. A rule that seems reasonable in selecting among relevant effect sizes within a study is to choose the one most likely to both exclude severe CP and to mini-mize shared method variance. To do otherwise would systematically increase the estimate of effect size with contaminated designs and with parents who use CP too severely.

The Yarrow et al. study illustrates the somewhat arbitrary nature of the myriad of decisions the synthesist must make in selecting which statistic should represent a study. Two tables summarized correlations of four punish-ment measures with three aggression measures. Gershoff based her effect size estimate on the largest of these 12 correlations. Furthermore, that correlation seems to be the poorest choice in terms of CP severity and validity threats. It was a correlation of .40 of "severity of punishment for aggression to parents" and aggression to adults at home, both based on the maternal interview. The most valid correlation was −.19 between maternal-reported physical punish-ment (overall) and teacher-reported aggression 2 months later. It was more valid because it was based on physical punishment overall, not severity of punishment in general, and because the CP and aggression measures were collected at different occasions from independent sources. Thus, the basis of an effect size between CP and child's aggression varies from −.19 in an uncontaminated design to .40 in a design contaminated by shared method variance, cross-sectional data, and overly severe punishment.

Furthermore, following the DSTAT manual's proscription against basing effect sizes on regression coefficients, even when controlling for third variables thought to be plausible confounds, Gershoff's effect sizes never reflected the most causally relevant statistics in longitudinal designs. Other metaanalytic experts recommend controlling for plausible confounds whenever possible, and some provide equations for calculating effect sizes from regression coefficients.

Reanalysis of the Data to Correct for Flaws in the Included Aggression Composite Studies

There are different views about whether poorly designed studies should be included in a meta-analysis. Mansfield and Busse recommended, and we concur, that all studies with severe methodological inadequacies should be eliminated from consideration and the remainder divided into two categories: those that have significant but not severe methodological limitations (e.g., retrospective longitudinal studies for which the likelihood of biased recall may be small) and those that are well designed in that they do not suffer from shared method variance, do use a prospective longitudinal or experimental design, and explicitly rule out severe corporal punishment. Unfortunately, as we show, that would leave too few studies for a meta-analytic review of the link between CP and most child behaviors (a situation in which one could conclude that a meta-analysis is premature).

Alternatively, methodological qualities of the studies can be coded and then used to see whether effect sizes from poorly designed studies are significantly different from those from the best-designed studies. Gershoff did attempt such analyses with her aggression composite variables, but these analyses were limited in two ways. First, almost all the studies had major methodological problems. More than half of the studies in the aggression composite used overly severe CP measures, more than half used cross-sectional or retrospective designs, and half had shared method variance. These problems were confounded with each other in unknown ways, making it difficult to sort out the differences those problems made by themselves or in combination. Second, Gershoff's analysis of study characteristics used a very conservative criterion for significance, especially considering the large number of categorical predictors (21) and small number of studies (22). This explains the unusual result of accounting for 86% of the variance in effect sizes without any of the categorical predictors being significant according to her conservative Bonferroni correction.

In contrast, we implemented more realistic analyses of whether effect sizes varied by CP severity, research design, or independence of data sources. We analyzed Gershoff's effect sizes in her aggression composite using the chi-square analyses of weighted effect sizes recommended by Hedges. Our analyses differ from Gershoff's analyses in the following ways: We treated each effect size as a separate case rather than combining effect sizes into one per study; we analyzed each methodological issue as a main effect rather than incorporating all predictors into one combined analysis; and finally, we used our codes for overly severe CP and corrected the design code for six cases.

As expected, effect sizes varied significantly by CP severity, by research design, and by independence of data sources. We found significantly higher effect sizes for overly severe than for nonsevere CP measures (mean weighted effect sizes, $d_+ = 0.46$ vs. 0.30, respectively, $\chi^2[1, N = 12{,}244] = 74.5$, $p < .001$). Effect sizes were also higher for cross-sectional than for longitudinal studies ($d_+ = 0.46$ vs. 0.37, $\chi^2[1, N = 7{,}807] = 16.1$, $p < .001$). Finally, effect sizes were higher for studies based partly or entirely on shared data sources than for independent sources of data ($d_+ = 0.35$ vs. 0.29, $\chi^2[1, N = 13{,}591] = 8.44$, $p < .01$). Only 3 of 54 studies in the aggression composite were methodologically sound on all three study characteristics. Their mean weighted effect size was 0.12, significantly less than the other 51 effect sizes in the aggression composite ($d_+ = 0.33$, $\chi^2[1, N = 13{,}591] = 5.99$, $p < .05$). This effect size is smaller than what Cohen labeled as small ($d = 0.20$).

Gershoff's analyses were limited in investigating important substantive distinctions as well. For example, there have been some discussions recently about whether the associations of CP differ by ethnicity. Gershoff could not investigate ethnic differences because none of her primary studies investigated ethnic minorities alone. Nonetheless, two of her primary studies included separate statistics for African American subsamples. In both studies, the mean effect sizes were negative, such that CP predicted less aggression subsequently at school in the African American subsample. Furthermore, Gunnoe and Mariner went beyond a longitudinal correlation by controlling statistically for baseline aggression, which resulted in stronger causal evidence that CP reduces subsequent school aggression in African American children ($\beta = -.30$). At least two other studies have also found that the association of CP with antisocial behavior differs significantly for African American and European American children.

Similarly, it is not clear that mild to moderate CP increases subsequent aggression and antisocial behavior at ages when parents are most likely to use CP (18 months to 6 years of age). Only one effect size in Gershoff's aggression construct was based on longitudinal and independent data on the use of nonsevere CP in this age range, and it was one of the smallest effect sizes ($d = 0.06$). Other primary studies had tiny effect sizes or ones for which CP predicted reductions in aggression for this age range when focusing on a young subsample and using data uncontaminated by the above three methodological problems. Furthermore, Gunnoe and Mariner showed that CP predicted significantly less fighting in 4- to 7-year-olds after controlling for baseline antisocial behavior. . . .

Conclusion

Gershoff acknowledged the necessity to distinguish between the harsh, punitive parental discipline that all experts would regard as both harmful and unethical (including such advocates of spanking as Dobson and Rosemond) and the more normative parental actions that involve the infliction of mild physical pain but not injury. In this response to Gershoff's article, we reanalyzed portions of Gershoff's meta-analyses to show that this separation was not in fact made in many primary studies. Because her measure included many instances of extreme and excessive physical punishment, her analyses are not relevant to the current political debate about whether normative spanking (a specific form of CP) is harmful for children.

Punishment by definition is aversive and therefore must be used sparingly and efficaciously to be acceptable. As Larzelere stated, "There may be more potential in identifying more vs. less effective ways to use each disciplinary tactic. The effect of any tactic may depend on the overall disciplinary style and the parent–child, family, and cultural contexts." Larzelere suggested a conditional sequence model as optimal in which parents begin with the mildest disciplinary tactic they think will be effective, such as reasoning, and resort to firmer tactics only if the child is defiant about a nonnegotiable request. If used efficaciously as a back-up at ages 2 to 6, both physical and nonphysical punishment are less likely to be needed as children learn to attain a reasonable level of behavioral compliance to mild disciplinary tactics such as reasoning.

Larzelere's conditional sequence model and Gershoff's process–context model should be tested with well-designed studies from culturally diverse populations. Even though randomized clinical trials are probably not practical, intervention studies are possible that would add to the knowledge base. To determine if normative physical punishment has any unique effect on 2- to 6-year-olds over and above that of otherwise optimal parenting, parents could be trained in techniques of authoritative discipline, which would include efficacious use of punishments of their choice. Some parents would choose to include spanking in their disciplinary repertoire, providing the opportunity for researchers to assess the child outcomes associated with disciplinary spanking when used efficaciously by comparing them with child outcomes associated with the alternative disciplinary tactics used by parents who choose to never spank. With a large and diverse enough sample, it should be possible to evaluate the moderating effects of third variables that would not be controlled, such as child and parent temperament and social stressors, in such quasi-experimental intervention studies. . . .

POSTSCRIPT

Is Spanking Detrimental to Children?

Both selections on corporal punishment addressed the issue of the need to define corporal punishment and to have researchers agree on the definition before they begin research on the subject. Gershoff found a relationship between children being spanked and 10 negative behavioral outcomes in childhood, some of which also extended into adulthood. Although spanking was associated with short-term compliance from the child, the 10 negative outcomes far outweighed the one short-term positive result.

Authors of the opposing selection showed that there was no support for a causal relationship between corporal punishment and detrimental child behaviors. The authors concede that no one feels abusive physical punishment is appropriate, but that mild spanking after 18 months of age and before puberty is OK. They feel spanking within the context of other discipline methods is useful.

Although these selections are more concerned with definitions and methodology than with resolving the spanking controversy, there is a real debate over what mild spanking is, and how it fits into the overall parenting discipline technique. Child development experts agree that reasoning, talking, and listening to children teaches them right from wrong and preserves their positive self-image. They admit this approach takes more time and effort but that in the long run, it is more effective and leads children to a better adjusted adulthood.

There are authorities in child development who believe spankings, when properly administered, and within the context of a loving home are effective in shaping children's behavior. Most agree to spank from about 2 years of age up until puberty and to only use an open hand and never use objects to hit children. They urge parents to explain to their children why they are being spanked.

Are spankings useful and justified, or is there a fine line between spanking and child abuse? Is it likely that parents who spank will cross that line to abuse in the heat of the moment? Is it really possible to spank with appropriate force and with logical thought? Can studies on the effects of spanking be designed to answer these questions? With all the studies already conducted, methodology and definitions are still being debated. It appears that there are many critical variables that need to be quantified before conducting research on the subject. In the meantime, parents are presented with the dilemma of how best to guide and discipline their children from childhood to becoming responsible adults.

Related Readings

Campbell, S. (September/October 2002). Spare the rod to spare the child? *Psychology Today, 35,* 26.

Davis, P. W., Chandler, J. L., & LaRossa, R. (December 2004). I've tried the switch but he laughs through the tears: The use and conceptualization of corporal punishment during the Machine Age, 1924–1939. *Child Abuse & Neglect, 28,* 1291–1310.

Deater-Deckard, K., Pettit, G. S., & Lansford, J. E. (September 2003). The development of attitudes about physical punishment: An 8-year longitudinal study. *Journal of Family Psychology, 17,* 351–360.

Giles-Sims, J., & Lockhart, C. (March 2005). Culturally shaped patterns of disciplining children. *Journal of Family Issues, 26,* 196–218.

Walsh, W. (2002). Spankers and nonspankers: Where they get information on spanking. *Family Relations, 51,* 81–88.

ISSUE 6

Are Fathers Really Necessary?

YES: W. J. Doherty, Edward F. Kouneski, and Martha F. Erickson, from "Responsible Fathering: An Overview and Conceptual Framework," *Journal of Marriage and the Family* (May 1998)

NO: Alexis J. Walker and Lori A. McGraw, from "Who Is Responsible for Responsible Fathering?" *Journal of Marriage and the Family* (May 2000)

ISSUE SUMMARY

YES: Professor of family social science W. J. Doherty, psychologist Edward F. Kouneski, and Martha F. Erickson, director of the University of Minnesota's Children, Youth and Family Consortium, explore the contextual influences on fathering and conclude that a quality marriage in the optimal context promotes responsible fathering.

NO: Professor of human development and family sciences Alexis J. Walker and Lori A. McGraw, 4-H program coordinator at Oregon State University, contend that there is no empirical evidence that children need active fathers in their lives.

There has been a dramatic rise in single-parent homes headed by men. Since the 1990 census, households headed by single fathers have risen from about 1.3 million homes in 1990 to over 2.1 million in 2000. As a consequence of this increase, an issue that has confronted researchers revolves around the necessity of two-parent families. One specific issue that has been hotly debated is whether or not fathers are necessary in raising children. Children need nurturing, guidance, and economic security, but must they receive these things from *both* father and mother? Some scholars argue that children need active, involved fathers throughout their childhood and adolescence. If this does not occur, the children may be more prone to involvement in crime, premature sexuality, out-of-wedlock childbirth, lower educational achievements, depression, substance abuse, and poverty.

Other scientists question whether or not the ability to meet children's needs is gender-specific. While few would argue that it is more challenging to raise a child in a single-parent home, well-socialized and successful children have come from single-parent homes. The vast majority of these homes are female-headed. In fact, there are over 7.5 million single mothers raising children in the United States today. Another consideration is that there has been an increase in adoption by gay and lesbian parents in two-parent homes. While these children may face challenges in dealing with the prejudice associated with being raised in such households, one might ask why children would be permitted to be adopted into these homes if there was evidence that children needed both a male and a female parent. Many scientists argue that there is little, if any, scientific evidence that suggests children must be raised by both a male and a female.

As you read the following selections, consider the type of family in which you were raised. Was your upbringing an optimal situation? Did the role that your father played have a positive or a negative effect on your life? W. J. Doherty, Edward F. Kouneski, and Martha F. Erickson contend that children need and deserve fathers who are actively involved with their children throughout childhood and adolescence. To achieve this, they promote responsible fathering as a way to help meet the needs of children. Alexis J. Walker and Lori A. McGraw believe that while there may be an ideological basis for the assumption that children need and deserve active and involved fathers, empirical support for this ideal is lacking.

YES ↩

W. J. Doherty, Edward F. Kouneski,
and Martha F. Erickson

Responsible Fathering: An Overview and Conceptual Framework

Responsible Fathering

The use of the term "responsible fathering," which was the original language used by the U.S. Department of Health and Human Services in commissioning our work, reflects a recent shift by academics and professionals away from value-free language and toward a more explicit value-advocacy approach. "Responsible" suggests an "ought," a set of desired norms for evaluating fathers' behavior. The term also conveys a moral meaning (right and wrong) because it suggests that some fathering could be judged "irresponsible." The willingness to use explicitly moral terms reflects a change in the social climate among academics, professionals, and policymakers, who until recently embraced the traditional notion that social science, social policy, and social programs could be value free. In the late twentieth century, there is more appreciation of the inevitability of value-laden and moral positions being part of social science and social interventions and a greater willingness to be explicit about values so that they can be debated openly and their influence on social science and policy can be made clear, rather than being covert (Doherty, 1995a; Doherty et al., 1993; Wolfe, 1989). Indeed, there has always been a strong but implicit undercurrent of value advocacy in fathering research, much of it conducted by men and women interested in promoting more committed and nurturing involvement by men in their children's lives. Similarly, there has always been a moral undertone to the focus on fathers' deficits that has characterized much of the literature on absent, "deadbeat," and emotionally uninvolved fathers (Doherty, 1990). The term "responsible fathering," as we use it, applies to fathers across all social classes and racial groups, not narrowly to men in lower social classes or minority groups. Now that value advocacy has become more explicit in the fathering area (Dollahite, Hawkins, & Brotherson, 1997), responsible fathering needs to be clearly defined. James Levine and Edward Pitt (1995) have made an important start in their delineation of responsible fathering. They write:

From Journal of Marriage and the Family, May 1998, pp. 278–279, 284–292. Copyright © 1998 by Blackwell Publishing, Ltd. Reprinted by permission.

A man who behaves responsibly towards his child does the following:

- He waits to make a baby until he is prepared emotionally and financially to support his child.
- He establishes his legal paternity if and when he does make a baby.
- He actively shares with the child's mother in the continuing emotional and physical care of their child, from pregnancy onwards.
- He shares with the child's mother in the continuing financial support of their child, from pregnancy onwards. (pp. 5–6)

Levine and Pitt's elements of responsible fathering have the advantage of referring to both resident and nonresident fathers, a reflection of the diversity of fathers' situations. The authors also assert that commitment to this ethic of responsible fatherhood extends beyond the father to the mother, to professionals who work with families, and to social institutions entrusted with the support of families. We employ Levine and Pitt's definition in this [selection], but we narrow our scope to men who are already fathers; we do not address the issue of postponing fatherhood.

The developmental backdrop for the discussion of fathering reflects children's needs for predictability, nurturance, and appropriate limit setting from fathers and mothers, as well as for economic security and a cooperative, preferably loving relationship between their parents (Hetherington & Parke, 1993). Furthermore, the specific needs of children vary by their developmental stage. Parents are required to provide higher levels of physical caregiving when their children are infants and greater levels of conflict management when their children become adolescents. Although we do not review the literature on the effects of active fathering on children, an assumption behind this [selection]—and our value stance—is that children need and deserve active, involved fathers throughout their childhood and adolescence. The prime justification for promoting responsible fathering is the needs of children. . . .

Influences on Fathering: A Conceptual Model

The fathering literature has been long on empirical studies and short on theory. Researchers mostly have adapted concepts from social sciences to fit their particular area, but work is beginning on overarching conceptual frameworks to guide research and program development. In his review of theory in fathering research, Marsiglio (1995) mentions life course theory (which emphasizes how men's experience of fatherhood changes with life transitions), social scripting theory (which emphasizes the cultural messages that fathers internalize about their role), and social identity theory (which focuses on how men take on the identity of a father in relation to their other social roles). Hawkins, Christiansen, Sargent, and Hill (1995), Hawkins and Dollahite (1997), and Snarey (1993) have used Erik Erikson's developmental theory in their work on how fathering can promote generativity among adult men. Other scholars have explored the utility of economic theories to understand fathers' decisions to invest in, or withdraw from, their children (Becker, 1991).

The most specific conceptual model frequently used in the fatherhood literature is Lamb's and Pleck's four-factor model of father involvement, which is not explicitly grounded in a broader theory such as Erikson's theory or social identity theory. (See Lamb et al., 1985.) Lamb and Pleck proposed that father involvement is determined by motivation, skills and self-confidence, social support, and institutional practices. These factors may be viewed as additive, building on one another, and as interactive, with some factors being necessary prior to others. For example, motivation may be necessary for the development of skills. Ihinger-Tallman, Pasley, and Buehler (1995) proposed an eight-factor model of mediators between father identity and actual involvement after divorce: mother's preferences and beliefs, father's perception of mother's parenting, father's emotional stability, mother's emotional stability, sex of child, coparental relationship, father's economic well-being, father's economic security, and encouragement from others. Recently, Park (1996) articulated a systems model of residential father involvement that includes individual, family, extrafamilial, and cultural influences.

Based on the research literature, prior theoretical work on fathering, and the systemic ecological orientation described earlier, we present a conceptual model of influences on responsible fathering. (See Figure 1.) Unlike prior work, the model is intended to include fathering inside or outside marriage and regardless of coresidence with the child. The focus is on the factors that help create and maintain a father-child bond. The model attempts to transcend the dyadic focus of much traditional child development theory by emphasizing first the child-father-mother triad and then larger systems' influences.

Figure 1

Influences on Responsible Fathering: A Conceptual Model

Contextual Factors
Institutional Practices
Employment Opportunities
Economic Factors
Race or Ethnicity Resources and Challenges
Cultural Expectations
Social Support

Father Factors
Role Identification
Knowledge
Skills
Commitment
Psychological Well-Being
Relations with Own Father
Employment Characteristics
Residential Status

Child Factors
Attitude toward Father
Behavioral Difficulties
Temperament
Gender
Age
Developmental Status

Coparental Relationship
Marital or Nonmarital Status
Dual vs. Single Earner
Custodial Arrangement
Relationship Commitment
Cooperation
Mutual Support
Conflict

Mother Factors
Attitude toward Father
Expectations of Father
Support of Father
Employment Characteristics

Father — Child
Mother

The model highlights individual factors of the father, mother, and child; mother-father relationship factors; and larger contextual factors in the environment. Within each of these domains, the model outlines a number of specific factors that can be supported by the research literature. The center of the model is the interacting unit of child, father, and mother, each formulating meanings and enacting behaviors that influence the others. The three are embedded in a broader social context that affects them as individuals and affects the quality of their relationships.

We are particularly interested in highlighting factors that pertain to fathers because one of the goals of this [selection] is to guide father-specific research, program development, and public policy. All of the factors in the model affect the mother-child relationship, as well, because they are generic to parenting (see Belsky, 1984), but many of them have particular twists for fathers. Because theory and research on parenting so often have been derived from work on mothers, it seems particularly important to illuminate the distinctive influences on fathering. The arrows point to the father-child relationship, in particular to the four domains of responsible fathering covered in this review—paternity, presence, economic support, and involvement. Although the model can depict fathers' indirect influence on their children through their support for the mother, the focus here is on direct father-child interaction. And although the influences depicted in the model also can be viewed as influencing the father directly, we prefer to focus on the effects on father-child relations because enhancing those relations and, therefore, the well-being of children is the ultimate goal of programs for fathers.

The research reviewed for this [selection] supports the notion that father-child relations are more strongly influenced than mother-child relations by three of the dimensions of the model: the coparental relationship, factors in the other parent, and larger contextual factors.

Coparental Relationship

A number of studies have shown that the quality of father-child relations both inside and outside marriage is more highly correlated with the quality of the coparental relationship than is true for the mother-child relationship (Belsky & Volling, 1987; Cox, Owen, Lewis, & Henderson, 1989; Feldman, Nash, & Aschenbrenner, 1983; Levy-Shiff & Israelashvili, 1988). Fathers appear to withdraw from their child when they are not getting along with the mother, whereas mothers do not show a similar level of withdrawal. This is one way to understand the tendency of fathers to remove themselves from their children's lives after a breakup with the mother, especially if they have a negative relationship with the mother (Ahrons & Miller, 1993). As Furstenberg and Cherlin (1991) have asserted, for many men, marriage and parenthood are a "package deal." Or one might say that in American culture, a woman is a mother all of her life, but a man is a father if he has a wife. Furthermore, if he has a wife but does not get along with her, he may be present as a father, but the quality of his relationship with his children is apt to suffer.

One reason that fathering is particularly sensitive to the marital or copa-rental relationship is that standards and expectations for fathering appear to be more variable than those for mothering. There is more negotiation in fam-ilies over what fathers will do than over what mothers will do and hence more dependence among fathers on the quality and outcome of those negotiations (Backett, 1987). As Lewis and O'Brien (1987) state, men have a less clear "job description" as fathers than women do as mothers. Therefore, fathers' behav-ior is strongly influenced by the meanings and expectations of fathers them-selves, as well as mothers, children, extended family, and broader cultural institutions.

One of the most sensitive areas of research on fathering is the impor-tance of fathers being married to the children's mothers. Because many fathers are not married to the mother, it can seem prejudicial to these men and their children—and perhaps to single-parent mothers—to emphasize the importance of marriage. On the other hand, an implication of our review of the research and our conceptual framework is that, for most American heterosexual fathers, the family environment most supportive of fathering is a caring, committed, and collaborative marriage. This kind of marriage means that the father lives with his children and has a good partnership with their mother. These are the two principal intrafamilial determinants of responsible fathering.

Some of the controversy over the role of marriage in responsible fathering can be circumvented by specifying the quality of the marriage, as we have done. It is the quality of the marital process, rather than the legal or coresidential sta-tus, that most affects fathering. One might argue, then, that being married is not important because cohabiting couples could have the same qualities of relation-ship. Although, in principle, this is true, the best national research on cohabita-tion indicates that cohabitation is a temporary arrangement for most heterosexual couples; they eventually either marry or break up (Bumpass et al., 1991). We conclude that, in practice, the kind of mother-father relationship most conducive to responsible fathering in contemporary U.S. society is a caring, committed, collaborative marriage. Outside of this arrangement, substantial barriers stand in the way of active, involved fathering.

Mother Factors

Among external influences on fathering, the role of the mother has particular salience because mothers serve as partners and sometimes as gatekeepers in the father-child relationship, both inside and outside marriage (De Luccie, 1995). Mother factors in the conceptual model, of course, interact with the coparental relationship because the mother's personal feelings about the father influence the coparental relationship. But there is also evidence that, even within satisfactory marital relationships, a father's involvement with his children, especially young children, is often contingent on the mother's atti-tudes toward, expectations of, and support for the father, as well as the extent of her involvement in the labor force (De Luccie, 1995; Simons, Whitbeck, Conger, & Melby, 1990). Marsiglio (1991), using the National Survey of Fami-lies and Households data set, found that mothers' characteristics were more strongly correlated with fathers' involvement than fathers' own characteristics were. Indeed, studies have shown that many mothers, both inside and outside marriage, are ambivalent about the fathers' active involvement with their children (Baruch & Barnett, 1986; Cowan & Cowan, 1987). Given the powerful cultural forces that expect absorption by women in their mothering role, it is not surprising that active paternal involvement would threaten some women's identity and sense of control over this central domain of their lives. The evolution of a social consensus on responsible fathering, therefore, will necessarily involve a consensus that responsible mothering means supporting the father-child bond.

Contextual Factors

Research demonstrates the particular vulnerability of fathering to contextual and institutional practices—from the establishment of legal paternity to the greater impact of unemployment on fathering than on mothering. Lack of income and poor occupational opportunities appear to have a particularly negative effect on fathering (Thomson, Hanson, & McLanahan, 1994). The prevalence of the abandonment of economic and psychological responsibilities among poor, unemployed men and among other men who undergo financial and employment crises is partly a function of the unique vulnerability of fathering to perceived success in the external environment (Jones, 1991; McLoyd, 1989). This analysis suggests that fathering is especially sensitive to changes in economic forces in the work force and marketplace and to shifts in public policy. It also suggests that fathering suffers disproportionately from negative social forces, such as racism, that inhibit opportunities in the environment. McLoyd (1990), in a review and conceptual analysis of economic hardship in African American families, describes how poverty and racism combine to create psychological distress, which is, in turn, associated with more negative parenting styles and more difficulty in the coparental relationship.

Our conceptual model also depicts the positive contribution of ethnic and cultural factors to fathering. One aspect of responsible fathering, that of economic support, is nearly universally expected of fathers by their cultures (Lamb, 1987b). LaRossa (1997), in his historical analysis, has demonstrated how changing cultural expectations in the first part of the twentieth century led to more nurturing father involvement in the U.S. Allen and Connor (1997) have examined how role flexibility and concern for children in the African American community create opportunities for men to become involved in surrogate father relationships with children who lack day-to-day contact with their biological fathers. Unfortunately, there has not been much empirical research that examines fathering in its cultural context, using representative samples of fathers to explore how cultural meanings and practices influence fathers' beliefs and behaviors.

The final contextual factor in the model is social support, which Belsky (1984) emphasized in his theoretical model of parenting and which McLoyd (1990) documented as a crucial factor in diminishing the negative effects of poverty on parenting behavior. However, most of the research on social support specifically for fathers has focused on mothers as sources of social support.

Pleck (1997) reviewed the limited research on extrafamilial social support for fathering and found the studies skimpy and inconsistent, except for the pattern that highly involved fathers tend to encounter negative attitudes from acquaintances, relatives, and fellow workers. Clearly, there is a need for studies that examine the sources and influences of social support on fathering, particularly the role of other fathers.

From the perspective of both the contextual factors and the mother factors discussed thus far, fathering can be conceptualized as a more contextually sensitive process than mothering is. Not that mothering is not also contextually sensitive, but the cultural norms are stricter on the centrality and endurance of the mother-child dyad, regardless of what is happening outside that relationship. Father-child relations, on the other hand, are culturally defined as less dyadic and more multilateral, requiring a threshold of support from inside the family and from the larger environment. Undermining from the mother or from a social institution or system may induce many fathers to retreat from responsible fathering unless their own individual level of commitment to fathering is quite strong.

This point about the ecological sensitivity of fathering is a principal conclusion of this [selection]. It suggests that fathering programs and policy initiatives that focus only on fathers will benefit mainly fathers who already have a supportive social and economic environment. Fathers whose context is less supportive—for example, fathers who do not live with their children, who have strained relationships with the mother, or who are experiencing economic stress—will need more extensive and multilateral efforts to support their fathering.

Child Factors

Individual child factors are included in the model for completeness, but the child factors studied in the research literature do not appear to be as important as the other dimensions in influencing fathering. Fathers do appear to find it easier to be more involved with their sons, especially older sons, presumably because they identify with them and are more comfortable communicating with them (Marsiglio, 1991). Most of the other child factors, such as age, appear to influence mothers as much as fathers, although Larson (1993) and Larson and Richards (1994) have documented how fathers withdraw more from parent-adolescent conflict than mothers do. More research is needed on the influence of the child's temperament and developmental status on relations with nonresidential fathers. Similarly, research is needed on how the child's beliefs about father involvement influence fathers' and mothers' expectations and behavior.

Mother-Child Relationship Factors

We include this domain for theoretical completeness, but we could find no research directly examining how the father-child relationship is affected by the mother-child relationship. Such effects may be tapped indirectly through other dimensions in the model, such as the mother's attitudes toward the father's involvement with the child. For example, a close mother-child bond, combined with an ambivalent maternal attitude toward paternal involvement, might lead to less closeness of the father than a situation in which a mother had the same attitude but, herself, was less close to the child.

Father Factors

Fathers' role identification, skills, and commitment are important influences on fathering (Baruch & Barnett, 1986; Ihinger-Tallman et al., 1995; Pleck, 1997). These three appear to fluctuate from low to high levels along with a number of interpersonal and contextual factors, such as the mother's expectations and the father's residential status with his children (Marsiglio, 1995; Ihinger-Tallman et al., 1995). In American culture, fathers are given more latitude for commitment to, identification with, and competence in their parental role. This latitude brings with it the price of confusion for many fathers about how to exercise their roles (Daly, 1995).

The variability of the individual father factors suggests two important implications of our conceptual model: that the positive support from mothers and the larger context can move men in the direction of more responsible parenting even in the face of modest personal investment, and that strong father commitment, knowledge, and skills are likely to be necessary to overcome negative maternal, coparental, and contextual influences. This latter point is similar to Lamb's (1987a) hypothesis that high levels of father motivation can override institutional barriers and the lack of social support.

As for the father's experience in his own family of origin, some research suggests that the father's relationship with his own father may be a factor— either through identifying with his father or compensating for his father's lapses—in contributing to his own role identification, sense of commitment, and self-efficacy (Cowan & Cowan, 1987; Daly, 1995). Snarey (1993), in a longitudinal study, documented the role of multigenerational connections between fathers.

The final father factors, psychological well-being and employment characteristics, have been studied extensively. Research examining psychological adjustment and parenting quality consistently shows a positive relationship between fathers' (and mothers') psychological well-being and their parenting attitudes and skills (Cox et al., 1989; Levy-Shiff & Israelashvili, 1988; Pleck, 1997). The research on job loss and economic distress generally has examined declines in psychological well-being as mediating factors leading to poorer fathering (Elder et al., 1984; Elder et al., 1985; Jones, 1991). And fathers' work situations have been shown to have mixed relationships with involvement with children. Specific work schedules are not strongly related to involvement, but greater flex time and other profamily practices are associated with more father involvement (Pleck, 1997). Indeed, consistent with other research on fathering, mothers' employment characteristics are more strongly associated with fathers' involvement than fathers' employment characteristics. When mothers are employed, fathers' proportionate share of parenting is greater, although studies are inconsistent about the absolute level of father involvement (Pleck, 1997).

Conceptual Overview

The conceptual model outlines multiple factors that influence fathering, from individual and relational to contextual. The factors can be viewed as additive. For example, low identification with the parental role, combined with low expectations from the mother, would be strongly associated with low involvement of the father in both residential and nonresidential contexts. High identification with the parental role, combined with high expectations from the mother, would lead to greater father involvement in any residential context.

The factors in the model also can be viewed as interactive. For example, high role identification and good employment and income might be sufficient to offset low expectations from the mother. Similarly, not living with the child could be offset by the father's strong commitment to his children and the support of the mother. And strong institutional support through public policies could mitigate unmarried fathers' and mothers' reluctance to declare paternity.

Although the conceptual framework is intended to apply to the four domains of responsible fathering (paternity, presence, economic support, and involvement), most of the research has focused on one or another of these areas. Indeed, the bulk of the empirical research has been on father involvement. Researchers have tended to assume that economic factors uniquely influence economic support and that father factors uniquely influence father involvement. Putting a range of factors into one model challenges researchers to examine how all the factors might influence all the domains of responsible fathering. We acknowledge that some components of the model are likely to influence some aspects of fathering more than others.

Finally, the model should be seen as depicting a dynamic set of processes, rather than a set of linear, deterministic influences. Systemic, ecological models run the risk of reducing the target behavior—in this case, responsible fathering—to a contextually determined phenomenon stripped of individual initiative and self-determination. We want to emphasize the pivotal role of fathers, themselves, in appropriating or discarding cultural and contextual messages, in formulating a fathering identity and developing fathering skills with their own children, in working out their feelings about their own fathers, and in dealing collaboratively with their children's mother. The social construction of fatherhood is an evolving creation of all stakeholders in the lives of children, and contemporary fathers have a central role in this creation. The active construction of fathering by fathers, themselves, is not a prominent theme in the research literature, although it is crucial to programs that work with fathers. More qualitative research is needed to explore the kinds of identity development and social negotiation that constitute the experience of fathering.

Conclusion

This [selection] delineates a conceptual model of influences on fathering that can serve as a stimulus for future research, programming, and policy development. The main premise, supported by a variety of studies, is that fathering is uniquely sensitive to contextual influences, both interpersonal and environmental. Fathering is a multilateral relationship, in addition to a one-to-one relationship. A range of influences—including mothers' expectations and behaviors, the quality of the coparental relationship, economic factors, institutional practices, and employment opportunities—all have potentially powerful effects on fathering. These contextual factors shape the major domains of responsible fathering discussed here: acknowledgment of paternity, willingness to be present and provide economic support, and level of involvement with one's children. When these influences are not supportive of the father-child bond, a man may need a high level identification with the father role, strong commitment, and good parenting skills to remain a responsible father to his children, especially if he does not live with them.

This review and conceptual model deal with factors that promote active, involved fathering, not with the effects of that kind of fathering on children. (See review by Pleck, 1997.) Nor do we take a position on whether there are essential characteristics of fathering versus mothering or whether having parents of two genders is necessary for the well-being of children. The growing literature on gay and lesbian parenting suggests that these kinds of questions are more complex than many scholars assumed in the past (Patterson, 1992; Patterson & Chan, 1997). However, it is not necessary to resolve these issues in order to address the factors that enhance and inhibit the parenting of men in the role of father in the late twentieth century.

A potentially controversial conclusion of this [selection] is that a high quality marriage is the optimal context for promoting responsible fatherhood. This position moves opposite the trend in contemporary family studies to disaggregate marriage and parenting. We do not suggest that men cannot parent adequately outside this context or that children must be raised in a married household in order to grow up well adjusted. However, we believe that the research strongly indicates that substantial barriers exist for most men's fathering outside a caring, committed, collaborative marriage and that the promotion of these kinds of enduring marital partnerships may be the most important contribution to responsible fathering in our society.

An encouraging implication of this systemic, ecological analysis is that there are many pathways to enhancing the quality of father-child relationships. Fathering can be enhanced through programs and policies that help fathers relate to their coparent, that foster employment and economic opportunities if needed, that change institutional expectations and practices to better support fathers, and that encourage fathers' personal commitment to their children.

References

Ahrons, C. R., & Miller, R. B. (1993). The effect of the postdivorce relationship on paternal involvement: A longitudinal analysis. *American Journal of Orthopsychiatry, 63*, 441-450.

Allen, W. D., & Connor, M. (1997). An African American perspective on generative fathering. In A. J. Hawkins & D. C. Dollahite (Eds.), *Generative fathering: Beyond deficit perspectives.* Newbury Park, CA: Sage.

Backett, K. (1987). The negotiation of fatherhood. In C. Lewis & M. O'Brien (Eds.), *Reassessing fatherhood: New observations on fathers and the modern family.* Newbury Park, CA: Sage.

Baruch, G. K., & Barnett, R. C. (1986). Consequences of fathers' participation in family work: Parent's role strain and well-being. *Journal of Personality and Social Psychology, 51,* 983–992.

Becker, G. S. (1991). *A treatise on the family.* Cambridge, MA: Harvard University Press.

Belsky, J. (1984). The determinants of parenting: A process model. *Child Development, 55,* 83–96.

Belsky, J., & Volling, B. L. (1987). Mothering, fathering, and marital interaction in the family triad during infancy. In P. W. Berman & F. A. Pedersen (Eds.), *Men's transitions to parenthood: Longitudinal studies of early family experience* (pp. 37–63). Hillsdale, NJ: Erlbaum.

Bumpass, L. L., Sweet, J. A., & Cherlin, A. (1991). The role of cohabitation in declining rates of marriage. *Journal of Marriage and the Family, 53,* 913–927.

Cowan, C. P., & Cowan, P. A. (1987). Men's involvement in parenthood: Identifying the antecedents and understanding the barriers. In P. W. Berman & F. A. Pedersen (Eds.), *Men's transitions to parenthood: Longitudinal studies of early family experience* (pp. 145–174). Hillsdale, NJ: Erlbaum.

Cox, M. J., Owen, M. T., Lewis, J. M., & Henderson, V. K. (1989). Marriage, adult adjustment, and early parenting. *Child Development, 60,* 1015–1024.

Daly, K. J. (1995). Reshaping fatherhood: Finding the models. In W. Marsiglio (Ed.), *Fatherhood: Contemporary theory, research, and social policy* (pp. 21–40). Thousand Oaks, CA: Sage.

De Luccie, M. F. (1995). Mothers as gatekeepers: A model of maternal mediators of father involvement. *The Journal of Genetic Psychology, 156,* 115–131.

Doherty, W. J. (1990). Beyond reactivity and the deficit model of manhood: A commentary on articles by Napier, Pittman, and Gottman. *Journal of Marital and Family Therapy, 17,* 29–32.

Doherty, W. J. (1995a). *Soul searching: Why psychotherapy must promote moral responsibility.* New York: Basic Books.

Doherty, W. J., Boss, P. G., LaRossa, R., Schumm, W. R., & Steinmetz, S. K. (1993). Family theories and methods: A contextual approach. In P. G. Boss, W. J. Doherty, R. LaRossa, W. R. Schumm, & S. K. Steinmetz (Eds.), *Family theories and methods: A contextual approach.* New York: Plenum Press.

Dollahite, D. C., Hawkins, A. J., & Brotherson, S. E. (1997). Fatherwork: A conceptual ethic of fathering as generative work. In A. J. Hawkins & D. C. Dollahite (Eds.), *Generative fathering: Beyond deficit perspective.* Newbury Park, CA: Sage.

Elder, G., Liker, J., & Cross, C. (1984). Parent-child behavior in the Great Depression: Life course and intergenerational influences. In P. Baltes & O. Brim (Eds.), *Life span development and behavior* (Vol. 6, pp. 109–158). Orlando, FL: Academic Press.

Elder, G., Van Nguyen, T., & Caspi, A. (1985). Linking family hardship to children's lives. *Child Development, 56,* 1628–1636.

Feldman, S. S., Nash, S. C., & Aschenbrenner, B. G. (1983). Antecedents of fathering. *Child Development, 54,* 1628–1636.

Furstenberg, F. S., & Cherlin, A. J. (1991). *Divided families: What happens to children when parents part.* Cambridge, MA: Harvard University Press.

Hawkins, A. J., Christiansen, S. L., Sargent, K. P., & Hill, E. J. (1995). Rethinking fathers' involvement in child care. In W. Marsiglio (Ed.), *Fatherhood: Contemporary theory, research, and social policy* (pp. 41–56). Thousand Oaks, CA: Sage.

Hawkins, A. J., & Dollahite, D. C. (1997). Generative fathering: Beyond deficit perspectives. Thousand Oaks, CA: Sage.

Hetherington, E. M., & Parke, R. D. (1993). *Child psychology: A contemporary view.* New York: McGraw-Hill.

Ihinger-Tallman, M., Pasley, K., & Buehler, C. (1995). Developing a middle-range theory of father involvement postdivorce. In W. Marsiglio (Ed.), *Fatherhood: Contemporary theory, research, and social policy* (pp. 57–77). Thousand Oaks, CA: Sage.

Jones, L. (1991). Unemployed fathers and their children: Implications for policy and practice. *Child and Adolescent Social Work Journal, 8,* 101–116.

Lamb, M. E. (1987a). Introduction: The emergent American father. In M. E. Lamb (Ed.), *The father's role: Cross-cultural perspectives* (pp. 3–25). Hillsdale, NJ: Erlbaum.

Lamb, M. E. (Ed.). (1987b). *The father's role: Cross-cultural perspectives.* Hillsdale: NJ: Erlbaum.

Lamb, M. E., Pleck, J., Charnov, E. L., & Levine, J. A. (1985). Paternal behavior in humans. *American Zoologist, 25,* 883–894.

LaRossa, R. (1997). *The modernization of fatherhood: A social and political history.* Chicago: University of Chicago Press.

Larson, R. W. (1993). Finding time for fatherhood: The emotional ecology of adolescent-father interactions. In S. Shulman & W. A. Collins (Eds.), *Father-adolescent relationships* (pp. 7–25). San Francisco: Jossey-Bass.

Larson, R. W., & Richards, M. H. (1994). *Divergent realities: The emotional lives of mothers, fathers, and adolescents.* New York: Basic Books.

Levine, J. A., & Pitt, E. W. (1995). *New expectations: Community strategies for responsible fatherhood.* New York: Families and Work Institute.

Levy-Shiff, R., & Israelashvili, R. (1988). Antecedents of fathering: Some further exploration. *Developmental Psychology, 24,* 434–440.

Lewis, C., & O'Brien, M. (1987). Constraints on fathers: Research, theory and clinical practice. In C. Lewis & M. O'Brien (Eds.), *Reassessing fatherhood: New observations on fathers and the modern family* (pp. 1–19). Newbury Park, CA: Sage.

Marsiglio, W. (1991). Paternal engagement activities with minor children. *Journal of Marriage and the Family, 53,* 973–986.

Marsiglio, W. (1995). Fathers' diverse life course patterns and roles: Theory and social interventions. In W. Marsiglio (Ed.), *Fatherhood: Contemporary theory, research, and social policy* (pp. 78–101). Thousand Oaks, CA: Sage.

McLoyd, V. C. (1989). Socialization and development in a changing economy: The effects of paternal job loss and income loss on children. *American Psychologist, 44,* 293–302.

McLoyd, V. C. (1990). The impact of economic hardship on Black families and children: Psychological distress, parenting, and socioemotional development. *Child Development, 61,* 311–346.

Park, R. D. (1996). *Fatherhood.* Cambridge, MA: Harvard University Press.

Patterson, C. J. (1992). Children of lesbian and gay parents. *Child Development, 63,* 1025–1042.

Patterson, C. J., & Chan, R. W. (1997). Gay fathers. In M. E. Lamb (Ed.), *The role of the father in child development* (3rd ed.). New York: Wiley.

Pleck, J. H. (1997). Paternal involvement: Levels, sources, and consequences. In M. E. Lamb (Ed.), *The role of the father in child development* (3rd ed.). New York: Wiley.

Simons, R., Whitbeck, L., Conger, R., & Melby, J. (1990). Husband and wife differences in determinants of parenting: A social learning and exchange model of parental behavior. *Journal of Marriage and the Family, 52,* 375–392.

Snarey, J. (1993). *How fathers care for the next generation: A four-decade study.* Cambridge, MA: Harvard University Press.

Thomson, E., Hanson, T., & McLanahan, S. S. (1994). Family structure and child well-being: Economic resources versus parent socialization. *Social Forces, 73,* 221–242.

U.S. Department of Health and Human Services (1995). *Report to Congress on out-of-wedlock childbearing* (Pub. No. PHS 95-1257-1). Washington, DC: U.S. Government Printing Office.

Wolfe, A. (1989). *Whose keeper? Social science and moral obligation.* Berkeley: University of California Press.

Alexis J. Walker and Lori A. McGraw  **NO**

Who Is Responsible for Responsible Fathering?

William Doherty, Edward Kouneski, and Martha Erickson proposed a conceptual framework on "Responsible Fathering." For both empirical and theoretical reasons, we found their essay to be problematic. The proposed model excludes key features of fatherhood and of motherhood, and researchers who attempt to operationalize it or practitioners who attempt to develop programs from it are destined to be misguided.

We are not concerned that the authors wrote from a position of advocacy. We agree that the new research on fatherhood primarily reflects a position valuing involved fathers and that discussions about absent fathers sometimes have a moral overtone. This is particularly evident in policy arenas. Congress, in fact, titled a 1998 child support bill, The Deadbeat Parents Punishment Act. As demonstrated by the plethora of empirical studies blaming mothers for their children's behavioral, psychological, and social problems (Caplan & Hall-McCorquodale, 1985), discussions about motherhood have moral overtones as well. Arguments grounded solely in ideology are inherent in the nature of public discourse. What is important for researchers who advocate a specific policy position in our journals is to adhere to principles and practices agreed upon within a scientific community, regardless of ideology (Furstenberg, 1999).

We appreciate the authors' willingness to make their underlying assumptions explicit. We draw attention to the empirical literature the authors neglected, however, and raise questions about their explicit and implicit reasoning. We take issue with their assumptions and their conclusions, and we critique their model by highlighting the sociohistorical context of fatherhood, childhood, and motherhood.

What Do Children Need?

A key, explicit assumption of the authors is "that children *need* [italics added] and deserve active, involved fathers throughout their childhood and adolescence" (p. 279). Although there might be an ideological basis for this assumption, it lacks empirical support. Members of the scientific community may

From Journal of Marriage and the Family, vol. 62, May 2000, pp. 563–569. Copyright © 2000 by Blackwell Publishing, Ltd. Reprinted by permission.

agree on what children need—broadly defined—for biological, physical, emotional, psychological, and social well-being. There is not agreement, however, that these needs must be met by a parent of a certain gender. In their study of children from single-parent households, Downey, Ainsworth-Darnell, and Dufur (1998) asked: "Do women and men play unique roles in shaping children's well-being?" (p. 878). They concluded that "the challenge for family researchers is to distinguish between familial characteristics that are necessarily important for creating positive family environments for children and those, such as sex of parent, that are not" (p. 892). We have no objection to children having actively involved fathers, but research has demonstrated that children's needs can be met within the full range of fathers' involvement, from no involvement to fathers raising children on their own (Acock & Demo, 1994; Risman, 1987).

Which Fathers Matter?

Doherty et al. focused on heterosexual, biological fathers "to delimit the review" (p. 279). Except for marital status, nothing in the authors' conceptual model accounts for their emphasis on biological fathers. Furthermore, there is no empirical evidence that biology predisposes fathers to be responsible and involved (Cooksey & Fondell, 1996). The authors deliberately excluded adoptive, gay, step, fictive kin, and other father surrogates, many of whom are involved, responsible fathers. They suggested that nonbiological and gay fathers deserve empirical and programmatic focus, but they saw such focus as beyond the scope of their paper. Given the authors' concerns about children's needs and the variety of ways through which men function as fathers in contemporary society (e.g., Hawkins & Eggebeen, 1991), we are at a loss to understand their decision. Because there are involved and engaged fathers who are meeting their children's needs in all of the excluded groups, a contextual model of responsible fathers would and should include them.

Mothers' "Gatekeeping," Fathers' Resistance

Doherty et al. exaggerated the problematic behavior of mothers and minimized the role fathers play in their own involvement with their children. They found three studies, two of them focused on young fathers, providing evidence that mothers and grandmothers act as gatekeepers between their husbands and their children. They also cited larger scale studies (e.g., Marsiglio, 1991), demonstrating that father involvement is tied more closely to mothers' than to fathers' characteristics. They relied on this research to argue that mothers control fathers' involvement. The authors concluded that "*many* [emphasis added] mothers are ambivalent about fathers' active involvement with their children" (p. 287). Because their essay was published, an additional study of mothers' gatekeeping has been reported (Allen & Hawkins, 1999).

Gatekeeping by mothers is an idea that has emerged to explain the relatively low levels of involvement of fathers with their children. It has been conceptualized in a variety of ways, most recently as a mother's cognitive schema that includes (a) high standards for housework and child care and enjoying control over family work; (b) an identity that is dependent on others' views of how well-groomed one's children are and how clean one's home is; and (c) a conventional attitude that women enjoy housework and find it easier to do housework and child care than men do (Allen & Hawkins, 1999). Note that interaction with children, other than through housework or child care, was neither part of this conceptualization nor measured as an outcome of gate-keeping. Allen and Hawkins did not include in gatekeeping the idea that fathers may play a direct or indirect role in setting standards for housework and child care or in influencing the division of labor in other ways. Although they attempted to include mothers' sense of responsibility for family work (these items were eliminated because of poor measurement properties), they did not consider fathers' sense of responsibility. Furthermore, neither moth-ers' desires nor their deliberate attempts to exclude fathers from interacting with their children were included. Even accepting this limited conceptualiza-tion, however, only one fifth of their sample of married mothers could be described as "gatekeepers."

In contrast to the idea that mothers keep fathers from their children, evi-dence suggests that women generally value and actively promote relationships between children and fathers (e.g., Haavind, 1984; Marsiglio, 1991; Pleck, 1985; Thompson, 1991). Even stepmothers function in this way. Consider recent evidence from the wives of remarried men over 60 in the Normative Study of Aging. Vinick and Lanspery (1998) described stepmothers as "'car-penters' of damaged family relationships" (p. 4) who worked to establish friendly contact with adult children who were hostile toward their fathers. Stepmothers encouraged their husbands to keep in touch with their children, reminding them to make phone calls, issuing invitations, or communicating with the stepchildren themselves. In separate interviews, their husbands spon-taneously supported these findings. Vinick and Lanspery concluded:

> Stepmothers often fulfilled pivotal roles in stepfamilies as rebuilders and nurturers of associations with the younger generation. Relationships with stepchildren, as well as husbands' relations with their own biologi-cal children, had frequently improved due, in large measure, to women's efforts, acting on their own behalf, and that of their husbands and their stepchildren. (p. 5)

To emphasize women who are ambivalent about or act as gatekeepers of fathers' involvement does a disservice to mothers. We do not deny that some mothers make it difficult for fathers to connect with their children, but any instance of gatekeeping must be viewed in the larger context of mothers' facil-itation and of men's authority in families. This empirical question has yet to be addressed: To what extent are mothers able to limit coresidential fathers' involvement when fathers have a strong interest in building connections with their children?

Doherty et al. wrote about mothers' gatekeeping but not about men's resistance. Fathers play a role in their limited involvement with children by resisting mothers' attempts to facilitate interaction. Arendell (1992, 1995) described how fathers' resistance to cooperating with mothers may become stronger after divorce. As husbands and fathers, men have legitimate control and authority in families. They expect, desire, and believe they have certain "rights to their parenthood" (1992, p. 569), and they see these rights as challenged after divorce. Similarly, Bertoia and Drakich (1993) demonstrated that, rather than involvement with and responsibility for children after divorce, noncustodial fathers felt they "deserved" access, information, and decision-making authority equal to that of custodial mothers. A focus on legitimacy and authority works against fathers' involvement with their children. As Arendell (1992) concluded, uninvolved nonresidential fathers do not see fathering "as an array of activities, interactional processes, and particular kinds of social relations" (p. 582). Instead, they focus on fatherhood as a status concomitant with certain rights. In part, then, men's conceptualization of fatherhood forecasts their involvement with their children.

Fathers and Financial Support

Doherty et al.'s model and discussion of responsible fathering minimized children's dependence on fathers' financial resources. There is ample and compelling empirical support that the most important activity fathers can do for their children's well-being is to support them financially (e.g., Crockett, Eggebeen, & Hawkins, 1993; King, 1994; McLanahan & Sandefur, 1994). Regardless of family structure, fathers who provide economic resources improve their children's developmental outcomes (Acock & Demo, 1994). In our society, men have greater access to resources than women do, and men are defined, in part, through their ability to be good providers (Bernard, 1981). Doherty et al. pay insufficient attention to this aspect of father involvement.

We intend neither to reduce men to their ability to provide money, nor to minimize the role mothers increasingly play in generating income for family members. Instead, we take issue with Doherty et al.'s decision to ignore the social context in which men's participation as fathers is grounded. There is simply no getting around the fact that men's financial contributions matter for both residential and nonresidential children, and that currently, these contributions have a greater impact on children than any other aspect of fathers' involvement.

That the social context creates differing financial imperatives and opportunities for women and men also makes it problematic to compare nonresidential mothers to nonresidential fathers. Doherty et al. minimized problems with noncustodial fathers' financial support by comparing it to that of noncustodial mothers. The causes and consequences of noncustodial motherhood are not the same as those for noncustodial fatherhood (e.g., Arditti & Madden-Derdich, 1993; Cancun & Meyer, 1998). At a minimum, being a noncustodial mother is far more nonnormative than being a noncustodial father. Furthermore, the reasons for noncustodial mothers' noncompliance with child support have yet to be determined. One cannot conclude, as Doherty et al. did, that "there is something in the structure of nonresidential parenting, rather than in the culture of fatherhood, that is the principal inhibitor of economic support for children outside of marriage" (p. 282).

The authors attributed fathers' noncompliance, in part, to mothers' role in "misusing the funds and . . . withholding the children from the father" (Doherty et al., p. 282). What fathers describe as misusing funds, mothers describe as meeting children's needs. What fathers see as withholding children from them, mothers see as a strategy to gain fathers' compliance with child support orders. Stephens (1996) reported county data from Texas in which 14,000 complaints were registered for noncompliance compared with 700 complaints regarding visitation. Most noncustodial fathers were satisfied with the frequency and duration of their visits with children, and fathers' complaints were unrelated to compliance (Stephens). Again, Arendell's (1992, 1995) research is relevant here. Some noncustodial fathers view child support payments as a loss of control over their income rather than as a way to enhance and support their children. This is lamentable because the problems caused by noncompliance are significant, particularly given the effect of such support on children's well-being.

Marriage and Father Involvement

The authors identified marriage as the best context for involved fathers. To support their position, they noted the problems fathers have interacting with and relating to their children, highlighting these problems for never-married and divorced fathers and minimizing the same problems for married fathers. For example, they cited research by Zill, Morrison, and Coiro (1993) showing that 65% of children aged 18 to 22 whose parents divorced reported poor relationships with their fathers. This same study found that nearly 1 in 3 (29%) children in the same age group with *married* parents also reported poor relationships with their fathers. Although the proportion is higher for divorced fathers, the proportion in stable families is alarmingly high. In contrast, mothers' relationships with their children, both inside and outside of marriage, are generally positive (Aquilino, 1994; Rossi & Rossi, 1990; Silverstein & Bengtson, 1997).

Doherty et al. also overstated the role of marriage in father involvement in other ways. For example, they exaggerated fathers' involvement when wives are employed. They reported that fathers with employed wives perform a greater proportion of parenting activities than do fathers with nonemployed wives. They did not explain that the proportion is greater primarily because employed wives do less than nonemployed wives. They stated that "fathers are a significant source of primary care when mothers work" (p. 284). Careful attention to this literature demonstrates that fathers serve as primary care providers in response to their wives' paid work schedules (e.g., Brayfield, 1995; Presser, 1988). Care-giving fathers of younger children typically work for pay during daytime hours, and their wives typically work for pay during evening and nighttime hours. Most of the time during which fathers are responsible for young children is when their children are asleep. In contrast, fathers provide daytime, after-school care for older children who have less demanding needs for care.

By not attending to the context in which fathers are fully responsible for their children, Doherty and his colleagues risk exaggerating fathers' involvement, as well as fathers' interest in being involved. We agree that fathers are capable of caring involvement with their children. It is not necessary to exaggerate what fathers do to support this view. That some serve as primary child care givers provides hope that fathers indeed may be more involved in the future.

Doherty and his colleagues argued that "a caring, committed, collaborative marriage" (p. 290) fosters responsible fatherhood. Unstated is the fact that husbands' behavior is a major contributor to this type of marriage (e.g., Gottman, 1998). Husbands who are responsive to and appreciative of their wives and who facilitate their wives' sense of partnership and equality have better quality marriages (Hochschild, 1989; Schwartz, 1994; Thompson, 1991). Coltrane (1989) found that fathers who participate in child care from infancy also have more egalitarian partnerships with their wives. The connection between a collaborative marriage and an involved father may reflect something other than marital quality. The type of man who helps to develop a cooperative marriage may be the type of man who will be an involved father.

Collaborative marriages are not inevitable. Furthermore, prescribing marriage as a solution to the lack of father involvement is not without risk. Marriages characterized by conflict have a negative influence on children (e.g., Buehler et al., 1998; Gottman, 1998). An emphasis on marriage or other aspects of family structure absent of consideration of family process is misguided (e.g., Cooksey & Fondell, 1996; King, 1994; Miller, Forehand, & Kotchick, 1999). Indeed, Demo (1992) concluded that family structure has far less influence on child outcomes than is assumed. Data on fathering demonstrate that marriage is neither a sufficient nor a necessary context for responsible fathering. In considering her findings and those of others, King concluded that relationship quality, an important precursor to marital stability, is not changed easily by intervention or by social policy.

Toward the end of their article, Doherty et al. stated that "a high quality marriage is the optimal context for promoting responsible fatherhood" (p. 290), suggesting that "the promotion of these kinds of enduring marital partnerships may be the most important contribution to responsible fathering in our society." They were concerned that their conclusion would be "potentially controversial" because it is opposite of a "trend in contemporary family studies to disaggregate marriage and parenting" (p. 290). It is inappropriate and unfair to take practitioners of the discipline to task in this way. The disaggregation of marriage and parenting is not a trend in the study of families. It is, instead, a trend in the lived experience of individuals in the United States and in other industrialized nations that is well documented by researchers in the field (e.g., Adler, 1997).

Father Involvement

The literature in family science has attended increasingly to fathers, highlighting their importance to their children, and arguing that their contributions have been minimized. Although the authors reviewed a chapter by Pleck (1997) concluding that heterosexual, married, biological fathers are significantly more involved now than they were 20 years ago, empirical evidence suggests otherwise (e.g., Perkins & DeMeis, 1996; Press & Townsley, 1998; Sanchez & Thomson, 1997). In 1988, Ralph LaRossa highlighted the disjunction between the culture and the conduct of fatherhood. All evidence suggests that this disjunction continues to exist. Doherty et al. stated their intention to avoid between-gender comparisons but pointed out that fathers' involvement remains well below that of mothers. Our point is that fathers' involvement is well below that of the cultural standard for fathers.

Studies using nationally representative data sets show little change in residential and nonresidential father involvement over time, and no influence or weak influence on child outcomes when fathers are involved (e.g., Cooksey & Fondell, 1996; Harris, Furstenberg, & Mariner, 1998; Stephens, 1996). For example, despite public and scholarly discourse to the contrary, except during the 1990–1991 economic recession, there was virtually no change from the mid-1960s to 1993 in the proportion of preschoolers cared for by fathers when mothers are employed (Casper & O'Connell, 1998). King's (1994) research is illustrative of the literature on the involvement of nonresidential fathers. Using the National Longitudinal Survey of Youth, she reported "that there is only limited evidence to support the hypothesis that nonresident father involvement has positive benefits for children" (p. 970). Other researchers (Mott, Kowaleski-Jones, & Menaghan, 1997) have found no significant long-term effects of father absence on children's behavior. (See also Argys, Peters, Brooks-Gunn, & Smith, 1998.) This does not mean that all fathers are uninvolved with their children or that fathers who are highly involved have no influence. It does mean that, on average, the level of fathers' involvement continues to be minimal and that there is insufficient variance in father involvement for it to have strong and significant associations with child outcomes.

One consistent and key predictor of father involvement is education (e.g., Amato & Booth, 1997; Cooksey & Craig, 1998; Cooney, Pedersen, Indelicato, & Palkovitz, 1993; King, 1994; Stephens, 1996). Highly educated men appear to have adopted a cultural standard for fathers that is at odds with fatherhood as practiced by the vast majority of men, most of whom have far less education. Given that education is so important in predicting fathers' involvement, policies and programs should stress greater access to and support for education for all men so as to encourage responsible fatherhood.

Fatherhood, Motherhood, and Social Location

Doherty and his colleagues suggested that, in comparison with mothers, fathers suffer disproportionately from negative social forces, such as racism, that inhibit them from being involved with their children. Fathers of color do suffer from racism, but so do mothers and children (e.g., Hill Collins, 1992). Oppression based on social location is a system of interacting influences: racism, classism, sexism, heterosexism, and ageism. Some individuals are affected by more of these influences than are others.

Additionally, fathers have greater access to economic resources than mothers do, and this fact shapes both fathering and mothering (Gerson, 1993;

LaRossa, 1988). There are fewer deterrents to fathers' than to mothers' participation in paid labor, a highly valued activity, and fathers have greater discretion than mothers to participate in child care, a less valued activity. Fathers lose status when they participate in labor defined as "women's work" (Gerson, 1993; Hochschild, 1989). Thus, not all fathers choose to be involved. For fathers to become more responsible for child care and more involved with their children would require a restructuring of paid and unpaid work. This restructuring would necessitate fathers giving up paternal privilege (Goode, 1982).

Who Is Responsible for Responsible Fathers?

We do not agree that Doherty et al.'s model is a contextual, social constructionist one. Any such model would attend to a number of features absent from their analysis. We note, for example, their failure to attend to a key feature of the needs of children: that they are socially constructed. Children's "needs" have evolved over time to shape and control the behaviors of mothers as much as they have been about promoting children's development (Ambert, 1994; Ehrenreich & English, 1978; Gerson, 1985). Fatherhood, motherhood, and childhood are *all* social constructions. A fully contextual model cannot ignore this key fact, nor the patriarchal context in which this social construction occurs.

Another context the authors ignored is the gendered nature of mothering and fathering in the United States. Their model disproportionately placed responsibility for fathers' involvement with their children on women. Instead of identifying things mothers can do to "move men in the direction of more responsible fathering" (p. 288)—activities destined to be described as nagging— we ask what responsibility *men* have for being responsible fathers?

We share the authors' inclusive and flexible definition of who can nurture, discipline, and provide for children. In an ideal world, parenting—the activities of nurturing, disciplining, and providing for children—would be work taken up by women *and* by men according to their individual proclivities and within a climate of economic justice and an ethic of care at all levels of society (Okin, 1989). We do not live in such a society, however. In our society, women and men do not have access to the same level of economic resources, nor are they held equally accountable for the undervalued activity of caring for dependent people. Any definition of responsible fathering must reflect the real world, even if it aims for a better world in the future.

References

Acock, A. C., & Demo, D. H. (1994). *Family diversity and well-being.* Newbury Park, CA: Sage.

Adler, M. A. (1997). Social change and declines in marriage and fertility in Eastern Germany. *Journal of Marriage and the Family, 59,* 37-49.

Allen, S. M., & Hawkins, A. J. (1999). Maternal gatekeeping: Mothers' beliefs and behaviors that inhibit greater father involvement in family work. *Journal of Marriage and the Family, 61,* 199-212.

Amato, P. R., & Booth, A. (1997). *A generation at risk: Growing up in an era of family upheaval.* Cambridge, MA: Harvard University Press.

Ambert, A. (1994). An international perspective on parenting: Social change and social constructs. *Journal of Marriage and the Family, 56,* 529–543.

Aquilino, W. S. (1994). Impact of childhood family disruption on young adults' relationships with parents. *Journal of Marriage and the Family, 56,* 295–313.

Arditti, J. A., & Madden-Derdich, D. A. (1993). Noncustodial mothers: Developing strategies of support. *Family Relations, 42,* 305–314.

Arendell, T. (1992). After divorce: Investigations into father absence. *Gender & Society, 6,* 562–586.

Arendell, T. (1995). *Fathers and divorce.* Thousand Oaks, CA: Sage.

Argys, L. M., Peters, H. E., Brooks-Gunn, J., & Smith, J. (1998). The impact of child support on cognitive outcomes of young children. *Demography, 35,* 159–173.

Bernard, J. (1981). The good provider role: Its rise and fall. *American Psychologist, 36,* 1–12.

Bertoia, C., & Drakich, J. (1993). The fathers' rights movement: Contradictions in rhetoric and practice. *Journal of Family Issues, 14,* 592–615.

Brayfield, A. (1995). Juggling jobs and kids: The impact of employment schedules on fathers' caring for children. *Journal of Marriage and the Family, 57,* 321–332.

Buehler, C., Krishnakumar, A., Stone, G., Anthony, C., Pemberton, S., Gerard, J., & Barber, B. K. (1998). Interparental conflict styles and youth problem behaviors: A two-sample replication study. *Journal of Marriage and the Family, 60,* 119–132.

Cancun, M., & Meyer, D. R. (1998). Who gets custody? *Demography, 35,* 147–157.

Caplan, P. J., & Hall-McCorquodale, I. (1985). The scapegoating of mothers: A call for change. *American Journal of Orthopsychiatry, 55,* 610–613.

Casper, L. M., & O'Connell, M. (1998). Work, income, the economy, and married fathers as child-care providers. *Demography, 35,* 243–250.

Coltrane, S. (1989). Household labor and the routine production of gender. *Social Problems, 36,* 473–490.

Cooksey, E. C., & Craig, P. H. (1998). Parenting from a distance: The effects of paternal characteristics on contact between nonresidential fathers and their children. *Demography, 35,* 187–200.

Cooksey, E. C., & Fondell, M. M. (1996). Spending time with his kids: Effects of family structure on fathers' and children's lives. *Journal of Marriage and the Family, 58,* 693–707.

Cooney, T. M., Pedersen, E. A., Indelicato, S., & Palkovitz, R. (1993). Timing of fatherhood: Is "on-time" optimal? *Journal of Marriage and the Family, 55,* 205–215.

Crockett, L. J., Eggebeen, D. J., & Hawkins, A. J. (1993). Father presence and young children's behavioral and cognitive adjustment. *Journal of Family Issues, 14,* 355–377.

Demo, D. H. (1992). Parent-child relations: Assessing recent changes. *Journal of Marriage and the Family, 54,* 104–117.

Doherty, W. J., Kouneski, E. E., & Erickson, M. F. (1998). Responsible fathering: An overview and conceptual framework. *Journal of Marriage and the Family, 60,* 277–292.

Downey, D. B., Ainsworth-Darnell, J. W., & Dufur, M. J. (1998). Sex of parent and children's well-being in single-parent households. *Journal of Marriage and the Family, 60,* 878–893.

Ehrenreich, B., & English, D. (1978). *For her own good: 50 years of the experts' advice to women.* Garden City, NY: Anchor Press.

Furstenberg, E. E., Jr. (1999). Children and family change: Discourse between social scientists and the media. *Contemporary Sociology: A Journal of Reviews, 28,* 10–17.

Gerson, K. (1993). *No man's land: Men's changing commitments to family and work.* New York: Basic Books.

Gerson, K. (1985). *Hard choices: How women decide about work, career, and motherhood.* Berkeley, CA: University of California Press.

Goode, W. J. (1982). Why men resist. In B. Thorne & M. Yalom (Eds.), *Rethinking the family: Some feminist questions* (pp. 131–147). New York: Longman.

Gottman, J. M. (1998). Toward a process model of men in marriages and families. In A. Booth & A. C. Crouter (Eds.), *Men in families: When do they get involved? What difference does it make?* (pp. 149–192): Mahwah, NJ: Erlbaum.

Haavind, H. (1984). Love and power in marriage. In H. Holter (Ed.), *Patriarchy in a welfare state* (pp. 136–167). Oslo, Sweden: Universitetsforlaget.

Harris, K. M., Furstenberg, F. F., Jr., & Marmer, J. K. (1998). Paternal involvement with adolescents in intact families: The influence of fathers over the life course. *Demography, 35,* 201–216.

Hawkins, A. J., & Eggebeen, D. J. (1991). Are fathers fungible? Patterns of coresident adult men in maritally disrupted families and young children's well-being. *Journal of Marriage and the Family, 53,* 958–972.

Hill Collins, P. (1992). Black women and motherhood. In B. Thorne & M. Yalom (Eds.), *Rethinking the family: Some feminist questions* (2nd ed., pp. 215–245). Boston: Northeastern University Press.

Hochschild, A., with Machung, A. (1989). *The second shift: Working parents and the revolution at home.* New York: Viking.

King, V. (1994). Variation in the consequence of nonresident father involvement for children's well-being. *Journal of Marriage and the Family, 56,* 963–972.

LaRossa, R. (1988). Fatherhood and social change. *Family Relations, 37,* 451–457.

Marsiglio, A. (1991). Paternal engagement activities with minor children. *Journal of Marriage and the Family, 53,* 973–986.

McLanahan, S., & Sandefur, G. (1994). *Growing up with a single parent: What hurts, what helps.* Cambridge, MA: Harvard University Press.

Miller, K. S., Forehand, R., & Kotchick, B. A. (1999). Adolescent sexual behavior in two ethnic minority samples: The role of family variables. *Journal of Marriage and the Family, 61,* 85–98.

Mott, E. L., Kowaleski-Jones, L., & Menaghan, E. G. (1997). Paternal absence and child behavior: Does a child's gender make a difference? *Journal of Marriage and the Family, 59,* 103–118.

Okin, S. M. (1989). *Justice, gender, and the family.* New York: Basic Books.

Perkins, H. W., & DeMeis, D. K. (1996). Gender and family effects on the "second-shift" domestic activity of college-educated young adults. *Gender & Society, 10,* 78–93.

Pleck, J. H. (1985). *Working wives/working husbands.* Beverly Hills, CA: Sage.

Pleck, J. H. (1997). Paternal involvement: Levels, sources, and consequences. In M. E. Lamb (Ed.), *The role of the father in child development* (3rd ed., pp. 66–103). New York: Wiley.

Press, J. E., & Townsley, E. (1998). Wives' and husbands' housework reporting: Gender, class, and social desirability. *Gender and Society, 12,* 188–218.

Presser, H. B. (1988). Shift work and child care among young dual-earner American parents. *Journal of Marriage and the Family, 50,* 133–148.

Risman, B. J. (1987). Intimate relationships from a microstructural perspective: Men who mother. *Gender and Society, 1,* 6–32.

Rossi, A. S., & Rossi, P. H. (1990). *Of human bonding: Parent-child relations across the life course.* New York: Aldine de Gruyter.

Sanchez, L., & Thompson, E. (1997). Becoming mothers and fathers: Parenthood, gender, and the division of labor. *Gender and Society, 11,* 747–772.

Schwartz, P. (1994). *Peer marriage: How love between equals really works.* New York: Free Press.

Silverstein, M., & Bengtson, V. L. (1997). Intergenerational solidarity and the structure of adult child-parent relationships in American families. *American Journal of Sociology, 103,* 429–460.

Stephens, L. S. (1996). Will Johnny see Daddy this week? An empirical test of three theoretical perspectives of postdivorce contact. *Journal of Family Issues, 17,* 466–494.

Thompson, L. (1991). Women's sense of fairness. *Journal of Family Issues, 12,* 181–196.

Vinick, B. H., & Lanspery, S. (1998, March). *Cinderella's sequel: Stepmothers' long-term relationships with adult stepchildren.* Paper presented at the annual meeting of the American Society on Aging, San Francisco.

Zill, N., Morrison, D. R., & Coiro, M. J. (1993). Long-term effects of parental divorce on parent-child relationships, adjustment, and achievement in young adulthood. *Journal of Family Psychology, 7,* 91–103.

POSTSCRIPT

Are Fathers Really Necessary?

What role does a father play in the development of a child? Is it the role of dad and what society says he "should" be that becomes important to the child rather than how he treats his child? Or, is it that is important? If the former is true, then anyone, regardless of how they treat the child, will be important to the child. We often see evidence of this phenomenon in dealing with abused children. No matter what the abuse, most children in this situation want to stay at home with abusive fathers rather than be placed in foster care. When confronted with "telling on" their fathers, children often will not say what abuse has occurred for fear of losing their father's love and being separated from them.

If the latter is true, the quality of interaction and events that children share with their fathers becomes key to their development. Then why couldn't women play that role? Women can interact with children in nearly all of the same ways that men can. Women can just as easily accompany children to baseball games, act as the soccer coach, or go to the school play as can men. Thus the question might not be "are fathers really necessary?" but might be "are men really necessary for the positive development of children?" To many, this would not only mean an assault on the role of fatherhood but also would constitute an attack on men in general.

As with most issues, extremes on either side make less sense than the middle ground. Child development experts would probably agree that the more adults, both male and female, involved in a child's life, the better. Having a variety of people in one's life brings a variety of experiences and an extensive social support network that can benefit children throughout their lives.

Significant research on fathering is becoming more prolific. Perhaps within the next few years scientists will be able to make more definitive statements with regard to the roles for both mother and father in a child's life. One could conclude that we are all responsible for fathering and mothering. This is especially true for families who do not have the choice of raising children in a two-parent system due to divorce or death of a spouse. We must continue to strive to find ways to support all families so that children will experience optimal need gratification as they grow and develop.

Suggested Readings

Amneus, D. (1995). The father's role in society; http://www.menweb.org/throop/nofather/articles/amneus.html.

Coley, R. L. (1990). Children's socialization experiences and functioning in single-mother households: The importance of fathers and other men. *Child Development, 69,* 219–230.

Popenoe, D. (2000). Life without father; http://www.themenscenter.com.

Sanchez, L., & Thompson, E. (1997). Becoming mothers and fathers: Parenthood, gender, and the division of labor. *Gender and Society, 11,* 747–772.

Stapleton, M. (2000). The unnecessary tragedy of fatherless children. *Policy and Practice of Public Human Services, 58,* 43–48.

Stephens, L. S. (1996). Will Johnny see Daddy this week? An empirical test of three theoretical perspectives of post-divorce contact. *Journal of Family Issues, 17,* 466–494.

ISSUE 7

Does Divorce Create Long-Term Negative Effects for Children?

YES: Judith Wallerstein, Julia Lewis, and Sandra Blakeslee, from *The Unexpected Legacy of Divorce: A 25-Year Landmark Study* (Hyperion, 2000)

NO: E. Mavis Hetherington and John Kelly, from *For Better or for Worse: Divorce Reconsidered* (W.W. Norton, 2002)

ISSUE SUMMARY

YES: Judith Wallerstein, Julia Lewis, and Sandra Blakeslee, authors of a long-term study on children of divorce, contend that children who experienced divorce carried the negative effects of post-divorce life into their adulthood. These children of divorce have difficulty developing trusting and intimate relationships with marriage partners.

NO: E. Mavis Hetherington, long-time researcher on children and divorce, and co-author John Kelly assert that children of divorce are mostly happy as adults. Although these children experienced unhappiness, they are able to develop normally and have successfully completed the tasks of young adulthood.

How does divorce affect children? Do they perceive it as positive or negative? How would their lives differ if their parents had worked out their problems and stayed together, even if only for the sake of the children? How do children from divorced families differ from those in intact homes—happy or unhappy? Do both groups have similarities, or are they significantly different? These are questions researchers ask when they study the effects of divorce on children.

According to some studies, children from divorced homes are more likely to divorce themselves. Other studies indicate that the quality of the home post-divorce is more likely to affect children's development than the actual divorce event. Is society setting children up for subsequent failed marriages by condoning divorce? Or is divorce simply a solution to the problem of choosing the wrong partner, giving individuals a way of correcting that mistake? Does the divorce spell disaster for children as they grow into adulthood, or are there other explanations for the problems, which children from divorced homes might exhibit?

As the divorce debate evolved from the 1960s to the 1980s, some professionals viewed divorce as an acceptable alternative to living in an unhappy home, while others saw divorce as having devastating effects on children and the family. In the 1990s, a movement to do away with no-fault divorce also spawned a renewed interest in the effects of divorce on children. Family scientists, therapists, and researchers questioned the belief that children eventually adjust to the effects of divorce and that it is better for children to live in a divorced home than in an unhappy, intact home. In the 2000s, longitudinal data on divorce's effects presented conflicting conclusions with more questions than answers to the issue.

There are numerous studies on effects of divorce on children. Some show that children benefit from divorce while others show it is the worst thing that ever happened. On the positive side, children from divorced homes reap benefits as a consequence of their divorce experience, particularly if parents model responsible coping skills. Some children do better in a home without the constant tension and fighting found in an unhappy intact home. These children appear more mature, more realistic about life, and more flexible.

Problems for children in divorced families are well documented. For these children, parents split physically and legally, but not emotionally. These family members might ride an emotional rollercoaster for years after the initial divorce decree. One parent pitted against the other with the child in the middle is all too common for divorced families. Family turmoil may result in children doing poorly in school, beginning to have sex at an early age, and displaying delinquent behavior. Children have no say in the divorce, but must live with the instability and confusion that occurs after the breakup.

If parents decide to divorce, there are things they can do to keep the divorce more healthy according to family life educators. They suggest not putting the other parent down in front of the children. This helps maintain some sense of stability and civility for the children. Seek outside help for the emotional turmoil associated with divorce, rather than using the children as a "sounding board." Make sure any heated discussions with the other parent are held in private where the children cannot hear. Also, try to accept the other parent's new mate so that children do not feel they are betraying the other parent when visiting the new family.

In the following selections, arguments are made about the long-term effects of divorce on children. Based on results of a 25-year study, Judith Wallerstein, Julia Lewis, and Sandra Blakeslee believe that children of divorce experience upheaval in their lives at every stage of development, but are most severely affected in adulthood when they begin looking for marriage partners. E. Mavis Hetherington and John Kelly report on a study about adults 20 years after they experienced divorce. They found that 80 percent of children from divorced homes eventually were able to adapt to their new life and become well-adjusted.

YES

Judith Wallerstein, Julia Lewis, and Sandra Blakeslee

The Unexpected Legacy of Divorce

Conclusions

"What's done to children, they will do to society."

Karl A. Menninger

Around the time I was finishing this book, a very important judge on the family law bench in a large state I shall not name invited me to come see him. I was eager to meet with him because I wanted to discuss some ideas I have for educating parents under court auspices that go beyond the simple advice "don't fight." After we had talked for a half an hour or so, the judge leaned back in his chair and said he'd like my opinion about something important. He had just attended several scientific lectures in which researchers argued that children are shaped more by genes than by family environment. Case in point, studies of identical twins reared separately show that in adulthood such twins often like the same foods and clothing styles, belong to the same political parties, and even bestow identical names on their dogs. The judge looked perplexed. "Do you think that could mean divorce is in the genes?" he asked in all seriousness. "And if that's so, does it matter what a court decides when parents divorce?"

I was taken aback. Here was a key figure in the lives of thousands of children asking me whether what he and his colleagues do or say on the bench makes any difference. He seemed relieved by the notion that maybe his actions are insignificant.

I told him that I personally doubt the existence of a "divorce gene." If such a biological trait had arisen in evolution, it would be of very recent vintage. But, I added, "What the court does matters enormously. You have the power to protect children from being hurt or to increase their suffering."

Now it was his turn to be taken aback. "You think we've increased children's suffering?"

"Yes, Your Honor, I do. With all respect, I have to say that the court along with the rest of society has increased the suffering of children."

"How so?" he asked.

We spent another half hour talking about how the courts, parents, attorneys, mental health workers—indeed most adults—have been reluctant to pay genuine attention to children during and after divorce. He listened respectfully

From *Psychoanalytic Psychology*, vol. 21, no. 3, Summer 2004, pp. 353–354, 359–360, 366–370.

to me but I must say I left the judge's chambers that day in a state of shock that soon turned to gloom. How can we be so utterly lost and confused that a leading judge would accept the notion of a "divorce gene" to explain our predicament? If he's confused about his role, what about the rest of us? What is it about the impact of divorce on our society and our children that's so hard to understand and accept?

Having spent the last thirty years of my life traveling here and abroad talking to professional, legal, and mental health groups plus working with thousands of parents and children in divorced families, it's clear that we've created a new kind of society never before seen in human culture. Silently and unconsciously, we have created a culture of divorce. It's hard to grasp what it means when we say that first marriages stand a 45 percent chance of breaking up and that second marriages have a 60 percent chance of ending in divorce. What are the consequences for all of us when 25 percent of people today between the ages of eighteen and forty-four have parents who divorced? What does it mean to a society when people wonder aloud if the family is about to disappear? What can we do when we learn that married couples with children represent a mere 26 percent of households in the 1990s and that the most common living arrangement nowadays is a household of unmarried people with no children? These numbers are terrifying. But like all massive social change, what's happening is affecting us in ways that we have yet to understand.

For people like me who work with divorcing families all the time, these abstract numbers have real faces. When I think about people I know so well, including the "children" you've met in this book, I can relate to the millions of children and adults who suffer with loneliness and to all the teenagers who say, "I don't want a life like either of my parents." I can empathize with the countless young men and women who despair of ever finding a lasting relationship and who, with a brave toss of the head, say, "Hey, if you don't get married then you can't get divorced." It's only later, or sometimes when they think I'm not listening, that they add softly, "but I don't want to grow old alone." I am especially worried about how our divorce culture has changed childhood itself. A million new children a year are added to our march of marital failure. As they explain so eloquently, they lose the carefree play of childhood as well as the comforting arms and lap of a loving parent who is always rushing off because life in the postdivorce family is so incredibly difficult to manage. We must take very seriously the complaint of children like Karen who declare, "The day my parents divorced is the day my childhood ended."

Many years ago the psychoanalyst Erik Erikson taught us that childhood and society are vitally connected. But we have not yet come to terms with the changes ushered in by our divorce culture. Childhood is different, adolescence is different, and adulthood is different. Without our noticing, we have created a new class of young children who take care of themselves, along with a whole generation of overburdened parents who have no time to enjoy the pleasures of parenting. So much has happened so fast, we cannot hold it all in our minds. It's simply overwhelming.

But we must not forget a very important other side to all these changes. Because of our divorce culture, adults today have a greater sense of freedom.

The importance of sex and play in adult life is widely accepted. We are not locked into our early mistakes and forced to stay in wretched, lifelong relationships. The change in women—their very identity and freer role in society—is part of our divorce culture. Indeed, two thirds of divorces are initiated by women despite the high price they pay in economic and parenting burdens afterward. People want and expect a lot more out of marriage than did earlier generations. Although the divorce rate in second and third marriages is sky-high, many second marriages are much happier than the ones left behind. Children and adults are able to escape violence, abuse, and misery to create a better life. Clearly there is no road back.

The sobering truth is that we have created a new kind of society that offers greater freedom and more opportunities for many adults, but this welcome change carries a serious hidden cost. Many people, adults and children alike, are in fact not better off. We have created new kinds of families in which relationships are fragile and often unreliable. Children today receive far less nurturance, protection, and parenting than was their lot a few decades ago. Long-term marriages come apart at still surprising rates. And many in the older generation who started the divorce revolution find themselves estranged from their adult children. Is this the price we must pay for needed change? Can't we do better?

I'd like to say that we're at a crossroads but I'm afraid I can't be that optimistic. We can choose a new route only if we agree on where we are and where we want to be in the future. The outlook is cloudy. For every person who wants to sound an alarm, there's another who says don't worry. For everyone concerned about the economic and emotional deprivations inherited by children of divorce there are those who argue that those kids were "in trouble before" and that divorce is irrelevant, no big deal. People want to feel good about their choices. Doubtless many do. In actual fact, after most divorces, one member of the former couple feels much better while the other feels no better or even worse. Yet at any dinner party you will still hear the same myths: Divorce is a temporary crisis. So many children have experienced their parents' divorce that kids nowadays don't worry so much. It's easier. They almost expect it. It's a rite of passage. If I feel better, so will my children. And so on. As always, children are voiceless or unheard.

But family scholars who have not always seen eye to eye are converging on a number of findings that fly in the face of our cherished myths. We agree that the effects of divorce are long-term. We know that the family is in trouble. We have a consensus that children raised in divorced or remarried families are less well adjusted as adults than those raised in intact families.

The life histories of this first generation to grow up in a divorce culture tell us truths we dare not ignore. Their message is poignant, clear, and contrary to what so many want to believe. They have taught me the following:

From the viewpoint of the children, and counter to what happens to their parents, divorce is a cumulative experience. Its impact increases over time and rises to a crescendo in adulthood. At each developmental stage divorce is experienced anew in different ways. In adulthood it affects personality, the ability to trust, expectations about relationships, and ability to cope with change.

The first upheaval occurs at the breakup. Children are frightened and angry, terrified of being abandoned by both parents, and they feel responsible for the divorce. Most children are taken by surprise; few are relieved. As adults, they remember with sorrow and anger how little support they got from their parents when it happened. They recall how they were expected to adjust overnight to a terrifying number of changes that confounded them. Even children who had seen or heard violence at home made no connection between that violence and the decision to divorce. The children concluded early on, silently and sadly, that family relationships are fragile and that the tie between a man and woman can break capriciously, without warning. They worried ever after that parent-child relationships are also unreliable and can break at any time. These early experiences colored their later expectations.

As the postdivorce family took shape, their world increasingly resembled what they feared most. Home was a lonely place. The household was in disarray for years. Many children were forced to move, leaving behind familiar schools, close friends, and other supports. What they remember vividly as adults is the loss of the intact family and the safety net it provided, the difficulty of having two parents in two homes, and how going back and forth cut badly into playtime and friendships. Parents were busy with work, preoccupied with rebuilding their social lives. Both moms and dads had a lot less time to spend with their children and were less responsive to their children's needs or wishes. Little children especially felt that they had lost both parents and were unable to care for themselves. Children soon learned that the divorced family has porous walls that include new lovers, live-in partners, and stepparents. Not one of these relationships was easy for anyone. The mother's parenting was often cut into by the very heavy burdens of single parenthood and then by the demands of remarriage and stepchildren.

Relationships with fathers were heavily influenced by live-in lovers or stepmothers in second and third marriages. Some second wives were interested in the children while others wanted no part of them. Some fathers were able to maintain their love and interest in their children but few had time for two or sometimes three families. In some families both parents gradually stabilized their lives within happy remarriages or well-functioning, emotionally gratifying single parenthood. But these people were never a majority in any of my work.

Meanwhile, children who were able to draw support from school, sports teams, parents, stepparents, grandparents, teachers, or their own inner strengths, interests, and talents did better than those who could not muster such resources. By necessity, many of these so-called resilient children forfeited their own childhoods as they took responsibility for themselves; their troubled, overworked parents; and their siblings. Children who needed more than minimal parenting because they were little or had special vulnerabilities and problems with change were soon overwhelmed with sorrow and anger at their parents. Years later, when contemplating having their own children, most children in this study said hotly, "I never want a child of mine to experience a childhood like I had."

As the children told us, adolescence begins early in divorced homes and, compared with that of youngsters raised in intact families, is more likely to include more early sexual experiences for girls and higher alcohol and drug use for girls and boys. Adolescence is more prolonged in divorced families and extends well into the years of early adulthood. Throughout these years children of divorce worry about following in their parents' footsteps and struggle with a sinking sense that they, too, will fail in their relationships.

But it's in adulthood that children of divorce suffer the most. The impact of divorce hits them most cruelly as they go in search of love, sexual intimacy, and commitment. Their lack of inner images of a man and a woman in a stable relationship and their memories of their parents' failure to sustain the marriage badly hobbles their search, leading them to heartbreak and even despair. They cried, "No one taught me." They complain bitterly that they feel unprepared for adult relationships and that they have never seen a "man and woman on the same beam," that they have no good models on which to build their hopes. And indeed they have a very hard time formulating even simple ideas about the kind of person they're looking for. Many end up with unsuitable or very troubled partners in relationships that were doomed from the start.

The contrast between them and children from good intact homes, as both go in search of love and commitment, is striking. (As I explain in this book, children raised in extremely unhappy or violent intact homes face misery in childhood and tragic challenges in adulthood. But because their parents generally aren't interested in getting a divorce, divorce does not become part of their legacy.) Adults in their twenties from reasonably good or even moderately unhappy intact families had a fine understanding of the demands and sacrifices required in a close relationship. They had memories of how their parents struggled and overcame differences, how they cooperated in a crisis. They developed a general idea about the kind of person they wanted to marry. Most important, they did not expect to fail. The two groups differed after marriage as well. Those from intact families found the example of their parents' enduring marriage very reassuring when they inevitably ran into marital problems. But in coping with the normal stresses in a marriage, adults from divorced families were at a grave disadvantage. Anxiety about relationships was at the bedrock of their personalities and endured even in very happy marriages. Their fears of disaster and sudden loss rose when they felt content. And their fear of abandonment, betrayal, and rejection mounted when they found themselves having to disagree with someone they loved. After all, marriage is a slippery slope and their parents fell off it. All had trouble dealing with differences or even moderate conflict in their close relationships. Typically their first response was panic, often followed by flight. They had a lot to undo and a lot to learn in a very short time.

Those who had two parents who rebuilt happy lives after divorce and included children in their orbits had a much easier time as adults. Those who had committed single parents also benefited from that parent's attention and responsiveness. But the more frequent response in adulthood was continuing anger at parents, more often at fathers, whom the children regarded as having been selfish and faithless.

Others felt deep compassion and pity toward mothers or fathers who failed to rebuild their lives after divorce. The ties between daughters and their mothers were especially close but at a cost. Some young women found it very difficult to separate from their moms and to lead their own lives. With some notable exceptions, fathers in divorced families were less likely to enjoy close bonds with their adult children, especially their sons. This stood in marked contrast to fathers and sons from intact families, who tended to grow closer as the years went by.

Fortunately for many children of divorce, their fears of loss and betrayal can be conquered by the time they reach their late twenties and thirties. But what a struggle that takes, what courage and persistence. Those who succeed overcome their difficulties the hard way—by learning from their own failed relationships and gradually rejecting the models they were raised with to create what they want from a love relationship. Those lucky enough to have found a loving partner are able to interrupt their self-destructive course with a lasting love affair or marriage.

In other realms of adult life—financial and security, for instance—some children were able to overcome difficulties through unexpected help from fathers who had vanished long before. Still others benefit from the constancy of parents or grandparents. Many men and women raised in divorced families establish successful careers. Their workplace performance is largely unaffected by the divorce. But no matter what their success in the world, they retain some serious residues—fear of loss, fear of change, and fear that disaster will strike, especially when things are going well. They're still terrified by the mundane differences and inevitable conflicts found in every close relationship.

I'm heartened by the hard-won success of these adults. But at the same time, I can't forget those who've failed to straighten out their lives. I'm especially troubled by how many divorced or remained in wretched marriages. Of those who have children and who are now divorced, many, to my dismay, are not protecting their children in ways we might expect. They go on to repeat the same mistakes their own parents made, perpetuating problems that have plagued them all their lives. I'm also concerned about many who, by their mid- and late thirties, are neither married nor cohabiting and who are leading lonely lives. They're afraid of getting involved in a relationship that they think is doomed to fail. After a divorce or breakup, they're afraid to try again. And I'm struck by continuing anger at parents and flat-out statements by many of these young adults that they have no intention of helping their moms and especially their dads or stepparents in old age. This may change. But if it doesn't, we'll be facing another unanticipated consequence of our divorce culture. Who will take care of an older generation estranged from its children?

What We Can and Cannot Do

Our efforts to improve our divorce culture have been spotty and the resources committed to the task are pitifully small. The courts have given the lion's share of attention to the 10 to 15 percent of families that continue to fight bitterly. Caught between upholding the rights of parents and protecting the interests of children, they have tilted heavily toward parents. Such parents allegedly speak in the name of the child just as those who fight bloody holy wars allegedly speak in the name of religion. Thus, as I explained to the judge with whom I began this chapter, our court system has unintentionally contributed to the suffering of children. At the same time, most parents receive little guidance. Some courts offer educational lectures to families at the time of the breakup, but the emphasis is on preventing further litigation. Such courses are typically evaluated according to how much they reduce subsequent litigation and not on how they might improve parenting. Curricula to educate teachers, school personnel, pediatricians, and other professionals about child and parenting issues in divorce are rare. Few university or medical school programs in psychiatry, psychology, social work, or law include courses on how to understand or help children and parents after separation, divorce, and remarriage. This lack of training persists despite the fact that a disproportionate number of children and adolescents from divorced homes are admitted as patients for psychological treatment at clinics and family agencies. In many social agencies, close to three-quarters of the children in treatment are from divorced families. Some school districts have organized groups for children whose parents are divorcing. And some communities have established groups to help divorcing parents talk about their children's problems. A few centers such as ours have developed programs to help families cope with high conflict and domestic violence. But such efforts are not widespread. As a society, we have not set up services to help people relieve the stresses of divorce. We continue to foster the myth that divorce is a transient crisis and that as soon as adults restabilize their lives, the children will recover fully. When will the truth sink in?

Let's suppose for a moment that we had a consensus in our society. Suppose we could agree that we want to maintain the advantages of divorce but that we need to protect our children and help parents mute the long-term effects of divorce on future generations. Imagine we were willing to roll up our sleeves and really commit the enormous resources of our society toward supplementing the knowledge we have. Suppose we gave as much time, energy, and resources to protecting children as we give to protecting the environment. What might we try?

I would begin with an effort to strengthen marriage. Obviously, restoring confidence in marriage won't work if we natively call for a return to marriage as it used to be. To improve marriage, we need to fully understand the nature of contemporary man-woman relationships. We need to appreciate the difficulties modern couples confront in balancing work and family, separateness and togetherness, conflict and cooperation. It's no accident that 80 percent of divorces occur in the first nine years of marriage. These new families should be our target.

What threats to marriage can we change? First, there's a serious imbalance between the demands of the workplace and the needs of family life. The corporate world rarely considers the impact of its policies on parents and children. Some companies recognize that parents need time to spend with their children but they don't understand that the workplace exerts a major influence on the quality and stability of marriage. Heavy work schedules and job insecurity erode married life. Families with young children especially postpone intimate talk, sex, and friendship. These are the ties that replenish a marriage. When the boss calls, we go to the office. When the baby cries, we pick up the child. But when a marriage is starving, we expect it to bumble along. Most Western European countries provide paid family leave. What about us? Why do we persist in offering unpaid leave and pretend that it addresses the young family's problem? One additional solution might be social security and tax benefits for a parent who wants to stay home and care for young children. That alone would lighten the burden on many marriages. Other suggestions for reducing the stresses on young families include more flex time, greater opportunities for part-time work, assurances that people who take family leave will not lose their place on the corporate ladder, tax advantages for families, and many other ideas that have been on the table for years. Public policy cannot create good marriages. But it can buffer some of the stresses people face, especially in those early, vulnerable years when couples need time to establish intimacy, a satisfying sex life, and a friendship that will hold them together through the inevitable challenges that lie ahead. Ultimately, if we're really interested in improving marriage so that people have time for each other and their children, we need to realign our priorities away from the business world and toward family life.

We might also try to help the legions of young adults who complain bitterly that they're unprepared for marriage. Having been raised in divorced or very troubled homes, they have no idea how to choose a partner or what to do to build the relationship. They regard their parents' divorce as a terrible failure and worry that they're doomed to follow in the same footsteps. Many adults stay in unhappy marriages just to avoid divorce. We don't know if we can help them with educational methods because we haven't tried. Our experience is too limited and our experimental models nonexistent. But when so many young people have never seen a good marriage, we have a moral obligation to try to intervene preventively. Most programs that give marital advice are aimed at engaged couples who belong to churches and synagogues. These are very good beginnings that should be expanded. But many offer too little and arrive too late to bring about changes in any individual's values or knowledge. Nor is the excitement that precedes a wedding the best time for reflection on how to choose a lifetime partner or what makes a marriage work. Academic courses on marriage mostly look at families from the lofty perch of the family scholar and not from the perspective of children of divorce who feel "no one ever taught me."

In my opinion, a better time to begin helping these youngsters is during mid-adolescence, when attitudes toward oneself and relationships with the opposite sex are beginning to gel. Adolescence is the time when worries about sex, love, betrayal, and morality take center stage. Education for and about relationships should begin at that time, since if we do it right, we'll have their full attention. It could be based in the health centers that have been established in many schools throughout the country. Churches and synagogues and social agencies might provide another launching place. Ideally, adolescents in a well-functioning society should have the opportunity to think and talk about a wide range of relationships, issues, and conflicts confronting them. As an opening gambit, think about asking the deceptively simple question: "How do you choose a friend?" A group of teenagers considering this problem could be drawn to the important question of how to choose a lover and life partner—and even more important, how not to choose one. Specific topics such as differences between boys and girls, cultural subgroups, and how people resolve tensions would follow based on the teenagers' interests and their willingness to discuss real issues. Colleges could also offer continuing and advanced courses on an expanded range of subjects, including many problems that young men and women now struggle with alone.

We are on the threshold of learning what we can and cannot do for these young people. Still one wonders, can an educational intervention replace the learning that occurs naturally over many years within the family? How do we create a corps of teachers who are qualified to lead meaningful courses on relationships? By this I mean courses that are true to life, honest, and respectful of students. I worry about the adult tendency to lecture or sermonize. In a society where the family has become a political issue, I'm concerned about attacks from the left and the right, about the many people who would attack such interventions the way they've attacked the Harry Potter books. Mostly I'm concerned about finding a constituency of adults who would rally behind an idea that has so many pitfalls. But I'm also convinced that doing nothing—leaving young people alone in their struggles—is more dangerous. We should not give up without a try.

For the Children

Except for those raised in divorced families, few people realize the many ways that divorce shapes not only the child's life but also the child. As we have seen in many homes, parenting erodes almost inevitably at the breakup and does not get restored for years, if ever. The changes in parenting and in the structure of the family place greater responsibilities on the child to take care of herself. And she, in turn, becomes a different person as she adjusts to the new needs and wishes of her parents and stepparents. All of the children I have described in this book took on new roles in direct response to changes that occurred during the postdivorce years. Many were acutely aware of their parents' distress and tried to rescue them. Others remained angry at their parents' diminished attention and judged them harshly. Others longed for the family they had lost and tried to reverse the divorce decision. And still others took responsibility for keeping the peace and walked on eggs throughout their childhoods. These children took many paths, but all changed significantly in the wake of divorce. And because the children's character and conscience were still being formed during the postdivorce years, the new roles they assumed in the family had profound effects on who they became and on the relationships they established when they reached adulthood.

As an adult child of divorce reading this book, I hope you have gained a better understanding of who you are today and how you got here. I hope you realize that you have millions of peers who share your worries about relationships and who understand the seriousness of your predicament. Your fears and feelings were forged in the crucible of your parents' divorce years ago and strengthened over the years that followed. These emotions, which are often hidden from consciousness, have the power to affect your marriage, your parenting, indeed the quality of your entire life.

An important task for your generation is to achieve better relationships. But how to go about it? You still wonder what motivated your parents' decision to divorce. Some people find that it helps to sit down and talk candidly with their parents. You may not believe or like the answers, but the exercise can provide new and useful perspectives. Not everyone can do this, nor should they, since it may cause both parent and child unnecessary suffering. But for many, it's worth trying to lift the curtain of silence that has troubled the parent and child relationship for years.

My next advice is to delay marriage or commitment until you have learned more about yourself and what you want in a partner. A good relationship cannot be created if you're expecting to fail. You can learn about people by observing them and by observing yourself together with them. Look around and try to see relationships that are working. You might learn something. You should consider individual or group therapy as a bridge to understanding yourself. You need to learn how to resolve conflict without becoming terrified. In mastering this skill, you'll gain confidence that you can influence your relationships instead of passively settling for whatever comes your way. Before you settle for disappointment, try to learn about the parts of life that you missed. In the end, each person finds his or her own way. Ultimately, your goal is to close the door on your parents' divorce, to separate the now from the then. By giving up wanting what you didn't have, you can set yourself free.

E. Mavis Hetherington
and John Kelly

 **NO**

For Better or for Worse:
Divorce Reconsidered

Mostly Happy: Children of Divorce as Young Adults

David Coleman has his father's imposing height and muscularity, but whereas on Richard, size added to his air of menace, making him look explosive even at rest, the son's six-foot-three frame has the opposite effect. It underscores his gentleness, makes you notice it in a way you wouldn't if he were a smaller, more delicate-looking man.

At a time when genetic theories threatened to reduce human development to a branch of biology, the difference between gentle David and violent Richard reminds us of the powerful role nurture plays in development. Genes are important, yes, certainly, but life experiences—especially with those closest to us—can take a given set of genes and make them add up in many different ways.

Much of the credit for the way David and his older sister, Leah, have ended up goes to Jenet. Both benefited immensely from her ability to maintain a stable, loving, emotionally safe environment through Richard's stalking, through the family's sojourn on welfare, and through Nick and Leah's fights. When the VLS ended, David had taken over much of the responsibility for running "Janet's Garden," and Leah was a happily married mother, with a young daughter.

In the 1970s, a fierce debate broke out about the future of children like David and Leah. Critics of the divorce revolution believed that as the generation of children from divorced families matured, American society would descend into disorder and chaos. The collapse of the two-parent family, the traditional engine of socialization, critics argued, would lead to a *Clockwork Orange* generation of unstable, reckless, indulgent young adults, who would overrun the nation's prisons, substance abuse centers, and divorce courts.

"Nonsense," declared supporters of the divorce revolution, who saw divorce as a kind of cleansing agent. At last, the dark gloomy oppressive Victorian house that was the nuclear family would get a long-overdue spring cleaning, one that would produce a new and more egalitarian, tolerant, and fulfilled generation of men and women.

While I found evidence to support both views, the big headline in my data is that *80 percent of children from divorced homes eventually are able to adapt to their new life and become reasonably well adjusted.* A sub-group of girls even become exceptionally competent as a result of dealing with the challenges of divorce, enjoy a normal development, and grow into truly outstanding young adults. The 20 percent who continue to bear the scars of divorce fall into a troubled group, who display impulsive, irresponsible, antisocial behavior or are depressed. At the end of the VLS, troubled youths were having difficulty at work, in romantic relationships, and in gaining a toehold in adult life. They had the highest academic dropout rate and the highest divorce rate in the study, and were more likely to be faring poorly economically. In addition, being troubled and a girl made a young woman more likely to have left home early and to have experienced at least one out-of-wedlock pregnancy, birth, or abortion.

However, coming from a non-divorced family did not always protect against growing into a troubled young adult. Ten percent of youths in non-divorced families, compared to 20 percent in divorced and remarried families, were troubled. Most of our troubled young men and women came from families where conflict was frequent and authoritative parenting rare. In adulthood, as was found in childhood and adolescence, those who had moved from a highly contentious intact home situation to a more harmonious divorced family situation, with a caring, competent parent, benefited from the divorce and had fewer problems. But the legacy of the stresses and inept parenting associated with divorce and remarriage, and especially with living in a complex stepfamily, are still seen in the psychological, emotional, and social problems in 20 percent of young people from these families.

A piece of good news about our youths was that their antisocial behavior declined as they matured. Much of the adolescent exploration, experimentation, and sense of invulnerability had abated. Although excessive use of alcohol remained a problem for one quarter, drug abuse and lawbreaking had declined in all of our groups; but the decrease had been most marked in those who married.

What about the other 80 percent of young people from divorced and remarried families?

While most were not exactly the New Man or New Woman that the divorce revolution's supporters had predicted, they were behaving the way young adults were supposed to behave. They were choosing careers, developing permanent relationships, ably going about the central tasks of young adulthood, and establishing a grown-up life.

They ranged from those who were remarkably well adjusted to Good Enoughs and competent-at-a-costs, who were having a few problems but coping reasonably well to very well.

Finally, it should be a reassuring finding for divorced and remarried parents, and their children, that for every young man or woman who emerged from postnuclear family life with problems, four others were functioning reasonably or exceptionally well.

I think our findings ultimately contain two bottom-line messages about the long-term effects of divorce on children. The first is about parents, especially mothers. If someone creates a Nobel Prize for Unsung Hero, my nominee will be the divorced mother. Even when the world was collapsing round them, many divorced mothers found the courage and resiliency to do what had to be done. Such maternal tenacity and courage paid off. Despite all the emotional and financial pressures imposed by marital failure, most of our divorced women managed to provide the support, sensitivity, and engagement their children needed for normal development. And while divorce creates developmental risks, except in cases of extraordinary stress, children can be protected by vigorous, involved, competent parenting.

The second bottom line is about flexibility and diversity. Divorce is not a form of developmental predestination. Children, like adults, take many different routes out of divorce; some lead to unhappiness, others to a rewarding and fulfilling life. And since over the course of life, new experiences are being encountered and new relationships formed, protective and risk factors alter, and the door to positive change always remains open.

We turn now to look at how some of these changing experiences and relationships contributed to the well-being of our younger generation from divorced and remarried families.

Parent-Youth Relationships in Perspective

At age twenty-four, Leah Coleman was a high school history teacher in a happy marriage to Brad Norton, and the mother of two-year-old Cindy. She commented, "I can't believe what a bitch I was to Nick. He tried so hard, but I just wanted to destroy him. When he gave up and avoided me, I thought it was a major victory. But you know, I gradually started to envy David and be jealous of Nick and David's relationship. David would go to Nick with things he didn't want to talk about with Mom, and they had such fun together, and I don't know, their relationship seemed so special."

Leah's reassessment of Nick advanced another step when she brought home Brad, her future husband, for the first time. "It would have been so easy for Nick to be standoffish and nasty," Leah told me later. "Instead, he was a real sweetie with Brad, friendly and warm and welcoming. He and Brad spent the whole afternoon drinking beer and working on an old beat-up wooden sailboat Nick had bought. They just hit it off right away. I felt absolutely terrible. I mean, here's this lovely man, and I've given him nothing but trouble since he stepped in the door."

Motherhood finally produced a complete rapprochement. "Nick's turned out to be the world's best grandfather," Leah declared. "Cindy's crazy about him, she calls him Gee-pa. She'll stop in the middle of playing and say, 'Where's my Gee-pa?' Did you ever think you'd hear me talk this way about Nick?"

Actually, I did.

Family relations do tend to improve in young adulthood. It may not always be the "Whoopie" experience described by some empty nesters, but it is often a mutually gratifying time for both parents and children. This is a time with more autonomy for both generations, less responsibility for parents, diminished conflict and acrimony, and continued affection and interest in each other's well-being. Parents get the satisfaction of launching a young life into the world, one they don't have to pay for or wait up for any more, while children are finally free of Mom and Dad's annoying foibles and demands. That, along with their grow-ing maturity, allows them to begin appreciating Mom and Dad's sacrifices and good points. Distance helps, too. When parents and children live apart, there are fewer opportunities to step on each other's toes, and when a toe is stepped on, everyone has a neutral corner to retreat to.

When our younger generation totaled up the balance sheet on how they felt about their parents, the mothers did well. Eighty percent of youths is non-divorced families and 70 percent in postnuclear families reported feeling close or very close to their biological mothers. Men didn't do as well. Although 70 percent of youths in non-divorced families felt close to their fathers, less than one third of males and one quarter of females reported being close to their stepfather or non-custodial fathers. Remarks like, "He was never around," "He never showed any interest in me," or, "He never played a real part in my life" were common.

Why do children feel so distant from fathers after divorce? Two reasons. First, often divorced fathers are not around because the kids are usually in the custody of their mothers, and children feel closer to custodial than non-custodial parents. Second, the disengaged parenting style common in step-fathers fails to promote close emotional bonds with stepchildren. In youth as in adolescence, when asked to list members of their family, only one third of those in stepfamilies included their stepparents. However, even these relation-ships in young adulthood were more likely to be characterized by disengage-ment than by confrontation and conflict.

Cross-gender parent-child relationships were found to be more fragile. Divorce was more likely to have undermined the quality of an adult son's than an adult daughter's relationship with their divorced mother, and of an adult daughter's relationship rather than an adult son's with their father.

Stepmothers, especially those in complex stepfamilies, had been able to build up the least closeness and goodwill with their stepchildren, with less than 20 percent of young adult stepchildren saying they felt close to their stepmothers. The competition between non-custodial mothers and stepmothers was remark-ably enduring, and youths with close ties to their non-custodial mothers were less likely to be close to their stepmothers.

A partial exception to the generalization that parent-child relations improve in young adulthood occurred in complex stepfamilies. Although relations did warm in some cases, in most, such as the Drew family, they did not.

The Drews were the complex stepfamily we met earlier. Anna Marie, the daughter who left early to escape her stepfather and half sister, grew into an embittered and alienated young woman, who refused to accept her mother's help even though, as a divorced single mother, she desperately needed it. "Anna Marie won't budge an inch," her mother told me the last time we talked. "I've offered to pay the tuition if Anna Marie goes back to school. But she says she doesn't want my help; she says she doesn't want to have anything to do with anyone related to Paul Drew."

Anna Marie later said, "Maybe I still love my mother, but I don't trust her. She never saved me from the Dastardly Duo." She laughs, rolls her eyes, and twirls an imaginary mustache like a villain in a Victorian melodrama. The

better regulators than young women from divorced, remarried, or high-conflict non-divorced homes, marriage to such a young woman is more likely to benefit a man like Richard Fredericks. Richard's online relationship blossomed into a full-blown romance and marriage with Hayden Moore, a remarkably sensitive, stable young woman. Richard said, "The only person I ever trusted other than Ed and Jeanie Dooley is Hayden. I feel really safe with her." Hayden, who came from a non-divorced family, gave Richard the love, support, and privacy and space he needed; she also recognized the importance of his involvement in his work. With Richard, some explosions were inevitable, but Hayden was careful not to reciprocate his irritable outbursts. Eventually, they were able to disagree, talk about, and even laugh over some of their differences. They called Richard's irritable, stressed days "black cloud days." When things were getting tense, Hayden often joshed, "I think I see a black cloud coming," and Richard would give a sheepish smile and calm down a bit or withdraw. . . .

What Protects against Marital Instability?

There are a number of ways to look at the higher divorce rate among young people from divorced families. Critics imagine that divorce-prone behaviors are being institutionalized and warn of a snowball effect: with each succeeding generation, a larger and larger proportion of young people will come of age knowing more about how to destroy a marriage than how to make it work.

But you can also look at the divorce rate as a triumph. When the study ended, there was less than a 10 percent difference in the marital failure rate between those from divorced and non-divorced families. Given all the developmental vulnerabilities that divorce creates, I think that is a remarkably small difference.

What promotes such resiliency?

Our research shows that several factors can protect against the intergenerational transmission of divorce.

The lessons children learn from adult mentors, authoritative parents and schools, and pro-social peers about self-respect, respecting others, and the importance of self-control all help them socially, in a marriage, and in dealing with the vicissitudes and setbacks of life.

Supportive friends with stable marriages also contribute to marital stability. Our youth were often helped through marital bad patches by other couples who acted as friends, advisers, sounding boards, and role models. And since immaturity can compound the effects of skill deficits, marrying later also has a protective effect.

However, the most important potential protective factor is the selection of a mate. Marriage is a relationship, not a one-person show. When a young person from a divorced family marries a stable, supportive spouse from a non-divorced family, his or her risk of marital failure falls back to that of a young man or woman from a non-divorced home. The reason? A mature spouse can teach skills like problem solving, sensitivity to others' needs, how to offer support in times of stress, and how to be a better parent.

In describing their marital histories, for young people from divorced families who were married to a caring, stable spouse, as well as those in other well-functioning marriages, the marital relationship seemed to be an entity in itself. These young people more often used the integrative "We" and "Us" and less often used the pronoun "I" in describing their marriage than did people from divorced families who had not married a supportive spouse. Moreover, like others in fulfilling marriages, they more often glorified and celebrated the building of their relationship. They spoke warmly and nostalgically of paint-ing their first apartment, of early shared financial struggles, and of the births of their children. In discussing their marriage, couples in mutually supportive relationships also seemed to have a different timeline. They shared vivid memories of their initial meeting and past history, excitement about the present, and plans for the future. Their less happily married peers seemed focused entirely on the present.

Twenty Years Later

The adverse effects of divorce and remarriage are still echoing in some divorced families and their offspring twenty years after divorce, but they are in the minor-ity. The vast majority of young people from these families are reasonably well adjusted and are coping reasonably well in relationships with their families, friends, and intimate partners. Most are moving toward establishing careers, eco-nomic independence, and satisfying social and intimate relationships. Some are caring spouses and parents. Although the divorce may resonate more in the memories of these children, most parents and children see the divorce as having been for the best, and have moved forward with their lives.

Points to Remember

- Parent, child, and sibling relationships that have been close in childhood seldom deteriorate in adulthood.
- Even if absence doesn't make the heart grow fonder, conflict usually diminishes once the protagonists are apart and contact becomes optional. Disengagement often replaces conflict in stepparent-stepchild and sibling relationships in divorced and remarried families in young adulthood.
- Biologically related siblings, whether in divorced, non-divorced, or remarried families, tend to have both more attached and more rivalrous relationships than those found in stepsiblings.
- Men remain reluctant to do their fair share. In most first- and second-generation VLS homes, the burden of household labor continued to fall predominantly on female shoulders. After a demanding eight- or ten-hour day at the office, many of our women would come home to cope with unmade beds, unwashed laundry, unfed children, and the morning's unwashed breakfast dishes in the sink.
- A family history of divorce does leave children of divorce relationship- and marriage-challenged. Children of divorce are often reluctant to commit wholeheartedly to a marriage, have fewer relationship skills, and in some cases show a genetic predisposition to destabilizing behaviors like antisocial behavior, impulsivity, and depression.

- Gender affects a person's divorce risk more than the kind of family the person was brought up in. In divorced, remarried, and non-divorced families alike, male belligerence, withdrawal, and lack of affection often produce thoughts of divorce in a woman; female contempt, nagging, or reciprocated aggression, thoughts of divorce in a man.
- Although marital instability is higher in offspring from divorced families, marriage to a stable, supportive spouse from a non-divorced family eliminates the intergenerational transmission of divorce. A caring, mature spouse can teach their partner from a divorced family skills they never learned at home.
- Young adults from complex stepfamilies continue to have more adjustment and family problems than young adults in other kinds of stepfamilies.
- For most youths, the legacy of divorce is largely overcome. Twenty years after divorce, most men and women who had grown up in divorced families and stepfamilies are functioning reasonably well. Only a minority still exhibited emotional and social problems, and had difficulties with intimate relationships and achievement.

POSTSCRIPT

Does Divorce Create Long-Term Negative Effects for Children?

$\mathbf{I}$s it the divorce event that creates problems for children in adulthood, or is it the poverty, family disorganization, and unmet needs of children often associated with divorce, that cause long-term problems? According to Wallerstein, Lewis, and Blakeslee, a common complaint of children of divorce is that there is no adult left in the family in which they can confide. They often lose both parents: one physically because the children must live primarily in one household, and the other parent psychologically, because the parent expects the child to become an adult-like confidant. This abandonment causes the child to take on different roles and become a different type of person than the child would normally have been, if there had been no divorce. This change in personality affects the child at every stage of development and eventually culminates in poor marital adjustment in adulthood.

Hetherington and Kelly believe that children experience unhappiness after a divorce, but that this life event helps them to become stronger and more flexible in their approach toward life. They believe that as adults, these children were able to develop permanent relationships due to the support of the parent (usually the mother) and other societal supports such as friends and other adult mentors.

When parents find that they are no longer happy in a marriage, which choice is better for their children? Should they stay together in order to maintain an intact home for their children, even though there may be constant conflict? Or should they divorce, creating two households for their children, with the hope that they will find happiness either as a single person or remarried to someone new? How will a remarriage, in addition to a divorce, affect their children? Obviously there are no easy answers to these questions as the opposing selections clearly indicate. One thing researchers know for sure is that no matter what traumatic event happens to children, whether it is a divorce, death of a parent, or natural disaster, the support and modeling of appropriate behavior by important adults in the child's life is critical. Children who have someone to talk to, who will listen to and guide the child, can make a significant difference in the way children adapt to negative life events.

Perhaps the answer is in making sure parents never have to face trying to end a marriage by divorce. Authors from each selection disagree on the long-term effects of divorce, but would probably agree on society making more of an effort to strengthen marriage in order to reduce the incidence of divorce. Strengthening marriage by providing marriage education for adolescents would help children learn how intact marriages work. Information on how to deal with current issues of balancing work and family as well as how to deal with conflict could be taught. This education could provide needed support to young adults as they choose marriage partners and help them develop healthy expectations of marriage.

Suggested Readings

Bernstein, Anne C. (2007). Re-visioning, restructuring, and reconciliation: Clinical practice with complex postdivorce families. *Family Process, 46*(1), 67–78.

Fabricius, William. (2003). Listening to children of divorce: New findings that diverge from Wallerstein, Lewis, and Blakeslee. *Family Relations, 52*(4), 385–396.

Hetherington, E. Mavis. (2002). Marriage and divorce American style: A destructive marriage is not a happy family. *The American Prospect, 13*(7), 62–64.

Wallerstein, Judith, & Blakeslee, Sandra. (2004). *Second chances: Men, women, and children a decade after divorce.* Houghton Mifflin.

ISSUE 8

Is Viewing Television Violence Harmful for Children?

YES: L. Rowell Huesmann, Jessica Moise-Titus, Cheryl-Lynn Podolski, and Leonard D. Eron, from "Longitudinal Relations between Children's Exposure to TV Violence and Their Aggressive and Violent Behavior in Young Adulthood: 1977–1992," *Developmental Psychology* (March 2003)

NO: Jib Fowles, from "The Whipping Boy: The Hidden Conflicts Underlying the Campaign against Violent TV," *Reason* (March 2001)

ISSUE SUMMARY

YES: L. Rowell Huesmann, Jessica Moise-Titus, Cheryl-Lynn Podolski, and Leonard D. Eron, from the Research Center for Group Dynamics, Institute for Social Research at the University of Michigan, found that both males and females are more likely to develop violent behavior in adulthood as a result of watching violent TV shows in early childhood.

NO: Jib Fowles, a professor of communication at the University of Houston, asserts that television violence has increased steadily, but the violent crime rate has in fact decreased.

The debate over television violence rages on. Ask any group of people you meet today about violence in contemporary society. The responses will be remarkably similar. "Violence is in epidemic proportions. There is a lot more violence out on the streets now than when I was a kid. It's just not safe to be out anymore. We live in such violent times." The anecdotes and nostalgia about more peaceful times seem to be endless. The unison in which society decries the rise in violence begins to disintegrate, however, when one attempts to discern causes for the increases in crimes like murder, rape, robbery, and assault.

One segment of society that is regularly targeted as a contributing cause to the rise in violence is the media, particularly television programming. A common argument is that television is much too violent, especially in children's programming. It has been suggested, for example, that a child will witness in excess of 100,000 acts of simulated violence depicted on television before graduating from elementary school! Lower socioeconomic status children may view even more hours of violent television. Many researchers suggest that this television violence is at least in part responsible for the climbing rates of violent crime, since children tend to imitate what they observe in life.

On the other side, critics argue that it is not what is on television that bears responsibility for the surge in violence. Programming is merely reflective of the level of violence in contemporary society. The argument is that while television watching may be associated with violence, it does not mean that it causes violence. As an example, the critics suggest that we have known for some time that aggressive children tend to watch more aggressive television programming. However, does the aggression predispose an interest in aggressive programming, or does the programming cause the aggression? This is a question that sparks hotly contested debates.

Those who believe television viewing is at least partly responsible for aggressive behavior in children want the U.S. Congress to more closely regulate the ratings, viewing times, and amount of violence that can be shown on American television. Those on the other side of the issue point to the infringement on First Amendment rights of freedom of expression if such intense regulation is imposed on the media.

Other factors that contribute to the issue of television viewing and violence are the types of programs and commercials that children watch. School-aged children are the most targeted when it comes to advertising. There are more commercial breaks per hour for children's programming than for other types of programs. Additionally, with the widespread access to cable television, children can watch violent adult programming, many times in unsupervised homes.

Several organizations have emerged to address the issue of television violence and its effects on society. The Center for Media Literacy provides practical information to children and adults by translating media literacy research and theory into easy-to-read resources. They also provide training and educational tools for teachers, youth leaders, parents, and caregivers of children. The National Institute on Media and the Family sponsors "Media Wise," which educates and informs the public, as well as encourages practices and policies that promote positive change in the production and use of mass media. According to their mission statement, they do not advocate censorship of any kind. They are committed to partnering with parents and other caregivers, organizations, and corporations in using the power of the free market to create healthier media choices for families, so that there are healthier, less violent communities.

The two articles that follow are typical of the debate centered around violence and television as it affects children. L. Rowell Huesmann, Jessica Moise-Titus, Cheryl-Lynn Podolski, and Leonard D. Eron studied children at age 6-10 and again 15 years later. They concluded that children are more likely to develop violent behavior in adulthood as a result of watching violent TV shows in early childhood. Children identify with aggressive TV characters and the realism they perceive from TV shows. Jib Fowles believes that television is used as a whipping boy, blamed for the ills of society including the perceived rise in violent acts. Although there are no champions that rise to television's defense, Fowles contends that the attack on television as the source of societal violence is a big lie and is used to cover up society's real problems.

YES

L. Rowell Huesmann et al.

Longitudinal Relations between Children's Exposure to TV Violence and Their Aggressive and Violent Behavior in Young Adulthood: 1977–1992

Over the past 40 years, a body of literature has emerged that strongly supports the notion that media-violence viewing is one factor contributing to the development of aggression. The majority of empirical studies have focused on the effects of watching dramatic violence on TV and film. Numerous experimental studies, many static observational studies, and a few longitudinal studies all indicate that exposure to dramatic violence on TV and in the movies is related to violent behavior. Furthermore, a substantial body of psychological theory has developed explaining the processes through which exposure to violence in the mass media could cause both short- and long-term increases in a child's aggressive and violent behavior. Long-term effects with children are now generally believed to be primarily due to long-term observational learning of cognitions (schemas, beliefs, and biases) supporting aggression, whereas short-term effects with adults and children are recognized as also due to priming, excitation transfer, or imitation of specific behaviors. Most researchers of aggression agree that severe aggressive and violent behavior seldom occurs unless there is a convergence of multiple predisposing and precipitating factors such as neurophysiological abnormalities, poor child rearing, socioeconomic deprivation, poor peer relations, attitudes and beliefs supporting aggression, drug and alcohol abuse, frustration and provocation, and other factors. The evidence is already substantial that exposure to media violence is one such long-term predisposing and short-term precipitating factor. The current longitudinal study adds important additional empirical evidence that the effects of childhood exposure to media violence last into young adulthood and increase aggressive behavior at that time for both males and females.

Theoretical Background

In discussing the alternative theoretical perspectives that have emerged to explain the obtained relations between exposure to violence (family, community,

From *Developmental Psychology*, March 2003, pp. 201–204, 217–219. Copyright © 2003 by American Psychological Association. Reprinted by permission.

or mass media) and subsequent aggressive behavior in the observer, it is important to distinguish between short-term effects and longer term effects.

In recent theorizing, long-term relations have been ascribed mainly to acquisition through observational learning of three social-cognitive structures: schemas about a hostile world, scripts for social problem solving that focus on aggression, and normative beliefs that aggression is acceptable. Building on the accumulating evidence that human and primate young have an innate tendency to imitate whomever they observe, these theories propose that very young children imitate almost any specific behaviors they see. Observation of specific aggressive behaviors around them increases children's likelihood of behaving in exactly that way. Proactive-instrumental aggressive behaviors in children 2 to 4 years old generally appear spontaneously, as may hostile temper tantrums. However, the observation of specific aggressive behaviors at that age leads to the acquisition of more coordinated aggressive scripts for social problem solving and counteracts environmental forces aimed at conditioning the child out of aggression. As the child grows older, the social scripts acquired through observation of family, peers, community, and the mass media become more complex, abstracted, and automatic in their invocation. In addition, children's social-cognitive schemas about the world around them begin to be elaborated. In particular, extensive observation of violence around them biases children's world schemas toward attributing hostility to others' actions. Such attributions in turn increase children's likelihood of behaving aggressively. As children mature further, normative beliefs about what social behaviors are appropriate become crystallized and begin to act as filters to limit inappropriate social behaviors. Children's own behaviors influence the normative beliefs that develop, but so do the children's observations of the behaviors of those around them, including those observed in the mass media. In summary, social-cognitive observational-learning theory postulates long-term effects of exposure to violence through the influence of exposure on the development of aggressive problem-solving scripts, hostile attributional biases, and normative beliefs approving of aggression.

A major alternative or complementary theory explaining long-term effects is desensitization theory. This theory is based on the empirical fact that most humans seem to have an innate negative emotional response to observing blood, gore, and violence. Increased heart rates, perspiration, and self-reports of discomfort often accompany such exposure. However, with repeated exposure to violence, this negative emotional response habituates, and the observer becomes desensitized. The presumption is that lack of a negative emotional response to observing violence also indicates a flat response to planning violence or thinking about violence. Thus, proactive-instrumental aggressive acts become easier to commit.

There are two other quite different theoretical perspectives that have attempted to explain long-term relations between exposure to violence and aggression without hypothesizing any direct effect of violence viewing on aggression. One theory is that aggressive behavior or a correlate of aggressive behavior stimulates exposure to violence and thus engenders the observed relation between them. Observational studies of aggressive children do show that the aggressive child is likely to provoke others, who then respond aggressively to the child, creating a violent environment that the child "observes." For media violence, however, the usual assumption is that the aggressive child simply "likes" watching media violence more than other children do. Drawing on social comparison theory, Huesmann elaborated on this theme by suggesting that aggressive children feel happier and more justified if they believe they are not alone in their aggression, and viewing media violence makes them feel happier because it convinces them that they are not alone.

The other alternative theory that has been widely discussed is best described as the "third variable" theory. A wide variety of demographic, family, and personal characteristics are known to be correlated both with TV viewing and with aggression, such as social class and IQ. These theories suggest that the observed long-term positive relations between aggression and exposure to media violence are spurious and are derived from their joint association with one or more of these third variables.

These "third variable" explanations should not be confused with the developmental perspectives on the observational learning and desensitization theories, which also assign important roles to parenting, intellectual ability, and social class as contributors to both exposure to violence and acceptability of aggressive behavior. Children of lower socioeconomic status (SES) and lower IQ are known to watch more TV, probably for multiple reasons including social norms, cost of alternative entertainments, and frustration with more intellectually demanding tasks. Parents' TV habits and child-rearing practices also influence the child's TV habits. Of course, early parenting factors such as harsh punishment, rejection of the child, and lack of discipline are also known to influence subsequent aggression by the child. The difference is that these factors are viewed not as explaining away the "effect" of exposure to violence on aggression but as explaining individual differences in exposure to violence and individual differences in the strength of the effect.

Any of these theoretical processes might also contribute to the shorter term relations between exposure to violence and aggressive behavior. However, two other processes have been widely discussed as playing a role in short-term relations: priming and arousal processes. The observation of stimuli that have been paired in the past with observed violence or that inherently suggest violence (e.g., weapons) activates memory traces for aggressive scripts, schemas, and beliefs sufficiently to make their utilization more probable. A provocation that follows a priming stimulus is more likely to stimulate aggression as a result of the priming. Although this effect is short-lived, the primed script, schema, or belief may have been acquired long ago and may have been acquired in a completely different context.

To the extent that observed violence (real world or media) arouses the observer, aggressive behavior may become more likely in the short run for two other possible reasons: excitation transfer and general arousal. First, a subsequent provocation may be perceived as more severe than it is because the emotional response stimulated by the observed violence is misattributed as being due to the provocation. Such excitation transfer could account for a more intense aggressive response in the short run. Alternatively, the increased general arousal stimulated by the observed violence may simply reach such a peak that the ability of inhibiting mechanisms such as normative beliefs to restrain aggression is reduced.

It is important to recognize that these theoretical processes are not mutually exclusive. It is perfectly possible both that observational learning, desensitization, priming, and excitation transfer all contribute to the stimulation of aggression by the observation of violence and that more aggressive children do like to watch more violence. However, there is one theory that is incompatible with all of these processes. Catharsis theory would predict that violence viewing should be followed by reductions in aggression. Because the empirical evidence for any such negative relation is almost nonexistent, catharsis theory seems untenable at this time.

Empirical Background

In contrived experimental studies, children (both boys and girls) exposed to violent behavior on film or TV behave more aggressively immediately afterward. The typical paradigm involves randomly selected children who are shown either a violent or nonviolent short film and are observed afterward as they play with each other. The consistent finding is that children who see the violent film clip behave more aggressively toward each other or toward surrogate objects. In these settings, exposure to violent film scenes clearly causes more aggressive behavior by children immediately afterward.

The demonstration of a relation between the observation of dramatic TV or film violence and the commission of aggressive behavior has not been limited to the laboratory. Evidence from field studies has clearly shown that the amount of TV and film violence a child is regularly watching is positively related to the child's aggressiveness. Children who watch more violence on TV and in the movies behave more violently and express beliefs more accepting of aggressive behavior. Although the correlations are modest by the standards used in the measurement of intellectual abilities (average = .41 for experiments and .19 for field studies), they are highly replicable and are substantial by public health standards. For example, as a comparison, the correlation between cigarette smoking and lung cancer was .34 in Wynder and Graham's classic study. Moreover, the correlation between childhood exposure to media violence and childhood aggression is highly replicable even across researchers who disagree about the reasons and across countries.

Although these one-shot field studies showing a correlation between media-violence viewing and aggression suggest that the causal conclusions of the experimental studies may well generalize to the real world, longitudinal studies with children can test the plausibility of long-term predisposing effects more directly. In perhaps the first longitudinal study on this topic, initiated in 1960 on 856 youth in New York State, Eron, Huesmann, Lefkowitz, and Walder found that boys' early childhood viewing of violence on TV was statistically related to their aggressive and antisocial behavior 10 years later (after graduating from high school) even after initial aggressiveness, social class, education, and other relevant variables were controlled. A 22-year follow-up of these same boys revealed that their early aggression predicted later criminality at age 30 and that early violence viewing also was independently but weakly related to their adult criminality.

A more representative longitudinal study was initiated by Huesmann and his colleagues in 1977. This 3-year longitudinal study of children in five countries also revealed that the TV habits of children as young as first graders also predicted subsequent childhood aggression even after initial levels of aggression were controlled. In contrast to earlier longitudinal studies, this effect was obtained for both boys and girls even in countries without large amounts of violent programming, such as Israel, Finland, and Poland. In most countries, the more aggressive children also watched more TV, preferred more violent programs, identified more with aggressive characters, and perceived TV violence as more like real life than did the less aggressive children. The combination of extensive exposure to violence coupled with identification with aggressive characters was a particularly potent predictor of subsequent aggression for many children. Still, there were differences among the countries. Although the synchronous correlations were positive in all countries, the longitudinal effect of violence viewing on aggression was not significant for girls in Finland or for all children in Australia. In Israel, there were significant effects for children living in a city but not for children raised on a kibbutz.

A few longitudinal studies have seemed to produce results at odds with the thesis that media-violence viewing causes aggression, but closer inspection of most of these studies reveals that their results are not discrepant but simply not strongly supportive of the thesis. For example, although the National Broadcasting Company's longitudinal study of middle-childhood youth conducted in the 1970s reported significant regression coefficients for only 2 out of the 15 critical tests of the causal theory for boys, an additional 10 were in the predicted direction. Furthermore, for girls, 3 out of the 15 critical tests were significant and an additional 7 were in the predicted direction.

The Current Study

As the above review indicates, over the past several decades, the correlation between TV-violence viewing and childhood or adolescent aggression has been unambiguously demonstrated. It has also been clearly confirmed that in the short run, exposure to violence causes an increase in immediate aggressive behavior. These effects have been obtained repeatedly for both boys and girls. The few completed longitudinal studies have also suggested that there is a long-term effect of early childhood exposure on aggression later in childhood, in the teen years, and, less strongly, into adulthood. However, these longer term effects have been found only for boys in the existing studies that were initiated in the 1960s.

The current study is a follow-up of the 1977 longitudinal study of 557 children growing up in the Chicago area that we described above and have reported on elsewhere. Our aim was to investigate the long-term relations between viewing media violence in childhood and young-adult aggressive behavior. The study was designed to provide data that could be used to compare the relative plausibility of the violence effects theories described earlier (observational learning theory or desensitization theory) with the plausibility of the preference-for-violence and "third variable" theories. However, the study was not designed to contrast observational learning theory with desensitization theory. In addition, the examination of the "third variable" hypotheses in this study, as always, is limited by the actual third variables included in the study.

In the follow-up study, we tracked down as many of the original boys and girls in that U.S. study as we could find 15 years later when they were in their early 20s. We interviewed them, interviewed their spouses or friends, and collected data on them from state archives. In this article, we address four major questions with data from this follow-up: (a) To what extent does early childhood exposure to media violence predict young-adult aggression and violence? (b) Are there gender differences in the predictability? (c) Does the extent to which the child viewer identifies with the aggressive character or believes the plot is realistic affect the strength of the prediction? and (d) To what extent does any long-term relation seem to be due to more aggressive children simply liking to watch violence or seem to be due to some environmental, family, or personal "third variable" that stimulates both childhood violence viewing and childhood and adult aggression? . . .

Discussion

In this 15-year longitudinal study of 329 youth, we found that children's TV-violence viewing between ages 6 and 9, children's identification with aggressive same-sex TV characters, and children's perceptions that TV violence is realistic were significantly correlated with their adult aggression. This was true for both male and female participants. It was true for physical aggression for both genders and for indirect aggression for women. Regression analyses that partialed out the effects of early aggression showed that these childhood TV habits were not just correlated with aggression but predicted increases or decreases in aggressive behavior. For both male and female participants, more childhood exposure to TV violence, greater childhood identification with same-sex aggressive TV characters, and a stronger childhood belief that violent shows tell about life "just like it is" predicted more adult aggression regardless of how aggressive participants were as children.

The longitudinal relations primarily reflected the adult behavior of the highest TV-violence viewing children. The upper 20% of boys and girls on any of the three child TV-viewing variables scored significantly higher on aggression as adults than did the rest of the participants. Furthermore, as adults they displayed a higher frequency of very serious antisocial and violent behaviors.

A longitudinal structural modeling analysis of the directionality of the effects suggested that it is more plausible that exposure to TV violence increases aggression than that aggression increases TV-violence viewing. These structural modeling analyses also demonstrated that the effects were not simply a consequence of lower SES children or less intellectually able children both watching more violence and being more at risk for aggressive and violent behavior. The structural models show that for both boys and girls, habitual early exposure to TV violence is predictive of more aggression by them later in life independent of their own initial childhood aggression, their own intellectual capabilities, their social status as measured by their parents' education or their fathers' occupations, their parents' aggressiveness, their parents' mobility orientation, their parents' TV viewing habits (including violence viewing), and their parents' rejection, nurturance, and punishment of them in childhood. Furthermore, the structural models suggest that being aggressive in early childhood has no effect on increasing males' exposure to media violence as adults and only a small effect for females.

Nevertheless, these results should not lead one to conclude that children's aggressiveness plays no role in their TV and film preferences. The paths from childhood aggression to adult TV-violence viewing were not significant, but they were all positive, and adult TV-violence viewing is not predicted much better by almost any childhood variable. Furthermore, in the childhood waves of this study, the comparable paths from aggression in one year to TV-violence viewing in the next were positive and significant. These results certainly are consistent with "justification theory"—that more aggressive children are more likely to watch media violence because it makes their own behavior seem normal. Their subsequent viewing of violence then increases their aggressive scripts, schemas, and beliefs through observational learning and makes subsequent aggression even more likely.

It is particularly interesting that we found longitudinal results that were of about the same magnitude for female as for male participants. In our 1960–1970 and 1960–1982 studies of New York children, longitudinal effects were found only for boys. One possibility is that the change in social norms for appropriate female behavior that occurred with the feminist movement of the late 1960s and 1970s has disinhibited female aggression. In addition, the increase in aggressive female models in movies and TV might have engendered a stronger observational learning effect. The combination of these two factors may have led to an increase in the size of the effect for female participants, making detection easier. It is not that girls were not subject to the observational effect in earlier years. Indeed, they were, as the laboratory experiments showed. Rather, it is that their use of the learned aggressive behaviors or aggressive scripts was inhibited by their existing normative beliefs about appropriate female roles. This explanation is consistent with the information-processing perspectives on learning aggressive behavior that Huesmann and Dodge have offered. According to Huesmann's model, learned scripts for aggressive behavior are not followed if they violate individuals' normative beliefs about what is appropriate for them.

Three notable gender differences in the results were found. First, early TV-violence viewing correlated with adult physical aggression for both male and female participants but correlated with adult indirect aggression only for female participants. Lagerspetz et al. pointed out that indirect aggression is more characteristic of females and more acceptable for them in most societies. The social-cognitive observational learning model suggests that normative beliefs about aggression, hostile biases about the world, and aggressive social scripts are all learned from observing violence. Female participants did not need to have observed indirect aggression to acquire it from observing violence. They only needed to have acquired beliefs more accepting of aggression. This reasoning also suggests that the lack of a finding of a relation between exposure to media violence and female aggression in earlier longitudinal studies may have been due to the failure to measure indirect aggression sufficiently in those studies.

Second, although identification with same-sex aggressive TV characters and the perception that violent TV shows tell about life "like it is" predicted adult aggression for both genders, these factors exacerbated the effect of TV-violence viewing only for male participants. Boys who viewed TV violence *and* identified with male aggressive TV characters or perceived TV violence as true to life were most at risk for adult aggression. The same gender difference had been found earlier for the childhood data relating TV viewing to subsequent aggression—identification was a moderator for boys but not for girls. Why would this exacerbating effect not occur for girls? Theoretically, it is difficult to believe that identification and perception of realism do not enhance observational learning in girls as well as boys. One possibility is that for girls, the relation between early exposure to violence and subsequent aggression is due more to cognitive and emotional desensitization to violence than to observational learning. Desensitization should not depend as much as observational learning on identification or perceptions of realism. Such a hypothesis cannot be tested with the current data but should be examined in future research.

The third notable gender difference was apparent in the structural models. For both male and female participants, there was no significant statistical effect of childhood aggression on adult TV-violence viewing. However, whereas for males the path coefficient from aggression to TV-violence viewing was virtually zero, for females it was a nontrivial positive value. This finding suggests that aggressive females may be more prone than aggressive males to use violent media to make themselves feel better and more justified about their own behavior. In a culture in which female aggressiveness is still less accepted than male aggressiveness, feeling justified about one's aggressive behavior could well be more important for females than for males.

Although longitudinal nonexperimental data do not provide a strong test of causation, they can be used to compare the relative plausibility of alternative causal perspectives. These results are certainly consistent with the observational learning and desensitization theories, which predict long-term statistical effects of early TV-violence viewing on later aggression after the effects of early aggression are statistically controlled. The results are much less consistent with the theoretical perspective that more aggressive children turn to watching more violence because they like it or because it serves as justification for their own aggression. Only for female participants was there a suggestion of such a long-term effect, and the effect estimate was not significant. The hypotheses that these longitudinal effects could be completely explained by "third" variables such as social class, intellectual ability, parent aggression, or parenting differences also did not receive much support. The effects remained even when the variance due to these factors was partialed out in our regression equations and structural models. However, intellectual ability and parents' education did seem to account for some of the effect in female participants. It may be that social norms for female behavior that inhibit the modeling of media violence are related to educational level or intelligence whereas for males this is not true.

Of course, a variety of parenting factors have been shown in the past to be related to both a child's exposure to media violence and that child's later aggression—for example, parents' intellectual ability and social class, parents' viewing habits, and parents' aggression. In the current study, many of these correlations were again found for at least one gender (e.g., for intellectual ability, parental rejection of the child, and parents' frequency of TV viewing). It seems plausible that these factors are indeed influencing both the child's aggressiveness and the child's exposure to media violence. Which children are placed most at risk of being exposed to media violence and of experiencing other learning conditions that reinforce the lessons taught by media violence is undoubtedly influenced by parent factors. However, given the pattern of results obtained, it is not very likely that the relations between early exposure to media violence and subsequent aggression are completely due to these "third" variables.

The effect sizes for media violence on aggression revealed in this longitudinal study are modest; however, there are few other factors that have been shown to have larger effects. That is not surprising considering the large number of factors that must converge before serious adult aggression occurs. Furthermore, as Rosenthal has pointed out, a correlation of .20 can represent a change in the probability of violence from 50/50 to 60/40, which is large enough to generate social concern.

One might also wonder whether the attrition in the sample made it unrepresentative and biased the results. This seems unlikely. Archival data were obtained on 80% of the original sample and interview data on 60%. An analysis of the attrition data showed that those who were not reinterviewed tended to be slightly more aggressive as children. Thus, it seems more plausible that, if anything, the attrition weakened the relations between TV-violence viewing and aggression.

Implications for Prevention of Violence

Overall, these results suggest that both males and females from all social strata and all levels of initial aggressiveness are placed at increased risk for the development of adult aggressive and violent behavior when they view a high and steady diet of violent TV shows in early childhood. The obvious follow-up question is whether society can do anything to prevent or at least moderate this effect.

Several points provide us with guidelines. First, we do not need to be as concerned about adults' or even teenagers' exposure to media violence as much as we do with childrens' exposure. Media violence may have short-term effects on adults, but the real long-term effects seem to occur only with children. This makes some societal controls more palatable in a society that places a high premium on the rights of adults to watch whatever they want.

Second, we need to be aware that media violence can affect any child from any family. The psychological laws of observational learning, habituation/

desensitization, priming, and excitation transfer are immutable and universal. It is not, as some have suggested, only the already violence-prone child who is likely to be affected. True, media violence is not going to turn an otherwise fine child into a violent criminal. But just as every cigarette one smokes increases a little bit the likelihood of a lung tumor some day, the theory supported by this research suggests that every violent TV show increases a little bit the likelihood of a child growing up to behave more aggressively in some situation.

Third, the violent films and TV programs that probably have the most deleterious effects on children are not always the ones that adults and critics believe are the most violent. What type of violent scene is the child most likely to use as a model for violent behavior? It is one in which the child identifies with the perpetrator of the violence, the child perceives the scene as telling about life like it is, and the perpetrator is rewarded for the violence. Thus, a violent act by someone like Dirty Harry that results in a criminal being eliminated and brings glory to Harry is of more concern than a bloodier murder by a despicable criminal who is brought to justice. Parents need to be educated about these facts.

Finally, we must recognize the economic realities of media violence. Violence sells. Both children and adults are attracted to violent scenes by the action and intense emotions. Many of the most popular shows and popular films for children have contained violence. Violent TV shows appear to be a little cheaper to produce on the average. Hamilton (1998) reported that from 1991 to 1993, the average production fee per hour for network prime time TV programming was about $1,094,000 for nonviolent shows and $998,000 for violent shows—about 10% cheaper in other words. A more telling statistic may be the finding that among shows with some violence, those with more violence actually cost less. Each additional violent act seems to reduce the cost by about $1,500. Of course, these are only averages for production costs. What really counts are the ability of a TV show to attract enough sponsors to cover its cost or to attract enough syndicated buyers and the ability of a video game to attract enough buyers to cover its cost. Here, a variety of marketing issues become important. For example, foreign markets become very important in these calculations, and generally violent shows and games are easier to sell in foreign markets than are other kinds of games or shows. More specifically, the probability of a TV show being exported successfully increases about 16% if it is violent.

The easiest way to reduce the effects of media violence on children, of course, is to reduce children's exposure to such violence. Prevention programs aimed at reducing exposure could obviously be targeted either at the production sources of the violence or at the child viewing the violence. In a society with strong protections for free speech, it is probably always going to be easier to target prevention efforts at the viewing child than at the producer. However, a more informed legal debate is needed on this subject. Broadcasters and film and program makers cannot avoid all responsibility for what children are exposed to. The argument that "people watch it so we give it to them" is not valid in a modern socially conscious society, and it is unrealistic to expect parents to control completely what children watch in a society with multiple TVs in each household, VCRs everywhere, and both parents working. Furthermore, it is the exposure of the 2- to 14-year-old child that is of the greatest concern here, as described in this article. The social value of reductions in the exposure of adults and even older teenagers is probably small compared to the social value of reducing younger children's exposure.

The ongoing V-chip social experiment is one such attempt to reduce children's exposure by giving parents a mechanism to control what the TV will allow to be broadcast through it. The problem is that the possibilities for this technology were greatly reduced from the start by the producers of violent shows, who managed to scuttle any idea of a content-based rating system that would actually allow parents to make judgments on the basis of violent content. Instead, only age guideline ratings are broadcast for most programs. Why did the producers do this? One can only speculate, but it is certainly likely that income from violent shows would be substantially reduced if violent labels were added—as much because sponsors would withdraw as because parents would actually program them out with the V-chip.

With regard to interventions aimed at the viewing child, there are a number of possibilities. Again, of course, simply reducing children's exposure through parental intervention is an obvious approach. However, the theory and results described in this article suggest a number of approaches aimed at changing the effect of any observed violence on the child as well. Nathanson recently found that parental co-viewing of and commenting on the programs seems to reduce the effects of TV violence on the child, probably because it reduces the child's identification with the perpetrator, reduces the child's perception of the violence as real, and reduces the likelihood that the child will rehearse the observed violent script in fantasy or play immediately after observation. Huesmann, Eron, Klein, Brice, and Fischer showed that the effects of violence on second graders could be reduced by a targeted school-based attitude change intervention that inculcates them with the beliefs that violence on TV does not tell about the world as it is and should not be imitated. A number of interventions based on teaching critical viewing skills in schools are being promoted, though few have yet to undergo rigorous evaluation. One of the problems with many of these interventions may be that they do not focus on those moderating variables that have been shown to be theoretically relevant, such as identification by the child with perpetrators, perception of violent acts as justified, and perception of violent scripts as realistic.

Although some questions remain to be resolved about the exact extent of the effect of observed violence on aggressive and violent behavior and its importance relative to other causal factors, the current study provides compelling additional evidence that habitual exposure of children to violence in the media (or in the real world around them) does have lasting effects on their propensity to behave aggressively and violently. Future research should probably be directed much more at elaborating and testing the kinds of interventions that parents, schools, producers, and the government can promote that will mitigate these long-term effects.

Jib Fowles

The Whipping Boy

Although television violence has never been shown to cause hostile behavior, its sinister reputation lives on. This is because the issue masks a variety of other struggles. Many of these conflicts are suppressed because they may pose a threat to social order or are considered unseemly topics for public discussion. Hence, we hear only the polite versions of the conflicts between races, genders, and generations, although these struggles roil national life. Because they are denied full expression, such conflicts are transferred into other debates, including and perhaps especially the issue of television violence.

Television violence is a whipping boy, a stand-in for other clashes, real or imagined. As one astute observer put it a few years back during a previous cycle of panic, "The debate about children and media violence is really a debate about other things, many of which have very little to do with the media."

There are several reasons why television violence has become such an exemplary whipping boy. First, it is a large target, present in one form or another in virtually every household in America. Second, if one puts on blinders, there might seem to be some correspondence between the mayhem on the television screen and real-life aggression; both televised entertainment and the real world deal in hostilities. Third and most important, television violence attracts no champions; the very idea of defending it seems silly to most people. Even industry representatives rarely get beyond conciliatory statements when they are compelled to address the matter. In one survey, 78 percent of entertainment industry executives expressed concern about the content of the action dramas they helped produce. In 1993 Ted Turner, perhaps the most conspicuous industry leader at the time, said in congressional testimony that television was "the single most important factor causing violence in America." The object of derision simply stands still and takes all the abuse that can be heaped on it.

What are the real conflicts that are being displaced? Most entail the stronger overwhelming the weaker, but in some conflicts the weaker retaliate through moral exertion. Here is a brief examination of the most important conflicts.

High vs. Low

The attack on television violence is, at least in part, an attack by the upper classes and their partisans on popular culture. In this interpretation, which has been broached repeatedly for a quarter-century, the push to reform television

From Jib Fowles, "The Whipping Boy: The Hidden Conflicts Underlying the Campaign Against Violent TV," *Reason* (March 2001). Adapted from *The Case for Television Violence* (Sage Publications, 1999). Copyright © 1999 by Jib Fowles. Reprinted by permission of Sage Publications, Inc.

is simply the latest manifestation of the struggle between the high and the low, the dominant and the dominated.

The United States is often regarded as a virtually classless society. Indeed, the overwhelming majority of Americans identify themselves as members of a "middle" class. Everyday experience, however, points in a different direction. Americans constantly make class judgments about one another. They quickly note outward appearances and speech patterns. When necessary, one person learns about the other's occupation and education, where he lives and what car he drives, and locates that person socially. Notions of class rank notoriously crop up in courtship and marriage. Characters in films and television programs radiate class information about themselves to audience members who know precisely how to read such clues.

Perhaps the preeminent living theorist and researcher into matters of class and culture is Pierre Bourdieu. He is best known for his work on the segmentation of society according to preferences in aesthetic taste (for instance, going or not going to art museums). At the center of Bourdieu's work is the concept of *habitus,* an idea similar to that of the English word, *habit.* Habitus is the system of predispositions ingrained in a particular group or social class. It manifests itself in similar thoughts, behaviors, expressions, and leisure pursuits. The shared habitus unites and defines the social entity. Habitus, however, does not shackle individuals; in Bourdieu's scheme, there is ample room for idiosyncratic action.

Another concept special to Bourdieu is *capital,* approximately equivalent to social power. In addition to conventional economic wealth, there are several other kinds of capital in Bourdieu's system. Cultural capital (preferences gained primarily through education), symbolic capital (prestige and honors), and social capital (whom one knows) work together with financial capital to define a person's location in the overall social structure. Social action then becomes a function of class habitus and personal capitals. A final term from Bourdieu's work is *reproduction,* which is the manner by which social classes reproduce themselves and, in doing so, preserve status differences. For Bourdieu, the reproduction of habitus is the key work of a social class.

Although Bourdieu does not discuss television in his magisterial work, *Distinctions* (1984), it does not take much imagination to extend his analysis. He writes in his opening pages that taste (cultural capital) functions as a marker of social class; therefore, different preferences (such as watching television violence or not) can be used to situate a person hierarchically. According to this system, an attack on the most popular medium, on television and especially its violent content, would also be an attack by the dominant class on the habitus of the dominated. To reconfirm social distinctions and maintain exclusivity, members of the dominant class need only profess an opposition to television violence. (Ironically, Bourdieu, mustering all the trappings of a French intellectual, himself attacked television in a series of lectures published in English in 1998, calling the medium "a threat to political life and to democracy itself.")

In the derisive vocabulary of this dominant class, violent content is delivered via the "mass media." This term is used so much that it seems unremarkable, but repetition has concealed its derogatory nature. Programming is not received by an undifferentiated horde; it is received by individuals. In fact, there is no mass, there are no masses. As the cultural critic Raymond Williams wrote in 1958, "The masses are always the others, whom we don't know, and can't know. . . . Masses are other people. There are in fact no masses; there are only ways of seeing people as masses." When dominant Americans chastise the nonexistent phenomena of the "masses" and their "mass medium" of television, with its evil content, what they are really endeavoring is to disparage and suppress the culture of dominated Americans.

The class nature of this conflict is evident in the string of congressional hearings that have addressed television violence. Consider the five such congressional hearings held between 1988 and 1995. Of the 36 non-industry witnesses who testified against television violence, only seven were women. None was black or Hispanic. The 29 white males were identified as presidents, professors, directors, representatives, senators, senior scientists, and other distinguished titles that suggested they were well advanced in their careers. It is this patrician sector of society that for reasons of its own leads the attack on rowdy television violence.

The means by which one enters into society's dominant segment, and in doing so learns to affect reproachful views on television violence, is the academy. The general veneration that greets the academy is a sign of its near-sacred station and of the importance of its role in, as Bourdieu would view it, the reproduction of the dominant class and its habitus. Although the rewards of academics are middling in terms of financial capital, the cultural capital they accrue cannot be surpassed. To have a college degree—only about one-quarter of American adults do—is to have the credential of the dominant; not to have a college degree is to remain forever among the dominated.

Academics strive to regard television with condescension or an affected indifference. "A studied, conspicuous ignorance about television," communication professor Ellen Seiter wrote in 1996, "is a mark of distinction (like all distinctions, it is valued because it is so difficult to maintain)." Professors' general attitude toward television becomes more pointed when the topic of television violence is discussed; they are quick to assert piously that television is dangerously violent. Among college communication teachers, two-thirds of a 1991 sample of 486 instructors agreed that television "increased aggressive behavior." Of 68 scholars who had published papers or reports specifically on television's effects, 80 percent concurred that television violence produced aggressiveness.

Professors researching television's effects, therefore, seem to occupy a doubly honored position. Not only are they, like their colleagues, performing the crucial service of reproducing the dominant classes, but they also are breathing life into a key issue in the struggle between the dominant and the dominated. They may devote their entire careers to demonstrating the dangers of television violence and are bound to receive approbation from the dominant class as a result. No wonder the position of television effects researcher has proven so attractive.

Yet when a given skirmish over violence has exhausted itself and a lull sets in, members of the dominant class revert to their un-self-conscious viewing of televised mayhem. Even college professors watch TV. During one lull in the violence debate, a 1982 study found that media professors did not restrict their children's viewing any more than the rest of the population did.

Us vs. Them

Perhaps the most striking conflict concealed in the debate over television violence involves the fabrication and control of "the Other." The best-known treatment of the concept of the Other is Edward Said's *Orientalism* (1978). The Orient, argued Said, was one of Europe's "deepest and most recurring images of the Other." It was "almost a European invention" that served as "a Western style for dominating, restructuring, and having authority over the Orient." Superiority over the Other was one motive for this phenomenon; another was self-definition. "The Orient," Said wrote, "has helped to define Europe (or the West) as its contrasting image, idea, personality, experience."

Thus the Other, the "not-us," is a fabrication used both to regulate those classified as the Other and to distinguish the culture of those doing the classifying. It is also a mechanism for emphasizing differences and disregarding similarities in order to maintain group solidarity. The Other differs conceptually from the mass in that the mass can be a part of "us," even if a discredited part, whereas the Other remains outside.

In the United States, the Other is often primarily a Dark Other—blacks and, to a lesser extent, Hispanics. The Dark Other is the recipient of an undeniable assault that plays out in racially charged terms. One form of the assault on the Dark Other is the War on Drugs. This "war" promotes definitions of legal and illegal drugs that have favored whites at the expense of the Dark Other; alcohol and prescription tranquilizers (both of whose records of extensive abuse and human damage are well documented) enjoy legal protection, whereas drugs associated with black culture, such as marijuana and cocaine (the health effects of which, on examination of the data, appear to be negligible), are proscribed. Of course, there is nothing inherent in these drugs that allocates them to the legal or illegal categories. These allocations are socially determined.

The anti–television violence crusades are part of this same assault. People do not worry about their own viewing of violent shows, and in fact they are so at peace with it that they are less likely to acknowledge the violence at all. They worry extensively, however, about what the Dark Other is watching. As British media scholar David Buckingham noted in 1997, "Debates about the negative effects of the media are almost always debates about other people."

"People like us" project a scenario onto the Dark Other in which viewing entertainment violence leads to real-life criminal behavior. This scenario is false in every detail—there exists no uniform Dark Other, and symbolic violence does not produce aggression—but it is upheld due to the emotional conviction behind it and the handy availability of rationalizing "scientific proof." Fears of the Dark Other—fears of difference, of being preyed on, of having one's culture overturned, of invalidating one's identity—are denied expression elsewhere but are allowed to sneak into the attack on television violence. In this way, the Dark Other, his culture, his viewing habits, and his behaviors are disparaged.

There is a curious twist to all this, however—a complexity revealing much about the intricacies of social life. Whereas whites push off the Dark Other with vigor, at the same time they subtly beckon him back. Cultural theorists Peter Stallybrass and Allon White observe that whatever is excluded and displaced to the Other then becomes an object of fascination and is summoned back. The desire for cultural homogeneity produces instead a heterogeneous mix. Thus whites are fascinated by the music, dance, clothing styles, and behavior of blacks. Whites study black athletes, seeking to learn about the prowess of the Other. Whites welcome black entertainers, even when (or especially when) black actors are involved in violent scenarios.

Old vs. Young

Adults who enlist in the anti-television crusade always insist that it is "impressionable youths" whom they wish to protect. In the guise of shielding youths, however, adults are trying to contain and control them.

This generational conflict emerges in contemporary polls: A 1997 survey by Steve Farkas and Jean Johnson of 2,000 randomly selected American adults found them ill disposed toward both younger children and adolescents. The majority of respondents used harsh terms to characterize 5-to-12-year-olds, such as "lacking discipline," "rude," and "spoiled." Two-thirds of the respondents were very critical of teenagers, calling them "irresponsible" and "wild." According to the report, "Most Americans look at today's teenagers with misgiving and trepidation, viewing them as undisciplined, disrespectful, and unfriendly." Six hundred teenagers were also surveyed, however; they viewed things differently. Most felt happy in their lives and in their relationships with adults. These discrepant attitudes indicate much about the essential nature of generational strife—of who deprecates whom.

Antagonism toward the young can be especially strong in an adult population configured like that of the United States—one that is aging rapidly due to the baby boom phenomenon. As subculture researcher Dick Hebdige observes, in the consciousness of adult society, "Youth is present only when its presence is a problem, or is regarded as a problem." Overall, adults feel threatened by the next generation.

Social scientist Charles Acland has argued that "youth's complex relationship with popular culture as a live and expressive domain is menacing because the uses of culture cannot be policed completely." With adults able only partially to supervise the "menace" of popular culture, children and adolescents turn to their television shows, their movies, their computer games, and their music as an escape from adult restraint. Passing through a difficult stage in life, indeed perhaps the most strenuous one of all, youths turn to television violence for the vicarious release it can offer.

The consumption of symbolic violent content correlates negatively with age. According to a 1993 study commissioned by the Times Mirror Center for People and the Press, age is the single most significant factor in the viewing of television violence: Younger viewers watch much more than do older viewers.

Cultural critic James Twitchell suggests that "if you study the eager consumers of vulgarities, you will soon see that this audience is characterized not so much by class (as we tend to assume, due in part to Marxist interpretations of the culture industry) as by maturity."

Youths do not think it probable that there could be any transfer from television's violence to aggression in the real world; of all age groups, they are the least likely to believe there is a connection. Elizabeth Kolbert, a *New York Times* reporter, interviewed three teenage felons on the subject in 1994 and noted, "The three teenagers . . . all scoffed at the notion that what young people see on the screen bore any relation to the crimes they committed."

Weaker vs. Stronger

There are at least two cases where the anti-television crusade allows a weaker group to mount an attack against a stronger target. The first relates to the struggle between masculinity and femininity. As the male expresses dominion and the female resists it, everything in culture becomes gendered, or has reference to gender. This pervasive rivalry would be expected to find its way into the anti-television campaign as another camouflaged conflict between the dominant and the dominated, but in this instance the thrust is completely reversed. That is, when the struggle between genders enters into the debate over television violence, it does so as an act of resistance by the female against the male—as a small counterstrike.

The power of males is most pointedly realized in the violence some of them direct toward women. Alert to the chance of male animosity, women are prone to feeling wary of violence even in its flattened, symbolic form on the television screen. The figment may draw too close to the real thing, whether experienced or imagined, to permit the degree of unimpeded pleasure that male viewers might enjoy. In surveys females are more likely than males to report there is "too much violence in television entertainment" and have been so since the general question was first asked in 1972. When queried about the amount of violence on specific action programs, women viewers will perceive more of it than will men, presumably because of their awareness of and uneasiness about the vicious content.

The recurring moral crusade against television violence affords women a choice opportunity for retribution. Seemingly untainted by any overt hostility on its own part, the movement to purify televised entertainment, one that all agree is to be rhetorical only, seems to be shielded from any possibility of retaliatory strikes. How much contention against males is bound up in the 1994 assertion of Barbara Hattemer, president of the National Family Foundation, that "as media violence is absorbed into a person's thoughts, it activates related aggressive ideas and emotions that eventually lead to aggressive behavior"? How much gender strife is exposed in the hyperbolic 1996 statement of Carole Lieberman, chairperson of the National Coalition Against Television, that "more lives are damaged or destroyed by the effects of on-screen violence than by any other medical problem"? She has forgotten heart disease, cancer, and other maladies, and she has done so for a particular reason.

The second case of a counterstrike against a stronger group involves religion. Many of the groups organized in opposition to television violence have religious ties. Here, neither the contestants nor their motives are camouflaged. The partisans on the attacking side are explicit and vociferous; they stand for religiosity, conservative beliefs, and "family values," and they are against licentiousness, media excesses, and symbolic violence. Those under attack—the entertainment industries and, by extension, all sorts of permissive people—respond first with incomprehension and then with annoyance, wishing the conservative and fundamentalist contingent would disappear. It would be easy for the political left to ignore the religious right if the latter did not comprise a well-defined and adamant voting bloc.

This cultural axis could hardly be more different from class antagonism. Social classes are stacked from bottom to top. Here, the axis and its poles can be understood as horizontal, stretching from the most conservative to the most free-thinking. Those gathered at the conservative and evangelical pole come from a wide range of social strata, although they are frequently depicted by their opponents as occupying lower-status positions exclusively. Seeking certainty in the literal word of the Bible, often believing in creationism and patriarchal traditions, and adhering to longstanding customs and attitudes, those clustered at this pole are often moved to take issue with the novelties of social transitions and the uncertainties of modern life.

Fundamentalists rail against the expanding, heaving tableau of television violence, and in organized fashion they strike out against it. The American Family Association (AFA), headed by the Rev. Donald Wildmon, has objected strenuously to video carnage. In 1993 Randall Murphree, editor of the association's *AFA Journal,* wrote: "Violence on the small screen continues to invade America's homes as television offers more graphic murders, bloodier assaults, and general mayhem. And all the while, the dramatic effects on society grow more and more alarming." In 1997 the AFA announced that, by its count, violent incidents in prime time network programs had increased 31 percent from the previous year—an increase far in excess of those measured by other monitors. As an example of the AFA's activities, in August 1997 its "Action Alert" roused its members to contact CBS and "express your concerns about their dangerous agenda of expanding the limits of violence on television through [the cop drama] *Brooklyn South."*

The issue of television violence affords groups such as the AFA the sanctioned opportunity to carry out a cultural attack—to have at their opponents, to condemn immoral depictions and the entertainment industry that produces and distributes them. Doing so, fundamentalism affirms its presence to others through an issue that is allowed to capture media attention and affirms its role to itself as a guardian of traditional mores. Television violence allows conservative forces the opportunity to carry their standard forward.

As religious conservatives react negatively to social changes of greater and lesser profundity, they may be performing an important service for American civilization. American culture is venturing into areas rarely if ever visited before, and never on such a large scale (for example, in matters of widespread individuality or of social inclusiveness). Some sort of conservative movement may prove useful, much like a sea anchor during turbulence, for steadying the vessel of culture.

The Big Lie

The widely held belief that television fantasy violence stimulates aggression in the real world and should be censured is what propaganda experts might call "a big lie"—a grotesque fabrication to which all unreflectingly subscribe. What makes this particular big lie different from the propagandists' is that it is not bestowed on an acquiescent population by some cabal; rather, this is one that we all repeatedly tell one another, duping ourselves as we dupe others. We do this for reasons of convenience: By repeating this uncontroverted big lie with ever-increasing volume, we can easily vent some of our own hostilities regarding other, truly confounding social conflicts.

While censure is generally directed by the stronger party toward the weaker, in some instances it flows in the opposite direction. Within the gender wars, and in the invectives of the religious right, condemnations are directed by weaker parties toward stronger targets. But whether the chastising energy flows from the stronger toward the weaker or from the weaker toward the stronger has nothing to do with the actualities of television violence.

Whatever its immediate source, the energy that breathes life into the whipping boy of television violence has its ultimate origins in fear—fear of disorder that, in the extreme, could overturn society. As Charles Acland has written, "A society is always concerned with normalization, with the organization of its order, to assure the continuation of its structures and distribution of power." Although social order is a perpetual preoccupation, at this point in history it would seem to be an obsessive one; witness the outsized emphasis on the containment of crime at a time when crime is on the decline and the reckless hysteria of the War on Drugs. Sociologist Graham Murdock refers to the "fear about the precarious balance between anarchy and order in the modern age." Exactly why this fearful fixation on social order should be occurring now is open to question. Its existence, however, should not be doubted. Indeed, the need to strengthen social controls has a correlate in Americans' increasing imposition of self-controls: Per capita alcohol consumption and cigarette smoking have been on the decline and health club memberships on the rise for most of the past 30 years.

Television is new enough that it is not embraced without reservations, and it has not yet accumulated the social equity that would allow it to be shielded by nostalgia. In addition to its relative novelty, it is enormous, filling up the day (television viewing trails only work and sleep in terms of expended time), and can be menacing on this count. Because everyone has access to television, its use cannot be regulated, and thus for those who want to control it, the medium is believed to be out of control and threatening. The rise of television, observes media scholar Richard Sparks, "has been taken to signify the drift of history beyond willed control or direction. The censure of television bears witness to the fear of the future."

General apprehension about the course of history is in several senses the opposite of video violence—the passivity of fear vs. the frenzy of aggression, the amorphous vs. the detailed, and the actual vs. the symbolic. The two find each other as if magnetized, whereupon the flaying of the whipping boy begins.

POSTSCRIPT

Is Viewing Television Violence Harmful for Children?

Almost everyone has access to television. There is hardly any other factor so pervasive in our society as television viewing. What is the relationship of television viewing to violent acts? Those who believe that television viewing is the root of all evil support unplugging the "boob tube" and going back to the good old days of reading, listening to the radio, and swapping stories while sitting by the fireplace. At the other end of the continuum, those who argue that television is merely the next evolution of communication technology would promote going with the flow, grinning and bearing television for it is surely here to stay, and stop worrying about television. After all, it is ultimately harmless. Television can't make you *do* anything you don't want to do.

What should be done to effectively address this problem? Is it realistic to revert back to the days prior to the television era? Or should we just relax and stop worrying about television? After all, children are resilient; they can eventually understand TV's impact on their lives just as we adults have. Anyone reading this book grew up with the "magic" box and probably turned out OK.

Huesmann, Moise-Titus, Podolski, and Eron contend that indeed children do not turn out OK. Based on their 15-year study, children identify with same-sex TV characters and believe that the violent TV shows they watch tell about life as it really is. They carry this learned aggression into adulthood and display more aggressive behavior. Previously it was believed that only males displayed more violent behavior based on childhood experiences, but this study showed that both males and females were more aggressive due to violent TV viewing in childhood. How do we respond to Fowles' contention that television is being used as the simple reason for societal violence when the reason is much more complex and difficult to flesh out?

There are numerous studies on children who watch violent TV shows, as well as on the amount of television children watch. Some research suggests that children who spend excessive amounts of time watching television tend to do poorly in school. Other studies show that children who spend moderate amounts of time in front of the set perform better scholastically than those who watch no television at all. Children are more likely to be overweight when they watch TV versus playing actively. If children are watching TV to excess, they are not communicating with adults in the family and are not learning family values. Logically, there must be middle-ground solutions to the issue of children, television viewing, and violence.

Perhaps if parents could accept the inevitable—that television is not only here to stay, but viewing choices are expanding almost daily—we, as a society, could move past this dichotomy of thinking television as simply good or bad. Television viewing could be thought of as an active endeavor rather than a passive one. Parents could become more involved with their children as they watch television by controlling the amount and type of TV shows their children are watching. Through modeling, parents could teach children to be skeptical about television advertisements, point out the differences between fantasy and reality, and argue that the moral values being portrayed on the tube are different from values that are important to the parents.

Suggested Readings

Bushman, B. J., & Huesmann, L. R. (2001). Effects of televised violence on aggression. In D. Singer & J. Singer (Eds.), *Handbook of children and the media* (pp. 223–254). Sage.

Freedman, Jonathan. (2002). *Media violence and its effect on aggression: Assessing the scientific evidence.* University of Toronto Press.

Sternheimer, Karen. (2003). *It's not the media: The truth about pop culture's influence on children.* Westview Press.

Walsh, David. (2007). *No, why kids of all ages need it and ways parents can say it.* Free Press.

Internet References . . .

Family: Single Parenting

This Single Parenting page of ParentsPage.com focuses on issues concerning single parents and their children. Although the articles cover issues concerning single parents of children from infancy through adolescence, most of the articles deal with middle childhood.

http://parenting.ivillage.com

National Institute on Out-of-School Time

Directed by the Wellesley College Center for Research on Women, this National Institute on Out-of-School Time project aims to improve the quality and quantity of school-age child care nationally.

http://www.niost.org

National Black Child Development Institute

At this site, the National Black Child Development Institute provides resources for improving the quality of life for African American children through public education programs.

http://www.nbcdi.org

National Clearinghouse for English Language Acquisition

This National Clearinghouse for English Language Acquisition was formely called the National Clearinghouse for Bilingual Education. This Web site is funded by the Department of Education and includes information on the latest legislation and conferences, as well as links to bilingual educational materials.

http://www.ncela.gwu.edu/

Action for Healthy Kids

This is a nonprofit organization formed specifically to address the epidemic of overweight, undernourished, and sedentary youth by focusing on changes at school. The organization's goal is to improve children's nutrition and increase physical activity, which will in turn improve their readiness to learn.

http://www.actionforhealthykids.org

Middle Childhood

*M*iddle childhood, or school age, is the period from ages five through twelve. The rate of a child's growth generally declines until the later part of this stage of development. Perhaps the most important experience during middle childhood is schooling. As a child progresses through this stage, new significant others outside the family emerge in the child's life. Children gain a broader understanding of the similarities and differences among them. The peer group (especially same-sex peers), teachers, and media personalities take on increased importance for the child. This section examines issues related to schooling, language development, and self-care.

- Does Marriage Improve Living Standards for Children?

- Are Stepfamilies Inherently Problematic for Children?

- Is Television Viewing Responsible for the Rise in Childhood Obesity?

- Do Bilingual Education Programs Help Non-English-Speaking Children Succeed?

- Is Gay Adoption and Foster Parenting Healthy for Children?

- Should the HPV Vaccination Be Mandatory for Girls in Later Childhood?

ISSUE 9

Does Marriage Improve Living Standards for Children?

YES: Wade F. Horn, from "Healthy Marriages Provide Numerous Benefits to Adults, Children, and Society," *Insight on the News* (March 18, 2002)

NO: Stephanie Coontz and Nancy Folbre, from "Marriage, Poverty, and Public Policy," *The American Prospect Online*, http://www.prospect.org/webfeatures/2002/03/coontz-s-03-19.html (March 19, 2002)

ISSUE SUMMARY

YES: Wade F. Horn, who heads the Marriage Initiative for President George W. Bush, asserts that marriage can remedy the ills of society, including family poverty and poor living standards for children.

NO: Stephanie Coontz, author and family advocate, and Nancy Folbre, professor of economics at the University of Massachusetts, contend that improving the living standards of children is a complicated issue, which needs to be approached from many different angles in order to make improvements.

There is no doubt that living with two parents who are married and who want to be together, is good for children, psychologically and economically. Having two married parents means that there is a possibility for two incomes, which would provide a higher standard of living for children and would make it more likely that the children will not grow up in poverty. Presently, the majority of children living in poverty live with a single parent, usually their mom.

And yet, is the issue that simple? Should we merely request or require that parents marry? Will that make everything all right? Will children's living standards improve if their parents get married? One-third of poor children live within a two-parent family. If the premise that marriage improves living standards for children is true, what happened to these families?

The complicated issue involving the living standards of children and marriage promotion has become intertwined with the issues of welfare reform fund reauthorization. The whole issue of how marriage influences children's living standards recently emerged in the American political agenda. Key personnel in the George W. Bush administration, led by Wade F. Horn, decided that parents need to be married to each other in order to move families out of poverty and to improve living standards for children. Horn asserts that marriage would solve the problem of children living in poverty. This idea prompted a slew of opposition from some family professionals and public-policy analysts.

As welfare reform has evolved, funding for Temporary Assistance for Needy Families (TANF) has also changed. While improving living standards for children has always been states' prominent goal, by moving families from welfare to work, states have been allowed to choose their own method of using federal dollars to accomplish this goal. The individuation of states has complicated this issue. Some states choose to provide affordable child care, education, and job training as a way to move families from welfare to work, and in so doing, they have managed to improve living standards for children. With the marriage promotion initiative, states that show higher levels of marriage rates receive more federal dollars for the welfare reform initiative. Although there is no empirical evidence that this type of programming works, states are likely to adopt programs that promote marriage, regardless of whether or not these programs are effective in improving living standards for children. Some states do this merely to increase funding levels.

The issue is not merely about living standards for children. It has evolved into the issue of making poor people get married in order to keep children from enduring a lifetime of poverty. In the following selections, the issue is debated within the present political climate. Horn presents the merits of marriage within the poor population. Horn states that the issue is simple: the government should promote marriage as a way to improve family life in general and more specifically for the children involved. In the opposing selection, Stephanie Coontz and Nancy Folbre describe why marriage within poor families is not always feasible or wise. They contend that this issue is more complicated than Horn suggests.

YES

Wade F. Horn

Healthy Marriages Provide Numerous Benefits to Adults, Children, and Society

The case for marriage is beyond debate. Marriage is the most stable and healthy environment for raising children. Men and women who are married have been shown to be happier and healthier. And they make more money over time than their single counterparts. Communities with more households headed by married couples are beset by fewer social ills, such as crime and welfare dependency, than communities where marriage is less prevalent.

We really can't argue—or, at least, the data say we shouldn't argue—about the benefits of marriage to children, adults and society. But I do grant that it is reasonable to debate the proper role of government in promoting marriage and that, indeed, reasonable people can disagree on whether government has a place in the marriage debate. I for one, noting that marriage is related directly to child well-being, conclude that government has no choice but to promote healthy marriages.

Let's pose the question this way: Since we know marriage can help adults be happier and healthier, and help children grow up happier and healthier, don't we have a responsibility to figure out ways to help low-income couples who want to be married enjoy a strong, supportive marriage? Of course we do.

Before I lay out my vision for how government can begin to make this happen, allow me a pre-emptive strike against the criticism that descends every time I unequivocally state that government should support and promote healthy marriages. Let me discuss four things that promoting marriage is not about.

First, it is not about government matchmaking or telling anybody to get married. Obviously, government has no business doing that. Choosing to get married is a private decision. Government should, and will not get into the business of telling people who, or even whether, to marry. I can state without hesitation that the Bush administration has no plans to create a federal dating service. We have no plans to add an entirely new meaning to the famous phrase, "Uncle Sam Wants You!"

Second, promoting marriage cannot, intentionally or inadvertently, result in policies that trap anyone in an abusive relationship. Seeing more Americans married is not our goal. Seeing more Americans enjoying healthy marriages is our goal. Healthy marriages are good for children and adults alike. Abusive marriages are not good for anyone.

Abuse of any sort by a spouse cannot be tolerated under any circumstances, and no marriage-promotion effort should provide comfort to spouse or child abusers. The good news is that good marriages are not a matter of luck but, rather, a matter of skill. We can teach couples the skills necessary to have good marriages. We can teach couples how to negotiate conflict and how not to allow unresolved anger to escalate. Marriages that last a lifetime and marriages that dissolve after a short while often face equal amounts of conflict. The difference is that couples who stay married have learned to manage this conflict constructively. We have proven strategies for teaching these skills to couples; standing by and not sharing these skills with low-income couples is irresponsible.

Third, when we talk about promoting marriage we are not talking about withdrawing support and services for single-parent families. As noted, we are for marriage because that's what the data say is best for kids. There is no data suggesting that taking away support from single mothers helps children in any way. Many single parents make heroic efforts to raise their children despite incredible pressures. Promoting marriage and supporting single parents is not, and must not be, mutually exclusive. Together, they are part of an integrated effort to promote child well-being.

Finally, marriage promotion is not the same as cohabitation promotion. For too long, we have treated marriage as if it were a dreaded "M" word. Too afraid to say "marriage," we have instead talked about "committed relationships." But shacking up isn't getting married. Common sense says so. So does research. There is something fundamentally different about the commitment two people make within a marriage relationship versus a cohabiting relationship. In a cohabiting relationship, the commitment of each of the partners primarily is self-serving. By contrast, the marriage commitment is about serving one's spouse. This is a fundamental difference, and one that ought to be reflected in our social policy.

I recommend the following principles for government marriage promotion:

Government must resolve that it will not merely be "neutral" about marriage. For many behaviors government is rightly neutral, for others it is not. For example, the government is not neutral about home ownership because it is good for communities when people own their homes. Furthermore, the government is not neutral about charitable giving because charitable giving is good for society. In the same way, government should not be neutral about healthy marriages because they contribute directly to the general strength of a good and sound society.

First of all, we must remove disincentives for marriage. Under current law if couples (especially low-income couples) marry, our tax code and social welfare system punish them. But striking these disincentives from our laws and policies, while a very important first step, only will bring us to the state of being neutral on marriage. We must go beyond that, into active support of marriage.

More than 90 percent of adults in the United States marry at some point during their lifetimes, and the vast majority enter marriage believing it to be a lifetime commitment. Surveys consistently document that most Americans see marriage as an important life goal. Clearly, providing active support for couples who want to marry and stay married is consistent with the values of the vast majority of Americans.

In doing so, government must not be paralyzed by the unknown. What we don't know about marriage promotion cannot be allowed to stand in the way of what we do know. Some have argued that we don't know enough about marriage promotion and, therefore, we should do nothing. They are partially correct. We have much to learn about promoting and supporting healthy marriages. But there is much we do know.

For example, thanks to a nascent marriage movement in our country, we do know that premarital-education programs work. We know that programs that assign mentoring couples to newlyweds do work. We know that good marriages are a result not of luck or chance but hard work and skill. We know that these skills can be taught. Finally, we know that programs designed to save even the most troubled marriages do work. Yes, there still is much to be learned, but we know enough about what works that standing by and doing nothing would be a tragic mistake.

New research constantly is shedding more light on our path. For example, research is debunking the myth that low-income, inner-city men and women who have children out of wedlock are not linked romantically and have no interest in marriage. A recent study by researchers at Princeton and Columbia universities revealed that 48 percent of unmarried urban couples were living together at the time their child was born. Eighty percent were involved in an exclusive romantic relationship. And half believed their chances of marrying—not at sometime to somebody, but to each other—were "certain" or "near certain." In other words, drive-by pregnancies are an especially insidious urban legend.

Now that we understand the goal for marriage promotion—helping couples who choose marriage develop the skills they need to build healthy marriages—it is time to explore specific actions the government can take. A number of proposals have been put forth. Here are five of my favorites—ideas that have the best chance of improving child well-being by strengthening the institution of marriage:

- Put marriage in the hospital. Hospitals should do more than talk about paternity establishment. They can talk about marriage as well. In most cases, hospital personnel stop at telling a young man that he must establish paternity. Doing so is extremely important. But hospital personnel should also ask the simple question, "Have you considered getting married?" If the answer is "yes," the couple can be referred to helpful services, such as premarital education. If the answer is "no," that's fine. But we can't be afraid to say the "M" word in the labor and delivery ward.
- Develop a referral system for premarital education. Schools, clinics, job-training sites and welfare offices all offer opportunities to provide referrals to premarital education.

- Provide marital-enrichment services through social programs dedicated to strengthening families. Head Start provides a perfect example. Many children in Head Start live with a married mother and father. While Head Start centers routinely provide parenting-education classes, I don't know of a single Head Start program providing marriage-education classes. Head Start represents a perfect opportunity to teach parents the skills they need to maintain a long-term, healthy marriage. We should seize this and similar opportunities.
- Create public-education campaigns highlighting the benefits of healthy marriages. The government funds numerous public-education campaigns promoting various healthy behaviors. Marriage can and should be added to this list.
- Increase support for intervention services, including mentoring programs, so that troubled marriages can be made whole and strong once again.

It no longer is a question of whether government should do this, but of how. It's time to get started right away, before another generation of children misses out on the benefits of a married mom and dad.

**Stephanie Coontz
and Nancy Folbre**

 **NO**

Marriage, Poverty, and Public Policy

One of the stated objectives of welfare legislation passed in 1996 was "to end dependence by promoting marriage." With this legislation coming up for reauthorization, many policymakers want to devote more public resources to this goal, even if it requires cutting spending on cash benefits, child care, or job training. Some states, such as West Virginia, already use their funds to provide a special bonus to couples on public assistance who get married.[1] In December 2001, more than fifty state legislators asked Congress to divert funds from existing programs into marriage education and incentive policies, earmarking dollars to encourage welfare recipients to marry and giving bonus money to states that increase marriage rates. On February 26, 2002, President Bush called for spending up to $300 million a year to promote marriage among poor people.[2]

Such proposals reflect the widespread assumption that failure to marry, rather than unemployment, poor education, and lack of affordable child care, is the primary cause of child poverty. Voices from both sides of the political spectrum urge us to get more women to the altar. Journalist Jonathan Rauch argues that "marriage is displacing both income and race as the great class divide of the new century."[3] Robert Rector of the Heritage Foundation claims that "the sole reason that welfare exists is the collapse of marriage."[4] In this briefing paper, we question both this explanation of poverty and the policy prescriptions that derive from it.

Marriage offers important social and economic benefits. Children who grow up with married parents generally enjoy a higher standard of living than those living in single-parent households. Two parents are usually better than one not only because they can bring home two paychecks, but also because they can share responsibilities for child care. Marriage often leads to higher levels of paternal involvement than divorce, non-marriage, or cohabitation. Long-term commitments to provide love and support to one another are beneficial for adults, as well as children.

Public policies toward marriage could and should be improved.[5] Taxes or benefit reductions that impose a marriage penalty on low-income couples are inappropriate and should be eliminated. Well designed public policies could

From Stephanie Coontz and Nancy Folbre, "Marriage, Poverty, and Public Policy," *The American Prospect Online,* http://www.prospect.org/webfeatures/2002/03/coontz-s-03-19.html (March 19, 2002). Copyright © 2002 by Stephanie Coontz and Nancy Folbre. Reprinted by permission of *The American Prospect,* 5 Broad Street, Boston, MA 02109 and the author.

play a constructive role in helping couples develop the skills they need to develop healthy and sustainable relationships with each other and their children. It does not follow, however, that marriage promotion should be a significant component of anti-poverty policy, or that public policies should provide a "bonus" to couples who marry.

The current pro-marriage agenda in anti-poverty policy is misguided for at least four reasons:

- Non-marriage is often a result of poverty and economic insecurity rather than the other way around.
- The quality and stability of marriages matters. Prodding couples into matrimony without helping them solve problems that make relationships precarious could leave them worse off.
- Two-parent families are not immune from the economic stresses that put children at risk. More than one third of all impoverished young children in the U.S. today live with two parents.

Single parenthood does not inevitably lead to poverty. In countries with a more adequate social safety net than the United States, single parent families are much less likely to live in poverty. Even within the United States, single mothers with high levels of education fare relatively well.

In this briefing paper, we summarize recent empirical evidence concerning the relationship between marriage and poverty, and develop the four points above in more detail. We also emphasize the need to develop a larger anti-poverty program that provides the jobs, education, and child care that poor families need in order to move toward self-sufficiency.

The Economic Context

Children living with married parents generally fare better than others in terms of family income. In 2000, 6 percent of married couple families with children lived in poverty, compared to 33 percent of female householders with children.[6] Mothers who never marry are more vulnerable to poverty than virtually any other group, including those who have been divorced.[7]

But the low income associated with single parenthood reflects many interrelated factors. Income is distributed far more unequally in the United States than in most other developed countries, making it difficult for low-wage workers (male or female) to support a family without a second income. Women who become single mothers are especially likely to have inadequate wages, both because of pre-existing disadvantages such as low educational attainment and work experience and because the shortage of publicly subsidized child care makes it difficult for them to work full time. In 2000, only 1.2 percent of children of single mothers with a college degree who worked full-time year round lived in poverty.[8] For single mothers with some college working full-time, the poverty rate was less than 8 percent.[9]

Whether single or married, working parents face high child care costs that are seldom factored into calculations of poverty and income. Consider the situation of a single mother with two children working full-time, full year round at the minimum wage of $5.15 an hour, for an income of $10,712. If she files for and receives the maximum Earned Income Tax Credit, she can receive as much as $3,816 in public assistance. But the EITC phases out quickly if she earns much more than the minimum wage, and her child care costs are very high. Unless she is lucky enough to have a family member who can provide free child care, or to find a federally subsidized child care slot, more than 20 percent of her income will go to pay for child care.[10] Federally subsidized child care remains quite limited. Most families who made a transition from welfare to employment in the 1990s did not receive a subsidy.[11]

The high cost of child care helps explain why the economic position of single parents has improved little in recent years despite significant increases in their hours of market work.[12] It may also explain why single parents are likely to live in households with other adults who can share expenses with them. About 40 percent of births to single mothers take place among cohabitors, and much of the increase in nonmarital childbearing in recent years reflects this trend rather than an increase among women living without a partner.[13] The economic stress associated with reductions in welfare benefits over the past six years may have increased the pressure on single mothers to cohabit, often with partners who are unwilling or unlikely to marry.[14]

On both a symbolic and a practical level, marriage facilitates the income pooling and task sharing that allows parents to accommodate family needs.[15] Not surprisingly, many low-income families consider marriage the ideal arrangement for child rearing.[16] The Fragile Families and Child Welfare project currently underway in about twenty cities shows that about 50 percent of unmarried parents of newborns live together and hope to marry at some point.[17] Lower expectations among some couples were associated not with disinterest in marriage but with reports of drug or alcohol problems, physical violence, conflict and mistrust.[18]

The advantages of marriage, however, do not derive simply from having two names on a marriage certificate, and they cannot be acquired merely by going through a formality. Rather, they grow out of a long-term and economically sustainable commitment that many people feel is beyond their reach.

Causality Works Both Ways

Liking the abstract idea of marriage and being able to put together a stable marriage in real life are two very different things. Unemployment, low wages, and poverty discourage family formation and erode family stability, making it less likely that individuals will marry in the first place and more likely that their marriages will deteriorate. These economic factors have long-term as well as short-term effects, contributing to changes in social norms regarding marriage and family formation and exacerbating distrust between men and women. These long-term effects help explain why African-Americans marry at much lower rates than other groups within the U.S. population. Poverty is a cause as well as a consequence of non-marriage and of marital disruption.[19]

Dan Lichter of Ohio State University puts it this way: "Marriage can be a pathway from poverty, but only if women are 'marriageable,' stay married, and marry well."[20] Precisely because marriage offers economic advantages, individuals tend to seek potential spouses who have good earnings potential and to avoid marriage when they do not feel they or their potential mates can comfortably support a family. Ethnographic research shows that low-income women see economic stability on the part of a prospective partner as a necessary precondition for marriage.[21] Not surprisingly, men increasingly use the same calculus. Rather than looking for someone they can "rescue" from poverty, employed men are much more likely to marry women who themselves have good employment prospects.[22]

Poor mothers who lack a high school degree and any regular employment history are not likely to fare very well in the so-called "marriage market." Teenage girls who live in areas of high unemployment and inferior schools are five to seven times more likely to become unwed parents than more fortunately situated teens.[23] A study of the National Longitudinal Survey of Youth confirms that poor women, whatever their age, and regardless of whether or not they are or have ever been on welfare, are less likely to marry than women who are not poor. Among poor women, those who do not have jobs are less likely to marry than those who do.[24]

It is easy to spin a hypothetical scenario in which marrying off single mothers to an average male would raise family incomes and reduce poverty. But unmarried males, and especially unmarried males in impoverished neighborhoods, are not average. That is often the reason they are not married. Researchers from the Center for Research on Child Well-Being at Princeton University report results from the Fragile Families Survey showing that unmarried fathers were twice as likely as married ones to have a physical or psychological problem that interfered with their ability to find or keep a job, and several times more likely to abuse drugs or alcohol. More than 25 percent of unmarried fathers were not employed when their child was born, compared to fewer than 10 percent of married fathers.[25]

Poor mothers tend to live in neighborhoods in which their potential marriage partners are also likely to be poorly educated and irregularly employed. Low-earning men are less likely to get married and more likely to divorce than men with higher earnings.[26] Over the past thirty years, labor market opportunities for men with low levels of education have declined substantially.[27] Several studies suggest that the decrease in real wages for low-income men during the 1980s and early 1990s contributed significantly to lower marriage rates in those years.[28]

This trend has been exacerbated by the high incarceration rates for men convicted of non-violent crimes, such as drug use. While in jail, these men are not available for women to marry and their diminished job prospects after release permanently impair their marriageability. High rates of incarceration among black males, combined with high rates of mortality, have led to a decidedly tilted sex ratio within the African-American population, and a resulting scarcity of marriageable men.[29] One study of the marriage market in the 1980s found that at age 25 there were three unmarried black women for every black man who had adequate earnings.[30] As Ron Mincy of Columbia University emphasizes, simple pro-marriage policies are likely to offer less benefit to African-American families than policies encouraging responsible fatherhood and paternal engagement.[31]

In short, the notion that we could end child poverty by marrying off impoverished women does not take into account the realities of life among the population most likely to be poor. It is based on abstract scenarios that ignore the many ways in which poverty diminishes people's ability to build and sustain stable family relationships.

Quality Matters

Happy, healthy, stable marriages offer important benefits to adults and children. But not all marriages fit this description. Marital distress leads to harsh and inconsistent parenting, whether or not parents stay together. Studies show that a marriage marked by conflict, jealousy and anger is often worse for children's well-being than divorce or residence from birth in a stable single-parent family.[32] For instance, research shows that while children born to teenagers who were already married do better than children born to never-married teens, children born to teen parents who married *after* the birth do worse on some measures, probably because of the high conflict that accompanies marriages entered into with ambivalence or under pressure. Some research suggests that, among low-income African-American families, children from single-parent homes show higher educational achievement than their counterparts from two-parent homes.[33]

The idea that marriage can solve the problems of children in impoverished families ignores the complex realities of these families. The Fragile Families study shows that many low-income parents of new born children already have children from previous relationships. Thus, their marriages would not create idealized biological families, but rather blended families in which child support enforcement and negotiation among stepparents would complicate relationships.[34] A recent study of families in poor neighborhoods in Boston, Chicago and San Antonio also reveals complex patterns of cohabitation and coparenting.[35]

Marriage to a stepfather may improve a mother's economic situation, but it does not necessarily improve outcomes for children and in some cases leads to more problems than continued residence in a stable single-parent family. Even if programs succeed in getting first-time parents married, there is no guarantee that the couples will stay married. Research shows that marriages contracted in the 1960s in order to "legitimate" a child were highly likely to end in divorce.[36] Multiple transitions in and out of marriage are worse for children psychologically than residence in the same kind of family, whatever its form, over long periods of time.[37]

Women and children in economically precarious situations are particularly vulnerable to domestic violence.[38] While it may be true that cohabiting couples are more prone to violence than married couples, this is probably because of what social scientists call a "selection effect": People in non-abusive relationships are more likely to get married. Encouraging women in an unstable cohabiting relationship to marry their partners would not necessarily protect them or their children. Indeed, the first serious violent episode in an unstable relationship sometimes occurs only after the couple has made a formal commitment.[39]

Even when it does not take a violent form, bad fathering can be worse than no fathering. For instance, the National Center on Addiction and Substance Abuse at Columbia University found that while teens in two-parent families are, on average, much less likely to abuse drugs or alcohol than teens in one-parent ones, teens in two-parent families who have a poor to fair relationship with their father are *more* likely to do so than teens in the average one-parent family.[40]

Furthermore, even good marriages are vulnerable to dissolution. The current risks of a marriage ending in divorce are quite high, although they have come down from their peak in 1979–81. It is now estimated that approximately 40 percent of marriages will end in divorce, and the risk of divorce is elevated among people with low income and insecure jobs. Sociologist Scott South calculates that every time the unemployment rate rises by 1 percent, approximately 10,000 extra divorces occur.[41] Comparing the income of single-parent families and married-couple families in any particular year leads to an overly optimistic assessment of the benefits of marriage, because it ignores the possibility of marital dissolution.

Marriage may provide a temporary improvement in a woman's economic prospects without conferring any secure, long-term protection for her children. Indeed, if marriage encourages mothers to withdraw time from paid employment, this can lower their future earnings and increase the wage penalty that they incur from motherhood itself.[42]

Two-Parent Families Are Also Under Stress

Poverty among children is not confined to single-parent families. In 2000, about 38 percent of all poor young children lived in two-parent homes.[43] These families have been largely overlooked in the debates over anti-poverty programs and marriage. Indeed, the campaign to increase marriage has overlooked one of the most important public policy issues facing the United States: the growing economic gap between parents, whether married or unmarried, and non-parents.

The costs of raising children have increased in recent years, partly because of the expansion of opportunities for women in the labor market and partly because of the longer time children spend in school. The lack of public support for parenting has also contributed to a worsening of the economic position of parents relative to non-parents.[44] Unlike other advanced industrial countries, the United States fails to provide paid family leaves for parents, and levels of publicly subsidized support for child care remain comparatively low. Most employment practices penalize workers who take time away from paid responsibilities to provide family care.[45] The high cost of parenting in this country helps explain many of the economic disadvantages that women face relative to men.[46] It may also help explain why many men are reluctant to embrace paternal responsibilities.

The Need for a Better Social Safety Net

The association of single parenthood with poverty is not inevitable. In Canada and France, single mothers—and children in general—are far less likely to live in poverty. Sweden and Denmark, with higher rates of out-of-wedlock births, have much lower rates of child poverty and hunger than does the United States. The reason for the difference is simple: These countries devote a greater percentage of their resources to assisting families with children than we do.[47] Similarly, dramatic differences in child poverty rates within our country reflect differences in tax, child care, and income assistance policies across states.[48]

Fans of the 1996 welfare reform law point to a dramatic decline in the welfare rolls since its enactment. Much of this decline is attributable to the economic boom and resulting low unemployment rates of the late 1990s. Despite promises that work requirements and time limits would lead to a more generous package of assistance for those who "followed the rules," cash benefits have declined. Between 1994 and 1999, the real value of maximum benefits fell in most states, with an overall decline in inflation-adjusted value of about 11 percent.[49] Average benefits declined even more, as recipients increased their earnings. Indeed, the declining value of benefits is another reason why caseloads have fallen.[50]

Punitive attitudes, as well as time limits, have discouraged many eligible families from applying for assistance. The Census Bureau estimates that less than 30 percent of children in poverty resided in a family that received cash public assistance in 1998.[51] Take-up rates for Food Stamps and Medicaid have declined in recent years.[52] The implementation of the new Children's Health Insurance program has been quite uneven. As a result, states have saved money, but many children have gone without the food or medical care they needed. Public support for child care increased on both the federal and the state level. Still, most families who made a transition from welfare to work in the late 1990s did not receive a subsidy.[53]

During the economic boom of the late 1990s, increases in earnings among single parents helped make up for declining welfare benefits. As a result, poverty rates among children declined from a high of about 21 percent in 1996 to about 16 percent in 2000.[54] But these figures do not take into account the costs of child care and other work-related expenses, and they offer little hope for the future of children in low-income families as unemployment rates once again begin to climb.[55]

The most important federal policy promoting the welfare of low income families is currently the Earned Income Tax Credit (EITC), a fully refundable tax credit aimed at low-income families with children. Because benefits are closely tied to earnings, and phase out steeply after family income reaches $12,460, the EITC imposes a significant penalty on two-earner married couples, who are less likely to benefit from it than either single-parent families or married couples with a spouse at home. This penalty is unfair and should be eliminated.

Other problems with the EITC, however, should be addressed at the same time. Families with two children receive the maximum benefit, which means that low-income families with three or more children do not receive any additional assistance. More than a third of all children in the country live in families with three or more children. Partly as a result of limited EITC coverage, these families are prone to significantly higher poverty rates.[56] Furthermore, the EITC is phased out in ways that penalize middle income families, who currently enjoy less public support for child rearing than the affluent.[57] An expanded unified tax credit for families with children could address this problem.[58]

Given the pressing need for improvements in basic social safety net programs and the threat of rising unemployment, it is unconscionable to reallocate already inadequate Temporary Assistance to Needy Families (TANF) funds to policies designed to promote marriage or provide a "marriage bonus." There is little evidence that such policies would in fact increase marriage rates or reduce poverty among children. Indeed, the main effect of marriage bonuses would probably be to impose a "non-marriage" penalty that would have a particularly negative impact on African-American children, who are significantly less likely to live with married parents than either whites or Hispanics.[59] As Julianne Malveaux points out in her discussion of the Bush proposal, "a mere $100 million can be considered chump change. But the chump who could have been changed is the unemployed worker who misses out on job training because some folks find those programs—but not marriage-promotion programs—a waste."[60]

Well-designed programs to help individuals develop and improve family relationships may be a good idea. However, they should not be targeted to the poor, but integrated into a larger provision of public health services, or built into existing health insurance programs (mandating, for instance, that both public and private health insurance cover family counseling). Such programs also should not be limited to couples who are married or planning to marry. Fathers and step-fathers who are not living with their biological children also need guidance and encouragement to develop healthy, nurturing relationships. Gay and lesbian families—who are currently legally prohibited from marriage—also merit assistance.

Public policies should not penalize marriage. Neither should they provide an economic bonus or financial incentive to individuals to marry, especially at the cost of lowering the resources available to children living with single mothers. Such a diversion of resources from public assistance programs penalizes the children of unmarried parents without guaranteeing good outcomes for the children of people who are married. A variety of public policies could help strengthen families and reduce poverty among all children, including a broadening of the Earned Income Tax Credit, expansion of publicly subsidized child care, efforts to promote responsible fatherhood, improvements in public education and job training, and efforts to reduce income inequality and pay discrimination. Unlike some of the pro-marriage policies now under consideration, these policies would benefit couples who wish to marry but would not pressure women to enter or remain in intimate relationships they would not otherwise choose.

Notes

1. Alexandra Starr, "Shotgun Wedding by Uncle Sam?" *Business Week,* June 4, 2001.

2. Cheryl Wetzstein, "States Want Pro-Family Funds," *The Washington Times,* December 10, 2001; Robin Toner and Robert Pear, "Bush Urges Work and Marriage Programs in Welfare Plan," *New York Times,* February 27, 2002.

3. Jonathan Rauch, "The Widening Marriage Gap: America's New Class Divide," *National Journal,* Friday, May 18, 2001.

4. Cheryl Weitzstein, "Unwed Mothers Set a Record for Births," *The Washington Times,* April 18, 2001.

5. See Jared Bernstein, Irv Garfinkel, and Sara McLanahan, *A Progressive Marriage Agenda,* forthcoming from the Economic Policy Institute.

6. U.S. Bureau of the Census, "Historical Poverty Statistics—Table 4. Poverty Status of Families, by Type of Family, Presence of Related Children, Race, and Hispanic Origin: 1959–2000." Available at. . . . In 1999, 36 percent of single-mother households lived in poverty. *Poverty in the U.S. 1999.* Current Population Reports, P60–210 (Washington, D.C.: Government Printing Office, 2000).

7. Alan Guttmacher Institute, "Married Mothers Fare the Best Economically, Even if They Were Unwed at the Time They Gave Birth," *Family Planning Perspectives* 31, no. 5: pp. 258–60, September, 1999; Ariel Halpern, "Poverty Among Children Born Outside of Marriage: Preliminary Findings From the National Survey of America's Families" (Washington, D.C.: The Urban Institute, 1999).

8. Calculations by Arloc Sherman, Children's Defense Fund, based on the March 2001 Current Population Survey.

9. Ibid. See also Neil G. Bennett, Jiali Li, Younghwan Song, and Keming Yang, "Young Children in Poverty: A Statistical Update," released June 17, 1999. New York: National Center for Children in Poverty. . . .

10. Linda Giannarelli and James Barsimantov, *Child Care Expenses of America's Families,* Occasional Paper Number 40 (Washington, D.C.: Urban Institute, 2000).

11. Rachel Schumacher and Mark Greenberg, *Child Care After Leaving Welfare: Early Evidence From State Studies* (Washington, D.C.: Center for Law and Social Policy, 1999).

12. Kathryn H. Porter and Allen Dupree, "Poverty Trends for Families Headed by Working Single Mothers, 1993–1999," Center on Budget and Policy Priorities, August 16, 2001. For full article. . . .

13. Pamela Smock, "Cohabitation in the U.S.: An Appraisal of Research Themes, Findings, and Implications," *American Review of Sociology* 26, no. 1 (2000): pp. 1–20.

14. Gregory Acs and Sandi Nelson, "'Honey, I'm Home.' Changes in Living Arrangements in the Late 1990s," *New Federalism: National Survey of America's Families* (The Urban Institute), June 2001, pp. 1–7. A new study by Johns Hopkins researchers, presented on February 20, 2002 at a welfare forum in Washington D.C., however, shows that these partnerships are unstable and may not be better for children than single-parent households. See Robin Toner, "Two Parents Not Always Best for Children, Study Finds," *New York Times,* February 20, 2002.

15. Many dual-earner families with preschool age children include a parent who works evenings and nights in order to provide care during the day while their husband or wife is at work. See Harriet Presser, "Employment Schedules Among Dual-Earner Spouses and the Division of Household Labor by Gender," *American Sociological Review* 59, no. 3 (June 1994): pp. 348–364.

16. Kristen Harknett and Sara McLanahan, "Do Perceptions of Marriage Explain Marital Behavior? How Unmarried Parents' Assessments of the Benefits of Marriage Relate to Their Subsequent Marital Decision"; and Marcia Carlson, Sara McLanahan, and Paula England, "Union Formation and Stability in Fragile

Families," papers presented at the meetings of the Population Association of America, Washington D.C., April 2001.

17. More details on the Fragile Families study are available at. . . .

18. Maureen Waller, "High Hopes: Unwed Parents' Expectations About Marriage," *Children and Youth Services Review* 23 (2001): pp. 457–84.

19. Sara McLanahan, "Parent Absence or Poverty: Which Matters More?" pp. 35–48 in Greg Duncan and Jeanne Brooks-Gunn, eds., *Consequences of Growing Up Poor* (New York: Russell Sage Foundation, 1997). On the impact of poverty in creating non-marriage and marital disruption, see Aimee Dechter, "The Effect of Women's Economic Independence on Union Dissolution," Working Paper Np. 92–98 (1992).

    Center for Demography and Ecology, University of Wisconsin, Madison, WI; Mark Testa et al., "Employment and Marriage Among Inner-City Fathers," *Annals of the American Academy of Political and Social Science* 501 (1989), pp. 79–91; Karen Holden and Pamela Smock, "The Economic Costs of Marital Dissolution: Why Do Women Bear a Disproportionate Cost?" *Annual Review of Sociology* 17 (1991), pp. 51–58. On the association of low income with domestic violence see Kristin Anderson, "Gender, Status, and Domestic Violence," *Journal of Marriage and the Family* 59 (1997), pp. 655–670; A. M. Moore, "Intimate Violence: Does Socioeconomic Status Matter?" in A. P. Gardarelli, ed., *Violence Between Intimate Partners* (Boston: Allyn and Bacon, 1997), pp. 90–100; A. J. Sedlack and D. D. Broadhurst, *Third National Incidence Study of Child Abuse and Neglect: Final Report* (Washington D.C.: Department of Health and Human Services, 1996).

20. Daniel T. Lichter, *Marriage as Public Policy* (Washington, D.C.: Progressive Policy Institute, September 2001).

21. Kathryn Edin, "A Few Good Men: Why Poor Mothers Don't Marry or Remarry?" *The American Prospect,* January 3, 2000, p. 28; Kathryn Edin and Laura Lein, Making Ends Meet: How Single Mothers Survive Welfare and Low-Wage Work (New York: Russell Sage, 1998).

22. Valerie Oppenheimer and Vivian Lew, "American Marriage Formation in the 1980s," in Karen Mason and An-Magritt Jensen, eds., *Gender and Family Change in Industrialized Countries* (Oxford: Oxford University Press, 1994), pp. 105–38; Sharon Sassler and Robert Schoen, "The Effects of Attitudes and Economic Activity on Marriage," *Journal of Marriage and the Family* 61 (1999): pp. 148–49.

23. John Billy and David Moore, "A Multilevel Analysis of Marital and Nonmarital Fertility in the U.S.," *Social Forces* 70 (1992), pp. 977–1011; Sara McLanahan and Irwin Garfinkel, "Welfare Is No Incentive," *The New York Times,* July 29, 1994, p. A13; Elaine McCrate, "Expectations of Adult Wages and Teenage Childbearing," *International Review of Applied Economics* 6 (1992), pp. 309–328; Ellen Coughlin, "Policy Researchers Shift the Terms of the Debate on Women's Issues," *The Chronicle of Higher Education,* May 31, 1989; Marian Wright Edelman, *Families in Peril: An Agenda for Social Change* (Cambridge: Harvard University Press, 1987), p. 55; Lawrence Lynn and Michael McGeary, eds., *Inner-City Poverty in the United States* (Washington, D.C.: National Academy Press, 1990), pp. 163–67; Jonathan Crane, "The Epidemic Theory of Ghetto and Neighborhood Effects on Dropping Out and Teenaged Childbearing," *American Journal of Sociology* 96 (1991), pp. 1226–59; Sara McLanahan and Lynne Casper, "Growing Diversity and Inequality in the American Family," in Reynolds Farley, *State of the Union,* vol. 2, pp. 10–11; Mike Males, "Poverty, Rape, Adult/Teen Sex: Why 'Pregnancy-Prevention' Programs Don't Work," *Phi Delta Kappan,* January 1994, p. 409; Mike Males, "In Defense of Teenaged Mothers," *The Progressive,* August 1994, p. 23.

24. Diane McLaughlin and Daniel Lichter, "Poverty and the Marital Behavior of Young Women," *Journal of Marriage and the Family* 59, no. 3 (1997): pp. 582–94.

25. Wendy Single-Rushton and Sara McLanahan, "For Richer or Poorer?" manuscript, Center for Research on Child Well-Being, Princeton University, July 2001, p. 4; Kathryn Edin, "What Do Low-Income Single Mothers Say About Marriage?" *Social Problems* 47 (2000), pp. 112–33.

26. Robert Nakosteen and Michael Zimmer, "Man, Money, and Marriage: Are High Earners More Prone than Low Earners to Marry?" *Social Science Quarterly* 78 (1997): pp. 66–82.

27. Francine D. Blau, Lawrence W. Kahn, and Jane Waldfogel, "Understanding Young Women's Marriage Decisions: The Role of Labor and Marriage Market Conditions," *Industrial and Labor Relations Review* 53, no. 4 (July 2000): pp. 624–48.

28. Robert Nakosteen and Michael Zimmer, "Men, Money, and Marriage," *Social Science Quarterly* 78 (1997); Frank F. Furstenberg, Jr., "The Future of Marriage," *American Demographics* 18 (June 1996), pp. 39–40; Francine Blau, Lawrence Kahn, and Jane Waldfogel, "Understanding Young Women's Marriage Decisions," *Industrial and Labor Relations Review* 53 (2000): pp. 624–48.

29. William A. Darity, Jr. and Samuel L. Myers, Jr., "Family Structure and the Marginalization of Black Men: Policy Implications," in *The Decline in Marriage Among African Americans: Causes, Consequences, and Policy Implications,* ed. M. Belinda Tucker and Claudia Mitchell-Kernan (New York: Russell Sage Foundation, 1995), pp. 263–308.

30. Daniel T. Lichter, D. McLaughlin, F. LeClere, G. Kephart, and D. Landry, "Race and the Retreat From Marriage: A Shortage of Marriageable Men?" *American Sociological Review* 57 (December 1992): pp. 781–99.

31. Ron Mincy, Columbia University, personal communication, February 18, 2002.

32. Mavis Hetherington, *For Better or for Worse: Divorce Reconsidered* (New York: W. W. Norton, 2001); Paul Amato and Alan Booth, "The Legacy of Parents' Marital Discord," *Journal of Personality and Social Psychology* 81 (2001), pp. 627–638; Andrew Cherlin, "Going to Extremes: Family Structure, Children's Well-Being, and Social Science," *Demography* 36 (November 1999): pp. 421–28.

33. Elizabeth Cooksey, "Consequences of Young Mothers' Marital Histories for Children's Cognitive Development," *Journal of Marriage and the Family* 59 (May 1997), pp. 245–62; Juan Battle, "What Beats Having Two Parents? Educational Outcomes for African American Students in Single- Versus Dual-Parent Families," *Journal of Black Studies* 28 (1998), pp. 783–802.

34. Ron Mincy and Chen-Chung Huang, "'Just Get Me to the Church . . .': Assessing Policies to Promote Marriage Among Fragile Families," manuscript prepared for the MacArthur Foundation Network on the Family and the Economy Meeting, Evanston, Illinois, November 30, 2001. Contact Ron Mincy, School of Social Work, Columbia University.

35. Research by Andrew Cherlin and Paula Fomby at Johns Hopkins University, as reported in Robin Toner, "Two Parents Not Always Best for Children," *New York Times,* February 21, 2002.

36. Frank Furstenberg, Jeanne Brooks-Gunn, and S. Philip Morgan, *Adolescent Mothers in Later Life* (New York: Cambridge University Press, 1987).

37. Frank Furstenberg, "Is the Modern Family a Threat to Children's Health?" *Society* 36 (1999): p. 35.

38. Richard Gelles, "Constraints Against Family Violence," *American Behavioral Scientist* 36 (1993), pp. 575–86; A. J. Sedlack and D. D. Broadhurst, *Third National Incidence Study of Child Abuse and Neglect: Final Report* (Washington, D.C.: Department of Health and Human Services, 1996); Kristin Anderson, "Gender,

Status and Domestic Violence," *Journal of Marriage and the Family* 59 (1997), pp. 655–670; Jacqueline Payne and Martha Davis, "Testimony of NOW Legal Defense and Education Fund on Child Support and Fatherhood Initiatives," submitted to the United States House Human Resources Subcommittee of the Ways and Means Committee, June 28, 2001.

39. Catherine Kenney and Sara McLanahan, "Are Cohabiting Relationship More Violent Than Marriages?" manuscript, Princeton University; E. D. Leonard, 1994, "Battered Women and Criminal Justice: A Review," doctoral dissertation cited in Todd Migliaccio, "Abused Husbands: A Narrative Analysis," *Journal of Family Issues* 23 (2002), pp. 26–52; K. D. O'Leary et al., "Prevalence and Stability of Physical Aggression Between Spouses: A Longitudinal Analysis," *Journal of Consulting and Clinical Psychology* 57 (1989), pp. 263–68.

40. National Center on Addiction and Substance Abuse at Columbia University, "Back to School 1999—National Survey of American Attitudes on Substance Abuse V: Teens and Their Parents," August 1999. See also Irvin Molotsky, "Study Links Teenage Substance Abuse and Paternal Ties," *New York Times,* Aug. 31, 1999.

41. "Census Bureau Reports Poor Two-Parent Families Are About Twice as Likely to Break Up as Two-Parent Families Not in Poverty," *New York Times,* January 15, 1993, p. A6; Don Burroughs, "Love and Money," *U.S. News & World Report,* October 19, 1992, p. 58; Scott South, Katherine Trent, and Yang Shen, "Changing Partners: Toward a Macrostructural-Opportunity Theory of Marital Dissolution," *Journal of Marriage and Family* 63, no. 3 (2001): 743–754. Also see note 17.

42. Michelle Budig and Paula England, "The Wage Penalty for Motherhood," *American Sociological Review* 66 (2001): pp. 204–225; Heather Joshi, Pierella Paci, and Jane Waldfogel, 1999, "The Wages of Motherhood: Better or Worse," *Cambridge Journal of Economics* 23, no. 5 (1999): pp. 543–564. Jane Waldfogel, "The Effect of Children on Women's Wages," *American Sociological Review* 62: 2 (1997): pp. 209–217.

43. "Young Children in Poverty: A Statistical Update," June 1999 Edition. Released June 17, 1999, prepared by Neil G. Bennett, Jiali Li, Younghwan Song, and Keming Yang. New York: National Center for Children in Poverty. . . . Data for 2000 from CPS. . . .

44. Nancy Folbre, *Who Pays for the Kids? Gender and the Structures of Constraint* (New York: Routledge, 1994); Ann Crittenden, *The Price of Motherhood* (New York: Metropolitan Books, 2001); Sylvia Ann Hewlett and Cornell West, *The War Against Parents* (New York: Houghton Mifflin, 1998).

45. Joan Williams, *Unbending Gender: Why Family and Work Conflict and What to Do About It* (New York: Oxford University Press, 2000).

46. Ann Crittenden, *The Price of Motherhood. Why the Most Important Job in the World Is Still the Least Valued* (New York: Henry Holt, 2001).

47. Timothy Smeeding, Barbara Boyle Torrey, and Martin Rein, "Patterns of Income and Poverty: The Economic Status of Children and the Elderly in Eight Countries," in John L Palmer, Timothy Smeeding, and Barbara Boyle Torrey, eds., *The Vulnerable* (Washington, D.C.: Urban Institute Press, 1988); Susan Houseknecht and Jaya Sastry, "Family 'Decline' and Child Well-Being: A Comparative Assessment," *Journal of Marriage and the Family* 58 (1996); Sara McLanahan and Irwin Garfinkel, "Single-Mother Families and Social Policy: Lessons for the United States From Canada, France, and Sweden," pp. 367–83, in K. McFate, R. Lawson, W. J. Wilson eds., *Poverty, Inequality, and the Future of Social Policy: Western States in the New World Order* (New York: Russell Sage Foundation, 1995). Michael J. Graetz and Jerry L. Mashaw, *True Security: Rethinking American Social Insurance* (New Haven: Yale University Press, 1999).

48. Marcia K. Meyers, Janet C. Gornick, and Laura R. Peck, 2001, "Packaging Support for Low-Income Families: Policy Variation Across the U.S. States," *Journal of Policy Analysis and Management* 20, no. 3: pp. 457–483.

49. Table 7–6, *Green Book 2000*. Committee on Ways and Means, U.S. House of Representatives, 106th Congress Available at. . . .

50. President's Council of Economic Advisors, *The Effects of Welfare Policy and the Economic Expansion of Welfare Caseloads: An Update* (Washington, D.C.: Council of Economic Advisors, 1999).

51. *2000 Kids Count Data Online.* . . .

52. Jennifer Steinhauer, "States Proved Unpredictable in Aiding Uninsured Children," *New York Times,* September 28, 2000. See also Leighton Ku and Brian Bruen, "The Continuing Decline in Medicaid Coverage," Series A, no. A–37 (Washington, D.C.: Urban Institute, 1999); Sheila Zedlewski and Sarah Brauner, "Are the Steep Declines in Food Stamp Participation Linked to Falling Welfare Caseloads?" Series B, no. B–3 (Washington, D.C.: Urban Institute, 1999).

53. Rachel Schumacher and Mark Greenberg, *Child Care After Leaving Welfare: Early Evidence From State Studies* (Washington, D.C.: Center for Law and Social Policy, 1999). On the added costs of child care and care-giving activities for low-income families, see Jody Heymann, *The Widening Gap: Why America's Working Families Are in Jeopardy and What Can Be Done About It* (New York: Basic Books, 2000).

54. Bureau of the Census, Current Population Reports, *Money Income and Poverty in the U.S.,* 1999. Figures for 2000 from. . . .

55. Patricia Ruggles, *Drawing the Line: Alternative Poverty Measures and Their Implications for Public Policy* (Washington, D.C.: The Urban Institute Press, 1990); Constance Citro and Robert Michael, eds., *Measuring Poverty: A New Approach* (Washington, D.C.: National Academy of Science, 1995); Jared Bernstein, Chauna Brocht, Maggie Spade-Aguilar, *How Much Is Enough? Basic Family Budgets for Working Families* (Washington, D.C.: Economic Policy Institute, 2000).

56. Robert Greenstein, "Should EITC Benefits Be Enlarged for Families With Three or More Children?" Washington, D.C.: Center on Budget and Policy Priorities, 2000. . . .

57. David Ellwood and Jeffrey B. Liebman, "The Middle Class Parent Penalty: Child Benefits in the U.S. Tax Code," manuscript, John F. Kennedy School of Government, Harvard University, Boston, MA, 2000.

58. Robert Cherry and Max Sawicky, "Giving Tax Credit Where Credit Is Due," Briefing Paper (Washington, D.C.: Economic Policy Institute, April 2000). Available at. . . .

59. Ronald B. Mincy, "Marriage, Child Poverty, and Public Policy," *American Experiment Quarterly,* 4: 2 (Summer 2001): pp. 68–71. See also Wendy Sigle-Rushton and Sara McLanahan, "For Richer or Poorer?" manuscript, Center for Research on Child Well-Being, Princeton University.

60. Julianne Malveaux, "More Jobs, Not More Marriages, Lift Poor," *U.S.A. Today,* February 22, 2002, p. 15A.

POSTSCRIPT

Does Marriage Improve Living Standards for Children?

In order to improve living standards for children, Horn maintains that parents need to be married. Horn asserts that the U.S. government must take a stand and become pro-marriage. In doing so, the government must remove tax disincentives for marriage and revamp the welfare system so that it does not punish married couples. Horn states that government programs should include pre-marriage education and teach couples the skills they need to help their marriage succeed. Horn provides specific techniques to encourage marriage among welfare recipients.

In the opposing selection, Coontz and Folbre cite evidence that shows that poor families need job training, increased education, and affordable child care in order to work their way out of poverty and to provide a higher standard of living for their children. Coontz and Folbre site the number of single parents who have high levels of education, work at well-paying jobs, and live at a middle-class standard of living. For these parents, the lack of marriage has not caused them to live in poverty.

Coontz and Folbre also show how dangerous marriage can be for single mothers and their children. The fathers to whom the mothers might marry are twice as likely to abuse alcohol or drugs and are likely to physically abuse them and their children. Marriage would not take these mothers and their children out of poverty and improve their standard of living, but might push them deeper into a desperate way of living, assert Coontz and Folbre.

Does marriage improve children's standard of living? Have we looked for complicated answers to this question and overlooked an obvious way to help children in our society by encouraging their parents to marry? Should the government promote marriage as a healthy lifestyle instead of being afraid to say the "M" word? What is wrong with promoting married parents and children? On the other hand, could this marriage promotion initiative backfire? Instead of helping children could it actually hurt them? Will the pressure to marry in order to move from welfare to work put additional stress on the family and cause increased child abuse and neglect? Society has a commitment to help children live at a standard of living that encourages positive growth and development. How society can achieve this goal is highly debatable.

ISSUE 10

Are Stepfamilies Inherently Problematic for Children?

YES: David Popenoe, from "The Evolution of Marriage and the Problem of Stepfamilies: A Biosocial Perspective," in Alan Booth and Judy Dunn, eds., *Stepfamilies: Who Benefits? Who Does Not?* (Lawrence Erlbaum, 1994)

NO: Lawrence A. Kurdek, from "Remarriages and Stepfamilies Are Not Inherently Problematic," in Alan Booth and Judy Dunn, eds., *Stepfamilies: Who Benefits? Who Does Not?* (Lawrence Erlbaum, 1994)

ISSUE SUMMARY

YES: Professor of sociology David Popenoe contends that children from single-parent families and stepfamilies are more likely to have emotional problems and health problems and to do poorly in school than children from intact families with two biological parents.

NO: Psychologist Lawrence A. Kurdek maintains that multiple-divorce families, not stepfamilies, differ from two-parent families and that stepfamilies are not inherently problematic for children.

$\mathbf{A}$sking the question, Are stepfamilies inherently problematic for children? triggers memories of the fairy tale "Cinderella," with her wicked stepmother and stepsisters. Although professional family associations such as the National Council of Family Relations and the Stepfamily Association have worked to dispel the Cinderella stepfamily myth, it is still a powerful image. Most people grow up believing that they will marry, have their own biological children, and live happily ever after. This does not always happen. All kinds of events can happen to change the way lives unfold. Changes in physical and mental health, abuse, loss of income, and changing needs of spouses are just a few of the things that can alter the fairy-tale ending of which many people dream.

For the past 20 years divorce has become more common, and, as a result, there is an increasing number of stepfamilies being formed. Most of these families result from divorce and remarriage, but some are formed due to the death of a spouse, single-parent marriage, or other circumstance. Because the research on divorce and stepfamilies is clouded with conflicting findings and research design flaws, how these family forms affect the development of children is also unclear.

Studies of children from divorced families and stepfamilies often take a negative approach. Researchers study what is wrong with the behavior of children from different family types rather than how children have adapted their behavior to survive life transitions. Conversely, society may have become so accustomed to validating divorce and remarriage that the needs of children have become ignored.

In the following selections, David Popenoe and Lawrence A. Kurdek present opposing views on the stepfamily's effect on children. Popenoe proposes that stepfamilies are not a useful alternative to the intact family and that they are a breeding ground for all kinds of problems for children. Kurdek refutes Popenoe's argument with four specific points of his own. He maintains that family life has changed and that family stability for stability's sake is not an appropriate societal value.

YES

David Popenoe

The Evolution of Marriage and the Problem of Stepfamilies: A Biosocial Perspective

One of the fastest growing family types in every advanced industrial nation has been the stepfamily. . . .

Since 1960 . . . the chances of spending part or all of one's childhood outside an intact family have grown dramatically. According to various estimates, the chances that a child born around 1980 will not be living at age 17 with both biological parents have increased to over 50% (Hernandez, 1993). . . . In 1960, an estimated 83% of all children are living with their two married, biological parents; by 1990, this figure was 58%. . . . More than 9 out of 10 stepchildren live with their biological mother and a stepfather. . . .

The Problem of Stepfamilies

Many, and perhaps most stepfamilies today lead contented home lives and produce happy and successful children. But a growing body of evidence suggests that the increase of stepfamilies has created serious problems for child welfare. . . . Contrary to the view of some social scientists in recent years, who believed that the effects of family fragmentation on children were both modest and ephemeral, there is now substantial evidence to indicate that the child outcomes of these alternative family forms are significantly inferior to those of families consisting of two biological parents. Compared to those in intact families, children in single-parent and stepfamilies are significantly more likely to have emotional and behavioral problems, to receive the professional help of psychologists, to have health problems, to perform poorly in school and drop out, and to leave home early. Moreover, some of these negative effects have been shown to persist into adult life.

Social scientists used to believe that, for positive child outcomes, stepfamilies were preferable to single-parent families. Today, we are not so sure. Stepfamilies typically have an economic advantage, but some recent studies indicate that the children of stepfamilies have as many behavioral and emotional problems as the children of single-parent families, and possibly more (e.g., Kiernan, 1992). . . .

From David Popenoe, "The Evolution of Marriage and the Problem of Stepfamilies: A Biosocial Perspective," in Alan Booth and Judy Dunn, eds., *Stepfamilies: Who Benefits? Who Does Not?* (Lawrence Erlbaum, 1994). Copyright © 1994 by Lawrence Erlbaum Associates, Inc. Reprinted by permission. Notes and some references omitted.

Certain problems are more prevalent in stepfamilies than in other family forms. A common finding is that stepparents provide less warmth and communicate less well with their children than do biological parents (Thomson, McLenahan, & Curtin, 1992). A number of studies have found that a child is far more likely to be abused by a stepfather than by the biological father. . . . Compared to children in intact and single-parent households, . . . "stepchildren are not merely 'disadvantaged,' but imperiled" (Wilson & Daly, 1987, p. 230).

As in single-parent families, a major problem of the stepfamily phenomenon is the net loss of fathering in children's lives. . . . Many studies have shown that stepfathering acts to diminish contact between original fathers and their biological children (Furstenberg & Nord, 1985; Furstenberg, Nord, Peterson, & Zill, 1983; Mott, 1990; Seltzer & Bianchi, 1988). In their turn, stepfathers take a considerably less active role in parenting than do custodial biological fathers, according to many studies, and frequently become disengaged from their stepchildren following the establishment of a stepfamily. . . .

Another problematic aspect of stepfamilies is their high breakup rate, higher than that of two-biological-parent families. According to the most recent census data, more than 62% of remarriages among women under age 40 will end in divorce, and the more that children are involved, the higher the redivorce rate. . . . By one estimate, about 15% of all children born in recent decades will go through at least two family disruptions before coming of age (Furstenberg, 1990).

In summary, according to the available evidence, stepfamilies tend to have less cohesive, more problematic, and more stressful family relationships than intact families, and probably also than single-parent families. Put more strongly by a recent article in *Psychology Today,* stepfamilies "are such a minefield of divided loyalties, emotional traps, and management conflicts that they are the most fragile form of family in America" ("Shuttle Diplomacy," 1993).

Biosocial Bases of Family Life

In order to better understand the special problems that stepfamilies pose, it is necessary to delve into the fundamental biosocial nature of human family life. . . .

From the perspective of evolutionary biology, the organization of the human nuclear family is based on two inherited biological predispositions that confer reproductive success, one that operates between parent and child, and the other between parent and parent. The first is a predisposition to advance the interests of genetic relatives before those of unrelated individuals. . . . With respect to children, this means that men and women have likely evolved to invest more in children who are related to them than in those who are not. . . .

The second biological predisposition is for males and females to have some emotional affinity for each other beyond the sexual act, and to establish pair bonds. We tend to fall in love with one person at a time. Although we think of love attachments as being highly social in character, they also have a strong biological component. There exists an "affective attachment" between men and women that causes us to be infatuated with each other, to feel a sense of well-being when we are together with a loved one, and to feel jealous when others attempt to intrude into our relationship. Around the world today, almost all adults pair-bond with someone of the opposite sex for at least a portion of their lives, and monogamous relationships are the rule. . . .

One fundamental reason for family instability is that, at heart, human beings are probably more self-interested than truly altruistic, even toward our own relatives and intimates. We act, first and foremost, in the interest of self-survival. But another reason is that the male–female bond, especially when compared to the mother–infant bond, is notoriously fragile. Although marriage is universal, divorce has also been a central feature of human social life. . . .

Possibly the most disintegrating force acting on the human pair bond is the male sexual drive. . . . Universally, men are the more sexually driven and promiscuous, while women are more relationship-oriented. . . .

Sexual and Reproductive Strategies

. . . Biologically, the primary reproductive function for males is to inseminate, and for females is to harbor the growing fetus. . . . Males, therefore, have more incentive to spread their numerous sperm more widely among many females, and females have a strong incentive to bind males to themselves for the long-term care of their more limited number of potential offspring.

The woman's best reproductive strategy is to ensure that she maximizes the survivability of the one baby she is able to produce every few years through gaining the provision and protection of the father. . . . The man's best strategy, however, may be twofold. He wants his baby to survive, yes, and for that reason he may provide help to his child's mother. But, at the same time, it is relatively costless to him . . . to inseminate other women, and thereby help to further insure that his genes are passed on. . . .

Why aren't all men promiscuous cads? Because, in addition to the pull of the biological pair-bonding and parenting predispositions discussed previously, virtually all human societies have established strong cultural sanctions that seek to limit male promiscuity and protect the sanctity of the family. . . .

If a man is to stay with one woman rather than pursue many different women, according to sociobiologists, the "paternal certainty" of his offspring is extremely important. A woman can be certain about her own offspring, but a man cannot be. . . . [A] male tends to invest in his mate's children only when his paternal confidence is high. . . .

Cultural Contexts

. . . During the most recent stages of the development of the human species, rapidly paced cultural evolution has overtaken slow-moving biological evolution as the main force of social change (Hallpike, 1986; Scott, 1989). One result is that family structures around the world today are widely variable, determined more by cultural differences than by biological predispositions. . . .

Associated with the rise of horticultural and agrarian societies was a fundamental shift in people's attitudes toward reproduction (Lancaster & Lancaster, 1987). . . .

[W]ith increased density of population and wealth, people came to perceive that resources were limited, that major differentials existed between who survived and who did not, and that survival was very much dependent on who controlled the most resources. It was no longer sufficient merely to rear as many offspring as possible and hope that they would survive to reproduce. Reproductive strategies became individually tailored to maximize the use and control of resources. It was necessary to try to guarantee children access to resources in the form of education or inheritance, for example, so that they would have an advantage over other parents' children.

Marriage and Divorce in Premodern Societies

The new perception of resource scarcity in complex societies generated a dramatic transformation in family life and kinship relations, including concern for the "legitimacy" of children, the rise of inheritance laws, and the careful control of female sexuality. The nuclear family gave way to the complex, extended family; the conjugal unit became imbedded in an elaborate kinship network. The father role of authority figure and head of household grew in importance, whereas the status of women deteriorated. . . .

Through the institutionalization of cultural norms and sanctions, complex societies have become heavily devoted to socially controlling male and female sexual strategies. The most important social institution serving this purpose is marriage. Marriage can be defined simply as "a relationship within which a group socially approves and encourages sexual intercourse and the birth of children" (Frayser, 1985, p. 248). . . . Throughout most of recorded history, until recently, most marriages were arranged (although the principals typically had a say in the matter); they were less alliances of two individuals than of two kin networks, typically involving an exchange of money or goods.

Various theories have been put forth to explain the fundamental purposes of marriage. But certainly one purpose is, as noted previously, to hold men to the pair bond, thereby helping to ensure high quality offspring and, at the same time, helping to control the open conflict that would result if men were allowed unlimited ability to pursue the "cad" strategy with other men's wives. . . .

Marriage and Divorce in Urban-Industrial Societies

. . . In urban-industrial societies, reproductive concerns about the quantity of children have largely given way to concerns about quality. Children in these societies require massive parental investments if they are to succeed, and childrearing has become extraordinarily expensive in terms of time and money. . . .

The modern nuclear family that accompanied the emergence of urban-industrialism and cultural modernity in the West was distinctly different from its preindustrial predecessor. . . . The new family form was emotionally intense, privatized, and child-oriented; in authority structure, it was relatively egalitarian; and it placed a high value on individualism in the sense of individual rights and autonomy. . . .

The big winners from the emergence of the modern nuclear family . . . were . . . children. In preindustrial Europe, parental care of children does not seem to have been particularly prominent, and such practices as infanticide, wet nursing, child fosterage, and the widespread use of lower status surrogate caretakers were common (Draper & Harpending, 1987). . . . Draper and Harpending (1987) suggested that one of the greatest achievements of the modern nuclear family was the return to the high-investment nurturing of children by their biological parents, the kind of parenting characteristic of our hunter-gatherer ancestors. . . .

Family stability during this era, together with parental investments in children, may have been greater than at any other time in history. Cultural sanctions concerning marriage were powerfully enforced, and thanks to ever lowering death rates and low divorce rates, both parents were typically able to see their children through to adulthood. This remarkably high family stability helps to explain why the family situation in the United States today appears so troubled, particularly in the minds of the older generation.

Recent Family and Cultural Change in America

In the past half century, the U.S. family has been on a social roller coaster. The ups and downs have been quite astonishing. Following World War II, the United States entered a two-decade period of extraordinary economic growth and material progress. Commonly referred to as simply "the 50s," it was the most sustained period of prosperity in U.S. history. Together with most other industrially developed societies of the world, this nation saw improvements in the levels of health, material consumption, and economic security that had scant historical precedent. For most Americans, the improvements included striking increases in longevity, buying power, personal net worth, and government-sponsored economic security.

The 1950s was also an era of remarkable familism and family togetherness, with the family as an institution undergoing unprecedented growth and stability within the middle and working classes. The marriage rate reached an all-time high, the birth rate returned to the high levels of earlier in the century, generating the baby boom, and the divorce rate leveled off. Home, motherhood, and child-centeredness reigned high in the lexicon of cultural values. A higher proportion of children were growing up in stable, two-parent families than ever before in U.S. history.

Beginning in the 1960s, however, a series of unanticipated social and cultural developments took place that shook the foundations of the modern nuclear family. . . . Men abandoned their families at an unprecedented rate, leaving behind broken homes and single-parent, female-headed households. Women relinquished their traditional mother/housewife roles in unexpectedly large numbers and entered the labor force. The percentage of births taking place outside of marriage skyrocketed. Highly permissive sexual behavior became acceptable. . . .

Not only did the modern nuclear family become fragmented, but participation in family life went into a precipitous decline. . . .

Underlying these family-related trends was an extraordinary shift in cultural values and self-definition. . . . Trust in, and a sense of obligation toward, the larger society and its institutions rapidly eroded; the traditional moral authority of social institutions such as schools, churches, and governments withered. What emerged, instead, was a new importance given by large segments of the population to the personal goal and even moral commandment of expressive individualism or "self-fulfillment" (Bellah, Madsen, Sullivan, Swidler, & Tipton, 1985). . . .

The institution of marriage was particularly hard hit. . . .

The marriage rate has steadily declined over the past few decades, from 76.7 marriages per 1,000 unmarried women in 1970, to 54.2 in 1990. The divorce rate, although it has leveled off, remains at an historically high level. Marriage has become a voluntary relationship which individuals can make and break at will. As one indicator of this shift, the legal regulation of marriage and divorce has become increasingly lax. In summary, fewer people ever marry, those who marry do so at a later age, a smaller proportion of life is spent in wedlock, and marriages are of a shorter duration (Espanshade, 1985).

. . . One of the significant attitudinal changes of recent years is the rising acceptance of divorce, especially when children are involved. . . .

The high voluntary dissolution of marriages might not be a serious problem if only adults were involved although, even then, it certainly generates considerable instability and anxiety. The problem is that young children, if they are to grow up successfully, still need strong attachments to parents. The evidence strongly suggests that parental bonds with children have suffered in recent years, and that the tremendous parenting advantages of the modern nuclear family are on the wane. . . .

The Social Response to Stepfamilies

The decline of marriage and the increase of divorce are, of course, the major contributors to the recent growth of stepfamilies. . . .

It is surely the case, especially in view of the diminution of kinship and neighborhood groupings, that stepfamilies need our collective help and understanding more than ever. But we should not confuse short-run actions aimed at helping stepfamilies with long-run solutions. If the argument presented [here] is correct, and the family is fundamentally rooted in biology and at least partly activated by the "genetically selfish" activities of human beings, childrearing by nonrelatives is inherently problematic. It is not that unrelated individuals are unable to do the job of parenting, it is just that they are not as likely to do the job well. Stepfamily problems, in short, may be so intractable that the best strategy for dealing with them is to do everything possible to minimize their occurrence.

Unfortunately, many members of the therapeutic and helping professions, together with a large group of social science allies, now take the view that the trend toward stepfamilies cannot be reversed. . . .

A close companion to this belief in stepfamily inevitability and optimum fit with a changing society is the view that we should now direct most of our attention toward understanding the familial processes of stepfamilies, and seek to develop social policies and interventions that will assist children's adjustment to them. . . . Once stepfamilies become more common and accepted, it is argued, and once our society comes to define the roles of stepparenthood more clearly, the problems of stepfamilies will diminish.

This may be a largely incorrect understanding of the situation. The reason why unrelated stepparents find their parenting roles more stressful and less satisfying than biological parents is probably due much less to social stigma and to the uncertainty of their obligations, as to the fact that they gain fewer intrinsic emotional rewards from carrying out those obligations. . . .

If, as the findings of evolutionary biology strongly suggest, there is a biological basis to parenting, we must question the view, widespread in the social sciences, that parenthood is merely a social role anyone can play if only they learn the part. . . .

The biosocial perspective presented in this essay leads to the conclusion that we as a society should be doing much more to halt the growth of stepfamilies. It is important to give great respect to those stepfamilies that are doing their job well, and to provide both assistance and compassion for those that are experiencing difficulties. But such efforts should not overshadow the paramount importance of public policies designed to promote and preserve two-biological-parent families, and of endeavors to reverse the cultural drift toward radical individualism and the decline of marriage.

References

Bellah, R. N., Madsen, R., Sullivan, W. M., Swidler, A., & Tipton, S. M. (1985). *Habits of the heart: Individualism and commitment in American life.* Berkeley: University of California.

Daly, M., & Wilson, M. (1987). The Darwinian psychology of discriminative parental solicitude. *Nebraska Symposium on Motivation.*

Draper, P., & Harpending, H. (1987). Parent investment and the child's environment. In J. B. Lancaster, J. Altmann, A. S. Rossi, & L. R. Sherrod (Eds.), *Parenting across the life span: Biosocial dimensions* (pp. 207–235). New York: Aldine De Gruyter.

Espenshade, T. J. (1985). The recent decline of American marriage. In K. Davis (Ed.), *Contemporary marriage* (pp. 53–90). New York: Russell Sage Foundation.

Frayser, S. (1985). *Varieties of sexual experience: An anthropological perspective on human sexuality.* New Haven, CT: HRAF Press.

Furstenberg, F. F., Jr. (1990). Divorce and the American family. *Annual Review of Sociology, 16,* 379–403.

Furstenberg, F. F., Jr., & Nord, C. W. (1985). Parenting apart: Patterns of childbearing after marital disruption. *Journal of Marriage and the Family, 47*(4), 893–905.

Furstenberg, F. F., Jr., Nord, C. W., Peterson, J. L., & Zill, N. (1983). The life course of children of divorce: Marital disruption and parental contact. *American Sociological Review, 48*(2), 656–658.

Hallpike, C. R. (1986). *The principles of social evolution.* Oxford: Clarendon.

Hernandez, D. J. (1993). *America's children.* New York: Russell Sage Foundation.

Kiernan, K. E. (1992). The impact of family disruption in childhood on transitions made in young adult life. *Population Studies, 46,* 213–234.

Lancaster, J. B., & Lancaster, C. S. (1987). The watershed: Change in parental-investment and family formation strategies in the course of human evolution. In J. B. Lancaster, J. Altmann, A. S. Rossi, & L. R. Sherrod (Eds.), *Parenting across the life span: Biosocial dimensions* (pp. 187–205). New York: Aldine de Gruyter.

Mott, F. L. (1990). When is father really gone? Paternal-child contact in father absent homes. *Demography, 27*(4), 499–517.

Scott, J. P. (1989). *The evolution of social systems.* New York: Gordon & Breach.

Seltzer, J. A., & Bianchi, S. M. (1988). Children's contact with absent parents. *Journal of Marriage and the Family, 50,* 663–677.

Shuttle diplomacy. (1993, July/August). *Psychology Today,* p. 15.

Thomson, E., McLanahan, S. S., & Curtin, R. B. (1992). Family structure, gender, and parental socialization. *Journal of Marriage and the Family, 54*(2), 368–378.

Wilson, M. I., & Daly, M. (1987). Risk of maltreatment of children living with step-parents. In R. J. Gelles & J. B. Lancaster (Eds.), *Child abuse and neglect: Biosocial dimensions* (pp. 215–232). New York: Aldine de Gruyter.

Lawrence A. Kurdek  **NO**

Remarriages and Stepfamilies Are Not Inherently Problematic

My strongest reactions to [professor of sociology David] Popenoe's chapter ["The Evolution of Marriage and the Problem of Stepfamilies: A Biosocial Perspective," in Alan Booth and Judy Dunn, eds., *Stepfamilies: Who Benefits? Who Does Not?*] were disappointment and irritation. . . . I had expected a critical review of the factors that determine both relationship commitment (e.g., Kurdek, 1993a) and relationship stability (e.g., Kurdek, 1993b) in remarriages involving children. No such review was presented.

Instead, Popenoe uses a biosocial perspective to make sweeping claims about the nature of family life that result in the conclusion that society should do more to halt the growth of stepfamilies. . . .

Children of Stepfamilies Have as Many Behavioral and Emotional Problems as the Children of Single-Parent Families, and Possibly More

My response to this claim has four parts: (a) comparisons between family structures should include mention of the size of any obtained differences between these family structures, (b) comparisons among divorce-related family structures need to take into account the number of parental divorces experienced, (c) the key family structure comparison involves stepfamilies and single divorced-parent families, and (d) comparisons involving stepfamilies need to consider the structural heterogeneity of stepfamilies. I expand on each of these parts.

In their influential meta-analysis of parental divorce and children's well-being, Amato and Keith (1991) presented information on the nature of differences between children in intact families and children in stepfamilies. True to the pattern Popenoe describes, relative to children in intact families, those in stepfamilies had more conduct problems, lower psychological adjustment, and lower self-esteem. . . . Although reliable, the differences between the two groups are fairly weak. . . .

Based on evidence from the life events, attachment, and family process literatures, there is reason to expect that the children and adolescents most at risk for behavioral and emotional problems are not those in stepfamilies, but those who have experienced multiple parental divorces and, consequently, multiple parenting transitions. Although evidence on this point is limited, it is consistent.

Studies that have examined the effects of parenting transitions on child and adolescent outcomes have typically compared four groups. These are children living continuously with both biological parents, children who have experienced one parental divorce and live with a single mother, children who have experienced one parental divorce and have made the additional transition to living with a mother and stepfather, and children who have experienced more than one parental divorce. Because of their relatively small numbers, children living with single divorced fathers and children living in stepmother families are usually excluded (see Kurdek & Fine, 1993).

Across a range of outcome variables and sources of information, it is the multiple divorce group—not the stepfamily group—that differs most strongly and negatively from the two-parent group. In fact, few differences emerge between children living continuously with both biological parents and either children living with a singly divorced mother or children living in a stepfather family. These findings lead to the plausible conclusion that what negatively affects children's well-being is not so much the kind of family structure in which they happen to reside, but the history of the quality and consistency of the parenting they receive. . . .

Despite the emphasis Popenoe places on family structure, he fails to recognize that stepfamilies themselves are quite structurally diverse. To his credit, he does note that stepfamilies may result from parental death, parental abandonment, or parental divorce. However, he does not mention that there may be important differences between stepfather families and stepmother families, or that the remarriage history of each spouse may affect the stability of the remarriage. Nor does he state that a joint consideration of the husbands' and wives' parent and custody status relevant to previous marriages leads to at least nine types of stepfamilies, and highlights the distinction between residential and nonresidential stepfamilies, or that a substantial number of children—as many as 300,000 children for women in second marriages alone—are born into stepfamilies (Wineberg, 1992). Given such diversity within stepfamily structures, the general and unqualified claim that stepfamilies are no better than single-parent families is unfounded.

Stepfamilies Are More Unstable than Intact Families

Popenoe claims that one problematic aspect of stepfamilies is their high breakup rate. However, a close reading of the limited data on this topic reveals that the findings on this issue are actually inconsistent. Most of the evidence concerns the stability of second marriages. Some of these studies report no difference in the marital stability of second marriers with and without children. Others report slightly higher instability rates for second marriers with children compared to those without children. Still others report that for second-marriers, a slightly increased instability rate occurs only for dissolutions occurring within the first 5 years of remarriage and that the birth of children to a mother in a second marriage increases the stability of that remarriage (Wineberg, 1992).

In short, because stepfamilies are a diverse group, it is misleading to characterize their stability as if they represented a homogeneous group. The current evidence gives every reason to expect that stability rates of remarriages vary by divorce history and parent history of each spouse; length of remarriage; age, gender, and pattern of residence for stepchildren; and whether mutual children are born to spouses in the stepfamily.

A Biosocial Perspective Leads to the Conclusion That Stepfamilies Are Intractably Problematic

Popenoe claims that in order to understand the special problems posed by stepfamilies, one must consider the biosocial nature of human family life. Based on an evolutionary biology perspective, Popenoe states that the organization of the human nuclear family is based on two inherited biological predispositions that confer reproductive success. The first predisposition operates between parents and children and entails advancing the interests of genetic relatives over those of unrelated individuals. The second predisposition operates between parents and concerns affective attachments between males and females. These seem like reasonable propositions.

Popenoe further notes that family instability can be linked to the fact that human beings are more interested in themselves than in their own relatives, results from men being more sexually driven and promiscuous than women, and that because human pair bonds are fragile, men and women follow different reproductive strategies: Men inseminate as many women as possible, whereas women withhold reproductive access until they can be certain that the male will commit his resources to his offspring.

I see two major problems with using these points to support the argument that childrearing by nonrelatives is inherently problematic. First, Popenoe ignores evidence that although the roles consistent with each gender's reproductive strategy do a reasonable job of accounting for differences between men and women in sexual attraction and mate selection, these same roles actually contribute to relationship problems and relationship instability. In what he termed the *fundamental paradox,* Ickes (1993) noted a tension between what genes predispose us to do in finding a mate and what current culture prescribes us to do in living happily with that mate. That is, although our evolutionary past may account for partner attraction, our cultural present accounts for how nonexploitative, equal partner relationships are established and maintained.

Second, Popenoe does not use the term *paternal investment* very clearly, but I assume he means that biological fathers in stable marriages are directly—and not just genetically—involved in childrearing. However, most of the normative descriptive data on this topic indicate that although fathers believe they should be directly involved in their children's lives, most are not (Thompson & Walker, 1989). . . .

Thus, the bystander role played by some stepfathers may be functionally similar to the indirect parenting role played by some biological fathers. . . .

Family Life in the 1950s Was Better than Contemporary Family Life

I agree with Popenoe that it is important to place family life within a larger sociocultural context. Further, no one could disagree that divorce rates began to accelerate in the 1960s. However, I strongly disagree with Popenoe's claim that the 1950s were an era of remarkable familism and family togetherness. Certainly, marital stability rates were high at this time in history. Nonetheless, there is ample evidence that stable marriages are not necessarily happy or healthy marriages. In addition, prospective longitudinal studies that have assessed the same group of children when they lived with both parents as well as when they lived with a divorced single parent indicate that the relatively adverse functioning of children who have experienced parental divorce is predicted by conditions in the intact family that existed well before the divorce. . . .

What irritates me most about the claim of familism in the 1950s is that it seems to value marital stability for stability's sake. Home, motherhood, and children did rank high among U.S. cultural values, yet current data on middle-aged persons who were children during this era strongly suggest that what transpired in many of these families belied these values. That is, the culture of the family was at odds with the conduct of the family. How can Popenoe extol the somewhat superficial endorsement of familism during this era in light of evidence that many children in these highly stable families were exposed to an interconnecting web of family conflict, domestic violence, harsh and inconsistent discipline, alcoholism, and, in some instances, abuse and neglect? Two biological parents were physically present in many of these families, but at what cost?

The Family Is Being Deinstitutionalized

Popenoe rightly notes that marriage as a social institution has evolved in form and function to adapt to new economic, social, cultural, and even psychological settings. But for some reason, Popenoe does not seem to think that the current nature of the institution of marriage reflects this continuous process of economic, social, cultural, and psychological change. One of the most peculiar aspects to Popenoe's chapter is that although he endorses a grand model of change (the biosocial, evolutionary perspective), he urges us as members of society to put an end to a family form that could be viewed as the result of the very economic, social, cultural, and psychological changes that preceded it.

. . . Like it or not, women are no longer economically dependent on their husbands. Like it or not, women no longer need to define themselves in terms of their social roles as wives and mothers. Like it or not, women benefit from participating in roles other than or in addition to that of mother. Like it or not, men and women are going to renege on vows of lifetime commitments to one person because life with that one person sometimes reaches intolerable limits that could not be foreseen at the time of marriage. Finally, like it or not, as a result of these economic, social, cultural, and psychological dimensions of contemporary life, many children will experience the stresses associated with parenting transitions.

References

Amato, P. R., & Keith, B. (1991). Parental divorce and the well-being of children: A meta-analysis. *Psychological Bulletin, 110,* 26–46.

Ickes, W. (1993). Traditional gender roles: Do they make, and then break, our relationships? *Journal of Social Issues, 49,* 71–85.

Kurdek, L. A. (1993a). *Determinants of relationship commitment: evidence from gay, lesbian, dating heterosexual, and married heterosexual couples.* Manuscript submitted for publication.

Kurdek, L. A. (1993b). Predicting marital dissolution from demographic, individual-differences, interdependence, and spouse discrepancy variables: A 5-year prospective longitudinal study of newlywed couples. *Journal of Personality and Social Psychology, 64,* 221–242.

Kurdek, L. A., & Fine, M. A. (1993). The relation between family structure and young adolescents' appraisals of family climate and parenting behavior. *Journal of Family Issues, 14,* 279–290.

Thompson, L., & Walker, A. J. (1989). Women and men in marriage, work, and parenthood. *Journal of Marriage and the Family, 51,* 845–872.

Wineberg, H. (1992). Childbearing and dissolution of the second marriage. *Journal of Marriage and the Family, 54,* 879–887.

POSTSCRIPT

Are Stepfamilies Inherently Problematic for Children?

Popenoe maintains that the intact, two-biological-parent family is the only type of family that is appropriate for children. He goes a step further by saying that stepfamilies are so harmful to children that they should be stopped.

Are stepfamilies inherently problematic for children? How do children in stepfamilies fare compared to families in which the mother lives with a number of boyfriends? This type of family form is not considered a stepfamily but could be very unstable for children. How do children from stepfamilies compare to children with two biological parents who are abusive to them? Is it better to be with stepparents who may not treat you warmly, as Popenoe argues, than to be with biological parents who beat you?

On the other hand, history is full of examples in which blood relatives were treated differently than relatives who came into the family through marriage or some other means. Inheriting land or a title as the first-born son or as the lineage associated with royalty has always depended upon being related by blood versus being adopted or being an in-law. Popenoe recognizes that having a son or daughter that is part of one's genetic material is a powerful concept. Whether or not this genetic tie interferes with parenting styles is debatable.

Suggested Readings

Amato, P. R. (1993). Children's adjustment to divorce: Theories, hypotheses, and empirical support. *Journal of Marriage and the Family, 55,* 23–38.

Cherlin, A. J., & Furstenberg, F. F. (1994). Stepfamilies in the United States: A reconsideration. *Annual Review of Sociology, 20,* 359–381.

Ganong, L. H., & Coleman, M. (1994). *Remarried family relationships.* Thousand Oaks: Sage Publications.

McLanahan, S., & Sandefur, G. (1994). *Growing up with a single parent: What hurts? What helps?* Cambridge, MA: Harvard University Press.

ISSUE 11

Is Television Viewing Responsible for the Rise in Childhood Obesity?

YES: The Henry J. Kaiser Family Foundation, from "The Role of Media in Childhood Obesity," *Issue Brief–The Henry J. Kaiser Foundation* (February 2004)

NO: Center for Science in the Public Interest, from "Dispensing Junk: How School Vending Undermines Efforts to Feed Children Well," *Report from Center for Science in the Public Interest* (May 2004)

ISSUE SUMMARY

YES: The Henry J. Kaiser Family Foundation, a private nonprofit foundation focusing on major health care issues facing the nation, cites research studies that show that the more children watch television, the more likely they will be overweight. They also contend that the rise in childhood obesity can be traced to the increased use of media.

NO: The Center for Science in the Public Interest, a consumer advocacy organization on nutrition and health, views the high-calorie, non-nutritious foods found in school vending machines as the culprit in the rise in childhood obesity rates.

The rise in childhood obesity is considered an epidemic because the rates of childhood overweight have grown so rapidly in such a short amount of time. According to the Centers for Disease Control and Prevention, National Center for Health Statistics, since 1980 the proportion of overweight children has more than doubled. The rate for teens has tripled since 1980. Currently, 10 percent of 2- to 5-year-olds are overweight, and 15 percent of 6- to 19-year-olds are overweight. The numbers go up to 20 percent for 2- to 5-year-old children, and 30 percent for 6- to 19-year-old children when you add in those at risk for being overweight. Children of color are at greater risk with four out of 10 Mexican-American and African-American children being overweight.

Childhood obesity is the term used to describe the problem in the population while individual children are generally referred to as being overweight. Children would not be referred to as obese, but would be classified as overweight. Overweight and at risk for being overweight are terms used to define children whose height and weight fall within a certain range on a chart referred to as the BMI (body mass index). The BMI measures the ratio of weight to height. BMI measures for children are age- and gender-specific because children's body fat varies with age and gender. A child's BMI is plotted on a growth curve that reflects that child's age and gender. This plotting yields a value, BMI for age, that provides a consistent measure across age groups. Percentile scores indicate how a particular child compares with other children of the same age and gender. The Centers for Disease Control classifies children above the 95th percentile for their age and gender as overweight. Children are considered at risk for being overweight if they fall between the 85th and 95th percentile for age and gender. Healthy children have a BMI of 6 to 85 percent, and underweight children have a BMI of less than 5 percent.

Why is the rise in childhood obesity considered such a problem? Along with being overweight comes a host of physical and mental health problems such as diabetes, high blood pressure, depression, and poor body image. The health care costs for these medical conditions are exorbitant, not to mention the reduced quality of life for the children. The probability that overweight children will become overweight adults is 50 percent; thus, these health care issues may follow the child into adulthood. The subsequent reduced productivity levels of adults, whose overweight condition follows them into adulthood, have economic and social implications. Instead of contributing to society and the economy, individuals may be relying on these institutions to take care of them.

What are the reasons that we are seeing such a rise in childhood overweight? In the following selections, personnel from The Henry J. Kaiser Family Foundation propose that the rise in childhood obesity is due to the influence of the media, specifically the huge numbers of hours of television that children watch. Personnel from the Center for Science in the Public Interest assert that the high-calorie, low-nutrient food found in school vending machines encourages children to develop poor eating habits and leads to their being overweight.

YES

The Role of Media in Childhood Obesity

Introduction

In recent years, health officials have become increasingly alarmed by the rapid increase in obesity among American children. According to the Centers for Disease Control and Prevention (CDC), since 1980 the proportion of overweight children ages 6–11 has more than doubled, and the rate for adolescents has tripled. Today about 10% of 2- to 5-year-olds and 15% of 6- to 19-year-olds are overweight. Taking into consideration the proportion who are "at risk" of being overweight, the current percentages double to 20% for children ages 2–5 and 30% for kids ages 6–19. Among children of color, the rates are even higher: 4 in 10 Mexican American and African American youth ages 6–19 are considered overweight or at risk of being overweight.

According to the American Academy of Pediatrics, the increase in childhood obesity represents an "unprecedented burden" on children's health. Medical complications common in overweight children include hypertension, type 2 diabetes, respiratory ailments, orthopedic problems, trouble sleeping, and depression. The Surgeon General has predicted that preventable morbidity and mortality associated with obesity may exceed those associated with cigarette smoking. Given that an estimated 80% of overweight adolescents continue to be obese in adulthood, the implications of childhood obesity on the nation's health—and on health care costs—are huge. Indeed, the American Academy of Pediatrics has called the potential costs associated with childhood obesity "staggering."

In an effort to seek the causes of this disturbing trend, experts have pointed to a range of important potential contributors to the rise in childhood obesity that are unrelated to media: a reduction in physical education classes and after-school athletic programs, an increase in the availability of sodas and snacks in public schools, the growth in the number of fast-food outlets across the country, the trend toward "super-sizing" food portions in restaurants, and the increasing number of highly processed high-calorie and high-fat grocery products.

The purpose of this issue brief is to explore one other potential contributor to the rising rates of childhood obesity: children's use of media.

From *Issue Brief*, February 2004. Copyright © 2004 by The Henry J. Kaiser Family Foundation. This information was reprinted with permission from The Henry J. Kaiser Family Foundation. The Kaiser Family Foundation, based in Menlo Prk, California, is a nonprofit, independent national health care philanthropy and is not associated with Kaiser Permanente or Kaiser Industries. References omitted.

During the same period in which childhood obesity has increased so dramatically, there has also been an explosion in media targeted to children: TV shows and videos, specialized cable networks, video games, computer activities and Internet Web sites. Children today spend an average of five-and-a-half hours a day using media, the equivalent of a full time job, and more time than they spend doing anything else besides sleeping. Even the very youngest children, preschoolers ages six and under, spend as much time with screen media (TV, videos, video games and computers) as they do playing outside. Much of the media targeted to children is laden with elaborate advertising campaigns, many of which promote foods such as candy, soda, and snacks. Indeed, it is estimated that the typical child sees about 40,000 ads a year on TV alone.

For the first time, this report pulls together the best available research, going behind the headlines to explore the realities of what researchers do and do not know about the role media plays in childhood obesity. In addition, the report lays out media-related policy options that have been proposed to help address childhood obesity, and outlines ways media could play a positive role in helping to address this important public health problem.

Pediatricians, child development experts, and media researchers have theorized that media may contribute to childhood obesity in one or more of the following ways:

- The time children spend using media displaces time they could spend in physical activities;
- The food advertisements children are exposed to on TV influence them to make unhealthy food choices;
- The cross-promotions between food products and popular TV and movie characters are encouraging children to buy and eat more high-calorie foods;
- Children snack excessively while using media, and they eat less healthy meals when eating in front of the TV;
- Watching TV and videos lowers children's metabolic rates below what they would be even if they were sleeping;
- Depictions of nutrition and body weight in entertainment media encourage children to develop less healthy diets.

The research to date has examined these issues from a variety of perspectives ranging from health sciences and public health, to child development and family relations, to advertising and mass communications. These investigations have been methodologically diverse, and the results have often been mixed. As with any research, caution must be used when comparing the outcomes of studies because of variations in the methods and measures used. For example, some studies are regional, while others use large, nationally representative samples. Some focus on specific demographic subsets, such as 6th-grade girls, while others are broader. Some studies rely on detailed data sets, others on fairly simplistic measures. For example, television use may be measured through self-reports, parental reports, or detailed diaries. Likewise, body fat may be assessed through multiple clinical measures or by self-reports of height and weight.

DEFINING CHILDHOOD OBESITY

The phrases "obese," "overweight," and "at risk for being overweight" are commonly used in the public health community. With regard to children, the terms "obese" and "overweight" are generally used interchangeably in the medical literature. The Body Mass Index (BMI), which measures the ratio of weight to height, is a standard tool used to define these terms. BMI definitions for children and adolescents are age- and gender-specific in order to accommodate growth patterns. The Centers for Disease Control and Prevention (CDC) classify children as "overweight" if they are above the 95th percentile for their age and sex, and "at risk of being overweight" if they are between the 85th and 95th percentile.

The following section of this report reviews the major research that has been conducted on the key issues concerning media and childhood obesity, and summarizes the major findings.

Research on Media and Childhood Obesity

Do major studies find a relationship between childhood obesity and the time children spend using media?   The first major evidence that children's media consumption may be related to their body weight came in a 1985 article by William Dietz and Stephen Gortmaker in the journal *Pediatrics*, and it was dramatic. An analysis of data from a large national study of more than 13,000 children, the National Health Examination Survey (NHES), found significant associations between the amount of time children spent watching television and the prevalence of obesity. The authors concluded that, among 12- to 17-year-olds, the prevalence of obesity increased by 2% for each additional hour of television viewed, even after controlling for other variables such as prior obesity, race, and socio-economic status. Indeed, according to the authors, "only prior obesity had a larger independent effect than television on the prevalence of obesity." In a commentary published in 1993, the authors went on to note that another interpretation of their findings is that "29% of the cases of obesity could be prevented by reducing television viewing to 0 to 1 hours per week."

Since then, several more studies have found a statistically significant relationship between media use and rates of obesity, while others have found either a weak relationship or no relationship at all. In addition to the Dietz and Gortmaker study, other large-scale national studies have found a correlation between media use and body weight:

- Analysis of data from a nationally representative survey of more than 700 kids ages 10–15, conducted in the late 1980s, concluded that "the odds of being overweight were 4.6 times greater for youth watching more than 5 hours of television per day compared with those watching for 0–1 hours," even when controlling for prior overweight, maternal overweight, race, and socio-economic status. The authors concluded, "Estimates of attributable risk indicate that more [than] 60% of overweight incidence in this population can be linked to excess television viewing time."

- Data from the 1988–1994 waves of the National Health and Nutrition Examination Surveys (NHANES) were analyzed to explore the relationship between TV watching and obesity among 8- to 16-year-olds. The study concluded that "television watching was positively associated with obesity among girls, even after controlling for age, race/ethnicity, family income, weekly physical activity, and energy intake." The study did not find a correlation for boys.

- Another analysis of the 1988–1994 NHANES data found that among 8- to 16-year-olds, both boys and girls "who watched the most television had more body fat and greater BMIs than those who watched less than 2 hours a day."

- A study based on the CDC's 1999 Youth Risk Behavior Survey which sampled more than 12,000 high school students nationwide, found that watching television more than 2 hours a day was related to being overweight; these findings were consistent for the entire student population, controlling for race, ethnicity, and gender.

- A later study found a link between television viewing and obesity using a different methodology. The Framingham Children's Study was a longitudinal study in which slightly more than 100 children were enrolled as preschoolers and followed into early adolescence. In this study, published in 2003, the authors found that "television watching was an independent predictor of the change in the child's BMI" and other measures of body fatness. They noted that the effect of TV viewing was "only slightly attenuated" by controlling for factors such as the child's body-fat measures at the time they were enrolled in the study, and their parents' BMI or education. The authors concluded that "television watching is a risk factor for change in body fat, not simply reflective of more obese children tending to watch more television as a consequence of their obesity making it difficult to exercise."

Other studies—one from a nationally representative cross-sectional sample and the others from specific regions or communities—have not found a relationship between television viewing and childhood obesity:

- A recent analysis of data from a national study of more than 2,800 children ages 12 and under, which relied on detailed time-use diaries, found a "striking" lack of relationship between time spent watching television and children's weight status. On the other hand, this study did find a relationship between obesity and time spent playing video games, although that relationship was not linear: Children with higher weight played moderate amounts of games, while those with low weight played electronic games either very little or a lot.

- A 1993 study of 6th- and 7th-grade girls in Northern California found that over a two-year period "baseline hours of after-school television viewing was not significantly associated with either baseline or longitudinal change in BMI." The authors argued that their study "refutes previous suggestions that . . . television viewing is causally related to obesity."

- A study of nearly 200 preschoolers in Texas observed the children for several hours on each of four different days a year, over the course of three years, recording the amount of TV the children watched and their physical activities. This study found that although television watching was weakly negatively correlated with physical activity levels, it was not associated with body composition.

In evaluating this research, it is important to note that some of these studies are cross-sectional rather than longitudinal—that is, they take a specific point in time and look at whether TV viewing is associated with obesity. One problem with this approach is that while a study may indicate a relationship between TV viewing and being overweight, it does not prove that the TV viewing *caused* the increased weight. Controlling for other risk factors such as socio-economic status and parental body weight (as many studies do) can help clarify the results. Another problem with the cross-sectional approach is that the causal relationship could run in the opposite direction: that is, being obese may cause children to engage in more sedentary (and isolated) activities, including watching more television.

Longitudinal studies can help address the causality issue; however, the results of these studies have varied. As noted above, the two-year longitudinal study of adolescent girls in Northern California did not find a causal relationship between children's weight and the time they spent with media. On the other hand, the Framingham Children's Study, which tracked preschoolers through early adolescence, did find such a relationship. The authors of the latter study have theorized that the effects of media use on body weight may emerge slowly over time, and hence were not revealed in the two-year study in Northern California. It has also been argued that the lack of effect in that study may be due to factors specific to the sample of 6th- and 7th-grade girls in Northern California. Additionally, the study of 700 10- to 15-year-olds referenced above used height and weight data from 1986 and compared it to TV viewing and BMI measures in 1990. These authors concluded that "no evidence was found for a selective effect of overweight; i.e., children who were overweight in 1986 were unlikely to watch more television in 1990 than were children who were not overweight."

Others argue that the only way to truly demonstrate a causal relationship is through an experimental trial; for example, reduce TV viewing and see whether that affects children's weight when compared to a control group. Several interventions of this nature have been found to have a positive impact in reducing children's body weight.

Do experimental interventions that reduce children's media time result in weight loss? Experimental trials are considered the best way of determining whether there is a causal relationship between television viewing and childhood obesity. Some experiments have incorporated reductions in media time as part of a more comprehensive program involving diet and increased physical activity as well. Another experiment used reduced media time as the only intervention, yet still found an impact on children's weight and body fatness.

- During the 1996–97 school year, Stanford University researchers conducted a randomized controlled trial in which they reduced the amount of time a group of about 100 3rd- and 4th-graders in Northern California spent with TV, videos, and video games. Two matched elementary schools were selected to participate, one of which served as the control group. The intervention involved a "turnoff" period of no screen time for 10 days followed by limiting TV time to 7 hours per week, as well as learning media literacy skills to teach selective viewing. At the end of a 6-month, 18-lesson classroom curriculum, students who received the intervention achieved statistically significant reductions in their television viewing and meals eaten in front of the TV set, as well as decreases in BMI, triceps skinfold thickness, waist circumference, and waist-to-hip ratio. While these changes were not accompanied by reduced high-fat food intake or increased physical activity, the findings do appear to demonstrate the feasibility of decreasing body weight by reducing time spent with screen media.
- Another school based intervention found improved diet, increased physical activity, and decreased television time to be effective. The study, which measured prevalence, incidence, and remission of obesity among ethnically diverse middle-school boys and girls, involved a randomized controlled field trial with five intervention and five control schools. Classroom teachers in math, science, language arts, social studies, and physical education incorporated lessons within the existing curricula over two years. The lessons focused on decreasing television viewing to 2 hours per day, increasing physical activity, reducing consumption of high-fat food, and increasing servings of fruits and vegetables. For each hour television viewing was reduced, the prevalence of obesity was reduced among girls in the intervention schools compared with the control schools; no similar effect was found for boys. The program also resulted in an increase in girls' consumption of fruits and vegetables.
- A family-based weight-control program found that decreasing sedentary behaviors (such as screen media use) is a viable alternative to increasing physical activity in treating childhood obesity. Families with obese children ages 8–12 were randomly assigned to one of four groups that included dietary and behavior-change information, but differed in whether they tried to decrease sedentary activities or increase physical activity. Results indicated that significant decreases in percent of overweight and body fat were associated with decreasing sedentary behaviors such as watching TV or videos, or playing video or computer games.

These interventions indicate that reducing the time children spend with media may indeed be an effective way to address childhood obesity. Researchers, health professionals, and advocates have theorized several ways media may contribute to childhood obesity. The following sections summarize some of the major scientific studies in order to provide an understanding of media's potential influence on the incidence of overweight among children and adolescents in the United States.

Does the time children spend using media displace time spent in more physical activities? From toddlers to teens, American youth are spending a substantial part of every day of their lives using media. But the time children spend using media does not necessarily mean a decrease in time spent in physical activities. Surprisingly, few studies have examined this relationship, and results have been mixed. Some studies have found a weak but statistically significant relationship between hours of television viewing and levels of physical activity, while others have found no relationship between the two.

- A study of 6th- and 7th-grade adolescent girls in four Northern California middle schools found that the number of hours they spent watching TV after school was negatively associated with their level of physical activity; however, the relationship accounted for less than 1% of the variance and there was no connection with body weight.
- A study of a small sample of preschool children in Texas, conducted in a naturalistic setting, found a weak but statistically significant relationship between TV viewing and physical activity, although it did not find a relationship between viewing and body weight.
- A recent national telephone survey of parents of children ages 4–6 found that children who spent more than two hours watching TV the previous day spent an average of a half-hour less playing outside that day than did other children their age.
- A review of data from the 1999 National Youth Risk Behavior Study, which includes a nationally representative sample of more than 15,000 high school students, found that among white female students only, time spent watching TV was associated with being sedentary.
- A survey of close to 2,000 9th-graders in Northern California found a weak but statistically significant relationship between TV viewing and physical activity for white males only.
- A study of national data from the 1988–1994 NHANES found no relationship between TV viewing and the number of bouts of vigorous physical activity, although it did find a statistically significant relationship between TV viewing and body weight.

While logic suggests that extensive television viewing is part of a more sedentary lifestyle, the evidence for this relationship has been surprisingly weak to date. In order for this relationship to be true, as one study noted, children who watch less TV would have to be choosing physically vigorous activities instead of TV, rather than some other relatively sedentary pastime such as reading books, talking on the phone, or playing board games.

Another possibility is that the act of watching TV itself actually reduces children's metabolic rate, contributing to weight gain. One study of 8- to 12-year-olds found that TV viewing decreased metabolic rates even more than resting or sleeping, but several other studies found no such effect.

The fact that most studies have failed to find a substantial relationship between the time children spend watching TV and the time they spend in physical activity may suggest that the *nature* of television viewing—that is, how children watch and what they watch—may be as or more important than the number of hours they watch.

Do the food ads children are exposed to on TV influence them to make unhealthy food choices? Many researchers suspect that the food advertising children are exposed to through the media may contribute to unhealthy food choices and weight gain. Over the same period in which childhood obesity has increased so dramatically, research indicates that the number of ads children view has increased as well. In the late 1970s, researchers estimated that children viewed an average of about 20,000 TV commercials a year; in the late 80s, that estimate grew to more than 30,000 a year. As the number of cable channels exploded in the 1990s, opportunities to advertise directly to children expanded as well. The most recent estimates are that children now see an average of more than 40,000 TV ads a year.

The majority of ads targeted to children are for food: primarily candy (32% of all children's ads), cereal (31%), and fast food (9%). One study documented approximately 11 food commercials per hour during children's Saturday morning television programming, estimating that the average child viewer may be exposed to one food commercial every 5 minutes. According to another study, even the two minutes of daily advertising targeted to students in their classrooms through Channel One expose them to fast foods, candy, soft drinks, and snack chips in 7 out of 10 commercial breaks.

A review of the foods targeted to children in commercials on Saturday morning television indicates that the nutritional value has remained consistently low over the past quarter-century. Over the years, the most prevalent foods advertised have been breakfast cereals. Up until the 1990s, the next most-advertised products were foods high in sugar, such as cookies, candy, and other snacks. By the mid-1990s, canned desserts, frozen dinners, and fast foods overtook ads for snack foods. The data indicate that ads for these high-fat and high-sodium convenience foods have more than doubled since the 1980s. While studies vary as to the exact percentages, the same pattern emerges: a predominance of ads for high-sugar cereals, fast food restaurants, and candy, and an absence of ads for fruit or vegetables.

The effect of food advertising on children The vast majority of the studies about children's consumer behavior have been conducted by marketing research firms and have not been made publicly available. Clearly, the conclusion advertisers have drawn is that TV ads can influence children's purchases—and those of their families. Fast food outlets alone spend $3 billion in television ads targeted to children. Recent years have seen the development of marketing firms, newsletters, and ad agencies specializing in the children's market. The New York Times has noted that "the courtship of children is no surprise, since increasingly that is where the money is," and added that marketing executives anticipate that children under 12 will spend $35 billion of their own money and influence $200 billion in household spending in 2004. The enthusiasm of marketers can be felt in the Februray 2004 edition of Harris Interactive's "Trends and Tudes" newsletter, which notes that "This generation has become a huge consumer group that is worthy of attention from many businesses seeking to maximize their potential. Kids, teens and young adults spend significant amounts of their own money, and they influence the shopping behavior of their parents, their siblings, their relatives, and other adults in their lives."

Scientific studies that are available in the public realm back up these marketing industry assessments of the effectiveness of advertising directed at children. Studies have demonstrated that from a very young age, children influence their parents' consumer behavior. As many parents can attest after a trip down the grocery aisle with their children, television viewing has also been found to impact children's attempts to influence their parents' purchases at the supermarket. For example, several studies have found that the amount of time children had spent watching TV was a significant predictor of how often they requested products at the grocery store, and that as many as three out of four requests were for products seen in TV ads. These studies have also found that children's supermarket requests do indeed have a fairly high rate of success.

One study found that among children as young as 3, the amount of weekly television viewing was significantly related to their caloric intake as well as their requests and parent purchases of specific foods they saw advertised on television. Another study manipulated advertising shown to 5- to 8-year-olds at summer camp, with some viewing ads for fruit and juice, and others ads for candy and Kool-Aid. This study found that children's food choices were significantly impacted by which ads they saw.

Experimental studies have demonstrated that even a brief exposure to food commercials can influence children's preferences. In one study, researchers designed a randomized controlled trial in which one group of 2- to 6-year-olds from a Head Start program saw a popular children's cartoon with embedded commercials, and the other group saw the same cartoon without commercials. Asked to identify their preferences from pairs of similar products, children who saw the commercials were significantly more likely to choose the advertised products. Preference differences between the treatment and control group were greatest for products that were advertised twice during the cartoon rather than only once.

Researchers are beginning to document a link between viewing television and children's consumption of fast foods and soda, a possible result of exposure to food advertising. A recent study found that students in grades 7–12 who frequently ate fast food tended to watch more television than other students. Another study found that middle-school children who watched more television tended to consume more soft drinks.

Other evidence of television's potential impact on children's dietary habits indicates a negative relationship between viewing television and consuming fruits and vegetables. The USDA's Dietary Guidelines recommend that youth eat three to five daily servings of fruits and vegetables, yet only 1 in 5 children meet the guideline, and one-quarter of the vegetables consumed reportedly are french fries. In a recent study, more than 500 middle school students from ethnically diverse backgrounds were studied over a 19-month period to determine whether daily television and video viewing predicted fruit and vegetable consumption. Using a linear regression analysis, researchers found that for each additional hour of television viewed per day, daily servings of fruits and vegetables decreased among adolescents. The researchers who conducted the study conclude that this relationship may be a result of television advertising.

Some researchers believe that TV ads may also contribute to children's misconceptions about the relative health benefits of certain foods. One of the earlier studies found that 70% of 6- to 8-year-olds believed that fast foods were more nutritious than home-cooked foods. Another study showed a group of 4th- and 5th-graders a series of paired food items and asked them to choose the healthier item from each pair (for example, corn flakes or frosted flakes). Children who watched more television were more likely to indicate that the less healthy food choice was the healthier one. These results replicated the results of an earlier study conducted with children of the same age.

Do cross-promotions between food products and popular TV and movie characters encourage children to buy and eat more high-calorie foods? Recent years have seen what appears to be a tremendous increase in the number of food products being marketed to children through cross-promotions with popular TV and movie characters. From SpongeBob Cheez-Its to Hulk pizzas and Scooby-Doo marshmallow cereals, today's grocery aisles are filled with scores of products using kids' favorite characters to sell them food. Fast food outlets also make frequent use of cross-promotions with children's media characters.

A recent article in the New York Times business section noted that "aiming at children through licensing is hardly new. What has changed is the scope and intensity of the blitz as today's youth become unwitting marketing targets at ever younger ages through more exposure to television, movies, videos and the Internet." One food industry executive was quoted as saying that licensing "is a way to . . . infuse the emotion and popularity of a current kids' hit into a product."

Some promotions involve toys based on media characters that are included in the food packages or offered in conjunction with fast food meals. McDonald's and Disney have an exclusive agreement under which Happy Meals include toys from top Disney movies. In the past, Happy Meals have reportedly also included toys based on the Teletubbies TV series, which is aimed at pre-verbal babies. Burger King has also featured Teletubbies tie-ins, along with Rugrats, Shrek, Pokemon and SpongeBob. More than a decade ago, researchers were finding that the typical "kid's meal" advertised to children consisted of a cheeseburger, french fries, soda, and a toy. One study found that about 1 in 6 (16.9%) food commercials aimed at children promise a free toy. In addition to the use of toys as an incentive in marketing food to children, many commercials use cartoon characters to sell products, which research has shown to be particularly effective in aiding children's slogan recall and ability to identify the product.

A recent example of the effectiveness of this technique is the growth in the dried fruit snack market. Almost half (45%) of fruit snacks had licensing agreements in 2003 compared to 10% in 1996. Sales have increased substantially every year since 1999: 5.6% in 2000, 8.7% in 2001, 3.2% in 2002, and

5.5% in 2003. Marketing experts attribute the sales growth to children's influence on their parents' purchasing decisions and parental beliefs that dried fruit snacks are healthier than other sweets.

Do depictions of nutrition and body type in entertainment media encourage children to develop less healthy diets and eating habits?   Over the years, some critics have argued that TV, movies, and magazines have promoted unrealistically thin body types as the ideal, possibly encouraging teen girls to engage in unhealthy dieting or eating disorders. But after years of an imbalance toward depictions of thin characters, the true weight-related health emergency among young people is, paradoxically, obesity. This paradox has yet to be explained.

Some advocates note that television gives children and teens contradictory messages about dietary habits and ideal body type: be thin but eat fatty foods, sugary sweets, and salty snacks. They point out that on the one hand, the stories media tell are about thin people who are popular and successful, while on the other hand, thin and average-size people on TV can eat whatever they want and almost never gain weight.

Some advocates and researchers also have criticized TV producers for not including more depictions of obese characters, and for negatively portraying the obese characters that do make it onto the screen. On the other hand, it could be argued that portraying obesity as an unhealthy and undesirable characteristic—and associating it with overeating—sends an *appropriate* message to youth. And while some critics fault the media for leaving obese characters off the screen, adding to stigmatization and isolation, other critics complain that too many minority characters are overweight.

Center for Science in the Public Interest

Dispensing Junk: How School Vending Undermines Efforts to Feed Children Well

Executive Summary

In September and October 2003, 120 volunteers in 24 states (including the District of Columbia) surveyed the contents of 1,420 vending machines in 251 schools, including 105 middle and junior high schools, 121 high schools, and 25 schools with other combinations of these grade levels (e.g., 7th–12th grades).

The results suggest that the overwhelming majority of options available to children in school vending machines are high in calories and/or low in nutrition. **In both middle and high schools, 75% of beverage options and 85% of snacks were of poor nutritional quality.** The most prevalent options are soda, imitation fruit juices, candy, chips, cookies, and snack cakes. The high prevalence of junk food in school vending machines does not support students' ability to make healthy food choices or parents' ability to feed their children well.

This is of concern because 1) 74% of middle/junior high schools and 98% of senior high schools have vending machines, school stores, or snack bars, 2) children are in school for a substantial portion of the week, and 3) obesity rates are rising rapidly in children and teens.

Given the rising obesity rates and children's poor eating habits, the time has come to ensure that school environments support healthy eating and parents' efforts to feed their children well. A number of policies and programs should be put in place or strengthened to address childhood obesity. **One important strategy is for federal, state, and/or local governments, schools, and school districts to enact policies to ensure that foods sold out of vending machines, school stores, fundraisers, a la carte, and other venues outside of the school meal programs are healthful and make a positive contribution to children's diets.**

At the federal level, Congress should give the U.S Department of Agriculture (USDA) authority to establish and enforce regulations for all food sales anywhere on school campuses throughout the school day as a condition for participating in the National School Lunch Program or School Breakfast Program. USDA has strong nutrition policies for school meals. It also should set nutrition standards for foods and beverages sold outside those meals.

States, cities, school districts, and schools also could implement strong nutrition standards for foods and beverages sold out of vending machines, school stores, a la carte (snack lines), fundraisers, and other venues outside of the school meal programs. We recognize that school budgets are tight and that the sale of foods in schools provides much-needed revenue. However, a number of schools around the country have replaced soda in school vending machines with healthier beverages and have not lost money.

Introduction

Vending machines are prevalent in schools, yet quantitative data regarding their contents are lacking. Such data would be important to have because most children eat diets of poor nutritional quality, with too much saturated fat, sodium, and refined sugars and too few nutrient-rich fruits, vegetables, and whole grains. Those nutrient imbalances can lead to heart disease, high blood pressure, cancer, dental cavities, and other health problems. In addition, children's calorie intake has increased (and they are insufficiently active) and, as a result, rates of overweight in children have increased. While obesity is a complex, multi-factorial problem, over-consumption of soft drinks and snack foods plays a key role.

Junk food in school vending machines undermines parents' efforts to feed their children well. (This is especially problematic when children have diet-related health problems, such as high cholesterol or diabetes.) When parents send their child to school with lunch money, they do not know whether the child will buy a balanced school lunch or a candy bar and a soda. Long cafeteria lines, short lunch periods, and activities during the lunch period mean that some students rely on foods from vending machines rather than buy lunch from the cafeteria line.

The food industry is taking advantage of schools' financial problems by offering them incentives to sell low-nutrition foods in schools. But bridging school budget gaps by selling junk food to students is a shortsighted approach. In the long run, society is sure to spend more money treating the resulting obesity and diet-related diseases, such as diabetes, heart disease, cancer, and osteoporosis, than schools can raise by selling soda and snack foods to students.

There are ways schools can raise money without jeopardizing children's health. A number of schools in Maine, California, Minnesota, Pennsylvania, and elsewhere have replaced soda with healthy beverages and not lost revenue. In addition to selling healthy foods, schools can sell gift wrap or candles, sponsor fun runs, host car washes, or conduct other profitable fundraisers that do not undermine children's health.

Methods

In late September and early October 2003, 120 individuals in 24 states (including Arkansas, California, Connecticut, the District of Columbia, Illinois, Iowa, Maine, Maryland, Michigan, Mississippi, Missouri, Montana, New Mexico, New York, North Carolina, North Dakota, Ohio, Oregon, Pennsylvania, South

Carolina, South Dakota, Vermont, Washington, and Wisconsin) surveyed the contents of vending machines in their local middle and high schools. The individuals collecting the data were primarily health professionals, employees of health organizations, and school employees. Volunteers surveyed a total of 1,420 vending machines in 251 schools, including 105 middle and junior high schools, 121 high schools, and 25 schools with other combinations of these grade levels.

School sites included both urban and rural schools, schools in a range of socioeconomic areas, and schools ranging in size from 110 to 2,600 students. Vending machines in areas accessible only to teachers and staff were not included.

The average number of vending machines per high school was eight. Some high schools had only one vending machine, while others had as many as 22 vending machines. The average number of vending machines per middle or junior high school was four. Some middle and junior high schools had only one vending machine, while others had up to 10 vending machines.

Vending machines were assessed by counting the number of slots per machine for each beverage or snack category and totaling the number of slots in all machines. Study participants were given a standardized survey form . . . and protocol. Participants had the opportunity to participate in a pre-survey conference call to discuss the protocol and methods for the survey. Participants sent their completed surveys to the Center for Science in the Public Interest (CSPI) for data aggregation and analysis.

The categorization of foods and beverages as "healthier" and "less healthful" was based on and generally in accordance with the nutrition standards for school foods developed by a national panel of experts convened by the California Center for Public Health Advocacy. The following types of beverages were categorized as "healthier" options: water, fruit juice containing at least 50% real juice, low-fat (1%) or fat-free milk (regular or flavored), and diet drinks. The following types of beverages were categorized as "less healthful" options: soda pop (regular), fruit drinks containing less than 50% real juice, whole or 2% milk, sports drinks, iced tea, and lemonade. Only 1% of the options in beverage vending machines ended up being categorized into the "other" category.

The following types of snacks were categorized as "healthier" options (which includes healthy foods and nutritionally-improved versions of unhealthy vending snacks): low-fat chips, pretzels, crackers, Chex Mix, fruits, vegetables, granola bars, cereal bars, nuts, trail mix, low-fat cookies, and other low-fat baked goods. While some of the options are not the healthiest products—high in sodium or made with refined flour—they are considered healthier alternatives to common vending options. The following types of snacks were categorized as being of "poor nutritional quality": regular chips, crackers with cheese, candy, cookies, snack cakes, and pastries. Foods that did not fit into these categories were categorized as "other." Just 2% of the options in snack vending machines ended up being categorized into the "other" category.

Table 1

Beverages Available in Middle and High School Vending Machines

Beverage Type	Middle Schools Percent of Total (Number of Slots)	High Schools Percent of Total (Number of Slots)	Middle Schools, High Schools, & Other Secondary Schools Combined Percent of Total (Number of Slots)
Soda (regular)	28 (1110)	39 (3489)	36 (4860)
Fruit drinks (less than 50% real juice)	17 (664)	12 (1079)	13 (1801)
Sports drinks	17 (671)	11 (994)	13 (1826)
Iced tea, lemonade, or other sweetened drink	9 (362)	8 (752)	9 (1167)
Whole or 2% milk (including flavored)	1 (46)	3 (268)	3 (367)
Water	13 (515)	11 (1001)	12 (1611)
Fruit juices (at least 50% real juice)	8 (295)	6 (563)	7 (896)
Diet soda	4 (149)	6 (555)	6 (769)
Low-fat/1% or fat-free milk (including flavored)	1 (47)	2 (177)	2 (276)
Other drinks	2 (64)	< 0.5 (13)	1 (77)
TOTAL	100 (3,923)	98 (8,891)	102 (13,650)

Results

The vending machine options in middle and high schools were markedly similar. In middle-school vending machines, 73% of beverage options and 83% of snack options were of poor nutritional quality. In high-school vending machines, 74% of beverage options and 85% of snack options were nutritionally-poor options.

The types of beverages available in middle and high school vending machines are listed in Table 1. **Seventy percent of those beverages were sugary drinks such as soda pop, juice drinks, iced tea, and sports drinks.** Of the sodas available in vending machines for both high schools and middle schools, 86% of soda slots were regular sugary sodas and 14% were diet. 12% of the beverages available were water. Of the "juices" offered, two-thirds (67%) were juice drinks that contained less than 50% juice. Only 5% of beverage options were milk. The majority (57%) of milks offered in school vending machines were the fattier types (either whole or 2%), with 43% of the milk either low-fat (1%) or fat-free.

The types of snacks available in middle and high school vending machines are listed in Table 2. The snack items most commonly available were: candy (42%), chips (25%), and sweet baked goods (13%), which together accounted for 80% of snacks available in school vending machines.

Children need fruits and vegetables to provide key nutrients and reduce future risk of heart disease and cancer. Yet of 9,723 total snack slots, only 26 slots

Table 2

Snacks Available in Middle and High School Vending Machines

Snack Type	Middle Schools Percent of Total (Number of Slots)	High Schools Percent of Total (Number of Slots)	Middle Schools, High Schools, & Other Secondary Schools Combined Percent of Total (Number of Slots)
Candy	38 (882)	43 (3028)	42 (4062)
Chips (regular)	24 (555)	25 (1787)	25 (2391)
Cookies, snack cakes, and pastries	14 (310)	13 (928)	13 (1270)
Crackers with cheese or peanut butter	7 (154)	4 (306)	5 (484)
Chips (low-fat) or pretzels	7 (152)	5 (332)	5 (489)
Crackers or Chex Mix	2 (52)	3 (235)	3 (303)
Granola/cereal bars	2 (56)	1 (103)	2 (171)
Low-fat cookies and baked goods	2 (44)	1 (106)	2 (155)
Nuts/trail mix	2 (41)	1 (89)	1 (141)
Fruit or vegetable	< 0.5 (8)	< 0.5 (18)	< 0.5 (26)
Other snacks	2 (39)	3 (178)	2 (231)
TOTAL	100 (2,293)	100 (7,110)	100 (9,723)

contained a fruit or vegetable. Only 7% of the beverage options were fruit juice (i.e., contained greater than 50% real juice). This finding highlights the potential value of increasing the number of refrigerated snack vending machines in schools to provide more fruits and vegetables to children.

Rationale for Improving School Foods

I. Schools Should Practice What They Teach

This study found that most choices available in school vending machines are of poor nutritional quality. Current school vending practices are not supportive of healthy eating.

Schools should practice what they teach. Selling low-nutrition foods in schools contradicts nutrition education and sends children the message that good nutrition is not important. The school environment should reinforce nutrition education in the classroom to support and model healthy behaviors.

II. The Sale of Low-Nutrition Foods in Schools Undermines Parents' Ability to Feed Their Children Well

Parents entrust schools with the care of their children during the school day. The sale of low-nutrition foods in schools makes it difficult for parents to ensure that their children are eating well. This is especially problematic when children have diet-related conditions, such as diabetes, high cholesterol, or overweight.

Without their parents' knowledge, some children spend their lunch money on the low-nutrition foods from vending machines rather than on balanced school meals. Long cafeteria lines, short lunch periods, or activities during the lunch period lead some students to purchase foods from a vending machine rather than a lunch from the cafeteria line.

III. Children's Eating Habits and Health

Obesity rates have doubled in children and tripled in adolescents over the last two decades. As a result, diabetes rates among children also have increased and type 2 diabetes can no longer be called "adult onset" diabetes. Also, 60% of obese children have high cholesterol, high blood pressure, or other risk factors for cardiovascular disease. While obesity is a complex, multi-factorial problem, over-consumption of soft drinks and snack foods plays a key role.

While low levels of physical activity are an important part of the problem, children are clearly eating more calories now than in the past. Between 1989 and 1996, children's calorie intake increased by approximately 80 to 230 extra calories per day (depending on the child's age and activity level). Soft drinks and low-nutrition snack foods are key contributors to those extra calories. Children who consume more soft drinks consume more calories and are more likely to be overweight than kids who drink fewer soft drinks. A recent study found that a school-based nutrition education program that encouraged children to limit their soda consumption reduced obesity among the children.

Consumption of soft drinks also can displace from children's diets healthier foods like low-fat milk, which can help prevent osteoporosis, and juice, which can help prevent cancer. In the late 1970s, teens drank almost twice as much milk as soda pop. Twenty years later, they are drinking twice as much soda pop as milk. The number of calories children consume from snacks increased by 30% (from 460 to 610 calories) between 1977 and 1996.

The health benefits of eating fruits and vegetables are well-documented; eating enough fruits and vegetables is important for preventing cancer, heart disease, high blood pressure, and other diseases. People who eat five or more servings of fruits and vegetables each day have half the cancer risk of those who eat fewer than two servings per day. However, children are not consuming enough fruits and vegetables to receive maximum health benefits. The average 6 to 11 year old eats only 3.5 servings of fruits and vegetables a day, achieving only half the recommended seven servings per day for this age group. Fewer than 15% of elementary-school-aged children eat the recommended five or more servings of fruits and vegetables daily. While fruit juices can have as many calories as soda, they provide important nutrients and health benefits that soda does not.

Milk is an important source in children's diets of essential vitamins and minerals, such as calcium and vitamins A and D. Since 98% of maximum bone density is reached by age 20, it is especially important that children get enough calcium. However, milk is also the largest source of saturated fat in children's diets. While low-fat and fat-free milk make important contributions to children's diets, whole and 2% milk contribute to children's risk of heart disease.

IV. Short-Term Profits from Selling Junk Food in Schools Pale in Comparison with the Long-Term Costs for Diet-Related Diseases

While schools are facing serious budget gaps, it is shortsighted to fund schools at the expense of our children's health. Diet- and obesity-related diseases, such as diabetes, heart disease, and cancer, cause disabilities and affect quality of life. The financial costs also are staggering. Annual medical spending attributed to obesity is estimated to be $75 billion per year, and half of that amount is financed by federal taxpayers through Medicare and Medicaid. From 1979 to 1999, annual hospital costs for treating obesity-related diseases in children rose threefold (from $35 million to $127 million).

The federal government also spends large amounts of money treating other diet-related diseases such as heart disease, cancer, diabetes, stroke, and osteoporosis through the Medicaid and Medicare programs and federal employee health insurance. Those diseases have their roots in childhood. According to the USDA, healthier diets could save at least $71 billion per year in medical and related costs.

V. Schools That Stop Selling Soda and Junk Food Are Not Losing Money

Even in the short-term, schools are finding that they can raise funds without undermining children's diets and health. A number of schools and school districts including Aptos Middle School (CA), Folsom Cardova Unified School District (CA), Monroe High School (CA), Venice High School (CA), Vista High School (CA), Fayette County Public Schools (KY), Old Orchard Beach Schools (ME), School Union 106 (ME), Shrewsbury School District (MA), North Community High School (MN), McComb School District (MS), Whitefish Middle School (MT), Sayre Middle School (PA), and South Philadelphia High School (PA) have improved the nutritional quality of school foods and beverages and not lost money.

Venice High School in Los Angeles eliminated unhealthy snack and beverage sales on campus. The school vending machines now offer a variety of waters, 100% juices and soy milk as well as a variety of healthy snacks including granola and cereal bars. After one year, snack sales in the student store were up by over $1,000 per month compared to the same time the previous year. Two years after the changes, snack sales per month had roughly doubled ($6,100 in May 2002 compared with $12,000 in March 2004). The students also raise significant funds with fundraisers that do not undermine children's health, such as a celebrity basketball game, car washes, and holiday gift wrapping.

Old Orchard Beach Schools in Maine wrote school vending policies that led to the removal of sodas and junk foods, and replaced them with water,

100% fruit juices, and healthier snack options. The vending machine signage was changed to advertise water instead of soda pop. Vending revenues have remained the same as they were prior to the changes.

North Community High School in Minneapolis replaced most of its soda vending machines with machines stocked with 100% fruit and vegetable juices and water and slightly reduced the prices of those healthier options. As a result, the sale of healthier items increased and the school has not lost money.

Though school vending is lucrative, it often represents only a small percentage of total school budgets. Soft drink contracts generate between $3 and $30 per student **per year;** even the most profitable contracts provide less than 0.5% of a school district's annual budget. In addition, the money raised from vending machines in schools is not a donation from the soft drink and snack food industries—it comes from the pockets of children and their parents.

VI. School Foods Can Be Improved at the Federal, State, or Local Level

States and localities have historically left the development of nutritional guidance to the federal government. The federal government has developed the Food Guide Pyramid, *Dietary Guidelines for Americans*, and nutrition facts labeling standards for packaged foods.

In addition, unlike other aspects of education that are primarily regulated at the state and local level, school foods have historically been regulated at the federal level—by Congress and the U.S. Department of Agriculture (USDA). The National School Lunch Program was created in 1946 under the Truman administration, "as a measure of national security, to safeguard the heath and well-being of the Nation's children and to encourage the domestic consumption of nutritious agricultural commodities and other food."

The federal government invests enormous resources in the school meal programs ($8.8 billion in FY 2003, including cash payments and commodities) and has strong nutrition standards for those meals, as well as provides technical assistance and support for states and local food service authorities to meet those standards. Selling junk foods in school vending machines undermines that investment.

USDA sets detailed standards and requirements for the foods provided through the school meal programs, including which foods are served, the portion sizes of those foods, and the amounts of specific nutrients that school meals must provide over the course of a week. In contrast, foods sold in vending machines, a la carte lines, fund-raisers, and other venues outside the school meal programs are not required by the USDA to meet comparable nutrition standards. The USDA currently has limited authority to regulate those foods.

For foods sold outside of school meals, USDA restricts only the sale of "Foods of Minimal Nutritional Value" (FMNV). A FMNV provides less than 5% of the Reference Daily Intake (RDI) for eight specified nutrients per serving. During meal periods, the sale of FMNV is prohibited by federal regulations in areas of the school where USDA school meals are sold or eaten.

However, FMNV can be sold anywhere else on-campus—including just outside the cafeteria—at any time. In addition, many nutritionally poor foods are not considered FMNV despite their high contents of saturated or trans fat, salt, or refined sugars, including chocolate candy bars, chips, and fruitades (containing little fruit juice), and thus can be sold anywhere on school campus anytime during the school day.

In order for USDA to set nutrition standards for all foods sold on school campuses throughout the school day, Congress needs to grant USDA additional authority. Implementation of those nutrition standards could be required as a condition for participating in the school meal programs.

States and cities have express authority to set nutrition standards in addition to the federal standards for foods sold out of school vending machines, a la carte lines, and other venues outside of the meal programs. A number of states have set or are working to set stronger nutrition standards for such foods (for examples, see http://cspinet.org/schoolfood/school_foods_kit_part3.pdf). Such state and local actions are needed given the limitations of current federal regulations.

Modest improvements in vending machine offerings can significantly reduce the calorie content of items purchased by students. . . .

Conclusions

This study found that the overwhelming majority of beverage and snack options in school vending machines are of poor nutritional quality. While foods and beverages sold in school vending machines are not the sole cause of childhood obesity, improving school nutrition environments is a key step toward ensuring that children have access to foods that promote their health and well-being. (For more information and model policies regarding other approaches to addressing nutrition, physical activity, and obesity, visit www.cspinet.org/nutritionpolicy.)

With skyrocketing childhood obesity rates, it is urgent that schools, school districts, and local, state, and federal governments enact policies to ensure that all foods and beverages available in schools make a positive contribution to children's diets and health. . . .

POSTSCRIPT

Is Television Viewing Responsible for the Rise in Childhood Obesity?

Authors of numerous research reports and surveys, which have appeared in the popular press as well as professional journal articles, agree that there is an increase in the rate of childhood obesity in the United States. Where the debate begins is over the reasons for this obesity epidemic. The Kaiser Foundation believes media is the culprit, while the Center for Science in the Public Interest feels vending machines in the schools are the cause of the problem. A balanced perspective would include both of these variables in explaining childhood overweight in addition to other factors such as parental influence, community access to exercise and nutritious food, economic cost of nutritious food, neighborhood safety, and education.

A review of the extensive literature that has been emerging on childhood obesity shows there are a multitude of reasons cited for the epidemic. Almost every American institution has been blamed as being responsible for the increase in children's weight. Grocery stores, schools, communities, families, restaurants, fast food, media, and the economy have had a role in making children overweight. Specifically, grocery stores are accused of stocking high-fat, high-calorie foods; the cost of healthy foods such as fruits and milk are more than processed snack foods and sodas. Schools house vending machines full of foods with little nutritive value and loads of calories; often school officials hesitate to get rid of the offending machines because they depend on them for revenue to purchase needed school supplies. There has been a reduction in the amount of hours and level of intensity of physical education classes in the schools, thus children do not get a chance to burn off calories in school the way they have in the past.

Other institutions have encouraged overeating while discouraging physical activity. Communities and neighborhoods do not lend themselves to exercise with few sidewalks for walking and few parks in which to play. Children do not feel safe enough in their neighborhoods to go out and play after school. Full-service restaurants and fast food venues have super sized their portions and encourage people to overeat. Buffets lure people to overeat by offering "all you can eat" for a lower price than a nutritious meal with vegetables and reasonable portions.

There is an overwhelming amount of media available to encourage sedentary behavior. Watching television, surfing the Web, and playing video games create an environment that discourages physical activity. Interestingly enough, research studies show that when children reduce time watching TV, physical exercise time does not necessarily increase; the children may replace this TV time with other sedentary activities like reading, talking on the phone, or playing board games.

The work/family dilemma of too little time shows up in family schedules that are hectic and leave little time for family meals together. Eating together as a family has been associated with reducing child weight. Parents may be contributing to childhood obesity by providing too much and the wrong type of food as well as not encouraging more physical activity of their children or themselves.

Although there are many factors that contribute to childhood obesity, will the concern for reducing childhood weight turn into an obsession with weight and lead to other types of problems? Already there is a concern among educators that more eating disorders such as anorexia or bulimia will emerge. In addition, there may be more of a tendency for overweight children to be discriminated against and develop a poor body image which can ultimately lead to mental illness and depression.

Related Readings

Bruss, M. B., Morris, J., & Dannison, L. (August 2003). Prevention of childhood obesity: Sociocultural and familial factors. *Journal of the American Dietetic Association, 103*, 1042–1046.

Golan, M., & Crow, S. (February 2004). Targeting parents exclusively in the treatment of childhood obesity: Long term results. *Obesity Research, 12*, 357–361.

Greaser, J., & Whyte, J. J. (September 2004). Childhood obesity: Is there effective treatment? *Consultant, 44*, 1349–1354.

McTaggart, J. (October 2004). The trouble with kids today: Childhood obesity is a complex problem, but supermarkets can be part of the solution. *Progressive Grocer, 83*, 26.

Van Staveren, T., & Dale, D. (September 2004). Childhood obesity problems and solutions: Food choices and physical activity at school and at home, underlie the childhood obesity problem. *The Journal of Physical Education, Recreation, and Dance, 75*, 44–51.

ISSUE 12

Do Bilingual Education Programs Help Non-English-Speaking Children Succeed?

YES: Stephen Krashen, from "Bilingual Education: Arguments for and (Bogus) Arguments Against," in James E. Alatis and Ai-Hui Tan, eds., *Georgetown University Round Table on Languages and Linguistics 1999: Language in Our Time: Bilingual Education and Official English, Ebonics and Standard English, Immigration and the Unz Initiative* (Georgetown University Press, 2001)

NO: Rosalie Pedalino Porter, from "The Case against Bilingual Education," *The Atlantic Monthly* (May 1998)

ISSUE SUMMARY

YES: Stephen Krashen, professor of education at the University of Southern California, contends that good bilingual education programs provide background knowledge of subject matter and literacy in the child's native language. Then, the program provides English input using English as a second language technique along with sheltered subject matter teaching in English. Krashen argues against assertions that immersion is more successful than bilingual education.

NO: Rosalie Pedalino Porter, director for the Institute for Research in English Acquisition and Development (READ), states that bilingual education is a failed endeavor. Porter cites drop-out rates and parental sentiment as evidence as to why bilingual education should be discontinued.

T here is little consistency among bilingual programs throughout schools in the United States. Numerous types of bilingual programs are being implemented. Each program is different, and each comes with its own set of advocates and opponents. For example, one school may have a program in which every subject is taught in the child's native tongue, with a small amount of class time reserved for English instruction. In another school, the child may start out being taught in Spanish, for example, and within 3–5 years be transitioned into an English-only classroom. In yet another school, a child may be immersed into English-only classes with a small amount of time reserved for tutoring in his or her native language.

Since bilingual education first became a political issue in the 1960s, it has been hotly debated. A child who does not speak English has as much of a right to an education as a child who does speak English. However, parents, politicians, researchers, and educators cannot seem to agree as to the best way to educate non-English-speaking children. When children are taught in their native language only, opponents argue that they may lack sufficient immersion into the culture and appropriate fluency in the dominant language (i.e. English), which is necessary to succeed in our society. When a child is taught in an English-only classroom, opponents argue that this leads to the student (especially one who is middle-school age and older) disliking school. These students do not understand what is being said. This, in turn, leads to disenchantment with the educational system and an alarmingly high number of non-English-speaking students becoming dropouts.

Even in more successful bilingual education programs, in which students are oriented to the language and happenings of an English-speaking classroom before being "immersed," there are other problems. These types of programs may take much longer to integrate the students into English-only classrooms. This, in turn, leaves the non-English-speaking students in danger of falling behind the other students academically, which could cause them to be in school more years than their English-speaking counterparts.

In the following selections, you will read two sides of the argument over whether or not bilingual education programs help non-English-speaking children succeed. Stephen Krashen details what successful bilingual education really is and then responds to the common criticisms of bilingual education. Rosalie Pedalino Porter discusses the origins of bilingual education. She calls it a "failed endeavor" and gives examples to support her case.

As you read the following selections, put yourself in the positions of politician, parent, educator, and student. Which approach to educating non-English-speaking students do you believe is most effective? Which teaching methods are economically and politically feasible? Which methods lead to integration into English-speaking society most effectively? And finally, is it the responsibility of the schools to preserve the child's native culture, or should that be left to the family?

Stephen Krashen

Bilingual Education: Arguments for and (Bogus) Arguments Against

Introduction

It is helpful to distinguish two goals of bilingual education. The first is the development of academic English and school success, and the second is the development of the heritage language. Good bilingual education programs achieve both goals, but my focus in this report is on the first.

Confusion about the first goal is understandable: How can children acquire English, their second language, while being taught in their first language? This occurs for two reasons: First, when we give a child good education in the primary language, we give the child knowledge, knowledge that makes English input more comprehensible. A child who understands history, thanks to good history instruction in the first language, will have a better chance understanding history taught in English than a child without this background knowledge. And more comprehensible English input means more acquisition of English.

Second, there is strong evidence that literacy transfers across languages, that building literacy in the primary language is a short-cut to English literacy. The argument is straightforward: If we learn to read by understanding the messages on the page (Smith, 1994; Goodman, 1982), it is easier to learn to read if we understand the language. And once we can read, we can read: The ability transfers to other languages.

The empirical support for this claim comes from studies showing that the reading process is similar in different languages, studies showing that the reading development process is similar in different languages, and that correlations between literacy development in the first language and the second language are high, when length of residence is controlled. All the above is true even when the orthographies of the two languages are very different (Krashen, 1996).

Good bilingual programs thus have these characteristics:

1. They provide background knowledge through the first language via subject matter teaching in the first language. This should be done to

the point so that subsequent subject matter instruction in English is comprehensible.
2. They provide literacy in the first language.
3. Of course they provide comprehensible input in English, through ESL and sheltered subject matter teaching. In sheltered classes, subject matter is taught to intermediate second language acquirers in a comprehensible way. (Sheltered classes are for intermediates; they are not for beginners and not for advanced acquirers or native speakers. It is extremely difficult to teach subject matter to those who have acquired none or little of the language. Beginners should be in regular ESL, where they are assured of comprehensible input. Including more advanced students in sheltered classes is problematic because their participation may encourage input that is incomprehensible to the other students. There is substantial evidence supporting the efficacy of sheltered subject matter teaching for intermediate level, literate students; Krashen, 1991.)

A Sample Program

The "gradual exit" model is one way of doing a bilingual program that utilizes these characteristics. In the early stage, non-English speaking students receive all core subject matter in the primary language. At the next stage, limited English proficient children receive sheltered subject matter instruction in those subjects that are the easiest to make comprehensible in English, math and science, which, at this level, do not demand a great deal of abstract use of language.

Putting sheltered subject matter classes at this stage insures that they will be comprehensible. Students in sheltered math, for example, have had some ESL, giving them some competence in English, and have had math in the primary language, giving them subject matter knowledge. These two combine to help make sheltered math comprehensible. Those forced to do subject matter in the second language immediately, without any competence in second language, have neither of these advantages. The gradual exit program appears to be the fastest way of introducing comprehensible subject matter teaching in English.

Note also that while the child is doing sheltered math, she is developing additional background knowledge and literacy through the first language in subjects that are more abstract, social studies and language arts. This will serve to make instruction in English at later stages more comprehensible.

In later stages, math and science are done in the mainstream and other subjects, such as social studies, are taught in sheltered classes in English. Eventually, all subjects are done in the mainstream. In this way, sheltered classes function as a bridge between instruction in the first language and the mainstream.

Once full mainstreaming is complete, advanced first language development is available as an option. This kind of plan avoids problems associated with exiting children too early from first language instruction (before the English they encounter is comprehensible) and provides instruction in the first language where it is most needed. This plan also allows children to have the advantages of advanced first language development.

In the gradual exit program, the second language is not delayed. It is introduced as soon as it can be made comprehensible. Quite early on, students in these programs do a considerable amount of serious academic work in English, well before they reach the very high levels required for official reclassification. The gradual exit model is thus not subject to the criticism that bilingual education programs delay exposure to English for years.

The Evidence for Bilingual Education

Evidence supporting bilingual education is of several kinds: (1) the results of program evaluations; (2) the effect of previous education on immigrant children's academic performance; (3) the effect of measured first language ability on immigrant children's second language acquisition. This framework also helps explain the strong impact of SES on school success for immigrant children and why some are successful without bilingual education.

Program evaluations. I would like to suggest a somewhat different approach in evaluating and reviewing research on bilingual education, relaxing one requirement that others adhere to strictly, but insisting on others. The one I insist on is the definition of bilingual education: A program can be considered a properly organized bilingual education program when it provides (a) subject matter teaching in the primary language without translation to the point that subject matter instruction in the second language is made comprehensible; (b) literacy development in the primary language; (c) comprehensible input in the second language. My prediction is that full bilingual programs, with all three conditions met, will be superior to those with fewer conditions met. I also insist that studies have adequate sample sizes and that the programs run for at least one year (which may be far too short to show an effect).

Other reviewers have required that there be some kind of control for experimental-comparison group differences that may have existed before the study began. Everyone agrees that randomization is the best way to do this. Lacking randomization, another technique is to statistically control for differences, in pretest scores and/or background differences. In this review, I relax this requirement and allow studies to enter the analysis where there is no compelling reason to suspect that the groups come from different populations. The logic behind this approach was presented in Krashen (1996): With a large number of post-test studies of this kind, randomization is present.

My conclusions are these: In all published studies in which these conditions are met, bilingual education is a winner. Children in bilingual programs acquire more of the second language than those in all-English programs (Mortensen, 1984), even eventually doing as well as native speakers of English (de la Garza and Medina, 1985; Burnham-Massey and Pina, 1990). Results of studies in other countries are similar (Fitzpatrick, 1987; Modiano, 1968 [literacy instruction in L1 only]; Appel, 1984; Verhoeven, 1991 [literacy only]).

In addition, apparent counterexamples, cases in which bilingual education was thought to be inferior, do not meet the conditions outlined above. In these comparisons, bilingual ed. is not described or inaccurately described, sample sizes are small, and/or real comparisons are not made.

For example, Rossell and Baker (1996) present ten studies in which "immersion" is considered to be better than bilingual education. Six are actually comparisons of different versions of Canadian immersion, a program that satisfies all three of the characteristics given above: They are all bilingual education. In all versions of Canadian immersion, children obtain enough background knowledge and develop enough literacy through the first language, both in school and at home, to make subject matter taught in the second language comprehensible (Krashen, 1996). Thus, those with more comprehensible input in the second language acquire more of it, since factors (a) and (b) are fully satisfied. In several other cases, categorization is inaccurate: What Rossell and Baker consider to be "immersion" and "submersion" are actually bilingual education; comparisons that Rossell and Baker consider to be between bilingual education and submersion or immersion are really comparisons of different versions of bilingual education (e.g., El Paso and McAllen; see Krashen, 1996). . . .

Natural experiments. Two natural experiments meet the criteria outlined above: Spanish-speaking children who had all their schooling in the U.S. were compared to those who had some of their education in Mexico. In one case, all children were in a bilingual program (Gonzales, 1989); the study thus compared the impact of some first language instruction with more. In the other study, education in the U.S. was all-English (Ferris and Politzer, 1981). In the former case, sixth graders with some education in Mexico did better than all-U.S. educated comparisons in English reading, while in the latter there was no difference between the groups in English writing in junior high school, but the Mexican-educated children had higher grades in English, and, according to teacher reports, were more dedicated students. Ferris and Politzer also report that the socioeconomic status of those with schooling in Mexico was lower than that of the all-U.S. educated group.

Impact of education in L1. Also consistent with this theoretical stance are studies showing that those with more education in the primary language are more successful in English language acquisition, a result that confirms the powerful influence of subject matter knowledge and literacy gained through the first language.

Here is just one example: Gardner, Polyzoi and Rampaul (1966) studied the impact of education in the first language on progress in intensive ESL classes for Kurdish and Bosnian adult immigrants to Canada who had "virtually no English" when they arrived (p. 3). The subjects were classified into three groups, those with a great deal of formal education (mean = 15 years), those with some (mean = 7 years) and those with no formal education.

[Another measure] presents the gains made by each group on tests of oral and written English after participation in intensive ESL (20 hours per week, for 1 to 1.5 years). For both measures, it is clear that the higher the level of literacy in the primary language, the greater the gains. This was true of both measures, and extremely powerful in the written test, in which preliterates' posttest scores were lower than the high literates' pretest scores.

The strong impact of first language education on English development has been confirmed in several other studies (Chiswick, 1991; Chiswick and Miller, 1995; Espanshade and Lu, 1997).

SES as defacto bilingual education.   Our framework helps explain the consistent positive relationship between SES and English language development (Krashen, 1996). Children from wealthier families have, most likely, more and better education in their primary language, caregivers who are better able to help them with schoolwork (in their primary language), and have more access to print in general.

Immigrant success.   The research presented here helps explain why some immigrants did well in school without bilingual education: They came with a good education in their own country, making instruction in English much more comprehensible (Krashen, 1996; Tse, 1997). Such cases are arguments for bilingual education, not against it.

Bogus Arguments against Bilingual Education

Many of the arguments used to attack the effectiveness of bilingual education violate one or more of the principles presented here.

Is immersion successful?   In several cases, the media has claimed success for "immersion" when no comparison was made at all with similar children under bilingual education.

Orange   According to the Los Angeles Times (Orange County edition) "A controversial new English immersion program in the Orange Unified School District appears to help many students learn to speak the language faster than traditional bilingual programs" (April 18, 1998). The article, which appeared in the middle of the Proposition 227 campaign, announced that "almost a quarter of the district's 4,132 elementary students in the immersion program had advanced their fluency by at least one level in the first five months of study." Orange, the Times reported, dropped bilingual education the year before and "went with English immersion."

A closer look shows that this did not occur at all: First, while Orange claimed that they dropped bilingual education, their current English immersion program used at least some first language support, supplied by paraprofessionals. Even more serious, no comparison was made of the progress made by children in the current program and children in the older program. Finally, the progress was not remarkable. I concluded (Krashen, 1999) that at the rate these children were progressing, for those starting with no English, after one year fewer than half would be ready for sheltered subject matter instruction in English, and fewer than 20% would be ready for the mainstream in one and a half years.

McQuillan (1998) analyzed a more recent report from the same district, and also concluded that children were not doing very well under the "immersion" plan. The district, for example, claimed that 81% of the immersion students could understand English in specially taught classes. McQuillan points out, however, that three-quarters of the children were already advanced enough in English to do a modified program before the new program began! In addition, only six of the 3,549 students were ready for regular classes after one year (the time limit imposed by Proposition 227), a dismal 1% reclassification rate, and, in agreement with my findings, only about half who began with no English were ready for "sheltered" classes after one year. Finally, once again Orange did not compare their students' progress with progress under older programs. . . .

Taft In another case, the comparison group was completely inappropriate. Children at the Taft School in Santa Ana scored at the 48th percentile in English reading on the CTBS in Spring, 1997, well above the district average of 22.5 and the highest in the district. Taft's principal credited the school's English immersion philosophy for some of this performance (*Education Week*, January 14, 1998). But Taft's students are clearly more advantaged than others in the district. . . .

Taft lies two standard deviations above the mean for free/reduced lunch as well as for percent of limited English proficient students. The correlation between reading scores and SES status (as measured by % free/reduced lunch) was nearly perfect ($r = .926$)(Krashen, 1999).

Taft's "success" has, most likely, nothing to do with the absence of bilingual education. In fact, some of it could be due to "de facto" bilingual education, the superior education in the primary language that more advantaged children tend to have. . . .

Is bilingual education responsible for dropouts? The circumstantial argument is this: Hispanic students have a large dropout rate. Hispanic students are the biggest customer of bilingual education programs. Therefore bilingual education causes dropouts.

False. Only a small percentage of Hispanic students are enrolled in bilingual education: In California, for example, only 15% were in full bilingual programs. In addition, the only empirical study of the impact of bilingual education on dropouts, Curiel, Rosenthal, and Richek (1986), reported fewer dropouts among bilingual education students than among comparison students.

What accounts for dropout rates? Not surprisingly, competence in English (McMillan, Kaufman and Klein, 1997). But if bilingual education results in better English development, as claimed above, this finding is an argument *for* bilingual education.

A large number of studies confirm that other factors count, such as socioeconomic class, time spent in the U.S., the presence of print, and family factors.

Hispanic students are well behind majority children in these areas. What is especially interesting is that *these background factors appear to be responsible for much if not all of the difference in dropout rates among different ethnic groups.* In other words, when researchers control for these factors, there is little or no difference in dropout rates between Hispanics and other groups (Rumberger, 1995; Rumberger, 1983; Fernandez, Paulsen, and Hiranko-Nakanishi, 1996; Warren, 1996; White and Kaufman, 1997; Pirog and Magee, 1997). Rumberger (1995), for example, concluded that " . . . Black, Hispanic, and Native American students have twice the odds of dropping out compared to White students . . . however, after controlling for the structural characteristics of family background—particularly, socioeconomic status—the predicted odds of dropping out are no different than those for White students" (p. 605). Rumberger (1983) confirms that Hispanic students often drop out because they have to go to work. When dropouts were asked why they dropped out, only 4% of the Hispanic students mentioned poor performance in school, compared to 8% of comparisons. But 38% of the Hispanic students mentioned economic factors, compared to 22% of the other students.

Bilingualism, Bilingual Education, and Earnings

. . . Chiswick and Miller (1998) suggest that bilingualism itself leads to lower earnings. On the basis of an analysis of data from the 1990 census, based on males ages 25–64 born in the U.S., they claim:

1. Those who speak only English earned more in 1989 than those who reported that another language was spoken in their home, even when factors such as schooling, years in the labor market, amount worked, marital status, and urban/rural were controlled. Overall, English-onlys (those who only heard English at home) earned about 8% more.
2. Even those who grew up in homes with another language who reported that they spoke English "very well" earned less than English-onlys.

Chiswick and Miller conclude that there is "no statistical support for the proposition that bilingualism, as measured in this study, enhances earning in the U.S. It does provide support for the proposition that whatever detracts from full proficiency in English has an adverse effect on earnings" (p. 15). However:

*   Those who really suffered were Native American, Hispanic, and "Mexican" men (for some reason, "Mexican" was not considered "Hispanic"). Even those who reported they spoke English "very well" earned less than English-onlys, 16%, 9%, and 7% respectively. Other groups had either a much smaller gap (3% for "white-non Hispanic) and none at all for Black and Asian-origin men. Chiswick and Miller also found that Hispanics who speak English "very well" but who live in "high concentration Spanish states" earned 11% less than English-onlys, but those other states were only 4% lower. These results suggest that language may

not have been the central issue in determining earnings, a possibility that Chiswick and Miller present.

- All other studies of heritage language show rather positive effects of bilingualism: Those who develop their heritage language, in addition to acquiring English, do slightly better in school and on the job market (research reviewed in Krashen, 1998). The overwhelming majority of children of immigrants report higher competence in English than in the heritage language by the time they are in high school (Krashen, 1996). Thus, most of those who speak another language at home probably do not develop it to high levels, for a variety of factors. Language shift is powerful. Most of Chiswick and Miller's subjects were, most likely, weak heritage language speakers. Their data is thus consistent with the hypothesis that high development of the heritage language is positive, and that weak development of the heritage language is a disadvantage.

Public Opinion

Our discussion of theory helps us interpret some opinion polls on bilingual education.

The polls clearly show that the public is not against bilingual education. Respondents last year in both Los Angeles and Texas agreed either that "Students should be taught in their native language for a brief time—a year or two" (Texas poll = 38% agreement. *Los Angeles Times* poll = 39%), or that first language instruction "should last as long as teachers and parents think it is necessary." (Texas poll = 36% agreement. Los Angeles Times poll = 25% agreement.) Thus, 74% of Texans surveyed supported some use of the first language in school and 64% of those surveyed in Los Angeles. Only a small percentage supported English only (Texas = 24%; Los Angeles = 32%). (Details in Krashen 1999.) . . .

When polls seem to indicate that the public is against bilingual education, a closer look reveals that this is not so.

- In some cases, the public is simply expressing support for children learning English, a goal we all agree with. In fact, this explains much of the success of Proposition 227: Many people thought they were simply "voting for English" (Krashen, 1999). Of course, when parents say they want children to learn English, this should not be interpreted as a rejection of bilingual education.
- When parents reject bilingual education explicitly, they reject versions of it that few bilingual education advocates would support, i.e., versions in which all instruction is in the first language "until children are ready to learn English." As noted earlier, I think children are ready for English the first day of school (Krashen, 1999).
- Some polls ask if parents are willing to delay subject matter for English, that is, take time for English study before children learn subject matter. This is an unreasonable question: In good bilingual education programs, children get both maximum subject matter instruction and make maximum progress in acquiring English at the same time. The former helps the latter, as explained earlier in this paper.

- Some polls ask if parents are willing to delay English while the children are instructed in their native language. This is also an unreasonable question: In good bilingual programs, there is no delay of English.

Postscript: What Happened in California?

I suspect that many voters did not know what they were voting for when they supported Proposition 227: They thought that a "yes" vote was simply a vote for English. My evidence comes not only from the countless number of people I talked to, people who told me that they were voting for Prop. 227 because "I'm for English," but also from the [Los Angeles] Times poll of April 13, discussed in the text, showing clear support for the use of the first language in school and little support for "English-only."

If voters had known what was really in 227, they would have voted differently. This was confirmed in our study. Jim Crawford noted that the following kind of question, closely following the description of 227 on the ballot, was typically asked of voters in polls: "There is an initiative on the June primary ballot that would require all public school instruction to be conducted in English and for students not fluent in English to be placed in a short-term English immersion program. If the June primary were being held today, would you vote for or against this measure?"

This kind of question can be easily interpreted as "Are you in favor of children getting intensive English instruction?" and did not reflect what was in Proposition 227. A more accurate question, Crawford suggested, would be one like this one: "There is an initiative on the June primary ballot that would severely restrict the use of the child's native language in school. This initiative would limit special help in English to one year (180 school days). After this time, limited English proficient children would be expected to know enough English to do school work at the same level as native speakers of English their age. The initiative would dismantle many current programs that have been demonstrated to be successful in helping children acquire English, and would hold teachers financially responsible if they violate this policy. If passed, schools would have 60 days to conform to the new policy. If the June primary were being held today, would you vote for or against this measure?"

Students in my language education class asked 251 voters either question 1 or question 2 and the data was analyzed by Haeyoung Kim. The difference between the responses to the two questions was huge (and statistically significant): While 57% supported the original version, only 15% supported the modified version, a result that confirmed our suspicions that few people knew what was in Proposition 227, and if they had known, most would have not supported it.

Unfortunately, despite numerous attempts, we were unable to get crucial information about 227 to many voters.

References

Appel, Rene. 1984. *Immigrant children learning Dutch*. Dordrecht, The Netherlands: Foris.

Burnham-Massey, Laurie, and Pina, Marilyn. 1990. Effects of reading instruction on English academic achievement of LEP children. *Reading Improvement* 27: 129–132.

Chiswick, Barry. 1991. Speaking, reading, and earnings among low-skilled immigrants. *Journal of Labor Economics* 9: 149–170.

Chiswick, Barry, and Miller, Paul. 1995. The endogeneity between language and earnings: International analyses. *Journal of Labor Economics* 13: 246–288.

Chiswick, Barry, and Miller, Paul. 1998. The economic cost to native-born Americans of limited English language proficiency. Report prepared for the Center for Equal Opportunity. August, 1998.

Crawford, James. 1999. *Bilingual education: History, politics, theory and practice.* Fourth Edition. Los Angeles: Bilingual Educational Services.

Cummins, Jim. 1989. *Empowering minority students.* Los Angeles, CA: California Association for Bilingual Education.

Curiel, Herman; Rosenthal, James; and Richek, Herbert. 1986. Impacts of bilingual education on secondary school grades, attendance, retentions and drop-out. *Hispanic Journal of Behavioral Sciences* 8(4): 357–367.

Curiel, Herman; Stenning, Walter; and Cooper-Stenning, Peggy. 1980. Achieved reading level, self-esteem, and grades as related to length of exposure to bilingual education. *Hispanic Journal of Behavioral Sciences* 2(4): 389–400.

Espenshade, Thomas, and Haishan Fu. 1997. An analysis of English-language proficiency among U.S. immigrants. *American Sociological Review* 62: 288–305.

Fernandez, Roberto; Paulsen, Ronnelle; and Hiranko-Nakanishi, Marsha. 1989. Dropping out among Hispanic youth. *Social Science Research* 18: 21–52.

Ferris, M. Roger, and Politzer, Robert. 1981. Effects of early and delayed second language acquisition: English composition skills of Spanish-speaking junior high school students. *TESOL Quarterly* 15(3): 263–274.

Fitzpatrick, Finbarre. 1987. *The open door.* Multilingual Matters.

Gardner, Sheena; Polyzoi, Eleoussa; and Rampaul, Yvette. 1996. Individual variables, literacy history, and ESL progress among Kurdish and Bosnian immigrants. *TESL Canada* 14: 1–20.

Gersten, Russell. 1985. Structured immersion for language minority students: Results of a longitudinal evaluation. *Educational Evaluation and Policy Analysis* 7: 187–196.

Glenn, Charles. 1998. Rethinking bilingual education: Changes for Massachusetts. *READ Abstracts, Research and Policy Review,* August, 1998.

Gonzales, L. Antonio. 1989. Native language education: The key to English literacy skills. In D. Bixler-Marquez, J. Ornstein-Galacia, and G. Green (Eds.), *Mexican-American Spanish in its societal and cultural contexts* (pp. 209–224). Rio Grande Series in Languages and Linguistics 3. Brownsville, Texas: University of Texas, Pan American.

Goodman, Kenneth. 1982. *Language, literacy, and learning.* London: Routledge & Kegan Paul.

Krashen, Stephen. 1991. Sheltered subject matter teaching. *Cross Currents* 18: 183–188.

Krashen, Stephen. 1996. *Under attack: The case against bilingual education.* Culver City, CA: Language Education Associates.

Krashen, Stephen. 1998. Heritage language development: Some practical arguments. In Stephen Krashen, Lucy Tse, and Jeff McQuillan (Eds.), *Heritage language development.* Culver City, CA: Language Education Associates.

Krashen, Stephen. 1999. *Condemned without a Trial: Bogus arguments against bilingual education.* Portsmouth, NH: Heinemann.

Krashen, Stephen, and Crawford, Jim. 1999. The research, the scientific method, and the Delaware-Massachusetts argument. *NABE News* 22(5): 14–15.

Krashen, Stephen, and McQuillan, Jeffrey. 1998. Do graduates of bilingual programs really earn less? A response to Lopez and Mora. *NABE News* 22(3): 506.

Lopez, Mark, and Mora, Marie. (1998). The labor market effects of bilingual education among Hispanic workers. *READ Perspectives* 5(2): 33–54.

McMillen, Marilyn; Kaufman, Phillip; and Klein, Steve. 1997. *Dropout rates in the United States: 1995.* Washington: US Dept of Education. NCES 97–473.

McQuillan, Jeff. 1998. Is 99% failure a "success"? Orange Unified's English immersion program. *Multilingual Educator* 21(7): 11.

Modiano, Nancy. 1968. National or mother tongue language in beginning reading: A comparative study. *Research in the Teaching of English* 2: 32–43.

Moore, Fernie Baca, and Parr, Gerald. 1978. Models of bilingual education: Comparisons of effectiveness. *The Elementary School Journal* 79(2): 93–97.

Mortensen, Eileen. 1984. Reading achievement of native Spanish-speaking elementary students in bilingual vs. monolingual programs. *Bilingual Review* 11(3): 31–36.

Pirog, Maureen, and Magee, Chris. 1997. High school completion: The influence of schools, families, and adolescent parenting. *Social Science Quarterly* 78: 710–724.

Ramos, Francisco, and Krashen, Stephen. 1997. Success without bilingual education? Some European cases of de facto bilingual education. *CABE Newsletter* 20(6): 7, 19.

Rumberger, Russell. 1983. Dropping out of high school: The influence of race, sex, and family background. *American Educational Research Journal* 20(2): 199–220.

Rumberger, Russell. 1995. Dropping out of middle school: A multilevel analysis of students and schools. *American Educational Research Journal* 32(3): 583–625.

Rossell, Christine. 1990. The effectiveness of educational alternatives for limited-English proficient children. In Gary Imhoff (Ed.), *Learning in two languages* (pp. 71–121). New Brunswick, NJ: Transaction Publishers.

Rossell, Christine, and Baker, Keith. 1996. The educational effectiveness of bilingual education. *Research in the Teaching of English* 30(1): 7–74.

Shin, Fay, and Gribbons, Barry. 1996. Hispanic parent perceptions and attitudes of bilingual education. *Journal of Mexican American Educators*, pp. 16–22.

Shin, Fay, and Lee, Bo V. 1996. Hmong parents: What do they think about bilingual education? *Pacific Educational Research Journal* 8(1): 65–71.

Shin, Fay, and Simon Kim, S. 1998. Korean parent perceptions and attitudes of bilingual education. In R. Endo, C. Park, J. Tsuchida, and A. Abbayani (Eds.), *Current issues in Asian and Pacific American education.* Covina, CA: Pacific Asian Press.

Smith, Frank. 1994. *Understanding reading.* Fifth edition. Hillsdale, NJ: Erlbaum.

Tse, Lucy. 1997. A bilingual helping hand. *Los Angeles Times*, Dec. 17, 1997.

Verhoeven, L. 1991. Acquisition of biliteracy. *AILA Review* 8: 61–74.

Warren, John. 1996. Educational inequality among White and Mexican-origin adolescents in the American Southwest: 1990. *Sociology of Education* 69: 142–158.

White, Michael, and Kaufman, Gayle. 1997. Language usage, social capital, and school completion among immigrants and native-born ethnic groups. *Social Science Quarterly* 78(2): 385–398.

Rosalie Pedalino Porter  **NO**

The Case against
Bilingual Education

Bilingual education is a classic example of an experiment that was begun with the best of humanitarian intentions but has turned out to be terribly wrongheaded. To understand this experiment, we need to look back to the mid-1960s, when the civil-rights movement for African-Americans was at its height and Latino activists began to protest the damaging circumstances that led to unacceptably high proportions of school dropouts among Spanish-speaking children—more than 50 percent nationwide. Latino leaders borrowed the strategies of the civil-rights movement, calling for legislation to address the needs of Spanish-speaking children—Cubans in Florida, Mexicans along the southern border, Puerto Ricans in the Northeast. In 1968 Congress approved a bill filed by Senator Ralph Yarborough, of Texas, aimed at removing the language barrier to an equal education. The Bilingual Education Act was a modestly funded ($7.5 million for the first year) amendment to the Elementary and Secondary Education Act of 1965, intended to help poor Mexican-American children learn English. At the time, the goal was "not to keep any specific language alive," Yarborough said. "It is not the purpose of the bill to create pockets of different languages through the country . . . but just to try to make those children fully literate in English."

English was not always the language of instruction in American schools. During the eighteenth century classes were conducted in German, Dutch, French, and Swedish in some schools in Pennsylvania, Maryland, and Virginia. From the mid nineteenth to the early twentieth century, classes were taught in German in several cities across the Midwest. For many years French was taught and spoken in Louisiana schools, Greek in Pittsburgh. Only after the First World War, when German was proscribed, did public sentiment swing against teaching in any language but English.

These earlier decisions on education policy were made in school, church, city, or state. Local conditions determined local school policy. But in 1968, for the first time, the federal government essentially dictated how non-English-speaking children should be educated. That action spawned state laws and legal decisions in venues all the way up to the Supreme Court. No end of money and effort was poured into a program that has since become the most controversial arena in public education.

From Rosalie Pedalino Porter, "The Case Against Bilingual Education," *The Atlantic Monthly* (May 1998). Copyright © 1998 by Rosalie Pedalino Porter. Reprinted by permission of the author.

In simplest terms, bilingual education is a special effort to help immigrant children learn English so that they can do regular schoolwork with their English-speaking classmates and receive an equal educational opportunity. But what it is in the letter and the spirit of the law is not what it has become in practice. Some experts decided early on that children should be taught for a time in their native languages, so that they would continue to learn other subjects while learning English. It was expected that the transition would take a child three years.

From this untried experimental idea grew an education industry that expanded far beyond its original mission to teach English and resulted in the extended segregation of non-English-speaking students. In practice, many bilingual programs became more concerned with teaching in the native language and maintaining the ethnic culture of the family than with teaching children English in three years.

Beginning in the 1970s several notions were put forward to provide a rationale, after the fact, for the bilingual-teaching experiment. José Cárdenas, the director emeritus of the Intercultural Development Research Association, in San Antonio, and Blandina Cárdenas (no relation), an associate professor of educational administration at the University of Texas at San Antonio, published their "theory of incompatibilities." According to this theory, Mexican-American children in the United States are so different from "majority" children that they must be given bilingual and bicultural instruction in order to achieve academic success. Educators were convinced of the soundness of the idea—an urgent need for special teaching for non-English-speaking children—and judges handed down court decisions on the basis of it.

Jim Cummins, a bilingual-education theorist and a professor of education at the University of Toronto, contributed two hypotheses. His "developmental interdependence" hypothesis suggests that learning to read in one's native language facilitates reading in a second language. His "threshold" hypothesis suggests that children's achievement in the second language depends on the level of their mastery of their native language and that the most-positive cognitive effects occur when both languages are highly developed. Cummins's hypotheses were interpreted to mean that a solid foundation in native-language literacy and subject-matter learning would best prepare students for learning in English. In practice these notions work against the goals of bilingual education—English-language mastery and academic achievement in English in mainstream classrooms.

Bilingual education has heightened awareness of the needs of immigrant, migrant, and refugee children. The public accepts that these children are entitled to special help; we know that the economic well-being of our society depends on maintaining a literate population with the academic competence for higher education and skilled jobs. The typical complaint heard years ago, "My grandfather came from Greece [or Sicily or Poland] and they didn't do anything special for him, and he did okay," no longer figures in the public discussion.

Bilingual education has brought in extra funding to hire and train paraprofessionals, often the parents of bilingual children, as classroom aides. Career programs in several school districts, among them an excellent one in Seattle that was in operation through early 1996, pay college tuition for paraprofessionals so that they may qualify as teachers, thus attracting more teachers from immigrant communities to the schools. Large school districts such as those in New York and Los Angeles have long had bilingual professionals on their staffs of psychologists, speech therapists, social workers, and other specialists.

Promoting parental understanding of American schools and encouraging parental involvement in school activities are also by-products of bilingual education. Workshops and training sessions for all educators on the historical and cultural backgrounds of the rapidly growing and varied ethnic communities in their districts result in greater understanding of and respect for non-English-speaking children and their families. These days teachers and school administrators make an effort to communicate with parents who have a limited command of English, by sending letters and school information to them at home in their native languages and by employing interpreters when necessary for parent-teacher conferences. In all these ways bilingual education has done some good.

But has it produced the desired results in the classroom? The accumulated research of the past thirty years reveals almost no justification for teaching children in their native languages to help them learn either English or other subjects—and these are the chief objectives of all legislation and judicial decisions in this field. Self-esteem is not higher among limited-English students who are taught in their native languages, and stress is not higher among children who are introduced to English from the first day of school—though self-esteem and stress are the factors most often cited by advocates of bilingual teaching.

The final report of the *Hispanic Dropout Project* (issued in February) states,

> While the dropout rate for other school-aged populations has declined, more or less steadily, over the last 25 years, the overall Hispanic dropout rate started higher and has remained between 30 and 35 percent during that same time period . . . 2.5 times the rate for blacks and 3.5 times the rate for white non-Hispanics.

About one out of every five Latino children never enters a U.S. school, which inflates the Latino dropout rate. According to a 1995 report on the dropout situation from the National Center on Education Statistics, speaking Spanish at home does not correlate strongly with dropping out of high school; what does correlate is having failed to acquire English-language ability. The NCES report states,

> For those youths that spoke Spanish at home, English speaking ability was related to their success in school. . . . The status dropout rate for young Hispanics reported to speak English 'well' or 'very well' was . . . 19.2 percent,

a rate similar to the 17.5 percent status dropout rate observed for enrolled Hispanic youths that spoke only English at home.

In the past ten years several national surveys of the parents of limited-English schoolchildren have shown that a large majority consider learning English and having other subjects taught in English to be of much greater importance than receiving instruction in the native language or about the native culture. In 1988 the Educational Testing Service conducted a national Parent Preference Study among 2,900 Cuban, Mexican, Puerto Rican, and Asian parents with children in U.S. public schools. Although most of the parents said they wanted special help for their children in learning English and other subjects, they differed on whether their children should be taught in their native languages. Asian parents were the most heavily opposed to the use of native languages in the schools. Among Latino groups, the Puerto Rican parents were most in favor, the Mexicans somewhat less, and the Cubans least of all. A large majority of the parents felt that it is the family's duty, not the school's, to teach children about the history and traditions of their ancestors. When Mexican parents were asked if they wanted the school to teach reading and writing in Spanish and English, 70 percent answered yes. But when they were asked if they wanted Spanish taught in school if it meant less time for teaching English, only 12 percent were in favor.

In the most recent national survey of Latino parents, published by the Center for Equal Opportunity, in Washington, D.C., 600 Latino parents of school-age children were interviewed (in Spanish or English) in five U.S. cities—Houston, Los Angeles, Miami, New York, and San Antonio. A strong majority favored learning English as the first order of business for their children, considering it more important than learning other subjects, and much more important than reading and writing in Spanish.

❧❦❧

Having begun quietly in the 1980s and gained momentum in the 1990s, Latino opposition to native-language teaching programs is now publicly apparent. Two actions by communities of Latino parents demonstrate this turn of events.

A hundred and fifty parents with children in Brooklyn public schools filed a lawsuit in September of 1995, charging that because their children routinely remained segregated in bilingual programs in excess of three years, and in some cases in excess of six years, contrary to section 3204 (2) of the State Education Law, these children were not receiving adequate instruction in English, "the crucial skill that leads to equal opportunity in schooling, jobs, and public life in the United States."

New York State law limits participation in a bilingual program to three years, but an extension can be granted for up to three years more if an individual review of the student's progress seems to warrant it. And here is the nub of the lawsuit: thousands of students are routinely kept in native-language classrooms for six years or longer without even the pretense of individual progress reviews.

Unfortunately, even with the help of a strong champion of their cause, Sister Kathy Maire, and the pro bono services of a prestigious New York law firm, Paul, Weiss, Rifkind, Wharton & Garrison, the parents lost their case. Under New York law these parents in fact have the right not to enroll their children in bilingual classes, or to remove them from bilingual classes, but in practice pressure from school personnel is almost impossible to overcome. Teachers and principals tell parents that their children will fail in English-language classrooms. They play on ethnic pride, asserting that children of a Latino background need to be taught in Spanish to improve their self-esteem.

In May of last year the Court of Appeals of the State of New York ruled that there could be no further appeals. But the publicity attracted by the case may encourage other Latino parents to take action on behalf of their children. And one concrete improvement has already occurred: the New York City Board of Education announced an end in 1996 to the automatic testing for English-language skills that children with Spanish surnames had undergone when they started school.

On the other coast an equally irate group of Latino parents moved against the Ninth Street School in Los Angeles. Seventy families of mostly Mexican garment workers planned the protest through Las Familias del Pueblo, a community organization that provides after-school child care. Typical of the protesters are Selena and Carlos (I have changed their names, because they are undocumented immigrants), who left the poverty of a rural Mexican village in 1985 to come to work in Los Angeles. Their children were born in Los Angeles, but the school insisted that they not be taught in English until they had learned to read and write in Spanish, by the fourth or fifth grade. The parents complained to the school for years that children who lived in Spanish-speaking homes and neighborhoods needed to study in English in the primary grades, when children find it easier to learn a language than they will later on.

Persistent stonewalling by administrators finally moved the parents to keep their children out of school for nearly two weeks in February of 1996, a boycott that made national news. The parents demanded that their children be placed in English-language classes, a demand that has since been met. The school administrators waited too long to make this change: the previous spring only six students (about one percent of enrollment) had been deemed sufficiently fluent in English to "graduate" to regular classrooms in the next school year.

In the early 1970s almost all the students in bilingual classes spoke Spanish. Today, of the three million limited-English students in U.S. public schools, more than 70 percent speak Spanish at home; the rest speak any of 327 other languages. California alone enrolls 1.4 million limited-English children in its schools—one of every four students in the state. According to the 1990 U.S. census, 70 percent of limited-English students are concentrated in California, Florida, Illinois, New Jersey, New York, and Texas.

⋅⟨⊚⟩⋅

Controversy over native-language education is at the boil in California. In our most multicultural state, where minorities now constitute 46 percent of the population, a revolution is brewing. In 1987 the California legislature failed to reauthorize the Bilingual-Bicultural Education Act, allowing it to expire. However, the California Department of Education immediately notified all school districts that even without the state law the same requirements would be enforced and bilingual programs continued. In July of 1995 the state Board of Education announced two major policy changes: the "preference" for native-language programs would henceforth be revoked and school districts would be given as much flexibility as possible in choosing their own programs; and school districts were ordered to be more diligent in recording evidence of student achievement than in describing the teaching methods used.

Yet in two years only four school districts have succeeded in obtaining waivers from the department, permitting them to initiate English-language programs for limited-English students. Why should schools have to seek waivers when no state or federal law, no court decision, no state policy, bars them from teaching in English? The most important case to date is that of the Orange Unified School District, with 7,000 limited-English students.

Orange Unified applied in early May of last year for permission to focus on English-language teaching in kindergarten through sixth grade while using a small amount of Spanish. The Department of Education strongly opposed the district, as did the California Association for Bilingual Education, California Rural Legal Assistance, and the organization Multicultural Education, Training, and Advocacy (META). Local Latino activists publicly criticized the district's change of plan, and some bilingual teachers resigned.

Nevertheless, the Board of Education last July granted Orange permission to try an English-language program for one year. A lawsuit was filed, and a temporary restraining order granted. But last September, U.S. District Court Judge William B. Shubb lifted the restraining order. In his seventeen-page decision the judge wrote, "The court will not second-guess the educational policy choices made by educational authorities." And he added a ruling with much broader application:

> It is clear that "appropriate action" does not require "bilingual educa-
> tion." . . . The alleged difference between two sound LEP [Limited-English
> Proficient] educational theories—ESL [English as a Second Language] and
> bilingual instruction—is inadequate to demonstrate irreparable harm.

The federal court ruling allowed Orange to proceed with its English-language program. But the case was returned to Sacramento County Superior Court, where Judge Ronald B. Robie ruled that nothing in California state law requires primary-language instruction, and therefore no waiver is needed for a district to provide an English-language program; and that federal law permits educational programs not to include native-language instruction. Soon after Robie's ruling the Board of Education rescinded the policy that schools must obtain waivers in order to eliminate bilingual programs. Although the court decision may be appealed, these two actions signal a victory for Orange Unified and have implications for other California districts as well. The legal battle has already cost the Orange district $300,000, which no doubt would have been better spent on students. It is estimated that the new program will cost an additional $60,000 the first year, but the superintendent of Orange Unified schools, Robert French, says, "We're not doing this to save money. We're doing this to save kids."

Ron Unz, a Silicon Valley entrepreneur, has long been concerned about the California education system's failures, especially as they affect its 1.4 million limited-English students. He has decided to put his time, energy, and money into an initiative—"English for the Children"—meant to give all California voters a say on the language of public education. If the initiative passes, in elections to be held on June 2, it will give "preference" to English-language programs for immigrant children, reduce the length of time children may remain in special programs, and make the state spend $50 million a year to teach English to adults. Bilingual programs will be allowed only in localities where parents actually request native-language teaching for their children.*

Last November, Unz and the co-chairman of the drive, Gloria Matta Tuchman, submitted more than 700,000 signatures to put the petition on the California ballot. The drive has the support of several Latino leaders in California, most notably Jaime Escalante, who is its honorary chairman. Escalante is the Los Angeles high school teacher whose success in teaching his Latino students advanced calculus gained him national fame in the film *Stand and Deliver.*

Though some opponents characterize the petition as "anti-immigrant," Unz and Matta Tuchman have strong pro-immigrant credentials. In 1994 Unz ran against the incumbent Pete Wilson in the Republican primary for governor and forcefully opposed the referendum to deny schooling and health benefits to illegal immigrants—a referendum that passed with Wilson's support. Matta Tuchman is a recognized Latina advocate for improved schooling for all immigrant children, but especially Spanish-speakers. The measure is likely to pass, some believe with strong ethnic support. A *Los Angeles Times* poll last October found Latino voters backing the initiative by 84 percent, and Anglos by 80 percent. A more recent survey showed a reduced amount of support— 66 percent of respondents, and 46 percent of Latinos, in favor. But whether or not the initiative passes, bilingual education has had a sufficient trial period to be pronounced a failure. It is time finally to welcome immigrant children into our society by adding to the language they already know a full degree of competency in the common language of their new country—to give these children the very best educational opportunity for *inclusion.*

---

*[It did pass.—Eds.]

POSTSCRIPT

Do Bilingual Education Programs Help Non-English-Speaking Children Succeed?

Is bilingual education effective? Depending on the way research is interpreted, and also what is considered "bilingual education," the answer to that question may vary. Even if research were consistent enough to determine the best way to handle bilingual education, we would still be left with the dilemma of dealing with bilingual education when more languages need to be taught. While the majority of children in bilingual classrooms speak Spanish as their native tongue, there are students who speak Portuguese, Korean, Chinese, and any number of other languages. Would it be necessary to implement bilingual programs in every school for every language needed?

Krashen gives three criteria for a successful bilingual program: providing background in the first language, providing literacy in the first language, and providing teaching in English through ESL or sheltered classes. Is this feasible? If it is feasible, is it enough to successfully integrate non-English-speaking students into American society? Will they be just as prepared for college as a native English speaker?

Porter states that parents of children in bilingual classrooms typically do not want their children there, and they are afraid that their child is missing out on valuable instruction in English. She suggests that we give up on bilingual education, but what does she suggest be implemented in its place? Is what she suggests just another form of bilingual education?

The controversy over the efficacy of bilingual education continues in states, provinces, counties, school districts, and even in individual schools and homes. Arguments ensue over the statistics and what the research means. But one must not lose sight of the most important thing in this battle—the children. What approaches provide the best possible education for the non-English-speaking students involved? As debates spiral round and round, we need to remember why we are debating in the first place. The reason for the debate is the children, who are more precious than the politics of securing funding for programs.

Suggested Readings

Crawford, J. (1999). *Bilingual education: History, politics, theory, and practice* (4th ed.). Los Angeles: Bilingual Educational Services.

Krashen, S. (1996). *Under attack: The case against bilingual education.* Culver City, CA: Language Education Associates.

Shin, F., & Gribbons, B. (1996). Hispanic parent perceptions and attitudes of bilingual education. *Journal of Mexican American Educators,* 16–22.

ISSUE 13

Is Gay Adoption and Foster Parenting Healthy for Children?

YES: National Adoption Information Clearinghouse, from "Gay and Lesbian Adoptive Parents: Resources for Professionals and Parents," *Adoption Information Clearinghouse* (April 2000)

NO: Paul Cameron, from "Gay Foster Parents More Apt to Molest," *Journal of the Family Research Institute* (November 2002)

ISSUE SUMMARY

YES: The National Adoption Information Clearinghouse (NAIC) presents facts regarding gay and lesbian adoptive parents. The NAIC gives current information on the background and laws regarding homosexual parenting, and confronts the issues and concerns many people have regarding homosexual adoption, including the idea that children are molested by homosexual parents.

NO: Dr. Paul Cameron, of the Family Research Institute, presents his case against allowing homosexuals to become parents—foster parents in particular. He mainly discusses case study information regarding the proclivity for homosexual parents to molest foster children.

A current topic being hotly debated in our society is gay and lesbian marriage. On the heels of this topic comes a closely related one regarding the fitness of homosexuals to raise children. Does sexual orientation affect parenting skills? Are gay and lesbian parents likely to promote homosexual behavior in their children? Will children learn to become homosexual from their gay parents? Are children at greater risk of molestation if they are raised in a homosexual household? These are just a sampling of the multitude of questions that some segments of our society have raised as we embrace this highly controversial and volatile issue. While there are segments of the heterosexual population that do not disfavor homosexual parenting, there are many concerns and fears that others have about homosexual parents. The question is whether or not any of those concerns have merit.

Those opposed to homosexual parenting, foster parenting, and adoption fear for the effects it may have on the children. Will children in these homes experience ridicule by their peers when a child tells a friend that they have two moms and no dad? Are young boys who are being raised by gay men being exposed to a lifestyle that is morally wrong? Will this exposure cause these boys to "turn gay"? Those opposed also worry about the safety of the children. In particular, they fear that children living in these environments could be molested by a parent or family friend. Furthermore, some groups have claimed that the children themselves will become gay because they are learning the lifestyle from their parents. The teasing children may endure from their friends because of having homosexual parents is a haunting concern. Those opposed to homosexual parenting also point to the need for children to have both a father and mother figure in order to grow up "normally." Some also contend that the vast majority of religions are vehemently against children being raised in a homosexual family because this is an "unnatural lifestyle."

There are not only homosexual, but heterosexual, segments of society that support the right of gays and lesbians to bear or adopt children and parent them. These groups contend that most of the concerns mentioned above are founded in the deep seated homophobia that exists throughout the world. They point to research on homosexuality which suggests that while homosexual parenting is challenging, especially with respect to children's relations with peers, most of the concerns of the opposition group are not based upon any scientific evidence and therefore are unfounded and without merit. They contend that homosexual parents face the same challenges as any other parent in raising their children. Gays and lesbians can be just as appropriately loving and nurturing as anyone else, and have the right to raise children and experience family life to the same degree that heterosexuals enjoy this right.

In the article that supports gay and lesbian parenting, the National Adoption Information Clearinghouse presents information about adoption in general and how gays and lesbians can initiate the adoption process as well. The article addresses many of the concerns that segments of society have regarding homosexual parenting. Current laws regarding adoption, by homosexual parents, are also presented. Dr. Paul Cameron, from the Family Research Institute, in his article that opposes homosexual parenting, argues that one of the most worrisome concerns that people have regarding homosexual parenting—children being molested—is occurring, yet social workers and placement agencies are choosing to overlook it.

As you read the following articles, realize that your personal beliefs and value system will heavily influence how you respond to each article. The issue of homosexuality and homosexual rights is one of the more divisive controversies in our society. As a personal challenge, read each article with the intent of not supporting one side or the other. Instead, try your best to understand the points made in the article that is more opposite of your views on homosexual parenting. Remember, to understand a point of view different than yours does not necessarily mean that you condone such a view. It merely aids you in seeing things from a different perspective.

Gay and Lesbian Adoptive Parents: Resources for Professionals and Parents

Introduction

Gay men and lesbians have always adopted, though in the past they usually hid their sexual orientation. Today, just as they are becoming visible in all other aspects of U.S. society, they are being considered more seriously as potential adoptive parents. This change has been aided by the increase in the number of gay and lesbian biological parents in the United States.

In 1976, there were an estimated 300,000 to 500,000 gay and lesbian biological parents; as of 1990, an estimated 6 to 14 million children *have* a gay or lesbian parent.[1] And, between 8 and 10 million children are being *raised* in gay and lesbian households.[2] The US Department of Health and Human Services, Adoption and Foster Care Analysis Reporting System (AFCARS), estimated in 1999 there were approximately 547,000 children in foster care in the United States, of which 117,000 are legally free and therefore eligible for adoption. But, in 1997, there were qualified adoptive families (including single parents) available for only twenty percent of these children. It is also estimated that approximately ten percent of the U.S. population—or 25 million individuals—are homosexual.[3]

Based on these increasing numbers, can gay and lesbian individuals be realistically and automatically excluded from consideration as potential adoptive parents?

Despite this increase in gay and lesbian parenting, social workers may have reservations when considering gay adoptive parents for a child. They might wonder how the children will be raised and how they will feel about themselves and their parents. Will they be embarrassed because they have two mothers or two fathers, or because their single mother dates women or their unmarried father has a boyfriend? Will their friends tease them? Will they be more likely to be homosexual than will children raised by heterosexual parents? And most important, how will having been raised by gay or lesbian parents affect them as they grow into adulthood?

This fact sheet addresses the issues faced both by social workers evaluating prospective gay or lesbian adoptive parents and by gays and lesbians considering

From *Adoption Information Clearinghouse*, April 2000.

adoption. An extensive list of sources of support and information that may be helpful to gay and lesbian adoptive parents and adoption professionals is available online at . . . , or by contacting the Clearinghouse at . . . or (888) 251–0075.

The Status of Gay and Lesbian Parenting

Defining the family structure of gay and lesbian parents can be a challenging task. The most common type of homosexual household is step or blended families. These are gay and lesbian parents who had their biological children in a former heterosexual relationship, then "came out," and created a new family with another partner. Other types of family structures include single gay or lesbian parents and couples having children together. Both of these family types may be created through adoption, but more frequently reproductive technology is being utilized.[4]

There has been some research on biological families with gay and lesbian parents. This research focuses mainly on children born to donor-inseminated lesbians or those raised by a parent, once married, who is now living a gay lifestyle. While research on these situations has not addressed all the issues relevant to adoptive parenting, this information is invaluable for social workers struggling with difficult decisions, for gay men and lesbians who want to be parents, for their families and friends, and for anyone seeking information on this nontraditional type of family.

Unfortunately, the effects on children of being raised by lesbian and gay adoptive parents cannot be predicted. The number of homosexuals who have adopted is unknown, and because of the controversial nature of the issue, their children are often reluctant to speak out. Testimony of children who have grown up in gay households may turn out to provide the best information about the results of gay parenting.

Research studies, often conducted by individuals or organizations with a vested interest in the outcome, are contradictory. Studies linked to conservative political and religious groups show negative effects on children of gay and lesbian parents; while studies which support homosexual parenting are said to reflect the bias of those who are themselves gay or who support gay rights. Clearly, what are needed are definitive studies that would follow larger numbers of children over a long period of time. That research, when completed, will provide more definitive information for the debate.

In the meantime, it is critical to address the issues and concerns so that social workers can examine their own personal biases to make informed decisions and gay and lesbian adoptive families can receive the support they need to thrive.

Issues and Concerns

"What Is Sexual Orientation?"

The American Psychological Association defines sexual orientation as "one of four components of sexuality and is distinguished by an enduring emotional, romantic, sexual or affectionate attraction to individuals of a particular gender. The three other components of sexuality are biological sex, gender identity (the psychological sense of being male or female) and social sex role (the adherence to cultural norms for feminine or masculine behaviors)."[5]

For most people sexual orientation emerges in early adolescence without any prior sexual experience. Sexual orientation is different from sexual behavior because it refers to innate feelings and self-concept and may not be expressed in behavior. Understanding the source of sexual orientation depends on which side of the nature versus nurture debate you fall. Some theories point to genetic or inborn hormonal factors; others to early childhood life experiences. Many believe sexual orientation is shaped at an early age through a combination of biological, psychological and social factors.[6]

"Children Will Be Molested by Homosexual Parents"

There is no legitimate scientific research connecting homosexuality and pedophilia. Sexual orientation (homosexual or heterosexual) is defined as an adult attraction to other adults. Pedophilia is defined as an adult sexual attraction or perversion to children.[7] In a study of 269 cases of child sex abuse, only two offenders where found to be gay or lesbian. More relevant was the finding that of the cases involving molestation of a boy by a man, seventy-four percent of the men were or had been in a heterosexual relationship with the boy's mother or another female relative. The conclusion was found that "a child's risk of being molested by his or her relative's heterosexual partner is over one hundred times greater than by someone who might be identifiable as being homosexual."[8]

"Children Will Be Teased and Harassed"

Children of gay men and lesbians are vulnerable to teasing and harassment, particularly as they approach adolescence, when any sign of difference is grounds for exclusion. How much of a problem is it? Is it likely to cause lasting psychological damage?

Gay and lesbian parents are well aware of the difficulties that a child may face—many have dealt with prejudice all of their lives. Most see it as an opportunity for ongoing discussion that will help their children grow as people.

Abby Ruder, a therapist, lesbian, and adoptive mother, acknowledges that children will be teased, and takes great pains to prepare her gay and lesbian clients for some of the problems that their children will face. She feels that families should have a plan for dealing with society's attitude toward them. "Children with gay or lesbian parents need to be taught when it's okay to tell people and when not to. A family doesn't have to be 'out' all of the time. My 9-year-old . . . has become very adept at knowing when to tell people that she has two mommies."

Wendell Ricketts and Roberta Achtenberg, in the article "Adoption and Foster Parenting for Lesbians and Gay Men: Creating New Traditions in Family" from *Homosexuality and Family Relations*, address social workers grappling with the issue by asking, ". . . should children be sheltered from every experience in which their difference might challenge prejudice, ignorance, or the status quo (or in which they would be 'exposed' to the difference of others)? Agencies conforming to such a standard must ask themselves whether it is their function to honor the system that generates stigma by upholding its constraints." They continue, "Teasing is what children do. Does this mean that child welfare policy must be set at a level no higher than the social interactions of children?"

In custody cases involving a gay or lesbian parent, courts have considered the fact that a child might be teased as contrary to the best interests of the child. They argue that the stigma attached to having a gay or lesbian parent will damage a child's self-esteem. This has been refuted in many studies. Research has found that although children of gays and lesbians do report experiencing teasing because of their parent(s), their self-esteem levels are no lower than those of children of heterosexual parents.[9]

In 1984 the Supreme Court heard a case, *Palmore v Sidoti*, in which a Florida man sought custody of his daughter on the grounds that his white ex-wife was now married to a black man and that this would expose his daughter to the stigma of living in an interracial family. The Court ruled that the girl should stay with her mother, saying that under the Equal Protection Clause of the Fourteenth Amendment, "private biases may be outside the reach of the law, but the law cannot, directly or indirectly, give them effect." Although the Court's ruling dealt specifically with racial prejudices, several researchers have mentioned the case as a rebuttal to the argument that placing a child in a family subject to social stigma is automatically contrary to the child's best interests.[10]

Nonetheless, social workers and even some gay men and lesbians considering adoption wonder if it is in the best interest of a child to be raised by homosexual parents. "It can be too hard a transition for some children, especially those who are older and have already formed preconceived notions about homosexuality," explains therapist Ruder. "Younger children usually have an easier time adjusting to a gay and lesbian parented home. They haven't learned the societal biases against gays and lesbians yet." When a gay person is being considered as a potential adoptive parent for an older child, the child should be told about the person's sexual orientation and asked his feelings about it. If the child is comfortable with the information, the caseworker can proceed to the next step.

Gay and lesbian adoptive parents must also think about how they will explain to younger children, in age-appropriate language, not only how and why the child was adopted but also about the parents' sexual orientation. Both are complex subjects that should be addressed a number of times as the child grows and matures, each time adding new information as the child asks and is able to absorb and understand more. Then both topics become accepted facts of family life.

"Children Raised in Homosexual Households Will Become Gay"

The bulk of evidence to date indicates that children raised by gay and lesbian parents are no more likely to become homosexual than children raised by heterosexuals. As one researcher put it, "If heterosexual parenting is insufficient to ensure that children will also be heterosexual, then there is no reason to conclude that children of homosexuals also will be gay."[11]

Studies asking the children of gay fathers to express their sexual orientation showed the majority of children to be heterosexual, with the proportion of gay offspring similar to that of a random sample of the population. An assessment of more than 300 children born to gay or lesbian parents in 12 different samples shows no evidence of "significant disturbances of any kind in the development of sexual identity among these individuals."[12]

"Children Will Develop Problems Growing Up in an 'Unnatural' Lifestyle"

Courts have expressed concern that children raised by gay and lesbian parents may have difficulties with their personal and psychological development, self-esteem, and social and peer relationships. Because of this concern, researchers have focused on children's development in gay and lesbian families.

The studies conclude that children of gay or lesbian parents are no different than their counterparts raised by heterosexual parents. In "Children of Lesbian and Gay Parents," a 1992 article in *Child Development*, Charlotte Patterson states, "Despite dire predictions about children based on well-known theories of psychosocial development, and despite the accumulation of a substantial body of research investigating these issues, not a single study has found children of gay or lesbian parents to be disadvantaged in any significant respect relative to children of heterosexual parents."

Psychiatrist Laurintine Fromm, of the Institute of Pennsylvania Hospital, agrees with that finding. "[The] literature . . . does not indicate that these children fare any worse [than those of heterosexual parents] in any area of psychological development or sexual identity formation. A parent's capacity to be respectful and supportive of the child's autonomy and to maintain her own intimate attachments, far outweighs the influence of the parent's sexual orientation alone."

What the Law Says

Only one state, Florida, specifically bars the adoption of children by gay and lesbian adults. Similar legislation was introduced in Utah prohibiting unmarried couples, including same-sex couples, from adopting children. The bill claims it is not in a child's best interest to be adopted by persons "cohabiting in a relationship that is not a legally valid (binding) marriage." The bill passed the State of Utah's House and Senate in February 2000 and is waiting the Governor's signature. The Governor has pledged to sign it.

Yet, in April 2000, Vermont lawmakers approved legislation that makes the State the first in the nation to recognize same-sex couples' right to form "civil unions." Partners in a civil union would be given the same benefits of married couples—the ability to transfer property, to make medical decisions for each other, to be eligible for inheritance, and the necessity to dissolve the union in Family Court (equivalent to a divorce). More than 30 other states have tried to avoid such unions through the passage of the Defense of Marriage Act. The act defines marriage as a union between a man and a woman and denies recognition of same-sex marriages performed elsewhere.

Legislation has also been introduced in Mississippi that would ban gay and lesbian couples from adoption and forbid the State of Mississippi from recognizing gay and lesbian adoptions that have previously been granted by other state courts—an unprecedented provision. Anti-sodomy statutes in 19 states and the lack of legal recognition of homosexual couples complicate adoption in the states that don't specifically prohibit gay and lesbian adoption.

Professor William Adams Jr., co-counsel in a case challenging Florida's ban on adoptions by gays and lesbians, has noted courts are increasingly turning to expert testimony to resolve questions in gay rights cases. He theorizes that there are several factors contributing to this trend, among them the courts' desire to justify their decisions in light of the controversy surrounding the issue and the efforts of gay litigants and civil rights organizations to provide the court with information. Although Adams sees this as a positive step, he comments, "citation to social science data should not be mistaken for a court's full understanding of it, however, because courts sometimes struggle to make sense of the research, or strain to ignore it."[13]

Nine states—California, Massachusetts, New Jersey, New Mexico, New York, Ohio, Vermont, Washington and Wisconsin—and the District of Columbia have allowed openly gay or lesbian individuals or couples to adopt. Although some joint adoptions have been successful, the most common practice is for a single person to apply as the legal adoptive parent of the child. Couples who both want custody then apply for a second parent, or coparent, adoption.

Second parent adoption or the adoption by non-marital partners, leaves the parental rights of one legally recognized parent intact and creates a second legally recognized parent for the adoptive children. Second parent adoption, which has become routine for children of heterosexual stepparents, is the only way for gay couples to both become legal parents of their children.[14] Although state statutes generally provide a "stepparent exception," these exceptions emphasize the existence of a legal marriage between the biological parent and the stepparent.[15]

This growing practice was tested in a landmark case in Vermont in 1993. Jane Van Buren had given birth to two boys through anonymous donor insemination. According to the law, only Ms. Van Buren was considered their parent—her partner, Deborah Lashman, had no legal standing. The couple filed a petition for a second parent adoption, asking the probate court to allow Ms. Lashman to adopt the children while leaving Ms. Van Buren's parental rights intact. The court denied the adoptions because Ms. Lashman was not married to the biological parent. On June 18, 1993, the Vermont Supreme Court unanimously reversed the decision of the lower court and awarded joint custody to the couple.[16] With this decision, the Vermont Supreme Court became the first State Supreme Court to recognize lesbian co-parent adoptions. As a result of this finding, other couples are likely to find second parent adoptions easier to accomplish in Vermont and other areas of the country.

Second parent adoptions (by unmarried couples) have been granted by the courts (the approvals were generally from the lower level courts) in 21 states and the District of Columbia: Alabama, Alaska, California, Illinois, Indiana, Iowa, Maryland, Massachusetts, Michigan, Minnesota, Nevada, New Jersey, New Mexico, New York, Ohio, Oregon, Pennsylvania, Rhode Island, Texas, Vermont and Washington.[17]

Types of Adoption

Depending on the type of adoption gay and lesbian parents are interested in—public, private, independent, open or international—there may be different considerations involved in disclosing sexual orientation. How open prospective adoptive parents are about their homosexuality depends upon the couples' personal feelings on disclosure, whether direct questions are asked and what the laws in the State of residency are.

One important point for all prospective adoptive parents to be aware of is—the difference between not sharing private information and deliberately lying at any time in the adoption process. Although it is completely legal to omit information regarding homosexuality, it is illegal to lie about it when confronted directly.[18] Let it be clear that failing to tell the truth is considered fraud and raises the opportunity for either an adoption not being finalized or a possible disruption.

Public Agency Adoption

Success in adopting from the public child welfare system depends on the State adoption law and the attitude of the agency. For example, in New York and California, gay and lesbian prospective adoptive parents are protected against discrimination. It is illegal for public agencies in those states to reject adoptive parents on the basis of sexual orientation. However, that is not a guarantee that prejudices don't exist. Social workers who are uncomfortable with homosexuality may find the prospective adoptive parents unsuitable for other reasons.[19]

Each state decides independently who can adopt. Since, the final decision is made by judges at the county level, the availability of adoption as an option to openly gay and lesbian couples is influenced by the political and social community in which the family lives. The court's decision hinges on the "best interest" of the child, a concept interpreted differently by different judges.

Private Agency Placements

Private agencies establish their own criteria for the prospective adoptive parents. Age, religion, fertility status, marital status and sexual orientation all may be agency considerations. Some private agencies may disregard sexual orientation, and present the prospective parent as a single adopter who lives with another adult who will share the responsibilities of raising the child. This omission of sexual orientation is based on the agency's judgement and relevancy to the applicant's parenting qualifications.

Independent and Open Adoption

An independent adoption is an adoption facilitated by those other than case-workers associated with an agency. They may be a physician, an attorney, or an intermediary and are illegal in some states. In an independent adoption the placement decision (within the provisions of the state statute) is completely up to the families involved. However, independent adoption does not necessarily mean an open adoption. An open adoption involves some amount of initial and/or ongoing contact of birth and adoptive families. The adoptive and birth parents agree upon the birth parents' role, future communication and the degree of openness prior to adoption. Being honest with the birth parents from the first contact allows gay and lesbian adoptive parents the opportunity to have a relationship without the possibility of a disrupting secret.

International Adoption

Adopting a child from a foreign country may involve finding an agency willing to accept the adoptive parents' sexual orientation, disclosing the information to the contacts in the sending country, and presenting the information to the foreign government. However, conservative, or religious and often developing countries may not be as receptive to gay and lesbian couples. Adoptive parents need to be aware that foreign governments and courts are making placement decisions based on their cultural standards and what they feel is in the best interest of the child.

The Social Worker's Dilemma

Placement Decisions

The debate goes on and will continue as long as there are conflicting views about homosexuality. Considering these different views, should social workers place children with gay men or lesbians? To make the best placement decision for children, social workers need to answer the following questions:

- Is this person or couple caring, nurturing, and sensitive to others?
- Do they have the qualities needed to parent a child?
- What are their individual strengths and weaknesses?
- How do their strengths/weaknesses complement the needs of the child?
- Do they have the capacity to nurture a child not born to them?

In addition, for prospective homosexual adoptive parents, Denise Goodman, Ph.D., a consultant and trainer in Ohio, firmly believes that workers need to have a holistic understanding that includes finding out answers to questions about their homosexuality:

> "I counsel workers to ask homosexual applicants where they are in their individual development. Have they recently come out? Are they comfortable with their self-image and with being gay? Having a positive self-image

will provide a model for an adopted child. I want to know about family support and how those who are important in their lives view them and their idea of adopting. I ask questions about the stability of their relationship and try to see how committed they are to each other. Do they have wills? Have they bought a home? Do they share finances? Once you know more about their situation, you can help them access appropriate resources and connect them with other gay or lesbian adoptive parents."

Goodman, who has trained thousands of social workers in Ohio, sees the opportunity for change, but has a few concerns:

"While it is gratifying to see social workers become more open, if agency administrators are not fully behind the workers, little will change. Families will be approved and never hear about an available child; those who aren't open about their sexuality will receive a child, while "honest" applicants will wait, or other issues will surface so that a family is not accepted."

If a sense of trust and openness is established between a social worker and applicant, the worker can help to decide when privacy is the best route or when an applicant can be more outspoken. It ultimately depends on state laws and the views of presiding judges.

Professional Prejudices and Policy Decisions

Adoption professionals need to be aware of their own personal prejudices and prejudgments when working with gay and lesbian prospective adoptive parents. Experiences and beliefs come from family background and values, religious beliefs, and community views on homosexuality and will affect social workers' and agency staff's ability to assess the couple.[20] Ann Sullivan, of the Child Welfare League of America, suggests in her article "Policy Issues in Gay and Lesbian Adoption," that professionals consider several key issues:

- The client is the child in need of an adoptive family. All families should be given equal consideration and the potential resources available weighed for the placement of the child.
- No single factor should be the determining factor in assessing suitability for adoption.
- In considering gay and lesbian prospective adoptive parents, sexual orientation and the capacity to nurture a child are separate issues and should not be confused in the decision making process.
- Each placement decision should be based on the strengths and needs of the individual child and the perceived ability of the prospective adoptive family to meet those needs and develop additional strengths.

Coping with the Agency Preference Hierarchy

Many gay and lesbian prospective adoptive parents are troubled by the feeling that adoption agencies offer them the children who are the most difficult to place: those with physical, mental, or emotional disabilities; those who are older; children of color; and members of sibling groups.

"Often gay parents will get harder children because it's the last resort," Bob Diamond, the former Executive Director of AASK Northern California in Oakland, admits. "A lot of social workers will say, 'Well, no one is going to take this kid except gay people.' Being homosexual is not usually seen as a positive factor," he adds, noting that single people in general are usually treated as "second-class citizens" by most adoption agencies.[21]

Roberta Achtenberg, Executive Director of the National Center for Lesbian Rights in San Francisco, bluntly confirms that there is an unspoken ranking within the adoption network. "The hierarchy prefers white, married, middle or upper middle class couples, and these couples don't want the special needs kids. The less preferred children then go to unmarried couples of all kinds, single individuals, and gay people. The children are less preferred, and the recipients are less preferred."

What strikes psychologist April Martin, author of *The Lesbian and Gay Parenting Handbook*, as ironic is that the same bureaucracies that believe that lesbians and gay men are not suitable parents will place children who require the most highly skilled parenting with them. She and others have pointed out that nontraditional families have unique strengths that make them excellent, and in some cases, the best homes for certain children. Among them is an ability to accept differences, to understand what it is like to be in the minority, to demonstrate flexible gender roles, to be open about sexuality with children who have been sexually abused, and to understand the special needs of homosexual children.

April Martin suggests that gays and lesbians who want to adopt younger, healthier children can find them by working with private agencies or by working directly with birthparents. Some birthparents have specifically chosen openly gay households for their children.

Life after Adoption

Explaining Sexuality to Children

All families at one time or another will have "the" discussion on sexuality. For gay and lesbian families this can be an even more sensitive subject. However, a healthy family, regardless of sexual orientation, shares the same core values—love and respect, commitment and understanding. It is especially important when talking with children to stress what these values mean to the family and to recognize that there are many different cultures, communities and families around the world.

The Family Pride Coalition, a national advocacy and support organization, offers several suggestions for parents discussing sexuality with their children:[22]

- Be honest about your own identity and comfort level.
- If you are uncomfortable, let your children know you find this hard to talk about, but that you feel it is important for families to talk about difficult things.

- Listen closely to your child and when possible, let your children take the lead. Let them ask questions. Take cues about their level of understanding from the questions they ask and interact at that level.
- Be as clear as you can be about your own feelings connected to sexuality, coming out, privacy, and family values.
- Consider your child's age and how much information they need.

Getting Support

Once an adoption is completed, the business of family life begins. Like all adoptive parents, gay men and lesbians are seeking ways to incorporate their children into their lives and to help them make a smooth transition. They also want to meet other homosexuals who have taken on the challenge of parenting. There are a growing number of support groups to meet these needs.

Len and Fernando, a multiethnic gay couple who adopted 3-year-old Isabel as a toddler, are members of an active group in the Philadelphia area. "Speaking to the parents of older children gives us ideas of how to cope with issues as they come up. Most of the members are women. We could use a few more men!"

Isabel, who is African-American, has the chance to meet other African-American adopted children and enjoys the many activities planned for families. Their group is part of a larger support network, Philadelphia Family Pride, that serves more than 250 gay and lesbian families in the Delaware Valley. In addition to giving its members a chance to socialize, the group's advocacy and educational projects encourage parents to work with teachers on adoption, race, and alternative family issues that affect their children. Members participate in conferences, receive local and national newsletters, and learn about books and articles for themselves and their children. Older children of gay parents have formed their own network, Colage—Children of Lesbians and Gays Everywhere.

A vital support network of family and friends is important for any family—adoptive, biological, one with heterosexual parents, or one with homosexual parents. Some gay and lesbian adoptive parents have found that even if their parents had a difficult time accepting their homosexuality, the parents readily accept their new role as grandparents. It is almost as if having children makes them more like mainstream families. "Our parents reacted to our desire to parent pretty much the same way they reacted to our coming out," says Tim Fisher, father of two and former Executive Director of the Family Pride Coalition (formerly Gay and Lesbian Parents Coalition International). "They said, 'We love you . . . but let's not talk about it.' With the kids, they have softened their tone a little. They are grandparents who adore their grandchildren."

Conclusion

The increasing number of gay men and lesbians choosing to adopt has brought the issue of gay and lesbian parenting to the forefront. Social workers are being asked to look carefully at their own feelings and to make reasonable judgments about what is in the best interest of children who need families. And, the increasing number of children needing adoptive families puts pressure on workers to find appropriate families.

The questions linger—should stable, nurturing, mature applicants be turned away on the basis of sexual orientation? What if a substantial number of children face the possibility of never achieving permanency, when they could have been adopted by a gay or lesbian family?

Endnotes

1. Sullivan, A., (1995). Issues In *Gay and Lesbian Adoption: Proceedings of the Fourth Annual Peirce-Warwick Adoption Symposium*, Washington, DC: Child Welfare League of America.
2. Editors of the *Harvard Law Review*. (1990). *Sexual Orientation and the Law.* Cambridge, MA: Harvard University Press.
3. Sullivan, A.
4. Rohrbaugh, J.B. Lesbian Families: Clinical Issues and Theoretical Implications. (1992). *Professional Psychology: Research and Practice,* 23: 467–473.
5. Blommer, S.J. (undated). Answers to Your Questions About Sexual Orientation and Homosexuality: A Fact Sheet. Washington, DC. American Psychological Association.
6. Blommer, S.J.
7. Lesbian and Gay Rights Project—ACLU. (1999). ACLU Fact Sheet—Overview of Lesbian and Gay Parenting, Adoption and Foster Care. New York, NY: American Civil Liberties Union.
8. Carole, J. Are Children at Risk for Sexual Abuse by Homosexuals? (1994). *Pediatrics,* 94 (1):
9. Huggins, S.L. A Comparative Study of Self-Esteem of Adolescent Children of Divorced Lesbian Mothers and Divorced Heterosexual Mothers. (1989). *Journal of Homosexuality,* 18 (1/2): 123–135.
10. Adams, W. E. Whose Family Is It Anyway? The Continuing Struggle for Lesbians and Gay Men Seeking to Adopt Children. (1996). *New England Law Review,* 30 (3): 579–621.
11. Bigner, J. J., Bozett, F. W. 1990. Parenting by Gay Fathers. In: *Homosexuality and Family Relations.* Bozett, F. W., Sussman, M. B. New York, NY: Haworth Press, Inc.
12. Patterson, C. J. Children of Lesbian and Gay Parents. (1992). *Child Development:* 1025–1039.
13. Adams, W. E.
14. Lambda Legal Defense and Education Fund. (1997). Lesbian and Gay Parenting: A Fact Sheet. New York: NY: Lambda Legal Defense and Education Fund.
15. Mishra, D. The Road to Concord: Resolving the Conflict of Law Over Adoption by Gays and Lesbians. (1996). *Columbia Journal of Law and Social Problems,* 30 (1): 91–136.
16. Patterson, C. J.
17. Lambda Legal Defense and Education Fund.
18. Martin, A. (1993). *The Lesbian and Gay Parenting Handbook.* New York, NY: HarperCollins Publishers, Inc.
19. Martin, A.
20. Sullivan, A. Policy Issues in Gay and Lesbian Adoption. (1995). *Adoption and Fostering,* 19 (4): 21–25.
21. Perry, D. Homes of Last Resort. (1993). *The Advocate:* 46.
22. Cronin, M. E. (1999). Guide to Talking with Your Child About California's Knight Initiative. San Diego, CA: Family Pride Coalition.

Paul Cameron  **NO**

Gay Foster Parents More Apt to Molest

No matter how professionals in our society extol the virtues of 'science,' if empirical evidence goes against their beliefs, they often ignore it or avoid it. The employment of homosexuals as foster parents is a perfect case in point.

When a 16-year-old foster son was molested and raped by two gay foster parents in Vermont, Tom Moore, Deputy of the State's Social and Rehabilitation Services, told me on June 25, 2002 that neither he nor the Commissioner knew of any evidence about the molestation rates of children by homosexual foster parents. He was apparently echoing his boss, Commissioner William Young, who the papers quoted as saying "I don't know of any screening instrument for [sexual molestation]. Certainly, sexual preference doesn't have anything to do with it, or religious beliefs or socioeconomic status. It's so frustrating because there isn't a predictor." (*Rutland Herald* 6/21/02)

Really? Traditional common sense holds that married parents are likely to be the best foster placement, and homosexuals among the worst, in part because of the risks of sexual molestation. But tradition holds almost no weight for these bureaucrats. How can this be? Can the traditions that worked to build arguably the world's most successful culture be ignored without injuring society? What kind of belief-system is so much better that it should be followed instead?

When I interviewed the reporter who wrote the story for the *Rutland Herald*, he refused to specify whether what he had called the "male couple" in the newspaper story was in fact a homosexual couple. He said that the *Rutland Herald* never released the sexual orientations of those accused of crimes. When I spoke with his editor, she repeated the policy. The "male couple" certainly acted as though they were gay, but the newspaper staff wasn't about to say or print it.

Fortunately, those at the District Court of Vermont were not so protective of 'sexual orientation privacy.' They provided the entire record. The rest of the story about the 16-year-old fit traditional common sense perfectly.

It turns out that the natural parents of the boy who was victimized strenuously objected to the placement of their hard-to-control son with these two gays. Yet, following a policy laid down 15 years ago, their objections were ignored. Additionally, when the boy complained to the Department that his new foster parents had asked him whether he had engaged in anal intercourse with his brother, the Department, through David Stanley, its Case Worker, concluded that the boy had been 'coached' to say this by his natural parents. Stanley said the gay foster parents denied saying such a thing and he believed them. So as far as the case worker was concerned, the boy had lied, so he was forced to stay with the 'male couple.'

Soon thereafter, the men gave the boy a magazine containing depictions of scantily clad men. They told the boy to 'masturbate to these pictures.' The boy complied, and hid the magazine under his bed.

Here, another factor of the case supported traditional common sense. Traditional thought holds that homosexuals have difficulty containing their sexual desires for youth. And sure enough, even in the face of all this investigation and conflict about possible molestation, the boy was with these homosexuals only two more weeks before they began to rape him!

Think of it. The investigation had already put these two gays 'on notice,' and yet this warning kept them from acting upon their temptation for only two weeks. Then, both men, who were in a 'committed relationship' with one another, had their way sexually with the boy. Sometimes, just one of them raped the boy alone, sometimes it happened when they were together. The boy managed to escape only by pretending that the sex was OK, and then fleeing to a hospital when the 'family' went to town to shop.

As it turned out, the men's magazine was the 'clincher' when the boy fingered his foster 'parents.' Because the magazine was where the boy said it was, the police were able to get the men to confess.

Notice what happened here. Vermont's child protective agency, without evidence of any sort, adopted a new policy 15 years ago that discarded tradition. Why? Because traditional common sense relegated homosexuals as 'not suitable for foster-placement' status. The child protective agency thought it had a 'better way.'

What was this 'better way?' What is this belief system that is so much better than traditional thought?

I filed a Freedom of Information request regarding this case and the policy changes that had been instituted by the agency, asking 17 specific questions. Some of these included: how many foster parents or foster parent pairs who have been involved in foster parenting a child or children were homosexual? Did your department conclude that the 16-year-old boy's claim was false that his foster parents had asked him whether he performed anal intercourse with his brother?

Less than a month later, Jody Racht, the Assistant Attorney General for Vermont, informed me that asking specific questions rather than "access to identified public records" fell outside of "any provision of state law."

So while certain policies had apparently been established to protect homosexuals—both in the child protective agency and at the *Rutland Herald*—neither institution would explain their basis. They just followed 'the policy.'

So what was this 'better way'?

Deputy Commissioner Moore said that, because of privacy and confidentiality concerns, no follow-up of placements with homosexuals had been conducted, nor were any contemplated. This strategy of 'deliberate ignorance' is not unique to Vermont. Over the past 10 years, I have talked with representatives of the District of Columbia, El Paso County (Colorado Springs, CO), and Seattle, WA—jurisdictions which place foster children with homosexuals—and gotten the same replies. In Colorado Springs, the wishes of the family regarding the placement of a 6-year-old boy—whose lesbian mother was judged unsuitable to parent—were overridden by child protective services in favor of the 'right of homosexuals to keep their children.' The little boy was given to a lesbian couple instead of his married aunt—an aunt who had been chosen by the extended family as the 'best fit' for the boy.

The social work representatives in the other three jurisdictions with whom I had contact said that since the National Association of Social Workers (NASW) declared homosexuals to be foster parents 'as fit' as heterosexuals, they believed that they were as unlikely to sexually abuse their charges as non-homosexuals. Indeed, the 1987 NASW resolution decrying "resistance to using single parents, . . . including lesbian and gay parents, as potential foster care and adoption resources" was passed, in substantial part, to counter the traditional belief that children placed with homosexual foster parents would be at higher risk of sexual exploitation.

NASW Influence

This NASW resolution and the new 'theory' behind it has informed social workers for the past 15 years. In one high profile case in 1992, the faculty of the Saint Cloud State University Social Work Department told potential students that this new 'theory' trumped not only traditional common sense, but also any religious beliefs. These faculty decreed that 'social homophobia' is a form of "human oppression." And citing the NASW code of ethics (Sec. 2.3), they noted that "accepting gay and lesbian people does not mean accepting them as individuals while simultaneously abhorring their behavior. . . . The only legitimate position of the social work profession is to abhor the oppression that is perpetrated in gay and lesbian people and to act personally and professionally to end the degradation in its many forms." That is, this 'new faith statement' must trump any other belief—including traditional religious beliefs like Christianity.

Is the NASW claim that homosexual and unmarried foster parents are 'as fit' as married heterosexuals warranted? No empirical literature concerning the issue appears to exist—although the evidence regarding the general parenting of homosexuals suggests that it is inferior to that of the married. Under the current system for placing foster children, putting the NASW claim to an empirical test cannot be done. The bureaucrats who could track the success of homosexual foster parents refuse to do so, and—citing privacy and confidentiality concerns—also prevent outsiders from doing it.

The 'faith' of the social worker profession, consisting of resolutions passed by a tiny committee within the NASW, is sufficient. No evidence is required! What a maddening mess! Fortunately, I found a way to bypass the current bureaucratic strategy of 'deliberate ignorance' regarding foster placements with homosexuals. My strategy exploited recent changes in the technology of newspaper publishing.

Here Is What I Did

While a successful foster-parenting outcome does not make the news, a highly unsuccessful outcome does. If homosexual foster parents do not differ from non-homosexuals, gross failure at foster parenting—such as the sexual molestation of foster kids—ought to occur at rates approximately proportionate to the frequencies of homosexual and heterosexual foster parents. Lexis-Nexis Academic Universe, an internet search service, scans the whole text of over 50 regional and national newspapers, largely in the U.S., but also including major papers in Australia, England, Canada, and New Zealand (e.g., *Baltimore Sun, Boston Globe, Independent* [England], *Ottawa Citizen* [Canada]).

This past summer, I examined every news story from 1989 through 2001 that included "child molestation"—a total of 5,492 stories. The findings were double-checked by also running "foster" against this database in early September, 2002. Only news stories or first-person accounts were tallied, not editorials nor opinion pieces, so the stories basically covered recent events, not reflections on older items.

This technique is obviously different from a comparison study where matched parents—homosexual and heterosexual—are randomly drawn from the total set of foster parents to see how they stack up. News stories are limited in the content they cover, nor are they necessarily consistent from reporter to reporter or paper to paper. Nonetheless, this method has its advantages. News stories are reports about 'the real world,' and not just responses to questionnaires from people who know they are being questioned or scrutinized.

Only a few of the news stories listed the sexual preferences of the perpetrators. Nevertheless, following the classification of method of infection for AIDS by the U.S. Centers for Disease Control, I was able to classify the perpetrators by the kinds of sex they engaged in (e.g., 'male with male' was considered homosexual, 'male with female' heterosexual). Since marital status is generally provided in stories about child molestation, where it was not reported, the perpetrator was assumed to be unmarried.

What I Found

Thirty stories about molestation of foster kids were located. They were numbered by date of the first newspaper story about the molestation, from 1 to 30. The location and date are given below. In 22 stories foster children were sexually abused. Five stories bore upon the character of the foster parent or guardian, though no foster child was reported as having been sexually molested. In three stories, foster caregivers molested their charges as they were held in group quarters.

Result #1. In 22 stories, the perpetrator(s) molested foster children:

1. Arlington, VA (3/2/89): An unmarried man, who had had boys placed in his home for 10 years, was charged with having sex with one of the foster boys (this was counted as one homosexual male perpetrator, one victim).

2. San Diego (3/1/89): A mother (who was married to an oft-absent husband in the military) and son lost their foster day care license when charges of possible molestation of two children were filed against her (counted as a female perpetrator and two victims of unknown sex).

4. Los Angeles (6/6/90): A man and wife lost their license when the man was accused of molesting two foster daughters (counted as a heterosexual male perpetrator and two girl victims).

7. St. Louis (10/21/90): An unmarried man, both a foster parent to one boy and the supervisor of a unit at a children's home, was convicted of molesting his foster son as well as 4 other boys at the home (counted as a homosexual male perpetrator and one boy victim).

8. British Columbia, Canada (3/26/92): A man (marital status not provided) was released from prison for molesting a 14-year-old foster daughter (counted as a male heterosexual perpetrator and one girl victim).

10. Los Angeles (7/8/93): A man and wife lost their foster care license when the man was charged with molesting 2 of his foster daughters (counted as a male heterosexual perpetrator and 2 girl victims).

11. St. Petersburg, FL (1/11/94): An unmarried man was convicted of molesting his 12-year-old foster son (counted as a homosexual male perpetrator and one boy victim).

12. Maryland (4/16/94): An unmarried judge was charged with molesting his 17-year-old foster son (counted as a homosexual male perpetrator and one boy victim).

13. San Francisco (12/13/94): A married man was convicted of molesting boys and girls, including 3 foster children (counted as one homosexual male perpetrator and 3 victims of unknown sex).

15. Atlanta (1/30/97): A married man molested his 12-year-old foster son (counted as a homosexual male perpetrator and one boy victim).

17. Connecticut (3/22/97): A man and wife lost their foster-care license when he was accused of molesting his foster son (counted as a homosexual male perpetrator and a boy victim).

18. New York (6/29/97): An apparently unmarried foster mother sexually molested her foster daughter from the time she was age 5 until she was 17 (counted as a homosexual female perpetrator and a female victim).

19. Seattle (12/3/97): An unmarried couple molested an 8-year-old foster daughter (counted as a homosexual female perpetrator and a male heterosexual perpetrator and a female victim).

21. England (12/5/98): An unmarried foster parent was convicted of molesting his 12-year-old foster son (counted as a homosexual male perpetrator and a boy victim).

22. Atlanta (2/27/99): An unmarried foster parent was convicted of molesting his 3 foster children, a girl and two boys (counted as a homosexual male perpetrator and a girl and two boy victims).

23. Boston (11/3/99): A married foster parent was convicted of molesting "foster children" (counted as a male perpetrator with 2 victims of unknown sex).

24. Toronto (4/3/00): A married foster parent was convicted of molesting a foster daughter (counted as a heterosexual male perpetrator and a girl victim).

25. San Diego (4/25/00): A married foster parent was convicted of molesting two twin 9-year-old foster daughters (counted as a heterosexual male perpetrator and two girl victims).

26. San Diego (6/23/00): A unmarried foster father was charged with sexual improprieties with his foster son, 11, and hiring him out for sex with other men (counted as a homosexual male perpetrator and a boy victim).

28. San Diego (9/24/00): An unmarried openly homosexual male, living with a partner who was a convicted homosexual child molester (the partner had sexually abused his own son and daughter), was given custody of an 11-year-old foster son. He then raped him. Over the years the foster father also offered his foster son to others who were sexually interested in the boy. At least three individuals accepted the foster-father's offer (counted as a homosexual male perpetrator and a boy victim).

29. Los Angeles (7/10/01): An unmarried woman pled no contest to the accusation of sexually abusing her 12-year-old foster daughter, and then lost her foster-care license (counted as a homosexual female perpetrator and a female victim).

30. St. Louis (12/31/01): An unmarried foster father was charged with molesting 2 foster sons, both 13 years old (counted as a homosexual male perpetrator and two boy victims).

Comment: It is noteworthy that in two of the 12 stories involving gays, the homosexual not only molested his foster son, but prostituted him as well. Something seems to be morally 'wrong' with homosexuals.

Result #2. Five stories concerned the character of the foster parent:

3. Boston (5/18/89): An unmarried man had illicit pictures of boys. Although he had been convicted of child molestation on a boy in 1967 (and given a suspended sentence), starting in 1977 the Massachusetts Probation Department used him as a placement for "24 adolescent males during the past 12 years."

5. Seattle (8/28/90): An unmarried man, with whom 5 foster children were currently living, admitted to molesting two boys, 14 and 15, in his Scout troop. He had been dishonorably discharged from the Navy for "similar incidents involving young boys."

6. St. Louis (8/31/90): An unmarried child molester had a 14-year-old boy placed in his home by the Missouri Division of Family Services. The boy's older brother also lived with the man. The child molester had been convicted of attempted rape of and then stabbing a 12-year-old boy. It is not clear whether he had had sex with the foster boys.

9. Los Angeles (12/29/92): A man and wife lost their foster care license when the man was charged with molesting 2 of his daughters from a previous marriage.

20. Seattle (11/3/98): An unmarried foster parent of a boy was accused of molesting 5 boys. The boys were apparently from a church youth group he assisted.

Comment: Is it a statistical fluke that 3 of the 4 gay foster parents above already had 'a record of child molestation' and yet were given boys to foster parent? Perhaps. But the bias that child protective services seem to exhibit in favor of homosexuals offers a more chilling possibility. While the 'fox' is not running the henhouse, there appear to be a considerable number of 'foxes' in these agencies—and in the current climate of ceding victimhood status to gays, even the non-foxes are inclined to 'give homosexuals a second chance.'

Result #3. In three stories, children in a group home were molested:

14. Los Angeles (5/2/96): For the second time in the year, the state initiated action to revoke the foster home license of Gay and Lesbian Adolescent Social Services because an additional number of boys reported having been molested by male staff members (counted as 3 homosexual male perpetrators and 6 boy victims).
16. Wales, Great Britain (2/4/97): Dozens of staff members at 30 children's homes sexually abused 180 victims, "most . . . were boys, some as young as 8."
27. Los Angeles (8/30/00): At least 3 male counselors raped at least 3 boys and a girl at group homes. One of the perpetrators was single, and at least one boy he raped obtained a judgment against him. There were no follow-up stories about the other perpetrators.

Comment: These stories suggest character flaws inherent to the homosexual lifestyle—flaws that put children under the care of homosexuals at considerable hazard. Note that although there are a lot of girls in children's homes, the boys appear to be at special risk. And why was a homosexual social service allowed to run group homes?

What Do These Stories Suggest?

A pattern of disproportionate molestation of foster children by those who engage in homosexuality is evident in each of the three sets of stories above. The 22 stories involving molestation of foster children, in particular, bear directly upon whether homosexual or unmarried foster parents commit more sexual offenses against their charges. Of the 22 stories, 15 (68%) involved homosexual molestation. Of the 23 perpetrators, 19 (83%) were men, and 4 (17%) were women. Of the 19 men, 12 (63%) engaged in homosexuality. Three (25%) of these 12 were married, while 9 were single. Seven (37%) of the 19 male perpetrators practiced heterosexuality. Of these 7, at least 5 (71%) were married and at least one was single.

Of the 4 women, 3 engaged in homosexuality and were unmarried. The other was married but her sexual proclivities were not revealed. Overall, of the 22 perpetrators whose marital status was known, 13 (59%) were single.

In the 22 stories, among the 32 foster children who were victimized, at least 12 (38%) were girls and at least 13 (41%) were boys. Since 2.5 of the girls were victimized by females (counting the girl who was victimized by the unmarried man and woman as being 0.5 homosexually and 0.5 heterosexually victimized), altogether, out of the 28 victims of perpetrators where a sexual preference could be determined, 8.5 (30%) were victimized by heterosexuals and 19.5 (70%) by homosexuals. Also, of the 32 children, at least 15 (43%) were victimized by the unmarried.

So What Does This Evidence Indicate about Gay Foster Parents?

Undoubtedly, only a fraction of child molestation by foster parents over the 13 years I examined was included in any news stories. If they did 'make the paper,' many—like the molestation of the boy in Vermont in 2002 that led me to conduct this study—only made the local newspaper, not the newspapers covered by Academic Universe. But there is no reason to believe that this sample was biased against those who engage in homosexuality. Indeed, a number of the newspapers included in Academic Universe have editorialized in favor of special social protections for those who engage in homosexuality (e.g., *Los Angeles Times, New York Times, Boston Globe*). And these same newspapers have also expressed support for 'marital status nondiscrimination.' So they would have seemingly little reason to 'pick on' gay foster parents.

That at least 15 of the 22 instances of molestation of a foster child by a foster parent involved those who engaged in homosexuality is sharply at odds with the National Association of Social Workers' (NASW) 1987 resolution decrying "resistance to using single parents, . . . including lesbian and gay parents, as potential foster care and adoption resources." It also flies in the face of the NASW's appeal to its members to 'correct' this 'injustice.'

The empirical evidence is lined up against the NASW—of the 21 stories where the sexual proclivities of the perpetrator could be determined, 71% implicated homosexuals! Likewise, at least 57% of the 22 perpetrators were unmarried, and they accounted for at least 47% of the 32 child victims.

Homosexuality was also a disproportionate problem in the other 8 stories. When they are around or 'in charge' of kids, homosexuals are far more apt to seek to have sex with them. Nevertheless, we hear a lot from talk show hosts that homosexuals are no more apt to molest kids—tell that to the children who were victimized in these stories!

These news stories suggest that homosexuals and unmarried individuals are more apt to molest their foster charges. Because of this, they would not seem to be 'as fit' foster parents as married heterosexuals. The boy in story number 28, despite being raped, desired to return to live with the perpetrator. So he was apparently willing to 'live with molestations,' perhaps because there were other compensatory benefits in the arrangement. However, no matter how 'great' a parent they might be otherwise, there is no way someone can be a 'fit' foster parent if they sexually abuse their placements.

In a study FRI published earlier this year, interviews with 57 children with gay parents revealed that living in a homosexual home was a trying experience for children. In addition, the largest comparison study done to date— 58 kids with married parents, 58 kids with cohabiting heterosexual parents, and 58 kids with homosexual parents—reported that the children with homosexual parents did less well at school, less well socially, and often gave evidence of personal distress. Thus, there is no particular reason to believe that either homosexuals or the unmarried generally compensate for their sexual weaknesses by offering exceptional foster-service in 'other areas.'

If the welfare of children is regarded as the most important consideration in foster-placement, these findings that the unmarried and those who engage in homosexuality are more likely to sexually molest their foster children suggest that the traditional aversion to their use as foster parents is rational and reasonable. Our society makes a lot of noise about 'protecting the children' and 'for the sake of the children.' But our foster system—which may process almost half a million kids every year—is being run throughout the country according to an alien, anti-child social philosophy.

Organizations like the NASW and many child protective service agencies across the land should lose their federal and state funding, until and unless they quit using kids' lives as bricks to reinforce unproven assertions that 'homosexuals are just as good' or that 'the unmarried are just as good.' Kids who need foster care are usually already under considerable stress—they don't need social revolutionaries putting them in highly sexually-charged environments.

POSTSCRIPT

Is Gay Adoption and Foster Parenting Healthy for Children?

There are increasing types of unique family forms that are coming to light as we move more deeply into the twenty-first century. Gay and lesbian-headed families are perhaps the most prominent of these forms. As a consequence, these new family forms challenge the traditional notions of who should be a parent and how families should look. Gay and lesbian families force us as a society to examine the relation between gender and parenting, the role of society in family life, and biological relations as prerequisite to the formation of a family. Is, for example, a lesbian mother, who is the biological parent of her seven-year-old daughter, and the mother's partner, who is committed to loving and caring for the seven-year-old, a family in the legal sense? Is it necessary for a family to be a "legal" family for the children within the family to develop into well-adjusted adults? Are these nontraditional homosexual families significantly different than common law–type heterosexual families?

With the need for qualified foster parents and adoptive parents for older children rising, should society automatically disqualify foster and adoptive parents because of their sexual orientation? It is true that there are many heterosexual married couples ready and waiting to adopt newborns in this country, but the need for reliable foster parents and adoptive parents for older children is great. Would it be better for a child to be raised in a loving home, rather than moved from placement to placement, regardless of the sexual orientation of the parents? Some advocates for homosexual parenting rights suggest that children raised in gay and lesbian families will develop a greater capacity for empathy, tolerance for others, and a healthy respect for differences among people than those children raised in traditional, heterosexual families because these children are forced to embrace these issues more overtly. Is teaching tolerance and respect for differences not a significant goal for *all* parents in the twenty-first century? If this is so, perhaps there is an advantage to being raised by homosexual parents!

The intensity of the beliefs and feelings behind the arguments for each side of the issue of homosexual parenting is immense. This is, however, but one issue in the ongoing dialogue of what is moral and what is immoral in our society. Some factions believe that it is immoral to raise a child without exposing that child to a religion. Atheists, however, are allowed to adopt and raise children and be foster parents. Others feel that adulterers, chronic gamblers, and those that abuse drugs and alcohol are immoral. Clearly, there are countless families where children are raised as parents grapple with these issues. Who decides where we draw the line as to who is moral and who is not when it comes to raising children? With such powerful feelings and emotions coming from the adults involved in this argument, it is most important to remember that we, as a community, should be working toward what is best for the children, rather than satisfying the urge to be right in our beliefs.

Related Readings

American Academy of Pediatrics. (February 2002). Technical report: Co-parent or second-parent adoption by same sex parents. *Pediatrics, 109,* 341–349.

American College of Pediatrics. (2004). Homosexual parenting: Is it time for a change? <http://www.acpeds.org/?CONTEXT=art&%20cat=22&art=50& BISKIT=2920801063>

Beaucar, K. (July 18, 2001). Homosexual parenting studies are flawed, report says. http://www.foxnews.com/story/0,2933,29901,00.html <http://www. foxnews.com/story/0,2933, 29901,00.html>

Cameron, P., & Perrin, E. (April 22, 2002). *Insight on the News, Symposium on Adoption by Gay or Lesbian Couples, 18,* 40–47.

Phillips, D., & Phillips, R. (July 2001). Homosexual parenting. *The Australian Family.* http://www.family.org.au/journal/2001/j20010728.html <http://www.family. org.au/journal/2001/j20010728.html>

Ray, V., & Gregory, R. (Winter 2001). School experiences of the children of lesbian and gay parents. *Family Matters,* 28–39.

Tasker, F. (1999). Children in lesbian-led families: A review. *Clinical Child Psychology and Psychiatry, 4,* 153–166.

ISSUE 14

Should the HPV Vaccination Be Mandatory for Girls in Later Childhood?

YES: Cynthia Dailard, from "Achieving Universal Vaccination Against Cervical Cancer in the United States: The Need and the Means," *Guttmacher Policy Review* (Fall 2006)

NO: Roni Rabin, from "A New Vaccine for Girls, but Should It Be Compulsory?" *The New York Times* (July 18, 2006)

ISSUE SUMMARY

YES: Cynthia Dailard, a senior public policy associate for the Alan Guttmacher Institute, suggests that the HPV vaccine be administered to females as a school entry requirement. She believes the vaccine is safe and effective and therefore should be universally administered to young girls. The best way to ensure the vaccine is available to these girls is by enacting state laws or policies requiring children to be vaccinated before school or day care enrollment.

NO: Roni Rabin, a columnist for *The New York Times*, objects to making the HPV vaccine mandatory for girls. She agrees that the vaccine is a significant development for the health and safety of our children. However, she does not believe every girl should be required to be vaccinated because the vaccine is costly and can be managed through current, less costly procedures such as Pap smears.

Human papillomavirus (HPV) is a common sexually transmitted disease that most infected individuals do not realize they have. It usually clears up within a few years on its own. The problem with HPV is that some strains (e.g., HPV-16 and HPV-18) cause most of the genital warts and the vast majority of cancers of the cervix, anus, and even the throat. People who contract the various strains of HPV do not always develop cancer or genital warts, but the risk of contracting the strains that cause these problems is ever present. Gardasil is the brand name for an HPV vaccine that was approved by the Food and Drug Administration in 2006 to prevent cervical cancer and genital warts.

The HPV vaccination may be one of the greatest health advances for women in the past several decades. In two studies by the Centers for Disease Control (CDC), the vaccine was 100 percent effective in preventing precancerous lesions and genital warts. In the second study, it was 98 percent effective in protecting against precancerous cervical lesions. Since, Gardasil prevents the human papillomavirus from infecting sexually active women, the CDC recommends that females obtain the vaccination prior to becoming sexually active. They suggest being inoculated at ages 11 to 12. However, girls as young as 9 can get the vaccination, and those aged 13 to 26 are still advised to receive the vaccine even though it is not as effective if sexual activity has already begun. Since the CDC has added Gardasil to the recommended childhood vaccination schedule, several states are currently considering whether to make the vaccine mandatory for public school attendance.

Advocates for the vaccine promote universal vaccination and support laws to mandate vaccination as a prerequisite to attending school. A recent CDC study found that nearly 25 percent of women aged 14 to 59 and 49 percent of women aged 20 to 24 currently have HPV. HPV is very prevalent not only in the United States but in less industrialized countries as well. In places where Pap tests are not as readily available, there is greater prevalence of cervical cancer. In order to minimize the spread of HPV, advocates for the vaccination believe young girls across the globe should be inoculated prior to any sexual activity. To prevent deaths from measles and Polio, vaccinations for these diseases had to reach the universal level. Advocates for the HPV vaccine hope the same should happen for Gardasil.

Opponents believe vaccination should be a personal choice for parents to make for their children. Mandating inoculation would further erode parents' rights to raise their children as they see fit. Other opponents are fearful that having the vaccination may actually encourage girls to engage in premarital sex because they would not be fearful of contracting HPV. Still others prefer having regular Pap screenings, which they believe are preferable in detecting HPV, because the long-term effects of the vaccine are still unknown. They argue that the virus is not transmitted through casual contact. Consequently, the vaccination should not be universally mandated. They do not believe all girls need to be vaccinated that young. Another argument states most cases of cervical cancer in the United States come from women who do not regularly receive Pap tests. Opponents also say the vaccine is expensive and contend that the women who can afford the HPV vaccine are not the women who need it because they are annually getting Pap tests, which detect the HPV virus.

The following selections convey points for and against universal use of the HPV vaccine. Are viruses that are transmitted through casual contact more easily approved and subsequently mandated by federal law? Is sexual contact such a controversial issue that it affects the judgment of policymakers and parents? Think about these questions as you read the next two articles arguing for and against making the vaccination for HPV mandatory for young girls.

YES

Cynthia Dailard

Achieving Universal Vaccination against Cervical Cancer in the United States: The Need and the Means

The advent of a vaccine against the types of human papillomavirus (HPV) linked to most cases of cervical cancer is widely considered one of the greatest health care advances for women in recent years. Experts believe that vaccination against HPV has the potential to dramatically reduce cervical cancer incidence and mortality, particularly in resource-poor developing countries where cervical cancer is most common and deadly. In the United States, the vaccine's potential is likely to be felt most acutely within low-income communities and communities of color, which disproportionately bear the burden of cervical cancer.

Because HPV is easily transmitted through sexual contact, the vaccine's full promise may only be realized through near-universal vaccination of girls and young women prior to sexual activity—a notion reflected in recently proposed federal guidelines. And history, as supported by a large body of scientific evidence, suggests that the most effective way to achieve universal vaccination is by requiring children to be inoculated prior to attending school. Yet the link between HPV and sexual activity—and the notion that HPV is different than other infectious diseases targeted by vaccine school entry requirements—tests the prevailing justification for such efforts. Meanwhile, any serious effort to achieve universal vaccination among young people with this relatively expensive vaccine will expose holes in the public health safety net that, if left unaddressed, have the potential to exacerbate long-standing disparities in cervical cancer rates among American women.

The Case for Universal Vaccination

Virtually all cases of cervical cancer are linked to HPV, an extremely common sexually transmitted infection (STI) that is typically asymptomatic and harmless; most people never know they are infected, and most cases resolve on their own. It is estimated that approximately three in four Americans contract HPV at some point in their lives, with most cases acquired relatively soon

From *Guttmacher Policy Review*, vol. 9, no. 4, Fall 2006, pp. 12–16. Copyright © 2006 by Alan Guttmacher Institute. Reprinted by permission.

after individuals have sex for the first time. Of the approximately 30 known types of HPV that are sexually transmitted, more than 13 are associated with cervical cancer. Yet despite the prevalence of HPV, cervical cancer is relatively rare in the United States; it generally occurs only in the small proportion of cases where a persistent HPV infection goes undetected over many years. This is largely due to the widespread availability of Pap tests, which can detect pre-cancerous changes of the cervix that can be treated before cancer sets in, as well as cervical cancer in its earliest stage, when it is easily treatable.

Still, the American Cancer Society estimates that in 2006, almost 10,000 cases of invasive cervical cancer will occur to American women, resulting in 3,700 deaths. Significantly, more than half of all U.S. women diagnosed with cervical cancer have not had a Pap test in the last three years. These women are dispro-portionately low income and women of color who lack access to affordable and culturally competent health services. As a result, the incidence of cervical cancer is approximately 1.5 times higher among African American and Latina women than among white women; women of color are considerably more likely than whites to die of the disease as well. Two new HPV vaccines—Gardasil, manufac-tured by Merck & Company, and Cervarix, manufactured by GlaxoSmithKline—promise to transform this landscape. Both are virtually 100% effective in preventing the two types of HPV responsible for 70% of all cases of cervical cancer; Gardasil also protects against two other HPV types associated with 90% of all cases of genital warts. Gardasil was approved by the federal Food and Drug Administration (FDA) in June; GlaxoSmithKline is expected to apply for FDA approval of Cervarix by year's end.

Following FDA approval, Gardasil was endorsed by the Centers for Disease Control and Prevention's Advisory Committee on Immunization Practices (ACIP), which is responsible for maintaining the nation's schedule of recom-mended vaccines. ACIP recommended that the vaccine be routinely adminis-tered to all girls ages 11–12, and as early as age nine at a doctor's discretion. Also, it recommended vaccination of all adolescents and young women ages 13–26 as part of a national "catch-up" campaign for those who have not already been vaccinated.

The ACIP recommendations, which are closely followed by health care professionals, reflect the notion that to eradicate cervical cancer, it will be necessary to achieve near-universal vaccination of girls and young women prior to sexual activity, when the vaccine is most effective. Experts believe that such an approach has the potential to significantly reduce cervical cancer deaths in this country and around the world. Also, high vaccination rates will significantly reduce the approximately 3.5 million abnormal Pap results expe-rienced by American women each year, many of which are caused by transient or persistent HPV infections. These abnormal Pap results require millions of women to seek follow-up care, ranging from additional Pap tests to more invasive procedures such as colposcopies and biopsies. This additional care exacts a substantial emotional and even physical toll on women, and costs an estimated $6 billion in annual health care expenditures. Finally, widespread vaccination fosters "herd immunity," which is achieved when a sufficiently high proportion of individuals within a population are vaccinated that those who go unvaccinated—because the vaccine is contraindicated for them or because they are medically underserved, for example—are essentially protected.

The Role of School Entry Requirements

Achieving high vaccination levels among adolescents, however, can be a difficult proposition. Unlike infants and toddlers, who have frequent contact with health care providers in the context of well-child visits, adolescents often go for long stretches without contact with a health care professional. In addition, the HPV vaccine is likely to pose particular challenges, given that it must be administered three times over a six-month period to achieve maximum effectiveness.

A large body of evidence suggests that the most effective means to ensure rapid and widespread use of childhood or adolescent vaccines is through state laws or policies that require children to be vaccinated prior to enrollment in day care or school. These school-based immunization requirements, which exist in some form in all 50 states, are widely credited for the success of immunization programs in the United States. They have also played a key role in helping to close racial, ethnic and socioeconomic gaps in immunization rates, and have proven to be far more effective than guidelines recommending the vaccine for certain age-groups or high-risk populations. Although each state decides for itself whether a particular vaccine will be required for children to enroll in school, they typically rely on ACIP recommendations in making their decision.

In recent months, some commentators have noted that as a sexually transmitted infection, HPV is "different" from other infectious diseases such as measles, mumps or whooping cough, which are easily transmitted in a school setting or threaten school attendance when an outbreak occurs. Some socially conservative advocacy groups accordingly argue that the HPV vaccine does not meet the historical criteria necessary for it to be required for children attending school; many of them also contend that abstinence outside of marriage is the real answer to HPV. They welcome the advent of the vaccine, they say, but will oppose strenuously any effort to require it for school enrollment.

This position reflects only a limited understanding of school-based vaccination requirements. These requirements do not exist solely to prevent the transmission of disease in school or during childhood. Instead, they further society's strong interest in ensuring that people are protected from disease throughout their lives and are a highly efficient means of eradicating disease in the larger community. For example, states routinely require school-age children to be vaccinated against rubella (commonly known as German measles), a typically mild illness in children, to protect pregnant women in the community from the devastating effects the disease can have on a developing fetus. Similarly, states currently require vaccination against certain diseases, such as tetanus, that are not "contagious" at all, but have very serious consequences for those affected. And almost all states require vaccination against Hepatitis B, a blood born disease which can be sexually transmitted.

Moreover, according to the National Conference of State Legislatures (NCSL), all 50 states allow parents to refuse to vaccinate their children on medical grounds, such as when a vaccine is contraindicated for a particular child due to allergy, compromised immunity or significant illness. All states except Mississippi and West Virginia allow parents to refuse to vaccinate their children on religious grounds. Additionally, 20 states go so far as to allow parents to refuse to vaccinate their children because of a personal, moral or other belief. Unlike a medical exemption, which requires a parent to provide documentation from a physician, the process for obtaining nonmedical exemptions can vary widely by state.

NCSL notes that, in recent years, almost a dozen states considered expanding their exemption policy. Even absent any significant policy change, the rate of parents seeking exemptions for nonmedical reasons is on the rise. This concerns public health experts. Research shows that in states where exemptions are easier to obtain, a higher proportion of parents refuse to vaccinate their children; research further shows that these states, in turn, are more likely to experience outbreaks of vaccine-preventable diseases, such as measles and whooping cough. Some vaccine program administrators fear that because of the social sensitivities surrounding the HPV vaccine, any effort to require the vaccine for school entry may prompt legislators to amend their laws to create nonmedical exemptions where they do not currently exist or to make existing exemptions easier to obtain. This has the potential not only to thwart the effort to stem the tide of cervical cancer, but to foster the spread of other vaccine-preventable diseases as well.

Financing Challenges Laid Bare

Another barrier to achieving universal vaccination of girls and young women will be the high price of the vaccine. Gardasil is expensive by vaccine standards, costing approximately $360 for the three-part series of injections. Despite this high cost, ACIP's endorsement means that Gardasil will be covered by most private insurers; in fact, a number of large insurers have already announced they will cover the vaccine for girls and young women within the ACIP-recommended age range. Still, the Institute of Medicine estimates that approximately 11% of all American children have private insurance that does not cover immunization, and even those with insurance coverage may have to pay deductibles and copayments that create a barrier to care.

Those who do not have private insurance or who cannot afford the out-of-pocket costs associated with Gardasil will need to rely on a patchwork system of programs that exist to support the delivery of subsidized vaccines to low-income and uninsured individuals. In June, ACIP voted to include Gardasil in the federal Vaccines for Children program (VFC), which provides free vaccines largely to children and teenagers through age 18 who are uninsured or receive Medicaid. The program's reach is significant: In 2003, 43% of all childhood vaccine doses were distributed by the VFC program.

THE POTENTIAL ROLE OF FAMILY PLANNING CLINICS IN AN HPV VACCINE 'CATCH-UP' CAMPAIGN

Family planning clinics, including those funded under Title X of the Public Health Service Act, have an important role to play in a national "catch-up" campaign to vaccinate young women against HPV. This is particularly true for women ages 19–26, who are too old to receive free vaccines through the federal Vaccines for Children program but still fall within the ACIP-recommended age range for the HPV vaccine.

Almost 4,600 Title X–funded family planning clinics provide subsidized family planning and related preventive health care to just over five million women nationwide. In theory, Title X clinics are well poised to offer the HPV vaccine, because they already are a major provider of STI services and cervical cancer screening, providing approximately six million STI (including HIV) tests and 2.7 million Pap tests in 2004 alone. Because Title X clients are disproportionately low income and women of color, they are at particular risk of developing cervical cancer later in life. Moreover, most Title X clients fall within the ACIP age recommendations of 26 and under for the HPV vaccine (59% are age 24 or younger, and 18% are ages 25–29); many of these women are uninsured and may not have an alternative source of health care.

Title X funds may be used to pay for vaccines linked to improved reproductive health outcomes, and some Title X clinics offer the Hepatitis B vaccine (which can be sexually transmitted). Although many family planning providers are expressing interest in incorporating the HPV vaccine into their package of services, its high cost—even at a discounted government purchase price—is likely to stand in the way. Clinics that receive Title X funds are required by law to charge women based on their ability to pay, with women under 100% of the federal poverty level (representing 68% of Title X clients) receiving services completely free of charge and those with incomes between 100–250% of poverty charged on a sliding scale. While Merck has expressed an interest in extending its patient assistance program to publicly funded family planning clinics, it makes no promises. In fact, a statement on the company's Web site says that "Due to the complexities associated with vaccine funding and distribution in the public sector, as well as the resource constraints that typically exist in public health settings, Merck is currently evaluating whether and how a vaccine assistance program could be implemented in the public sector."

The HPV vaccine, however, is not just recommended for children and teenagers; it is also recommended for young adult women up through age 26. Vaccines are considered an "optional" benefit for adults under Medicaid, meaning that it is up to each individual state to decide whether or not to cover a given vaccine. Also, states can use their own funds and federal grants to support the delivery of subsidized vaccines to low-income or uninsured adults. Many states, however, have opted instead to channel these funds toward childhood-vaccination efforts, particularly as vaccine prices have grown in recent years. As a result, adult vaccination rates remain low and disparities exist across racial, ethnic and socioeconomic groups—mirroring the disparities that exist for cervical cancer.

In response to all this, Merck in May announced it would create a new "patient assistance program," designed to provide all its vaccines free to adults who are uninsured, unable to afford the vaccines and have an annual household income below 200% of the federal poverty level ($19,600 for individuals and $26,400 for couples). To receive free vaccines, patients will need to complete and fax forms from participating doctors' offices for processing by Merck during the patients' visits. Many young uninsured women, however, do not seek their care in private doctors' offices, but instead rely on publicly funded family planning clinics for their care, suggesting the impact of this program may be limited (see box).

Thinking Ahead

Solutions to the various challenges presented by the HPV vaccine are likely to have relevance far beyond cervical cancer. In the coming years, scientific breakthroughs in the areas of immunology, molecular biology and genetics will eventually permit vaccination against a broader range of acute illnesses as well as chronic diseases. Currently, vaccines for other STIs such as chlamydia, herpes and HIV are in various stages of development. Also under study are vaccines for Alzheimer's disease, diabetes and a range of cancers. Vaccines for use among adolescents will also be increasingly common. A key question is, in the future, will individuals across the economic spectrum have access to these breakthrough medical advances or will disadvantaged individuals be left behind?

When viewed in this broader context, the debate over whether the HPV vaccine should be required for school enrollment may prove to be a healthy one. If the HPV vaccine is indeed "the first of its kind," as some have characterized it, it has the potential to prompt communities across the nation to reconsider and perhaps reconceive the philosophical justification for school entry requirements. Because the U.S. health care system is fragmented, people have no guarantee of health insurance coverage or access to affordable care. School entry requirements might therefore provide an important opportunity to deliver public health interventions that, like the HPV vaccine, offer protections to individuals who have the potential to become disconnected from health care services later in life. Similar to the HPV vaccine's promise of cervical cancer prevention, these benefits may not be felt for many years, but nonetheless may be compelling from a societal standpoint. And bearing in mind that school dropout rates begin to climb as early as age 13, middle school might be appropriately viewed as the last public health gate that an entire age-group of individuals pass through together—regardless of race, ethnicity or socio-economic status.

Meanwhile, the cost and affordability issues raised by the HPV vaccine may help draw attention to the need to reform the vaccine-financing system in this country. In 2003, the Institute of Medicine proposed a series of reforms designed to improve the way vaccines are financed and distributed. They included a national insurance benefit mandate that would apply to all public and private health care plans and vouchers for uninsured children and adults to receive immunizations through the provider of their choice. Legislation introduced by Rep. Henry Waxman (D-CA) and Sen. Edward Kennedy (D-MA), called the Vaccine Access and Supply Act, adopts a different approach. The bill would expand the Vaccines for Children program, create a comparable Vaccines for Adults program, strengthen the vaccine grant program to the states and prohibit Medicaid cost-sharing requirements for ACIP-recommended vaccines for adults.

Whether the HPV vaccine will in fact hasten reforms of any kind remains to be seen. But one thing is clear: If the benefits of this groundbreaking vaccine cannot be enjoyed by girls and women who are disadvantaged by poverty or insurance status, then it will only serve to perpetuate the disparities in cervical cancer rates that have persisted in this country for far too long.

Roni Rabin  **NO**

A New Vaccine for Girls, but Should It Be Compulsory?

Around the time report cards came home this spring, federal health officials approved another new vaccine to add to the ever-growing list of recommended childhood shots—this one for girls and women only, from 9 to 26, to protect them from genital warts and cervical cancer.

One of my own daughters, who just turned 9, would be a candidate for this vaccine, so I've been mulling this over. A shot that protects against cancer sounds like a great idea, at first. States may choose to make it mandatory, though the cost for them to do so would be prohibitive.

But let's think carefully before requiring young girls to get this vaccine, which protects against a sexually transmitted virus, in order to go to school. This isn't polio or measles, diseases that are easily transmitted through casual contact. Infection with this virus requires intimate contact, of the kind that doesn't occur in classrooms.

Besides, we already know how to prevent cervical cancer in this country, and we've done a darn good job of it. In the war against cancer, the battle against cervical cancer has been a success story.

Why, then, did federal health officials recommend the inoculation of about 30 million American girls and young women against the human papillomavirus, a sexually transmitted disease that in rare cases leads to cervical cancer?

Vaccine supporters say that some 3,700 American women die of cervical cancer each year, and close to 10,000 cases are diagnosed. Cervical cancer has a relatively high survival rate, but every death is tragic and treatment can rob women of their fertility.

Still, you have to see the numbers in context. Cervical cancer deaths have been dropping consistently in the United States—and have been for decades.

Cervical cancer has gone from being one of the top killers of American women to not even being on the top 10 list. This year cervical cancer will represent just 1 percent of the 679,510 new cancer cases and 1 percent of the 273,560 anticipated cancer deaths among American women. By contrast, some 40,970 women will die of breast cancer and 72,130 will die of lung cancer.

According to the American Cancer Society Web site, "Between 1955 and 1992, the number of cervical cancer deaths in the United States dropped by 74 percent." Think about it: 74 percent.

The number of cases diagnosed each year and the number of deaths per year have continued to drop, even though the population is growing.

From 1997 to 2003, the number of cervical cancers in the United States dropped by 4.5 percent each year, while the number of deaths dropped by 3.8 percent each year, according to a government Web site that tracks cancer trends, called SEER or Surveillance, Epidemiology and End Results. . . . This, while many other cancers are on the rise.

If current trends continue, by the time my 9-year-old daughter is 48, the median age when cervical cancer is diagnosed, there will be only a few thousand cases of the cancer in women, and about 1,000 deaths or fewer each year, even without the vaccine.

The secret weapon? Not so secret. It's the Pap smear. A simple, quick, relatively noninvasive test that's part and parcel of routine preventive health care for women. It provides early warnings of cellular changes in the cervix that are precursors for cancer and can be treated.

An American Cancer Society spokeswoman said that most American women who get cervical cancer these days are women who either had never had a Pap smear or had not followed the follow-up and frequency guidelines. So perhaps we could redirect the public money that would be spent on this vaccine—one of the most expensive ever, priced at $360 for the series of three shots—to make sure all women in the United States get preventive health care.

Because even if you have the new vaccine, which protects against only some of the viral strains that may bring on cervical cancer, you still need to continue getting Pap smears.

To be clear, I'm talking only about American women. Sadly, hundreds of thousands of women worldwide die of cervical cancer each year because they don't have access to Pap smears and the follow-up care required. For them, and for American women at high risk, the vaccine should be an option.

Black, Hispanic and some foreign-born women are at higher risk, though rates have dropped precipitously among blacks. Certain behavior—smoking, eating poorly, having multiple sexual partners and long-term use of the pill, for example—are also associated with an increased risk. But most people infected with the human papillomavirus clear it on their own.

Vaccine supporters, including the American Cancer Society, say the immunization will reduce abnormal Pap test results, and the stress, discomfort and cost of follow-up procedures and painful treatments. That's a strong argument for the vaccine.

But vaccines carry risks. In recent years, children have been bombarded with new immunizations, and we still don't know the full long-term implications. One vaccine, RotaShield, was removed from the market in 1999, just a year after being approved for infants.

Merck has tested the cervical cancer vaccine in clinical trials of more than 20,000 women (about half of them got the shot). The health of the subjects was followed for about three and a half years on average. But fewer than

1,200 girls under 16 got the shots, among them only about 100 9-year-olds, Merck officials said, and the younger girls have been followed for only 18 months.

Public health officials want to vaccinate girls early, before they become sexually active, even though it is not known how long the immunity will last.

But girls can also protect themselves from the human papillomavirus by using condoms; a recent study found that condoms cut infections by more than half. Condoms also protect against a far more insidious sexually transmitted virus, H.I.V.

So yes, by all means, let's keep stamping out cervical cancer. Let's make sure women and girls get Pap smears.

POSTSCRIPT

Should the HPV Vaccination Be Mandatory for Girls in Later Childhood?

As stated in the introduction, HPV is a common type of sexually transmitted disease. In most cases, those infected with the virus recover with no medical intervention. The Centers for Disease Control and Prevention (CDC) state that most of those infected do not know that they have contracted the virus since they do not have any symptoms. Do you think that the benign nature of most of the cases of HPV is the reason for the reluctance of some to support universal vaccination? Does the support and recommendation of the CDC to have girls universally vaccinated prior to the time they may become sexually active offer a sense of safety and security to parents who are leaning toward having their daughters vaccinated? Or does it encourage parents to be suspect as they may be about other government-supported initiatives? Perhaps, as one of the selections suggests, vaccination at such an early age would send a message of a false sense of security and encourage sexually active females to engage in unprotected sex?

If there is such controversy about universal vaccination, should American tax dollars be used for research in areas such as this one? However, if one of America's goals is to find cures for various types of cancers, shouldn't young girls be vaccinated in order to eliminate cervical cancer?

Finally, at what point do federal laws requiring universal vaccination "fly in the face" of parental and family morals and values? If this vaccination is required by federal laws, will some young girls see it as a ticket to early promiscuity? If this vaccine becomes mandatory, what message does it send? Will other vaccines for other diseases also become mandatory? If so, at what point will there be too many mandated inoculations? What about the long-term safety implications of injecting our children with so many different vaccines?

Suggested Readings

Dempsey, A. F., et. al. (2006). Factors that are associated with parental acceptance of Human Papillomavirus Vaccines: A randomized intervention study of written information about HPV (Human Papillomavirus). *Pediatrics, 117*(5).

HPV Vaccine. (2007). National Conference of State Legislatures: U.S. Department of Health & Human Services. www.ncsl.org/programs/health/HPVvaccine.htm.

MacKenzie, Debora. (April 2005). Will cancer vaccine get to all women? www.newscientist.com/channel/sex/mg18624954.500.

The New England Journal of Medicine (May 10, 2007). (This entire issue contains various articles on HPV and the vaccine.)

Vaccine Protects Against Virus Linked to Half of All Cervical Cancers. (2005). National Cancer Institute; U.S. National Institutes of Health. www.cancer.gov/clinicaltrials/results/cervical-cancer-vaccine1102.

Internet References . . .

Positive Parenting

This Positive Parenting site contains information and articles related to how parents and educators can communicate more effectively with children and adolescents. Most of the linked information is specific to adolescence.

http://www.positiveparenting.com

CYFERNet

The Children, Youth, and Families Education and Research Network (CYFERNet), sponsored by the U.S. Department of Agriculture's Cooperative Extension Service, provides practical research-based information in health, child care, family strengths, science, and technology.

http://www.cyfernet.org

The American Academy of Child and Adolescent Psychiatry Home Page

Here the American Academy of Child and Adolescent Psychiatry provides information as a public service to assist families and educators in socializing children and adolescents.

http://www.aacap.org

Adolescent Health On-Line

This Adolescent Health On-Line site of the American Medical Association (AMA) provides extensive information on adolescent health issues and the AMA's Guidelines for Adolescent Preventive Services (GAPS) program. It also links to numerous other sites related to adolescent health issues.

http://www.ama-assn.org/ama/pub/category/1974.html

UNIT 4

Adolescence

*M*any people use the term teenage years to describe adolescence. This is the period of time from ages 13 through 19. During this period of development the child experiences puberty, and there are dramatic physical changes that occur as the child becomes a young adult. Much less obvious than the physical changes are the cognitive and emotional changes in children at this stage of development. In early adolescence the child is increasingly able to think on an abstract level. Adolescents also undertake the process of identity development, defining who they are. This final section considers some of the key issues related to decisions about values and sexuality that teens make as they move through adolescence.

- Should Children Who Are at Risk for Abuse Remain with Their Families?

- Is Abstinence-Only Sex Education the Best Way to Teach about Sex?

- Is the Internet a Safe Place for Teens to Explore?

ISSUE 15

Should Children Who Are at Risk for Abuse Remain with Their Families?

YES: Lisa Kolb, from "Family Preservation in Missouri," *Public Welfare* (Spring 1993)

NO: Mary-Lou Weisman, from "When Parents Are Not in the Best Interests of the Child," *The Atlantic Monthly* (July 1994)

ISSUE SUMMARY

YES: Lisa Kolb, a public information specialist, asserts that the family preservation model is the best way to help families in crisis. Family preservation keeps all the family members together in the home while helping the family solve its problems.

NO: Freelance writer Mary-Lou Weisman argues that orphanages and out-of-home placements are necessary for children whose parents abuse or neglect them. She maintains that society has an obligation to take children away from parents who are doing serious harm to them and that some children have their only real family experience when living in an institutional setting.

Newspaper headlines and television accounts of parents who neglect, abuse, or even kill their children show that the unthinkable does happen. Parents, the very people who are obligated to nurture and protect their children, do not always meet their children's needs. Parents may forfeit their responsibility to nurture and provide for their children because of drug addiction, mental illness, an abusive childhood, or poor parenting skills.

In the past, children who did not have parents or family members to care for them were sent to orphanages, but presently these children are placed in foster homes, residential treatment centers, or small group care homes. In addition to these types of placements, another alternative, family preservation, has emerged. In the 1980s the large numbers of children who needed foster care exceeded the number of foster homes available. Thus, the idea of family preservation became a popular alternative to out-of-home placement for needy children.

Family preservation is a model of intervention that is family centered and available 24 hours a day, seven days a week. Social workers spend a lot of time with families in their caseload and try to build on the strengths of the family to help create a more functional family unit. At first family preservation was seen to be a cost-effective answer to helping battered children. Now it has come under fire from some critics, who contend that it does more harm than good because the characteristics and standards of the programs have become so varied.

Can all families be served by the family preservation model, and are children protected from abuse during the treatment period? Are children in out-of-home placements or foster care protected from abuse? Studies provide conflicting answers to these questions. Proponents from each side point to cases of abuse and poor care in foster care as well as in family preservation situations.

How can society best care for children who are at risk for abuse or worse? Should the whole family (including children) be kept together and worked with in that context? Should children be placed in foster care until the family's problems are solved? Should children be taken away from parents entirely and sent to an institution for the rest of their childhood?

What do the children think about these choices? When faced with being removed from their home, no matter what the reason, most children probably want to stay at home. Often children will defend their parents before authorities even if their home situation is not safe. In these cases, who intervenes for children when parents cannot meet their responsibilities and when the children themselves want what may be harmful to them? How can society keep its children safe?

In the following selections, Lisa Kolb states that children are further damaged when they are removed from their homes as their families deal with crises. She sees family preservation as a successful way to solve families' problems while keeping children at home and argues that it works because parents value the family unit. On the other hand, Mary-Lou Weisman presents evidence that some children are not safe with parents who physically and emotionally scar their children. She maintains that society must bite the bullet, take children out of their abusive homes, and put them where they will survive and thrive.

YES

Lisa Kolb

Family Preservation in Missouri

It's 3:00 A.M. in a small, rural town in southwest Missouri. Vanessa Johnston, a family preservation services (FPS) worker, is combing the streets looking for Heidi, one of her clients. Earlier that night, Vanessa learned that Heidi, a 19-year-old single mother, had been accosted by "Stacey," a "friend." Stacey had heard a rumor that Heidi was involved with Stacey's boyfriend, so she had set out to even the score: she surprised Heidi in the dark stairwell leading to her apartment and beat her up.

Heidi has a habit of running when things get rough. Finding no trace of her client, and knowing Heidi's penchant for hitching rides with truckers, Vanessa heads for the local truck stop. She has to talk with only a few drivers to find out that Heidi, with her infant son in tow, has hitched a ride to Oklahoma City.

Vanessa goes back to her office and waits. She knows the rumor about Heidi and Stacey's boyfriend is unfounded, and she wonders how Heidi has been affected by Stacey's assault. She knows that Heidi has felt that Stacey was her only friend, the one person she could trust.

After several hours, the telephone rings: it's Heidi, asking for help to get back home. Vanessa arranges for the bus ride back to Missouri, goes home, and gets ready for work.

Welcome to the world of an FPS worker. The work is harried, and time is a precious commodity. The job is frustrating: one step forward can be followed by two steps backward. And it is emotionally draining—six weeks of being on 24-hour call can take its toll. But it is encouraging: to see a family learn from its mistakes is what this job is all about. Frustrated and eager for a change, many social workers, caseworkers, and others are willing to accept the challenge and take on the daunting job description that comes with FPS.

. . . [F]amily preservation services are designed to protect children who are at immediate risk of out-of-home placement, by providing immediate, intensive, comprehensive, 24-hour, in-home services to these children and their families. FPS is guided by these premises:

- Children have a right to their families.
- The family is the fundamental resource for nurturing children.
- Parents should be supported in their efforts to care for their children.

From Lisa Kolb, "Family Preservation in Missouri," *Public Welfare,* vol. 51 (Spring 1993), pp. 8–19. Copyright © 1993 by The American Public Welfare Association. Reprinted by permission. Notes omitted.

- Families are diverse and have a right to be respected for the special cultural, racial, ethnic, and religious traditions that make them distinct.
- Children can be reared well in different kinds of families, and one family form should not be discriminated against in favor of another.

Operating statewide since October 1992, FPS is working for a large number of Missouri families. The state measures success by the number of children who remain safely in their homes rather than being removed and placed in foster care. From October 1991 to September 1992—roughly the year before FPS was operating statewide—the program reported serving 656 families. According to the Department of Social Services, Division of Family Services (DFS), which administers the program, 128 of those families ended up having children placed outside the home.

Since it began operating statewide, the program has succeeded in diverting about one-third of the children who otherwise would have entered foster care. Statewide preliminary data show that in the six months to a year following completion of FPS, 81.93 percent of FPS families are intact. A year or more following FPS, 77.89 percent of FPS families are intact.

Vanessa started with the program in November 1991 and had worked with only eight other families before Heidi and her baby. Vanessa identifies the benefits of a program like FPS, which is designed to deal with long-term issues by meeting immediate needs: "We know families will still cycle [in and out of various services] after they've gone through the program, but we hope that what they learned through FPS will help them to pull themselves up and not sink so low the next time."

For Vanessa, one of the most attractive qualities of FPS is the program's flexibility. FPS allows her the latitude to tailor her services to meet the specific needs of her client families. Typically, FPS workers

- teach problem-solving skills to family members;
- teach families how to cope with future crises without relying on harmful behavior;
- provide information to families regarding other sources of assistance;
- teach family members life skills, such as finding an apartment, bargain hunting, nutrition, and money and management;
- focus all services on empowering families to solve their own problems and avert crises.

Statewide, FPS has 114 full-time workers: 36 are employees of DFS, and 78 are working under contract. FPS also has four part-time workers, three in-house and one contractual.

FPS workers must meet a number of requirements:

- They must have a master's degree in social work, counseling, psychology, or a related field. Or, with the approval of DFS, they can have a bachelor's degree and extensive experience in treatment of families in crisis. Vanessa has a bachelor of arts degree in psychology and five and a half years' experience with DFS in investigations, foster care, and casework.

- They must have experience working with children and their families.
- They must demonstrate knowledge of crisis intervention, communications skills, and family education methods.
- They must demonstrate a willingness to work a nonstructured, flexible schedule, routinely including evenings and weekends.
- Contracted workers must meet applicable state licensing criteria.

FPS workers are assigned two families at a time and work with those families for six weeks. The two assignments rarely begin and end at the same time, so there is frequent overlap of cases. Though she could use as much as two weeks between cases to complete the required paperwork—since she has little time to work on anything but the family's needs while the case is in progress—the demand for FPS is so great that Vanessa usually gets no more than two to five days between family assignments.

Vanessa's personality is ideally suited for FPS's nondirective approach. Her ability to act as mother, confidant, and counselor, coupled with her innate sense of when to advise, when to pull back, and when to listen, are key to her rapport with families in crisis. Vanessa admits she works best when encouraging family members to identify their problems and arrive at their own solutions. Although each FPS worker has his or her own style, Vanessa emphasizes that the priority in each FPS case is the same—to make all families safe. If she accomplishes nothing else in her six weeks with a family, Vanessa strives to instill one vitally important attitude: "respect for the kids and their view of the world."

The six-week time frame forces FPS workers to prioritize the elements that are critical to keeping a family together. Vanessa's work with Heidi on parenting and other life skills had to wait until mother and son had a roof over their heads. Kima and Jerry, Vanessa's other FPS family, were not searching for food and shelter, but rather salvation for their marriage.

Heidi and Zach

Like many clients, Heidi chose FPS as the less of two evils. Faced with the removal of her son, Heidi reluctantly allowed FPS into her life for one simple reason: "Zach is all I have." Many of Vanessa's clients have a history of physical or sexual abuse, and Heidi's background is no different. Her childhood in Alabama was little more than a series of new addresses and new guardians, and she did not develop relationships with any of them. Her parents divorced when she was very young. The few times she lived with them were brief, unpleasant interruptions in her travels from one foster home to another. When she turned 18, Heidi aged out of the Alabama foster care system and finally escaped the instability of foster care; but she found that life in an Alabama group home was not much better. She soon ran away to Arkansas, then to Mt. Vernon, Missouri, where she met Micky.

Within a year, Heidi found herself homeless and pregnant with Micky's child. She delivered Zach while living in an area home for unwed mothers. But, restless and longing for her old lifestyle, Heidi soon left to run with her baby's 15-year-old father and his friends. The drugs, alcohol, and delinquency of the group led to the intervention of DFS and Vanessa.

Immediately, Vanessa learned that, with Heidi, she would have to shelve her counselor's hat. Heidi's past had left her stubborn and independent, with a deep mistrust of adults and no tolerance for advice. Heidi likes the fact that FPS allows her to retain control over her own life: "Vanessa doesn't tell me what to do—the decisions are mine to make. I'm learning to trust in myself. I'm a good person."

With Vanessa's help, Heidi was able to begin pursuing her lifelong dream of becoming a nurse. Daycare, provided by FPS, allowed Heidi to work on her general equivalency diploma (GED); and she scored well in preliminary testing. For the first time in her life, she not only is setting goals but also is working to meet them. "I'll do it," she says, "if it takes me till I'm 80."

Vanessa's teaching methods allowed Heidi to learn by example. "My families learn much more from what I do," she says, "than from what I say." For Heidi, many of life's most mundane tasks—including looking for an apartment—were a mystery; and, as Vanessa explained, "You can't ask about something you know nothing about." Armed with a newspaper, a telephone book, and a map, Vanessa talked Heidi through the procedure—looking in the classified section, calling apartment managers for details, and filling out applications.

The scarcity of rental housing in the area limited Heidi's options, and her monthly income—$234 from Aid to Families with Dependent Children and $200 in food stamps—prevented her from qualifying for federal housing. Finding nothing more suitable, Vanessa and Heidi were forced to make do with a small, windowless basement apartment for $100 a month. With money from the Crisis Intervention Fund, an FPS emergency fund earmarked for high-priority needs, Vanessa took Heidi to garage sales, teaching her to bargain-shop for kitchen items, other household goods, and baby clothes for Zach. One of Vanessa's FPS coworkers obtained a used sleeper sofa, chairs, and a lamp to complete the apartment's furnishings.

Although the apartment soon looked livable, Vanessa worried about the steep, dark stairwell leading to the apartment and the lack of heating or air conditioning. Heidi objected to turning on the gas stove for fear of an explosion, but Vanessa explained that utilities are a good way to establish credit. Meanwhile, Vanessa would look for a used microwave oven.

Vanessa also subtly tried to change Heidi's nutritional habits and attitudes about medical care. Heidi, a frail 80 pounds, frequently skipped meals; and this sometimes would carry over to 4½-month-old Zach, who needed regular feedings of formula. Vanessa was concerned that Heidi would not prepare balanced meals for Zach as his nutritional needs changed. She learned that Heidi occasionally would fix instant soup or other one-step preparation foods if she had access to a microwave. Vanessa knew that Heidi was concerned about Zach staying on target with his weight gain, and she hoped this would entice Heidi to do more cooking.

Whereas Heidi did not seem very concerned about her own health, Vanessa did begin to see improvements in her concern for Zach's health. Heidi would become defensive at the suggestion of seeking medical care for herself, and she ignored her doctor's diagnosis of strep throat and recommendation for a tonsillectomy. With Vanessa's encouragement, however, Heidi began to understand the importance of regular checkups for Zach, who had developed a chronic cough soon after he was born. Heidi was afraid of the "hurt" that doctors cause and the bad-tasting medicine they prescribe, but Vanessa helped her to see that these were the only ways to make Zach better. Watching Heidi follow Zach's medication schedule gave Vanessa a renewed sense that mother and son would make it—together.

As determined as she was to become a better mother, Heidi experienced an equally strong pull to return to her old lifestyle on the streets, running with Micky and his friends. Vanessa had to suppress her own maternal instincts. As a mother of three, she knew that if Heidi were her own child, she likely would have reacted to Heidi's involvement with Micky and his friends by criticizing their behavior and prohibiting Heidi from seeing them. But Vanessa knew that reaction not only would be a waste of time, but also would damage her relationship with Heidi.

As an FPS worker, Vanessa strongly believes that it is neither her position nor beneficial to her clients for her to judge them. She realizes that Micky's role as Zach's father is important to Heidi and that it is unlikely that his influence and that of his friends will diminish.

During a scheduled visit, Vanessa found Micky and his friends at Heidi's apartment. Vanessa's theory is that every moment spent with a family is "teachable," so she turned what could have been a wasted afternoon into a group counseling session by including the entire group in her discussion with Heidi. By opening a discourse about their influence on Zach's well-being, Vanessa believes Micky, and perhaps some of his friends, came away with a sense of the consequences of their actions. Heidi says Micky likes her involvement with FPS and that he admits he has gained a new perspective through Vanessa.

Vanessa's presence gradually began to have a calming effect on Heidi's life. Heidi describes her past experiences with the Department of Social Services (DSS) as having had a "bad thing" with the agency. But she says her relationship with Vanessa is "okay"—a glowing endorsement from the reserved teenager. "DDS has always been rude," Heidi says. "They make me feel like they don't have the time. FPS is making me think some of them do care. Maybe they do."

Kima and Jerry

Vanessa met Kima and Jerry as their two-year marriage was showing signs of breaking up. Jerry, a 25-year-old unemployed welder, was starting to drink; and drinking made him mean. Kima had plenty of experience with abusive men, and she wasn't going to risk Jerry's angry words turning to violence. Fed up, she had filed for divorce; and, as a would-be single mother of three with no job, she saw FPS as the only way to keep her family together.

Kima's nightmare had begun in her early teens. After months of sexually abusing her, Kima's stepfather one day had escalated his assault to a violent rape, after which he had left her tied in an abandoned barn. She escaped by breaking a window and sawing herself free with a shard of glass. The stepfather, serving an eight-year sentence for the crime, was threatening Kima from prison. Family members who were in contact with him warned her about his plans to find her when he was released. In fact, shortly after his release early in 1993, he was rearrested for attempting to poison the water supply of Sarcoxie, Missouri, a town close to where Kima lived.

Although her stepfather's incarceration gave Kima a sense of release from the pain he had caused, she had had other equally devastating relationships in the years since—sadly, a common occurrence for sexual abuse victims. Kima's oldest son, Travis, 7, was born out of a later rape. Then a boyfriend killed his and Kima's 6½-month-old son. Kima has two other children, Megan, 5, and Miles, 11 months; only Miles is Jerry's child.

Kima and Jerry's first contact with DFS came after Jerry jerked a crying Miles out of his crib, breaking his arm. Although the doctor who treated Miles's injury originally suspected abuse, his final report called the incident "accidental." Jerry now feels DFS is suspicious of him, and his disdain for what he believes was an unfair investigation has left both Kima and Jerry with a blatant distrust of DFS.

Despite this mistrust, Kima saw FPS as the only way to save her marriage, something she very much wanted to preserve. Middle-class values are important to Kima. Her father, killed when she was 11, was a positive influence on her life; and she wants the same for her children. Referred to the program by a DFS worker, the couple was willing to work with FPS because they saw it as an answer to their marital troubles, not acknowledging that the children were at issue.

"I just wanted Jerry to realize he is an equal partner," Kima said. "You can't take 90 percent and give 10. I realize he had a lot of problems growing up. I guess I just wanted us both to start fresh. It's easier for Jerry to talk with someone else present—he's not as apt to walk out."

Jerry says he and Kima immediately accepted Vanessa by "detaching" her from DFS. "I kind of had feelings . . . I didn't know Vanessa or anything about her. I wasn't sure if I was ready to talk to an outsider. But she's strong on offering suggestions. She's even told us several times she'd leave if we wanted her to. I thought we'd have to sit in a circle and play a game. Everything was to our advantage, because it helped."

Kima and Jerry's problems escalated after Kima lost her job with a local trucking company. Until then, it had not been important to Kima that Jerry work—she was willing to do almost anything to keep the peace: "When Jerry is unhappy, the whole house suffers." But when the loss of Kima's paycheck forced Jerry to look for employment, the tension began to mount. Although Jerry eventually landed a job at an area factory, one with good wages and benefits as well as safe working conditions, he found many excuses to skip work. After three weeks, Jerry had clocked in for only seven shifts.

Now that Kima was unemployed, she had time to begin work on her GED, and FPS enabled her to do that. Since Travis was in the first grade and Megan was enrolled in Head Start, Miles was the only child needing daycare. Unfortunately, Mt. Vernon happens to have the highest teen pregnancy rate in Missouri, which makes state-funded daycare scarce. After Kima completes her GED, she plans to attend college full-time. Through Vanessa, Kima learned that many area colleges have daycare facilities on campus. "FPS points out opportunities," Kima says. "I always knew I had college potential, but until I met Vanessa, I wasn't aware what was available in this area."

Kima and Jerry seemed to be getting past the communication barriers that had caused so many of their problems. "Overall, I feel Jerry has more consideration and respect for me," Kima said. "He has learned to voice his anger rather than just letting it build up. He has been harsh with the kids in the past; but he has learned that if we are to respect his feelings, he has to respect ours. You can't solve your problems when you're angry."

Vanessa points out that FPS's nondirective approach doesn't always work for her. Sometimes, she explains, the atmosphere is just right for physical violence to erupt: "After all, FPS strives to build a rapport while family members are learning to vent their frustrations. Some families become so comfortable with my presence that they forget I'm there and start swinging. That's the time to become very directive."

During counseling, Jerry admitted that he often became frustrated with the children when they would not help Kima around the house. Vanessa helped turn a major point of conflict between Kima and Jerry into a workable solution by developing a chore chart with a reward system for the children. "They learned that there are certain things that have to be done," Kima said. "Now they know that Mom isn't going to do everything for them."

Jerry admitted he had been self-centered and that his moods had made life hard for Kima and the children, but he seemed unwilling to share the decision-making with his wife. Money management had been a problem, and Jerry's new role as the breadwinner gave him a sense of ownership over his paycheck. For instance, the rent was due and the family needed a second car; but Jerry went out and bought a motorcycle. Vanessa worried that Kima and Jerry would be evicted since they were already behind on their rent. Their finances for the coming month looked no better. Because Jerry had missed so much work, his paycheck was going to be short; and, though they had applied, the family was not yet receiving food stamps.

Vanessa's first inclination was to dip into the program's Crisis Intervention Fund. FPS workers have discretion over how and when to use the money, and they do not usually make clients aware that the money is available, so that families do not become dependent on it. FPS workers spend an average of $350 from this fund per family, and Vanessa already had nearly depleted Kima and Jerry's share. Vanessa thought better of bailing Kima and Jerry out of their financial troubles. "Jerry lost his safety net when Kima lost her job," Vanessa said. "These are hard lessons for Jerry, and it's too bad the whole family has to suffer. He needs to learn." The family did manage to scrape by, but later had to move when the landlord raised the rent.

Most FPS workers are women, but Jerry's respect for male authority made Vanessa wonder if he would be more inclined to open up with a male counselor. Jerry dispelled those fears, however: "To me it doesn't matter whether it's a male or female counselor as long as they are helping. Vanessa taught me to stop and think before I say anything—but there are still times I wish I would do more thinking."

"I can't speak for all families, but it's been very beneficial for us," Kima said. "Jerry and I talk more than we ever would have before. Jerry's focus used to be on the bad side of things. He would always focus on the bad things the kids did. I guess something from his childhood made him feel like he didn't measure up. Vanessa has helped him see the good things."

FPS workers and their families often develop a closeness that makes it difficult to let go at the end of six weeks. This was the case between Vanessa and Kima and Jerry. When asked if he felt that the progress he and Kima had made with Vanessa would continue, Jerry said, "She's not going to leave our lives—we know where she lives." Vanessa's first FPS family still calls her on occasion, she says, just for reassurance that what they are doing is okay.

After leaving the FPS program, families are assigned aftercare (AC) workers from their home counties. AC workers continue the case plan that the FPS worker has started with the family. To make the transition easier for families, Vanessa is in constant communication with the AC workers to prepare them for the next phase of a family's treatment. "From the very first day I'm with a family, I begin pulling in other services that they can rely on when I'm gone," Vanessa says. "Actually, I guess you could say aftercare begins with that very first session."

~~~

Vanessa winds up a whirlwind week with Heidi, Kima, and Jerry with a trip to McDonald County, Missouri, where she will attend a "staffing"—a periodic screening of clients to determine progress and alternative services. The two-hour drive will account for part of the 2,000 miles she puts on her family van each month. Accompanying Vanessa are Angela, a private provider of outpatient therapy from a nearby county, and Keith, an FPS coworker.

The room is filled with social workers, FPS workers, and private providers such as Angela, all of whom offer additional insight to the cases they hear. Amid the often horrifying stories of the plight of area families are the occasional lighthearted jokes and repeated trips to the coffeepot—both necessary for the long meetings. Vanessa relates Heidi's progress, and all are impressed. Vanessa appreciates the recognition from her colleagues, but she warns that Heidi has much work ahead of her. Then Vanessa says she is not taking any more FPS families until she returns from a much-needed vacation. Everyone in the room nods in enthusiastic agreement.

Having already had its final staffing, Kima and Jerry's case is closed for Vanessa. She speaks hopefully of their chances for success, knowing they are better prepared for the inevitable rough turns their lives will continue to take. The AC worker has taken over and will continue to guide them toward services should they need assistance.

Families receive a follow-up survey up to one year after they have completed FPS, and this is an FPS worker's final barometer of the program's impact on each family. Vanessa is not ready to say that FPS has succeeded in Kima and Jerry's case. If the survey shows that the children still are living with their family, and if Kima and Jerry are talking and not yelling, then she can say that FPS was successful for this family.

Meanwhile, Vanessa steals a few minutes each day for her own family's needs. Her private life is sandwiched between FPS families, but she has no complaints; and the sparkle in her eye reveals her firm belief that she is doing the right thing. She smiles as she relates how her clients' gratitude is rewarding, but misguided. "It's great that some families say they are doing it for me," says Vanessa. "But if I'm the motivation, then I'm out of there, and where do they go? Believe me, they are doing all the work, and they are doing it for their family."

Mary-Lou Weisman  **NO**

When Parents Are Not in the
Best Interests of the Child

Orphanages are not what they used to be. They aren't even called orphanages anymore. The residents no longer sleep in metal beds, twenty to a dormitory room. At the Boys Town campus, just outside Omaha, Nebraska, children
live eight to a suburban-style home, two to a bedroom. Bureaus have replaced
lockers. Uniforms and standardized haircuts are gone. So are the long wooden
tables where, in the orphanages of legend, children sat awaiting their portions
of cornmeal mush for breakfast, or bread and gravy for dinner. For instance,
at the former St. James Orphanage, in Duluth, Minnesota, known since 1971 as
Woodland Hills, young people wearing clothes from places like The Gap and
Kmart push plastic trays through a cafeteria line, choosing baked chicken or
shrimp and rice. The weight-conscious detour to the salad bar.

In 1910 some 110,000 orphans lived in 1,200 orphan asylums throughout the United States. At the end of 1990, according to data from the American
Public Welfare Association, there were approximately 406,000 children in
out-of-home placements. About three-quarters of these children were in adoptive and foster homes. About 16 percent, or 65,000, were emotionally disturbed children in need of therapy, most of whom lived in the group homes
and residential treatment centers that are the institutional descendants of the
orphanage. (The remainder, less than 10 percent, were cared for by a variety of
temporary and emergency services.) What little research is available indicates
that most of this smaller subset of "homeless" children have been physically
or sexually abused, often by the adults charged with their care. At Boys Town,
now a residential treatment center—and no longer just for boys—virtually all
the girls and nearly half the boys have been sexually abused. The director,
Father Val J. Peter, tells of a teenager who asked him on the day she arrived,
"Who do I have to sleep with to get along here?"

Child-care workers agree that children in residential treatment today are
likely to be far more disturbed than the children who were in need of protective
services twenty years ago and who, in turn, were probably more disturbed than
the good-hearted orphans with chips on their shoulders who preceded them.
These kids have had it with parents—biological, adoptive, or foster—and the feeling is usually mutual. These kids do not trust adults, especially parents. They

From Mary-Lou Weisman, "When Parents Are Not in the Best Interests of the Child," *The Atlantic
Monthly,* vol. 274 (July 1994), pp. 43–63. Copyright © 1994 by Mary-Lou Weisman. Reprinted by
permission.

cannot tolerate the intensity of family life, nor do they behave well enough to attend public school. During a first screening at a residential treatment center a psychiatrist often asks a child, "If you had three wishes, what would they be?" Twenty years ago a typical answer was "I want a basketball," or "I wish my father didn't drink." Today, according to Nan Dale, the executive director of The Children's Village, a residential treatment center for boys in Dobbs Ferry, New York, one is likely to hear "I wish I had a gun so I could blow my father's head off." Child-care professionals call these young people "children of rage." Some of them take antidepressants and drugs to control hyperactivity. In addition to the behavior and attachment disorders common to children who have been abused and moved around a lot, some suffer from having been exposed *in utero* to crack and some from other neurological problems.

Most of the children who live in institutions are between the ages of five and eighteen. According to a 1988 study 64 percent of children in residential treatment centers were adolescents thirteen to seventeen years old. Approximately 31 percent were younger than thirteen, a percentage that has been increasing. According to the same study, the majority, about 70 percent, were male, a factor attributed to the more aggressive nature of the sex. Approximately 25 percent of the children were black, and eight percent were Hispanic.

A group home may house as few as four children, whereas a residential treatment center may be home to a hundred or more, although in either facility usually no more than eight to twelve are housed together, supervised by house parents or by child-care personnel working eight-hour shifts. At Woodland Hills an old three-story red-brick orphanage building has been renovated so that the first floor can be used for administration, classrooms, and the cafeteria. The second- and third-floor dormitory rooms have been divided into meeting rooms, staff offices, and apartments with bedrooms that sleep two.

Unlike the orphanages from which they are descended, most group homes and residential treatment centers are not meant to be long-term abodes. A typical stay at such a center lasts from several months to two years, after which most children return to their birth, foster, or adoptive families. A significant minority, those who either have no homes to return to or do not wish to go home, move on to less restrictive group homes or to independent living arrangements, also under the aegis of the child-welfare system.

History

The first orphan asylum in the United States was established in 1729 by Ursuline nuns, to care for children orphaned by an Indian massacre at Natchez, Mississippi. Thereafter the number of orphanages increased in response to wars, especially the Civil War, and to epidemics of tuberculosis, cholera, yellow fever, and influenza. (Contemporary epidemics such as AIDS, the resurgence of tuberculosis, and the rampant use of crack cocaine have the potential to create another orphan crisis in the twenty-first century. By the year 2000, it is estimated, 100,000 children, most of them from female-headed households, will lose their mother to AIDS. Senator Daniel Patrick Moynihan, among others, foresees the return of the orphanage as inevitable.)

In spite of the Dickensian reputation that outlives them, orphanages, which began to proliferate in this country in the mid-1800s, represented a significant social reform for their time, just as the group homes and residential treatment centers that took their place are now seen as reforms. Before orphan asylums were common, orphaned, homeless, and neglected children, if they were not living, stealing, and begging on the streets, were housed, along with adults, primarily in almshouses, but also in workhouses and jails. The Victorian conviction that childhood was a time of innocence influenced attitudes toward destitute children. People came to believe that even street urchins could be rescued—removed to a better environment and turned into productive citizens.

Most orphanages were private institutions, the result of the combined efforts of passionately committed "child savers," children's-aid societies, and a variety of mostly religious but also ethnic organizations that raised the money to build and maintain them. But even as the orphanage was becoming the nation's dominant mode of substitute child care, an anti-institutional effort called "placing out" was under way, setting the stage for a debate that continues to this day. By the mid-1800s children were being transported on "orphan trains" from crowded eastern slums and institutions to the West, where they were adopted by farm families in need of extra hands. By the late nineteenth century, in a further move away from institutionalization, cottage-style "homes," which more closely mimicked family life and each of which housed about twenty-five children, began to take the place of large orphanages.

In the twentieth century, psychology—first psychoanalytic theories and then behaviorism—has dominated the field of child welfare. Unlike psychoanalytic theories, which focus on the child's inner personality, behaviorism emphasizes the way the child interacts with his world. In this view a child is not "bad"; his unacceptable behavior is. By changing the behavior, so the thinking goes, one changes the child. Behavioral theories replaced psychoanalytic theories, which were used only to limited effect by Bruno Bettelheim and others in the "homes" and "schools" for emotionally disturbed children which appeared mid-century. The therapeutic hour remains important, but what goes on in the child's life during the other twenty-three hours of the day is seen as potentially even more valuable. (A book by that name, *The Other 23 Hours,* by Albert E. Trieschman, James K. Whittaker, and Larry K. Brendtro, is the classic text of residential treatment.) The goal of residential treatment is to create a "therapeutic milieu," an environment in which everyday events are turned to therapeutic use. Any activity in a child's day—from refusing to get dressed in the morning to answering a question correctly at school to picking a fight—offers the child-care worker an opportunity to teach, change, or reinforce behavior through therapeutic intervention. Residential treatment aims to seize the moment while it is happening and the child's feelings are still fresh.

Policy versus Reality

Orphanages as such had virtually disappeared by the late 1970s as a result of a decrease in the number of orphans and a growing conviction that children belong in families. That every child needs parents and a home has become an article of faith and a guiding principle for social-policy makers and a matter of federal law as well. The philosophy of "permanency planning," as set forth in the Adoption Assistance and Child Welfare Act of 1980, considers the goal of the foster-care system to be keeping children in families. The law allows for but discourages "out-of-home placement"—institutionalization in group homes or residential treatment centers—and calls for the return of the children to a family, biological or otherwise, whenever possible and as quickly as possible. But for many practitioners in residential treatment the law has become increasingly irrelevant.

Richard Small is the director of The Walker Home and School, in Needham, Massachusetts, a residential and day treatment center for severely disturbed pre-adolescent boys. Writing recently in a professional journal with Kevin Kennedy and Barbara Bender, Small expressed a concern shared by many of his colleagues.

> For at least the past decade, we in the field have been reporting, usually to each other, a worsening struggle to work with a much more damaged group of children and families, and a scramble to adjust our practice methods to meet both client needs and policy directives that may or may not have anything to do with client needs. . . . Those of us immersed in everyday residential treatment practice see these same guidelines as less and less applicable to the real children and families with whom we work. Many of our child clients and their families suffer from profound disruptions of development that we believe are likely to require long-term, multiple helping services, including (but not limited to) one or more time-limited stays in residential treatment. Despite a policy that seems to see clear boundaries between being "in care" (and therefore sick and vulnerable) and "reunified" (and therefore fixed and safe) our experience tells us that many of our clients are likely to live out their lives somewhere between these poles.

In keeping with the goal of permanency planning, institutions are supposed to maintain close communication with the parents of the children they treat. Many centers offer counseling for parents and for the entire family. The Children's Village runs evening and weekend programs especially for parents who have abused their children. At institutions that adhere most closely to the goal of reuniting parent and child, parents are encouraged to visit, and good behavior on the part of children is rewarded with weekend visits home. Green Chimneys, a residential treatment center that serves primarily inner-city kids, regularly transports parents and children in vans between New York City and its campus in Brewster, New York. Nationally, nobody really knows how many families are reunited, for how long or how successfully. Those who work with children in institutions complain that the pressure from departments of social service to reunite parent and child is so intense that the workers sometimes yield to it despite their better judgment.

The objective of residential care is to discharge healthier children into the care of healthier parents—an outcome that authorities agree is desirable in theory but not always likely in fact. In their recent casebook for child-care workers, *When Home Is No Haven*, Albert J. Solit, Barbara Nordhaus, and Ruth

Lord write that "one of the hardest tasks for a new worker is becoming reconciled to the inherent contradictions in the Protective Services worker's role. The worker is expected to aim for two goals, which in some instances may be mutually exclusive: reunification of the family, and protection of the child and the child's best interests." . . .

Institutional Family Values

In the paradoxical world of "child protective services," an institution may be the first home some children have ever known, providing their first chance to sit down to meals with other people at regular times, blow out birthday candles, and be taken care of by adults who do not hit or even yell. All but one of the staple ingredients of a happy home life are replicated in the best group homes and treatment centers. Intimacy is purposely missing. Love and family bonding may be what these children will need and be capable of having eventually, but for the moment the emotional thermostat must be set at neutral. These children are believed to be too disturbed to handle the intensity of real family life; that is precisely why they have been institutionalized.

The best institutions offer emotionally disturbed children a chance at a second childhood. They are given the opportunity to shed cynicism, develop self-esteem, and grow back into innocence and vulnerability. Candy will become a treat. This time they will be protected from harm. This time they will come to think of adults as kind and dependable. They will learn to play. They will learn to care about others.

Treatment communities teach Judeo-Christian values—the work ethic and the golden rule. Institutions offer vocational training and courses in computer literacy. At The Children's Village the best computer students teach their newfound skills to other children and adults in the surrounding communities, and The Children's Village has its own Boy Scout troop. The kids at Woodland Hills collect and pack supplies for national and international relief efforts. In addition, they split wood and deliver logs to the elderly in the Duluth community. Boys Town children host Special Olympics games.

A highly controlled environment is required to create a second childhood for severely disturbed children. Safety is the key issue. Keeping these children from harm involves more than keeping them safe from sexual abuse, physical abuse, drugs, and crossfire; they must be kept safe from themselves and their peers. Newly institutionalized children often try to run away. When a young person at Woodland Hills forgets to bring the appropriate book to class, two peers accompany the student back to the dormitory to retrieve it, thereby minimizing the possibility of an escape attempt. At The Children's Village burly guards equipped with walkie-talkies and trained in firm but gentle techniques of physical restraint stand ready to intervene should fights or tantrums develop beyond the regular staff's ability to control them. Children are never left unattended, not even when they sleep. In every one of the twenty-one cottages at The Children's Village one staff member remains awake throughout the night. The children in these cottages are sometimes suicidal. The bedroom doors in all the cottages open into the corridor, so that youngsters cannot barricade themselves in their rooms. Sexually abused children sometimes become sexual predators. At The Villages in Kansas some young girls will not allow anyone to comb their hair; for girls who have been sexually abused, even grooming can be too threatening.

This antidotal second childhood must be highly structured and predictable as well as safe. Treatment communities impose rules, chores, and schedules, and emphasize neatness, cleanliness, and order. "Everybody wakes up at 7:30 in the morning," writes eleven-year-old Robert, describing his day at The Children's Village, where hairbrushes, combs, toothbrushes, and toothpaste tubes are lined up with military precision on bureau tops. "The first thing we do is make our bed, wash our face, brush our teeth, last but not least put on some clothes. We eat our breakfast by 8:15 and do our chores. At 8:45 we go to school. In school the first thing we do is math, then reading and spelling. We go to lunch at 12:00 noon. . . ." Homer, the orphan hero of John Irving's *The Cider House Rules,* thrives on the routine of orphanage life. He enjoys "the *tramp, tramp* of it, the utter predictability of it." "An orphan," Irving writes, "is simply more of a child than other children in that essential appreciation of the things that happen daily, on schedule." A well-structured day serves the child as a kind of armature within which to build a new, less chaotic, inner self. "How to succeed and how to fail is very clear here," says Daniel Daly, the director of research at Boys Town. "These children are looking for consistency and for an environment they can understand." . . .

Paradigms and Politics

[Five] years ago legislation called the Family Preservation Act was vetoed by President George Bush. The bill asked for about $2 billion to strengthen families. About half of that amount was earmarked for "family preservation"—programs to preserve troubled families *before* they broke up, so that fewer children would enter the foster-care system in the first place. Families in crisis would be assigned a licensed social worker, who would be available to them around the clock for a period of about three months, for help with problems ranging from substance abuse to landlord-tenant relations. Parents in imminent danger of abusing their children could find relief in a "respite program." Last year's [1993] budget legislation provided $1 billion for similar purposes, with a substantial portion also to be spent on family preservation. It had the backing of leading child-advocacy groups, including the Child Welfare League of America, the Children's Defense Fund, and The National Association of Homes and Services for Children. The Edna McConnell Clark Foundation has produced media kits claiming that family-preservation programs cost less per family ($3,000 for one family for a year) than family foster care, which it says costs $10,000 per *child,* or institutional care, which costs $40,000 per child.

Directors of some children's institutions are convinced that "family preservation" will take money directly out of institutional pockets. Sam Ross, [founder and executive director of Green Chimneys,] likes to point out that the family, theoretically the best way to rear children, also happens to be the least expensive. He calls this coincidence good news for advocates of family preservation, whom he calls "the liberal-conservative conspiracy." The way Ross sees it, liberal family preservationists believe that residential treatment centers are warehouses for children who could best be served in homes in their own communities. Conservative preservationists are horrified by the cost of residential treatment and are looking for a cheaper alternative. "For once in their lives," Ross says, "they agree on something: let's get rid of residential treatment."

"It makes about as much sense as closing down emergency rooms and intensive-care units in order to lower hospital costs," says Brenda Nordlinger, the executive director of the National Association of Homes and Services for Children.

"Family preservation? Who can be opposed to that?" says David Coughlin, of Boys Town. "But," he warns, "some kids are going to be in trouble all their lives. These kids are always going to need help. You can't just blow across the top of a family for three months and expect their woes to go away."

As of this year [1994] The Villages in Kansas will be responding to pressure from the state, which provides 78 percent of its operating expenses, to institute a family-preservation program in addition to its group-foster-care program. One of the eight Kansas residences will be rededicated as a ninety-day "home away from home" for abused children. Meanwhile, therapists trained by The Villages will work with the abusing parents and the abused children in an effort to reunite the family. "We want to provide the services that the state wants to purchase. We'd be foolish not to," says Mark Brewer, who has been the executive director since last June [1993].

Nan Dale, of The Children's Village, thinks that the fervor to reduce the numbers of children in residential treatment is reminiscent of what is now generally considered the disastrous policy of de-institutionalizing adult mental patients in the 1970s. Program directors are very skeptical about whether preventive-intervention programs are really as successful as their advocates claim. Those who believe that family preservation is being oversold see an ally in John Schuerman, a professor of social work at the University of Chicago. Schuerman has studied preventive-intervention programs and believes that many of the families that were treated and did not split up were not likely to split up in the first place.

Nan Dale is feeling the anti-institutional heat and resenting it. "We're as pro-family a place as you can find. The fact that we serve a child who has been removed from a family does not make us anti-family. We involve parents." Nevertheless, she says, "the lines have been drawn. When the words 'preventive service' got applied to everything up to the doorstep of residential care, some of us had apoplectic fits. We all would have told you that what we did here *was* preventive. We prevent lifetimes in mental hospitals, lifetimes in prisons. All of a sudden some bureaucrat in Washington defines preventive service as preventing placement outside the home, and we become the thing to be prevented." For the first time in anyone's memory The Children's Village, one of the largest and considered one of the best residential treatment centers in the country, has no waiting list. Dale says that children who might once have been sent there are being diverted to less restrictive, less expensive, and less appropriate options, such as foster-home care, on the presumption that a family setting is always better.

"What's in vogue right now is family preservation," says Father Val, of Boys Town. "Just follow the trend. Watch the little lemmings dashing toward the sea. They will tire of family preservation the way they tired of de-institutionalization. It's as if they just discovered that it's a good idea to try to keep kids in families. It's an exegesis of the obvious." Father Val thinks that the need to frame the debate as either anti-family or anti-institution is inevitable, given the longing that human beings feel for simple answers to complex questions. Certainly the people who make child-welfare policy, as well as those who carry it out, believe that the either-or approach is self-defeating. Nevertheless, it persists. Earl Stuck, who was one of the supporters of the Family Preservation Act, acknowledges the problem. "When you try to sell something politically, you have to oversell your case."

David Fanshel was until retirement a professor at the Columbia University School of Social Work. A leader in the field of social work, and foster care in particular, Fanshel was the principal investigator in two major longitudinal studies on foster children in homes and institutions. At a time when many experts are questioning the value of residential treatment and promoting family preservation, Fanshel is going against the tide. He foresees a greater need for residential care in the near future. In fact, Fanshel, for decades one of the leading proponents of permanency planning, has modified his views. He now believes that permanent placement with a family is not an appropriate goal for about a quarter of the older, more seriously damaged and criminally inclined children in the system. He would like to see foster care reorganized into a two-tiered system in which permanent placement would remain the goal for the larger group, and the forestalling of criminal behavior through treatment would be the goal for the other group, which he calls "Subsystem B." He sees institutions playing a significant role in treating such dangerous children. The creation of two subsystems, Fanshel argues, "might help to avoid the inappropriate underfunding of Subsystem B now taking place in the interest of permanency planning."

The debate between family preservationists and those who advocate the wider use of institutions has been going on for decades. Until as late as the 1920s pro-family reformers used the "orphan trains" to place children with farm families. Today their anti-institutional counterparts, in their determination to provide a home for every child, sometimes resort to "adoption fairs," where difficult-to-adopt children are viewed by prospective parents. The social worker who organized one such event told a reporter from *Vogue* that although these fairs can result in the adoption of as many as half the children, "it felt like a slave auction."

Richard Small tells prospective adoptive parents, "If you're going to adopt a child from The Walker School, you're going out of your way to ask for trouble." Small is uncertain about whether it will be possible to find parents for six of the eight children at the school who were recently freed for adoption. One is a very disturbed twelve-year-old boy who has already suffered two failed adoptions. Small is faced with the opposite of King Solomon's conundrum: this time no mothers want the child. How hard should he try to find another adoptive family?

"Another adoption with this boy would be likely to fail," says Small, who also knows that another rejection might harm the boy more than a life-time without parents. On the other hand, can he consign the child to such permanent and profound loneliness? "He has no one," Small says, "absolutely no one."

Small talked at length with the boy about the pros and cons of risking another adoption. Together, they had just about made up their minds in favor of life without parents when the boy wondered out loud, "Then who will take me for my driver's license?"

"I wish," Small says, "that there were a place, a group home, where kids could live at those times when they couldn't live at home. We've got a number of youngsters in this society—who knows how many?—who are capable of being connected to people, who wish to be connected, who should be con-nected, but who can't live full-time with the people they're connected to. When they do, terrible things happen to both sides, the kids and the caretak-ers. These kids get placed in families repeatedly and they repeatedly fail. What are we going to do with these children? Right now we either put them in an institution or we put them in a family."

Going Home

A good children's institution is a hard place to leave. In the institutional world the child has the advantage; in the real world the child does not. The experts consult. Parents and children consult. Is the family ready? Is the child ready?

Twenty-five years ago 80 percent of the children who "graduated" from The Children's Village went home to some family member, most likely the mother. But starting about five years ago the percentage began to drop. Today only 55 percent go home to family. Nan Dale, citing her own subjective stan-dard of measurement, the "GFF" (gut-feeling factor), estimates that half of that narrow majority are returning to a home situation that is fragile. At Woodland Hills, where most of the kids are released to the care of their families, David Kern says he feels uneasy about the prospects for success almost half the time. He calls sending vulnerable children home the worst part of the job. While he was at The Villages, Don Harris felt uneasy about returning kids to their parents about 80 percent of the time. "The reality is we can help these kids build some bridges to their families, but they probably will never be able to live with them."

Not sending vulnerable children home can also be the worst part of the job. People who work with institutionalized children continually face a quan-dary to which they have no satisfactory solution: What should they do when, in spite of everyone's best efforts, family seems not to be in the best interests of the child? What the system has to offer is life in a group home followed by independent apartment living, and then nothing.

Life without parents is a difficult sentence to pronounce upon a child, but it's happening more and more often. "Sometimes children have gone beyond the opportunity to go back and capture what needed to be done between the ages of three and eight," says Gene Baker, the chief psychologist at The Children's Village. "Sometimes the thrust of intimacy that comes with family living is more than they can handle. Sometimes the requirement of bonding is more than they have the emotional equipment to give. As long as we keep pushing them back into what is our idealized fantasy of family, they'll keep blowing it out of the water for us."

POSTSCRIPT

Should Children Who Are at Risk for Abuse Remain with Their Families?

Kolb summarizes the family preservation model and documents its success in Missouri. In that program family preservation workers teach family members problem-solving skills and ways to cope with family crises while keeping family members, including children, together as a unit. Family preservation workers in Missouri meet certain educational and experiential requirements and work with two families at a time for six weeks.

Parents choose the family preservation treatment to avoid removal of their children from the home and, according to Kolb, want to preserve the family unit because they value it and want to make it work. Whereas traditional social service focuses on the individual for an indefinite amount of time, Kolb reports that family preservation is more successful because it focuses on the family system for a specific amount of time—four to six weeks.

Policymakers have been instrumental in child welfare in that they have diverted funds from one treatment program to another. When family preservation became a lower-cost alternative to foster care in the 1980s, money was diverted into the family preservation model in lieu of other child protection programs. Was this action in the best interests of the children? Who should decide? Parents? Policymakers? Protective service workers?

Suggested Readings

Berliner, L. (1993, December). Is family preservation in the best interest of children? *Journal of Interpersonal Violence, 8,* 556–557.

Carp, E. W. (1996, June). Two cheers for orphanages. *Reviews in American History, 24,* 277–284.

Craig, C. (1995, Summer). What I need is a mom. *Policy Review, 73,* 41–49.

Ingrassia, M. (1994, April). Why leave children with bad parents? *Newsweek, 123,* 52–58.

McKenzie, R. (1996, May). Revive the orphanage (but don't expect help from child care professionals). *American Enterprise, 7,* 59–62.

Shealy, C. (1995, August). From Boys Town to Oliver Twist: Separating fact from fiction in welfare reform and out-of-home placement of children and youth. *American Psychologist, 50,* 565–580.

Van Biema, D. (1994, December). The storm over orphanages. *Time, 144,* 58–62.

ISSUE 16

Is Abstinence-Only Sex Education the Best Way to Teach about Sex?

YES: Robert E. Rector, Melissa G. Pardue, and Shannan Martin, from "What Do Parents Want Taught in Sex Education Programs?" *Backgrounder* (January 28, 2004)

NO: Advocates for Youth and the Sexuality Information and Education Council of the United States (SIECUS), from "Toward a Sexually Healthy America: Roadblocks Imposed by the Federal Government's Abstinence-Only-Until-Marriage Education Program," SIECUS (2001)

ISSUE SUMMARY

YES: Robert Rector, who is a research fellow for the Heritage Foundation, and Melissa Pardue and Shannan Martin, policy analysts for the Heritage Foundation, argue that comprehensive sex education approaches are misleading because they do little to promote abstinence. Under the auspices of the Heritage Foundation, a conservative organization based in Washington, D.C., they present the results of a poll they conducted that sought to measure parental support for ideas taught in "abstinence-only" and "comprehensive sex education" programs.

NO: Advocates for Youth and the Sexuality Information and Education Council of the United States (SIECUS) promote comprehensive education about sexuality and advocate for the right of individuals to make responsible sexual choices. SIECUS compares abstinence-only sex education to comprehensive sex education and finds shortcomings regarding abstinence-only programs.

Most people agree about the need for some type of sex education for our children in our schools. There is little argument that abstinence is the safest choice an adolescent can make regarding sexual activity. It is the only 100 percent effective way to avoid pregnancy and the hundreds of sexually transmitted diseases that are epidemic in our society. However, the reality is that adolescents do engage in premarital sexual behaviors. The problem is that parents and educators cannot agree on the best way to teach children and adolescents about the implications of premarital sex. One group believes that the best approach is comprehensive sex education, which encourages abstinence but also provides information on birth control, protection against sexually transmitted diseases, and the emotional aspects of engaging in sex. Other groups promote abstinence-only sex education, which provides information on the hazards of sex (i.e., pregnancy, STDs, broken hearts, etc.) and sometimes includes information on self-esteem and dealing with peer pressure to have premarital sex.

Advocates for comprehensive sex education argue that many adolescents will have premarital sex; as a consequence, adolescents need to be taught about birth control methods and STD prevention techniques. Those supporting abstinence-only sex education believe that teaching about birth control methods and STD prevention sends mixed messages about premarital sex. It could give teens the impression that teachers and parents accept that adolescents cannot help themselves from having sex, which is contrary to the pro-abstinence movement's goals.

To intensify the debate, the government has established a federal entitlement program for "abstinence-only-until marriage" education. When schools and other agencies accept these grants, they must adhere to the program's rules, which include requiring schools to teach little about sexuality but instead to send a strong message that sexual activity outside of marriage is psychologically and physiologically harmful. Therefore, premarital sex should be avoided. This is worrisome for comprehensive sex education advocates because they believe that education about sexuality is the best way to empower adolescents to make sound decisions regarding premarital sex.

Rector, Pardue, and Martin's selection argues against comprehensive sex education on the grounds that they do not do enough to promote abstinence and that according to their poll, parents overwhelmingly prefer their children to be taught abstinence-only programs in sex education. The Advocates for Youth and SIECUS present a history of abstinence-only sex education in the United States. They offer definitions of both abstinence and comprehensive sex education, suggest shortcomings of abstinence-only programs, and conclude with research supporting comprehensive sex education programs.

As you read both selections, think back to your days in high school and the sources and types of education about sexuality you received. Was the education sufficient? Should it have been different? If so, in what ways? Also, put yourself in the place of a parent of an adolescent. Consider what approach to sex education this parent would support and why.

YES ⬅

Robert E. Rector, Melissa G. Pardue,
and Shannan Martin

What Do Parents Want Taught in Sex Education Programs?

Debates about sex education have focused on two different approaches: "safe sex" courses, which encourage teens to use contraceptives, especially condoms, when having sex, and abstinence education, which encourages teens to delay sexual activity.

In recent years, advocacy groups such as SIECUS (the Sex Information and Education Council of the United States) and Advocates for Youth have promoted another apparent alternative, entitled "comprehensive sexuality education" or "abstinence plus." These curricula allegedly take a middle position, providing a strong abstinence message while also teaching about contraception. In reality, this claim is misleading. Comprehensive sexuality education curricula contain little or no meaningful abstinence material; they are simply safe-sex programs repackaged under a new, deceptive label.

Abstinence programs teach that:

- Human sexuality is primarily emotional and psychological, not physical, in nature;
- In proper circumstances, sexual activity leads to long term emotional bonding between two individuals; and
- Sexual happiness is inherently linked to intimacy, love, and commitment—qualities found primarily within marriage.

Abstinence programs strongly encourage abstinence during the teen years, and preferably until marriage. They teach that casual sex at an early age not only poses serious threats of pregnancy and infection by sexually transmitted diseases, but also can undermine an individual's capacity to build loving, intimate relationships as an adult. These programs therefore encourage teen abstinence as a preparation and pathway to healthy adult marriage.

By contrast, comprehensive sex-ed curricula focus almost exclusively on teaching about contraception and encouraging teens to use it. These curricula neither discourage nor criticize teen sexual activity as long as "protection" is used. In general, they exhibit an acceptance of casual teen sex and do not encourage teens to wait until they are older to initiate sexual activity. For

From Backgrounder, no. 1722, January 28, 2004. Copyright © 2004 by The Heritage Foundation. Reprinted by permission.

example, the curricula do not encourage teens to abstain until they have finished high school. "Protected" sex at an early age and sex with many different partners are not treated as problems. Sexuality is treated primarily as a physical phenomenon; the main message is to use condoms to prevent the physical problems of sexually transmitted diseases and pregnancy. Comprehensive sex-ed curricula ignore the vital linkages between sexuality, love, intimacy, and commitment. There is no discussion of the idea that sex is best within marriage.

Determining Parental Attitudes toward Sex-ed Curricula

This paper presents the results of a recent poll on basic issues concerning sex education. The poll questions seek to measure parental support for the themes and values contained in abstinence curricula as well as support for the values embodied in comprehensive sex education.

The data presented are drawn from a survey of parents conducted by Zogby International in December 2003. Zogby conducted telephone interviews with a nationally representative sample of 1,004 parents with children under age 18. Parents were asked 14 questions concerning messages and priorities in sex education; the questions used were designed by Focus on the Family. The margin of error on each question is plus or minus 3.2 percent points. The responses to the questions showed only modest variation based on region, gender of the parent, or race.[1] The poll questions were designed to reflect the major themes of abstinence education. The descriptions of the messages contained in abstinence and comprehensive sex-ed curricula in the following text are based on a forthcoming content analysis of major sex-ed curricula conducted by The Heritage Foundation. . . .

"Sex Should Be Linked to Marriage; Delaying Sex Until Marriage Is Best"

Abstinence education curricula stress a strong linkage between sex, love, and marriage. The Zogby poll shows strong parental support for this message.

Parents want teens to be taught that sexual activity should be linked to marriage.

Parents Want Teens to Be Taught to Delay Sexual Activity until They Are Married or Close to Marriage

Some 47 percent of parents want teens to be taught that "young people should not engage in sexual activity until they are married." Another 32 percent of parents want teens to be taught that "young people should not engage in sexual intercourse until they have, at least, finished high school and are in a relationship with someone they feel they would like to marry."

When these two categories are combined, we see that 79 percent of parents want young people taught that sex should be reserved for marriage or for an adult relationship leading to marriage. Another 12 percent of parents believe that teens should be taught to delay sexual activity until "they have, at least, finished high school." Only 7 percent of parents want teens to be taught that sexual activity in high school is okay as long as teens use contraception.

These parental values are strongly reinforced by abstinence education programs, which teach that sex should be linked to marriage and that it is best to delay sexual activity until marriage. By contrast, comprehensive sex-ed programs send the message that teen sex is okay as long as contraception is used; the underlying permissive values of these programs have virtually no support among parents.

Parents Want Teens to Be Taught That Sex Should Be Linked to Love, Intimacy, and Commitment and That These Qualities Are Most Likely to Occur in Marriage

Some 91 percent of parents want teens to be taught this message about sexuality.

This is a predominant theme of all abstinence curricula. By contrast, comprehensive sex-ed programs do not discuss love, intimacy, or commitment and seldom mention marriage. Casual sex is not criticized; sex is presented largely as a physical process; and the main lesson is to avoid the physical threats of pregnancy and disease through proper use of contraception. Comprehensive sex-ed programs do not present sexuality in a way that is acceptable to most parents.

Parents Want Teens to Be Taught That It Is Best to Delay Sex until Marriage

Some 68 percent of parents want schools to teach teens that "individuals who are not sexually active until marriage have the best chances of marital stability and happiness."

This theme is strongly supported by abstinence programs, all of which urge teens to delay sexual activity until marriage. It is ignored completely by comprehensive sex-ed courses, which do not criticize casual sex and seldom mention marriage.

General Support for Abstinence

The poll shows overwhelming parental support for other abstinence themes as well.

Parents Want Teens to Be Taught to Abstain from Sexual Activity during High School Years

Some 91 percent of parents support this message. However, for most parents, this is a minimum standard; 79 percent want a higher standard taught: abstinence until you are married or near marriage.

All abstinence curricula strongly encourage abstinence at least through high school, and preferably until marriage. By contrast, comprehensive sex-ed curricula do not encourage teens to delay sex until they have finished high school; most do not even encourage young people to wait until they are older.

Parents Want Teens to Be Taught That Abstinence Is Best

Some 96 percent of parents support this message.

Abstinence curricula obviously support this theme. Comprehensive sex-ed programs may claim to support this message, but in reality they do not. They teach mainly that abstinence is the "safest" choice, but that teen sex with protection is safe. Their overall message is that abstinence is marginally safer than safe sex. Beyond this, they have little positive to say about abstinence.

"Sex at an Early Age, Sex with Many Partners, and Casual Sex Have Harmful Consequences"

Parents believe that sex at an early age, casual sex, and sex with many partners are likely to have harmful consequences. They want teens to be taught to avoid these behaviors.

Parents Want Teens to Be Taught That the Younger the Age an Individual Begins Sexual Activity, the Greater the Probability of Harm

Some 93 percent of parents want teens taught that "the younger the age an individual begins sexual activity, the more likely he or she is to be infected by sexually transmitted diseases, to have an abortion, and to give birth out-of-wedlock."

Abstinence programs strongly support this message; they teach teens to delay sex until they are older, preferably until they are married. Comprehensive sex-ed programs teach about the threat of unprotected sex, not about the harm caused by sex at an early age. They do not urge young people to delay sex until they are older; voluntary sex at any age is depicted as okay as long as "protection" is used.

Parents Want Teens Taught That Teen Sexual Activity Is Likely to Have Psychological and Physical Effects

Some 79 percent of parents want teens to be taught this message.

Abstinence curricula clearly teach this message; comprehensive sex-ed curricula do not. Comprehensive sex-ed curricula focus on encouraging condom use; they do not criticize or discourage teen sex as long as "protection" is used.

Parents Want Schools to Teach That Teens Who Are Sexually Active Are More Likely to Be Depressed

Some 67 percent of teens who have had sexual intercourse regret it and say they wish that they had waited until they were older. (The figure for teen girls is 77 percent.)[2] Sexually active teens are far more likely to be depressed and to attempt suicide than are teens who are not sexually active.[3] Nearly two-thirds of parents support the message that sexually active teens are more likely to be depressed; a quarter of parents oppose it.

Abstinence curricula inform teens about the basic facts of regret and depression; comprehensive sex-ed curricula ignore this topic.

Parents Want Sex Education to Teach That the More Sexual Partners a Teen Has, the Greater the Likelihood of Physical and Psychological Harm

Some 90 percent of parents want this message taught to teens.

Abstinence curricula emphasize the harmful effects of casual teen sex; comprehensive sex-ed curricula do not.

Parents Want Teens Taught That Having Many Sexual Partners at an Early Age May Undermine One's Ability to Develop and Sustain Loving and Committed Relationships as an Adult

Some 85 percent of parents want teens to be taught that "having many sexual partners at an early age may undermine an individual's ability to develop love, intimacy and commitment." Another 78 percent of parents want teens to be taught that "having many different sexual partners at an early age may undermine an individual's ability to form a healthy marriage as adult."

These are major themes of abstinence programs. They teach that teen sexual relationships are inherently short-term and unstable and that repeated fractured relationships can lead to difficulties in bonding and commitment in later years. This perspective is accurate; women who begin sexual activity at an early age will have far more sexual partners and are less likely to have stable marriages as adults.[4] Comprehensive sex-ed curricula ignore this topic completely.

"What's More Important, Abstinence or Contraception?"

Parents believe that abstinence should be given emphasis that is more than, or equal to, that given to contraception. Some 44 percent of parents believe that teaching about abstinence is more important than teaching about contraception; another large group (41 percent) believe that abstinence and contraception should be given equal emphasis. Only 8 percent believe that teaching about contraception is more important than teaching about abstinence.

Regrettably, government spending priorities directly contradict parental priorities. Currently, the government spends at least $4.50 promoting teen contraceptive use for every $1.00 spent to promote teen abstinence.[5]

Parents Overwhelmingly Reject Main Values and Messages of Comprehensive Sex Education

Despite the claims of advocacy groups such as SIECUS and Advocates for Youth, comprehensive sex education curricula contain weak to non-existent messages about abstinence. These programs focus almost exclusively on (1) explaining the threat of teen pregnancy and sexually transmitted diseases and (2) encouraging young people to use contraception, especially condoms, to combat these threats. Many of these curricula appear to be written from a limited health perspective. Sexuality is treated as a physical process (like nutrition), and the goal is to reduce immediate health risks.

While comprehensive sex-ed curricula do not explicitly and directly encourage teen sexual activity, they do not discourage it either. As long as "protection" is used, teen sexual activity is represented as being rewarding, normal, healthy, and nearly ubiquitous. While "unprotected" sex is strongly criticized and discouraged, "protected" teen sex is presented as being fully acceptable. There is little or no effort to encourage young people to wait until they are older before becoming sexually active. By presenting "protected" teen sex activity as commonplace, fulfilling, healthy, and unproblematic, comprehensive sex-ed courses send a strong implicit anti-abstinence message to teens.

The new poll of parental attitudes shows that less than 10 percent of parents support the main values and messages of comprehensive sex education programs. Specifically:

Parents Oppose Teaching That Teen Sex Is Okay If Condoms Are Used

In comprehensive sex-ed curricula, "protected" teen sex is neither criticized nor discouraged. These courses explicitly or implicitly send the strong message that "it's okay for teens in school to engage in sexual intercourse as long as they use condoms." Only 7 percent of parents support this message; 91 percent reject it.

At a Minimum, Parents Want Teens to Be Taught to Abstain from Sexual Activity until They Have Finished High School

Some 91 percent of parents want teens to be taught this minimum standard; most want a far higher standard. But comprehensive sex-ed curricula do not teach that teens should abstain until they have finished high school; in fact, these courses do not provide any clear standards concerning when sexual activity should begin. For the most part, they do not even encourage young people to wait until they are vaguely "older"; they are simply silent on the issue.

Comprehensive Sex-Ed Courses Are Silent on Vital Issues Such as Casual Sex, Intimacy, Commitment, Love, and Marriage

. . . Parents overwhelmingly support the main themes of abstinence education and want these topics to be taught to their children. These themes are conspicuously absent from comprehensive sex-ed. These courses therefore fail to meet the needs and desires of most parents.

Should Abstinence Programs Teach about "Safe Sex" or Contraception?

The poll shows an apparent divergence between abstinence education and parental attitudes on only one issue: Some 75 percent of parents want teens to be taught about both abstinence and contraception. Except for describing the likely failure rates of various types of birth control, abstinence curricula do not teach about contraception.

However, the fact that abstinence programs, per se, do not include contraceptive information does not mean that teens will not be taught this material. Abstinence and sex education are seldom taught as stand-alone subjects in school; they are usually offered as a brief part of a larger course, most typically a health course.[6]

In addition, sex education is usually taught not once, but in multiple doses at different grade levels as the student matures. When students are taught about abstinence, in most cases, they will also receive biological information about reproduction and contraception in another part of their course work. By 11th or 12th grade, some 91 percent of students have been taught about birth control in school.[7]

There is no logical reason why contraceptive information should be presented as part of an abstinence curriculum. Not only would this reduce the limited time allocated to the abstinence message, but nearly all abstinence educators assert that it would substantially undermine the effectiveness of the abstinence message.

In general, parents tend to agree that abstinence and contraceptive instruction should not be directly mixed. . . . Some 56 percent of parents believe either that contraception should not be taught at all or that, if both abstinence and contraception are taught, they should be taught separately. (Some 22 percent believe that contraception should not be taught, while 35 percent want the two subjects taught separately.)

Although most parents want teens to be taught about both abstinence and contraception, there is no strong sentiment that these topics must be combined into one curriculum. The stronger a parent's support for abstinence, the less likely he or she is to want abstinence and contraception merged into a single curriculum.

The fact that 75 percent of parents want both abstinence and contraception taught to teens should not, in any way, be interpreted to mean support for comprehensive sex-education. Comprehensive sex-ed curricula are focused almost exclusively on promoting contraceptive use and contain little or no mention of abstinence, yet only 8 percent of parents believe that schools should give greater emphasis to contraception than to abstinence.

Moreover, parents have reservations concerning the type of contraceptive education these curricula contain. While 52 percent of parents want schools to provide "basic biological and health information about contraception," only 23 percent want schools "to encourage teens to use condoms when having sex, teach teens where to obtain condoms, and have teens practice how to put on condoms." The latter aggressive type of contraceptive promotion is typical of comprehensive sex-ed curricula, though it lacks wide support among parents.

In general, parents want teens to be taught a strong abstinence message as well as being given basic biological information about contraception. The polls suggest that most parents would be satisfied if young people were given a vigorous abstinence course and were taught about the basics of contraception separately. This is probably the typical situation in most schools where authentic abstinence is taught. On the other hand, extremely few parents (7 percent to 8 percent) would be happy if abstinence education were to be replaced by comprehensive sex-ed.

Conclusion

The newly released poll shows strong (in many cases, nearly unanimous) support for the major themes of abstinence education. Abstinence programs provide young people with the strong, uplifting moral messages desired by nearly all parents.

Multiple evaluations show that abstinence programs are effective in encouraging young people to delay sexual activity.[8] The effectiveness of these programs is quite remarkable, given that they typically provide no more than a few hours of instruction per year. In those few hours, abstinence instructors seek to counteract thousands of hours of annual exposure to sex-saturated teen media, which strongly push teens in the opposite direction.

Most parents not only want vigorous instruction in abstinence, but also want teens to be taught basic biological information about contraception. Such information is not contained in abstinence curricula themselves but is frequently provided in a separate setting such as a health class. Overall, the values and objectives of the overwhelming majority of parents can be met by providing teens with a strong abstinence program while teaching basic biological information about contraception in a separate health or biology class. This arrangement appears common in schools where abstinence is taught.

In recent years, groups such as Advocates for Youth and SIECUS have sought to eliminate funding for abstinence or to replace abstinence education with comprehensive sex-ed. This is always done under the pretext that comprehensive sex-ed contains a strong abstinence message and, thereby, renders traditional abstinence superfluous. In reality, comprehensive sex-ed curricula have weak to nonexistent abstinence content. Replacing abstinence education with these programs would mean eliminating the abstinence message in most U.S. schools; nearly all parents would object to this change.

Only a tiny minority (less than 10 percent) of parents support the values and messages taught in comprehensive sex education curricula. Since the themes of these courses (such as "It's okay for teens to have sex as long as they use condoms") contradict and undermine the basic values parents want their children to be taught, these courses would be unacceptable even if combined with other materials.

The popular culture bombards teens with messages encouraging casual sexual activity at an early age. To counteract this, parents want teens to be taught a strong abstinence message. Parents overwhelmingly support abstinence curricula that link sexuality to love, intimacy, and commitment and that urge teens to delay sexual activity until maturity and marriage.

Regrettably, this sort of clear abstinence education is not taught in most schools. As a result, the sexual messages that parents deem to be most important are not getting through to today's teens.

Notes

1. Responses to individual questions categorized by region, gender, and race are available upon request.
2. National Campaign to Prevent Teen Pregnancy, *America's Adults and Teens Sound Off About Teen Pregnancy,* December 2003, p. 17.
3. Robert E. Rector, Kirk A. Johnson, Ph.D., and Lauren R. Noyes, "Sexually Active Teenagers Are More Likely to Be Depressed and to Attempt Suicide," Heritage Foundation Center for Data Analysis Report No. 03-04, June 3, 2003.
4. Robert E. Rector, Kirk A. Johnson, Lauren Noyes, and Shannan Martin, *The Harmful Effects of Sexual Activity and Multiple Sexual Partners Among Women: A Book of Charts,* The Heritage Foundation, June 23, 2003, pp. 4, 10.
5. Melissa G. Pardue, Robert E. Rector, and Shannan Martin, "Government Spends $12 on Safe Sex and Contraceptives for Every $1 Spent on Abstinence," Heritage Foundation Backgrounder No. 1718, January 14, 2004.
6. Some 85 percent of the sex education taught in the United States is part of a larger course on a broader subject, most typically a health or biology class. See *Sex Education in America* (Menlo Park, Cal.: Kaiser Family Foundation, 2000), p. 90.
7. Ibid., p. 18.
8. Robert E. Rector, "The Effectiveness of Abstinence Education Programs in Reducing Sexual Activity Among Youth," Heritage Foundation Backgrounder No. 1533, April 8, 2002.

Toward a Sexually Healthy America: Roadblocks Imposed by the Federal Government's Abstinence-Only-Until-Marriage Education Program

A Brief History of Abstinence-Only-Until-Marriage Education

Government funding of abstinence-only-until-marriage programs is not new. In fact, the federal government has poured large sums of money into such programs for the past 20 years.

AFLA: the birthplace of abstinence-only programs   The U.S. Office of Population Affairs began administering the Adolescent Family Life Act (AFLA) in 1981. This program was designed to prevent teen pregnancy by promoting chastity and self-discipline.[1] During its first year, AFLA received $11 million in federal funds. In fiscal year 2000, AFLA received $19 million.

AFLA's early programs taught abstinence as the only option for teens and often promoted specific religious values. As a result, the American Civil Liberties Union filed suit in 1983 charging that AFLA violated the separation of church and state as defined in the U.S. Constitution. In 1985, a U.S. district judge found AFLA unconstitutional. On appeal in 1988, the U.S. Supreme Court reversed that decision and remanded the case to a lower court.[2]

Finally, an out-of-court settlement in 1993 stipulated that AFLA-funded sexuality education programs must: (1) not include religious references, (2) be medically accurate, (3) respect the "principle of self-determination" regarding contraceptive referral for teenagers, and (4) not allow grantees to use church sanctuaries for their programs or to give presentations in parochial schools during school hours.[3] Within these limitations, AFLA continues to fund abstinence-only programs today.

Abstinence-only-until-marriage education as defined in AFLA has been taught for over two decades and yet there is still no peer-reviewed research that proves it is effective in changing adolescents' behavior. To the contrary, a meta-evaluation of AFLA program evaluations found them "barely adequate" to "completely inadequate."[4]

Congress institutes similar programs through Doolittle amendment The first Congressional attempt to censor sexuality education using an abstinence-only provision came in 1994 during the reauthorization of the Elementary and Secondary Education Act. Representative John Doolittle (R-CA) introduced an amendment to limit the content of HIV-prevention and sexuality education in school-based programs.

Fortunately, four federal statutes required alterations to the Doolittle amendment. The Department of Education Organization Act (Section 103a), the Elementary and Secondary Education Act (Section 14512), Goals 2000 (Section 319 (b)), and the General Education Provisions Act (Section 438) all prohibited the federal government from prescribing state and local school curriculum standards.

Proponents of abstinence-only programs learned from this that even though they could not legally restrict state and local education programs that they could restrict and define the scope of state and local health policy and funding. They applied their new-found lesson in 1996.

Federal entitlement program promotes abstinence-only-until-marriage That year, the federal government attached a provision to the popular welfare-reform law establishing a federal entitlement program for abstinence-only-until-marriage education.

This entitlement program, Section 510(b) of Title V of the Social Security Act, funneled $50 million per year for five years into the states. Those states that choose to accept Section 510(b) funds are required to match every four federal dollars with three state-raised dollars and then disperse the funds for educational activities.[5]

Programs that use the funds are required to adhere to a strict eight-point definition, which, among other things, requires them to teach that "sexual activity outside of marriage is likely to have harmful psychological and physical effects."[6] The section 510(b) abstinence-only-until-marriage funds are up for reauthorization in 2001.

Other federal abstinence legislation Funding for unproven abstinence-only-until-marriage education has increased nearly 3,000 percent since the federal entitlement program was created in 1996.[7] In November 1999, opponents of comprehensive sexuality education, family planning, and reproductive rights began a process that successfully secured an additional 50 million federal dollars for abstinence-only-until-marriage programs over the next two years. Although these funds are not part of Section 510(b), they are only available for programs that conform to the strict eight-point definition in 510(b).[8]

These new funds will be awarded directly to state and local organizations by the Maternal and Child Health Bureau through a competitive grant process instead of through state block grants as is the case for 510(b) funds. Many viewed this decision as an attempt by conservative lawmakers to control the funding and prevent money from supporting media campaigns, youth development, and after-school programs that they saw as diluting the abstinence message.[9]

Sexuality Education: Definitions and Comparisons

This section compares two contrasting approaches to teaching young people about their sexuality: *comprehensive sexuality education* and *abstinence-only-until-marriage education.* The differences point to the real public health threat imposed by current federal policy.

Comprehensive sexuality education   These programs emphasize the benefits of abstinence while also teaching about contraception and disease-prevention methods. Ideally, they start in kindergarten and continue through twelfth grade. They provide developmentally appropriate information on a broad variety of topics related to sexuality such as sexual development, reproductive health, interpersonal relationships, affection, intimacy, body image, and gender roles. Comprehensive programs provide opportunities for students to develop communication, decision-making, and other personal skills.

Abstinence-only-until-marriage   These programs, many of which are federally-funded, teach abstinence from all sexual activity as the only morally correct option for unmarried young people. They teach that "a mutually faithful monogamous relationship in the context of marriage is the expected standard of human sexual activity" and that "sexual activity outside of the context of marriage is likely to have harmful psychological and physical effects."[10] These programs, also referred to as abstinence-only programs, censor information on contraception for the prevention of sexually transmitted diseases and unintended pregnancies.

Abstinence-only-until-marriage programs and curricula are, by their very nature, very limited in scope. They typically limit discussion to sexually transmitted diseases, unplanned pregnancies, contraceptive failure rates, and the need to refrain from sexual activity outside of marriage. They often fail to mention basic sexual health information relating to puberty and reproduction and contain no information about pregnancy and disease-prevention methods other than abstinence. Consequently, these abstinence-only-until-marriage programs deny young people the information necessary to make informed, responsible sexual decisions. Some, however, go beyond withholding information by using fear as an educational tool. These programs, often referred to as fear-based, are designed to control young people's sexual behavior by instilling fear, shame, and guilt. They often contain biased information about gender, family structure, sexual orientation, and abortion. . . .

What Is Wrong with Abstinence-Only-Until-Marriage Education Requirements?

SIECUS, Advocates for Youth, and other organizations who support comprehensive sexuality education also support teaching young people about abstinence. They do not, however, support teaching young people *only* about abstinence or using fear and negative messages to motivate behavior.

One of the four primary goals of sexuality education—as set forth by the National Guidelines Task Force, a group of leading health, education, and sexuality professionals—is to "help young people exercise responsibility regarding sexual relationships, including abstinence [and] how to resist pressures to become prematurely involved in sexual intercourse." SIECUS' *Guidelines for Comprehensive Sexuality Education; K–12,* which was created by the Task Force, includes 36 sexual health topics. Abstinence is one of these topics.[11]

SIECUS and Advocates for Youth believe that abstinence is a healthy choice for adolescents and that premature involvement in sexual behavior poses risks. However, data has consistently shown that 50 percent of high school students have engaged in sexual intercourse.[12]

Whether adults agree with young people's actions or not, they cannot ignore the fact that millions of teenagers in the United States are engaging in a range of sexual behavior.[13] That is why all young people need the information, skills, and access to services necessary to make and carry out informed, responsible decisions about their sexuality.

Federally-funded abstinence-only-until-marriage education programs deny young people this very information. In fact, they must adhere to a strict eight-point definition, many aspects of which are in direct opposition to the goals and tenets of comprehensive sexuality education. While the law does not require programs to focus equally on each aspect of the definition, it does state that a federally-funded project "may not be inconsistent with any aspect of the abstinence definition."[14] While some aspects of the law's definition are not objectionable, others run counter to common sense, research, and genuine public health realities and responsibilities. The following section highlights some of the more problematic points of the eight-point definition.

> *Federal Requirement B ". . . teaches that abstinence from sexual activity outside marriage is the expected standard for all school age children."*

Although adults may want this as a standard, it is far from accurate in describing the world of today's teenagers. The reality is that sexual behavior is almost universal among American adolescents. A majority of them date, over 85 percent have had a boyfriend or a girlfriend and have kissed someone romantically, and nearly 80 percent have engaged in deep kissing.[15]

The majority of young people move from kissing to more intimate sexual behaviors during their teen years. Seventy-two percent of teens report "touching above the waist," 54 percent report "touching below the waist," 26 percent report engaging in oral sex, and 4 percent report engaging in anal sex.[16]

According to data from the most recent *Youth Risk Behavior Surveillance System* of the Centers for Disease Control and Prevention (CDC), 50 percent of high school students have had sexual intercourse, a rate virtually unchanged since the study began in 1990.[17] A similar survey of college students found that 80 percent of students 18 to 24 years of age had engaged in sexual intercourse.[18]

In addition, a recent study found that even those young people who remain virgins during their teen years engage in some forms of sexual behavior. Nearly one third of teens who identified themselves as virgins in that study had engaged in heterosexual masturbation of or by a partner, 10 percent had participated in oral sex, and one percent had engaged in anal intercourse.[19]

Teens are engaging in a variety of sexual behaviors every day that place them at risk for unintended pregnancy and STDs, including HIV. There is no research to support the notion that they will stop sexual behavior simply because adults ask them. Yet, the federal definition of abstinence-only-until-marriage education clearly prohibits programs from discussing pregnancy and disease-prevention methods other than abstinence. Such education denies teens the information they need to make informed responsible sexual decisions.

Federal Requirement C ". . . teaches that abstinence from sexual activity is the only certain way to avoid out-of-wedlock pregnancy, sexually transmitted diseases, and other associated health problems."

On the surface, it is hard to argue with this statement. The *Guidelines* state that "abstinence from sexual intercourse is the most effective method of preventing pregnancies and STDs/HIV."[20] However, this point clearly prevents funded programs from discussing the effectiveness of condoms and contraception in preventing unintended pregnancy and disease transmission. In fact, many abstinence-only-until-marriage programs discuss methods of contraception only in terms of their failure rate. After learning that abstinence is the "only certain way" to avoid pregnancy and disease and that condoms and contraceptive methods are not reliable, young people who do become sexually active are less likely to practice prevention techniques.

Some strict abstinence-only-until-marriage programs actually discourage the use of contraception, especially condoms. These programs give teens exaggerated and outdated information about effectiveness and tell them that correct condom use is difficult. In reality, research has shown that using a condom for protection from HIV is 10,000 times safer than not using a condom. But people need to learn how to use condoms correctly if they are going to protect themselves.[21] The CDC states that "studies of hundreds of couples show that consistent condom use is possible when people have the skills and motivations to do so." The CDC pointed out, however, that "people who are skeptical about condoms aren't as likely to use them—but that doesn't mean they won't have sex."[22]

Programs that teach students that condoms or contraception do not work will not necessarily prevent students from having sexual intercourse but will likely prevent them from using protection. These students will, therefore, put themselves at risk for STDs and unintended pregnancy.

In 1979, fewer than 50 percent of adolescents used contraception at first intercourse. In 1988, more than 65 percent used them. In 1990, more than 70 percent used them.[23] Unfortunately, abstinence-only-until-marriage education is likely to reverse these significant strides that youth in the United States have made toward safer sexual behavior in the past two decades.

> *Federal Requirement D ". . . teaches that a mutually faithful monogamous relationship in the context of marriage is the expected standard of human sexual activity."*

Again, while members of Congress or society might wish this as a standard, it is clearly not true in American culture. The concept of chastity until marriage is unrealistic in an age when young people are reaching puberty earlier than ever before, when half of high school students have engaged in sexual intercourse,[24] when 80 percent of college students 18 to 24 years of age have engaged in sexual intercourse,[25] and when the median age of first marriage is 25.9 for men and 24 for women.[26]

A brief look at Americans' behavior indicates that this "expected standard" is highly unlikely in American society. The vast majority of Americans begin having sexual relationships in their teens, fewer than seven percent of men and 20 percent of women 18 to 50 years old were virgins when they were married, and only 10 percent of adult men and 22 percent of adult women report their first sexual intercourse was with their spouse.[27] It is likely this "standard" was never true in America. A third of all Pilgrim brides were pregnant when they were married.[28]

Federally-funded abstinence-only-until-marriage programs are required to teach young people that all unmarried individuals (both adults and youth) *must* remain celibate. While this is a value held by many people in America, it is clearly not universally accepted as truth. Today, there are almost 80 million American adults who are classified as single because they have either delayed marriage, have decided to remain single, have divorced, are widowed, or have entered into gay or lesbian partnerships.[29] It is unreasonable to expect these adults to adhere to this "standard" and it is inaccurate and misleading to tell students that adults are adhering to it.

This part of the definition also seems to assume that all people have an equal chance or desire to enter into a "mutually faithful monogamous relationship in the context of marriage." Many people choose not to marry. Others— like gays and lesbians—are legally barred from marrying. Students enrolled in abstinence-only-until-marriage programs are now essentially learning that the sexual relationships of these people—whether same-sex or opposite-sex—are in conflict with society's standards.

Finally, this part of the definition may prove particularly harmful to young people who are or have been sexually abused. It requires telling these students that the behaviors in which they have involuntarily participated go against society's "expected standard." Such statements are likely to produce additional feelings of guilt and shame in these abused individuals.

> *Federal Requirement E ". . . teaches that sexual activity outside of marriage is likely to have harmful psychological and physical effects."*

There is no sound public health data to support this statement. It is true that unprotected sexual activity can lead to unplanned pregnancies, STDs, and HIV. It is also true that intimate relationships can be harmful for some people. However, the reality is that the majority of people have had sexual relationships prior to marriage with no negative repercussions.

> *Federal Requirement F ". . . teaches that bearing children out-of-wedlock is likely to have harmful consequences for the child, the child's parents, and society."*

In order to comply with this part of the definition, abstinence-only-until-marriage programs must present one family structure as morally correct and beneficial to society. In reality, any American classroom is likely to have children of never-married or divorced parents as well as children of gay, lesbian, and bisexual parents who can never legally marry. Telling these students that their families are the cause of societal problems will likely alienate them and could cause negative feelings about themselves and their families.

In sum, much of this eight-point definition written by Congressional staff under the influence of special interest groups has no basis in public health research.

Research Supports Comprehensive Sexuality Education

Abstinence-only-until-marriage education relies on the notion that young people will "just say no" if they are told to do so. Proponents of this type of education conclude that this is the only way to encourage young people to delay sexual activity until marriage, and consequently, to avoid becoming involved in a pregnancy, infected with an STD, or even emotionally hurt by a failed romance.

There is no proof that these claims are true. There are no published studies in the professional literature that show that abstinence-only programs will result in young people delaying the initiation of sexual intercourse.

To date, there are six published studies of abstinence-only programs. None have found consistent and significant program effects on delaying the onset of intercourse. In fact, at least one has provided strong evidence that the program did not delay the onset of intercourse.[30]

Proponents of abstinence-only-until-marriage programs often conduct their own in-house evaluations and cite them as proof that their programs are effective. However, outside experts have found them inadequate, methodologically unsound, or inconclusive based on methodological limitations.[31]

The CDC's *Research to Classroom Project* identifies curricula that have *shown evidence* of reducing sexual risk behaviors.[32] A recent paper written by the White House Office of National AIDS Policy points out that "none of the curricula on the current list of programs uses an 'abstinence-only' approach." The paper goes on to say that ". . . it is a matter of grave concern that there is such a large incentive to adopt unproven abstinence-only approaches."[33]

Comprehensive sexuality education is effective   On the other hand, numerous studies and evaluations published in peer-reviewed literature suggest that comprehensive sexuality education is an effective strategy to help young people delay their involvement in sexual intercourse.

A review commissioned by the Joint United Nations Programme on HIV/AIDS (UNAIDS) looked at 22 HIV-prevention and comprehensive sexuality education programs and found that they delayed the onset of sexual activity, reduced the number of sexual partners among sexually active youth, and reduced the rates of unintended pregnancy and STDs.[34]

A report titled *No Easy Answers,* written by Dr. Douglas Kirby, one of the leading researchers in the field of sexuality education, also considered evaluations of HIV-prevention and sexuality education programs—both abstinence-only-until-marriage and comprehensive. It concluded that HIV-prevention and sexuality education programs that cover both abstinence *and* contraception can delay the onset of sexual intercourse, reduce the frequency of sexual intercourse, and reduce the number of sexual partners. It also found that many of these programs significantly increased the use of condoms and other forms of contraception.[35]

Critics of comprehensive sexuality education often suggest that giving youth information about sexuality and contraception will encourage them to engage in sexual activity earlier and more often. However, research has consistently found that "sexuality and HIV education programs that include the discussion of condoms and contraception do not increase sexual intercourse, either by hastening the onset of intercourse, increasing the frequency of intercourse, or increasing the number of sexual partners."[36]

The conclusion reached by these studies is echoed in a review by the World Health Organization of evaluations of 35 sexuality education programs. The review concluded that the programs that are most effective in reducing sexual risk-taking behaviors among young people are programs that provide information on abstinence, contraception, and STD prevention.[37]

According to Dr. Kirby, effective programs:

- focus narrowly on reducing one or more sexual behaviors that lead to unintended pregnancy or STDs/HIV infection
- are based on theoretical approaches that have been successful in influencing other health-related risky behaviors
- give a clear message by continually reinforcing a clear stance on particular behaviors
- provide basic, accurate information about the risks of unprotected intercourse and methods of avoiding unprotected intercourse
- include activities that address social pressures associated with sexual behavior
- provide modeling and the practice of communication, negotiation, and refusal skills

EVALUATIONS SUPPORT COMPREHENSIVE SEXUALITY EDUCATION

Reviews of published evaluations of sexuality education, HIV-prevention, and adolescent pregnancy prevention programs have consistently found that such programs:

- do not encourage teens to start having sexual intercourse
- do not increase the frequency with which teens have intercourse
- do not increase the number of a person's sexual partners

Instead many of these programs:

- delay the onset of intercourse
- reduce the frequency of intercourse
- reduce the number of sexual partners
- increase condom or contraceptive use

- incorporate behavioral goals, teaching methods, and material that are appropriate to the age, sexual experience, and culture of the students
- last a sufficient length of time to complete important activities adequately
- select teachers or peers who believe in the program they are implementing and then provide training for those individuals[38]

There is no credible evidence that a "just say no" attitude toward teen sexual activity will work. On the other hand, study after study clearly support an approach to sexuality education that includes teaching young people about abstinence, contraception, and disease-prevention methods.

References

1. R. Saul, "Whatever Happened to the Adolescent Family Life Act?," *Guttmacher Report on Public Policy,* vol. 1, no. 2, April 1998.

2. Ibid.

3. D. Daley, "Exclusive Purpose: Abstinence-Only Proponents Create Entitlement in Welfare Reform," *SIECUS Report,* April/May 1997.

4. C. Bartels, et al., *Adolescent Abstinence Promotion Programs: An Evaluation of Evaluations.* (Paper presented at the Annual Meeting of the American Public Health Association, Nov. 18, 1996, New York, NY.)

5. Daley, "Exclusive Purpose" *SIECUS Report,* April/May 1997.

6. Section 510, Title V of the Social Security Act (Public Law 104–193).

7. C. Dailard, "Fueled by Campaign Promises, Drive Intensifies to Boost Abstinence-Only Education Funds," *The Guttmacher Report on Public Policy,* vol. 3, no. 2, April 2000.

8. W. Smith, "Public Policy Update: More Federal Funds Targeted for Abstinence-Only-Until-Marriage Programs," *SIECUS Report,* June/July 2000.

9.   Ibid.

10. Section 510, Title V of the Social Security Act (Public Law 104–193).

11. National Guidelines Task Force, *Guidelines for Comprehensive Sexuality Education: Kindergarten–12th Grade* (New York: SIECUS, 1991, 1996).

12. "Youth Risk Behavior Surveillance System—United States, 1999," *Morbidity and Mortality Weekly Report,* June 9, 2000, vol. 49, no. SS-5.

13. Ibid.

14. Section 510, Title V of the Social Security Act (Public Law 104–193).

15. R. Coles and F. Stokes, *Sex and the American Teenager* (New York: Harper and Row, 1985); Roper Starch Worldwide, *Teens Talk About Sex: Adolescent Sexuality in the 90s* (New York: Sexuality Information and Education Council of the United States, 1994).

16. Ibid.

17. "Youth Risk Behavior Surveillance System—United States, 1999," *Morbidity and Mortality Weekly Report,* June 9, 2000, vol. 49, no. SS-5.

18. "Youth Risk Behavior Surveillance System—National College Health Risk Behavior Survey, 1995," *Morbidity and Mortality Weekly Report,* Nov. 14, 1997, vol. 46, no. SS-6.

19. M. A. Schuster, R. M. Bell, D. E. Kanouse, "The Sexual Practices of Adolescent Virgins: Genital Sexual Activities of High School Students Who Have Never Had Vaginal Intercourse," *American Journal of Public Health,* 1996, vol. 86, pp. 1570–76.

20. National Guidelines Task Force, *Guidelines for Comprehensive Sexuality Education: Kindergarten–12th Grade* (New York: SIECUS, 1991, 1996).

21. R. F. Carey, et al., "Effectiveness of Latex Condoms As a Barrier to Human Immunodeficiency Virus-sized Particles under the Conditions of Simulated Use," *Sexually Transmitted Diseases,* vol. 19, no. 4, p. 230.

22. Centers for Disease Control and Prevention (CDC), "Questions and Answers about Male Latex Condoms to Prevent Sexual Transmission of HIV," *CDC Update* (Centers for Disease Control and Prevention: Atlanta, GA: April 1997).

23. D. Haffner, editor, *Facing Facts: Sexual Health for America's Adolescents* (New York: Sexuality Information and Education Council of the United States, 1994).

24. "Youth Risk Behavior Surveillance System—United States, 1999," *Morbidity and Mortality Weekly Report,* June 9, 2000, vol. 49, no. SS-5.

25. The Alan Guttmacher Institute, *Sex and America's Teenagers* (New York: The Alan Guttmacher Institute, 1994).

26. U.S. Bureau of the Census, Statistical Abstract of the US 1998 (118th edition), Washington, DC, 1998. p. 112.

27. E. Laumann, et al., *The Social Organization of Sexuality—Sexual Practices in the United States* (Chicago: The University of Chicago Press, 1994).

28. J. D'Emilio and E. Freedman, *Intimate Matters: A History of Sexuality in America* (New York: Harper and Row, 1988).

29. U.S. Census Bureau. Marital Status and Living Arrangements of Adults 18 Years Old and Over, March 1998.

30. D. Kirby, *No Easy Answers* (Washington, DC: National Campaign to Prevent Teen Pregnancy, 1997).

31. C. Bartels, et al., *Federally Funded Abstinence-Only Sex Education Programs: A Meta-Evaluation.* Paper presented at the Fifth Biennial Meeting of the Society

for Research on Adolescence, San Diego, CA, Feb. 11, 1994; B. Wilcox, et al., *Adolescent Abstinence Promotion Programs: An Evaluation of Evaluations.* Paper presented at the Annual Meeting of the American Public Health Association, New York, NY, Nov. 18, 1996; D. Kirby, M. Korpi, et al., *Evaluation of* Education Now and Babies Later (ENABL): *Final Report* (Berkeley, CA: University of California, School of Social Welfare, Family Welfare Research Group, 1995); D. Kirby, *No Easy Answers.*

32. Office of National AIDS Policy, The White House, *Youth and HIV/AIDS 2000: A New American Agenda* (Washington, DC: Government Printing Office, 2000), p. 14. (Individuals can download the report as a PDF file at. . . .)

33. Office of National AIDS Policy, *The White House, Youth and HIV/AIDS 2000,* p. 14.

34. Joint United Nations Programme on HIV/AIDS, "Sexual Health Education Does Lead to Safer Sexual Behaviour," press release, Oct. 22, 1997.

35. D. Kirby, *No Easy Answers: Research Findings on Programs to Reduce Teen Pregnancy* (Washington, DC: National Campaign to Prevent Teen Pregnancy, 1997), p. 27.

36. D. Kirby, *No Easy Answers,* p. 31.

37. A. Grunseit and S. Kippax, *Effects of Sex Education on Young People's Sexual Behavior* (Geneva: World Health Organization, 1993).

38. D. Kirby, "What Does the Research Say about Sexuality Education?," *Educational Leadership,* Oct. 2000, p. 74.

POSTSCRIPT

Is Abstinence-Only Sex Education the Best Way to Teach about Sex?

In our culture, it's impossible to avoid the constant presence of sexual references. Sex is the number one marketing tool to sell a product in our society. Sex is pervasive on television, on the Internet, and in the movies. The media oftentimes gives a false image of what sex really is, so that teens may see sex in unrealistic contexts, with no responsibility associated to sex-related decisions. Sex education in schools may be the only sound information sources available to adolescents.

Many questions should be considered when deciding on a sex education curriculum. Should parents or professionals have the sole decision-making power to decide what type of sex education a student receives? Should students have a voice in this decision? Should religion and moral values be a factor when deciding which type of sex education is best? Will comprehensive sex education encourage teens to have more casual sex as long as they use protection? Will comprehensive sex education encourage teens to start having sex sooner? Is abstinence-only sex education very realistic? Are we as a society being realistic if we believe that most teens will abstain from premarital sex?

As a society, we need to be cognizant of the fact that schools are not the only place where children receive sex education. All one has to do is listen to students during lunchtime at an elementary school, middle school, or high school to hear that they are receiving information about sex from peers. The Internet and other mass media are full of information about sex as well. Also, our own behaviors that we model to our children send strong messages about sexuality. It seems that the true mission of schools is to empower our children with accurate, developmentally appropriate information about their sexuality as a way to counterbalance the sometimes erroneous messages they receive from other aspects of their lives. Which approach most effectively addresses this goal?

Suggested Readings

The Kaiser Family Foundation. (2000). *Sex education in America: A view from the inside of the nation's classrooms.* The Kaiser Family Foundation.

Kirby, D. (2000). What does the research say about sexuality education? *Educational Leadership, 74.*

Sex Education in America: An NPR/Kaiser/Kennedy School Poll (2004). National Public Radio. www.npr.org/templates/story/story.php?storyId= 1622610.

Teicher, Stacy. (November 2004). In Texas, a stand to teach 'abstinence only' in sex ed. *Christian Science Monitor.* www.csmonitor.com/2004/ 1109/p12s01-legn.html

ISSUE 17

Is the Internet a Safe Place for Teens to Explore?

YES: Michele Fleming and Debra Rickwood, from "Teens in Cyberspace: Do They Encounter Friend or Foe?" *Youth Studies Australia* (vol. 23, no. 3, 2004)

NO: Chang-Hoan Cho and Hongsik John Cheon, from "Children's Exposure to Negative Internet Content: Effects of Family Content," *Journal of Broadcasting and Electronic Media* (December 2005)

ISSUE SUMMARY

YES: Michele Fleming and Debra Rickwood, professors at the University of Canberra in Australia, contend that parents need to be vigilant about their teens surfing the Web, but that it is generally a safe place and that the prevalence of cyber predators is overstated.

NO: Chang-Hoan Cho, assistant professor at the University of Florida, and Hongsik John Cheon, assistant professor at Frostburg State University, believe that the Web can be a dangerous place for teens to explore. They conducted a study that found that children are exposed to more negative Internet content than parents expect. Factors that reduced children's exposure to negative Internet content included parental interaction and family cohesion.

Parents want to protect their children. When children are young, they are under parental control and easier to protect because they are physically in parents' sight. They are dependent on parents for physical needs such as food and shelter. As children get older, they are more mobile, particularly when they learn to drive. Parents of teens are usually sleep deprived because they cannot sleep until they know their teens are home safely from a night activity with their friends. But how can parents protect their children from the dangers of the Internet? Teens can be right in front of them in the house working on the computer and still be in possible danger. They don't even have to be out of the house to be exposed to dangers on the Internet such as sexual predators.

Is this true or is it an exaggeration? Although media reports suggest that children and teens are being sexually solicited on the Internet at an alarming rate, some researchers state that the incidence of sexual predators on the Internet is grossly overstated. Media reports often quote the statistic that one in five children, aged 10 to 17, per year, are sexually solicited online. What they don't tell you is that this statistic comes from a report that defines sexual solicitation as anything from a classmate asking his girlfriend if she is a virgin to something more serious like adults asking children to meet for a sexual encounter. One is a simple question, while the other is an example of the serious problem of online predators.

Studies on Internet use and its effects report conflicting and varied results. Some studies on children's use of the Internet show that it has positive effects on academic achievement and no negative effects on social or psychological development. Other studies report children experience lasting psychological damage as a result of surfing the Web. For example, one study stated that 42 percent of Internet users aged 10 to17 had seen online pornography in the past year, with the majority saying that they did not seek it out and were very disturbed by it. Of the more than 450 million porn Web sites, 3 percent ask for proof of age and are more than willing to show scenes that are sexually explicit.

Not only is there confusion over how much real danger the Internet poses, but parents must also contend with the new language that children and teens use when surfing the Web. For example, "lol" means laughing out loud; "pos" means parents over shoulder. In order to protect and guide children in the new world of the Internet, parents must learn about hardware, software, and a new language!

Common Sense Media and Media Wise from the National Institute on Media and the Family list Internet safety by age and stage as well as rules on Internet safety. For children aged 2 to 6, they suggest keeping children away from the Internet, even the games. For ages 7 to 9, e-mailing is OK, but not instant messaging (IM) as it is too difficult to control. Web surfing can be done if a filter is installed. No chat rooms, online games, or downloading should be allowed for this age group. For ages 10 to 12, children begin exploring the Web much more at school, at home, and at their friends' homes. They insist on IMing and surfing the Web for games and need to be supervised closely. MySpace, which is a Web site for social networking for young people, is inappropriate at this age. Children age 13 to 16 can e-mail, IM, surf the Web, download, and play games as long as they follow the rules of Internet safety.

In the following selections, Internet safety for children and teens is debated. Michele Fleming and Debra Rickwood recognize that dangers on the Internet exist, but that children use the Web mostly to interact with friends from their existing social networks, for homework, and for entertainment. From their study of 178 families, Chang-Hoan Cho and Hongsik John Cheon found that children are exposed to more negative Internet content than most parents had previously thought.

YES

Michele Fleming and Debra Rickwood

Teens in Cyberspace: Do They Encounter Friend or Foe?

Recent media reports of relationships developed "online" have fuelled parents' concerns about the safety of their children using the Internet ('Runaway schoolgirl contacts family after Internet liaison', The *Canberra Times*, 17 July 2003, p. 15). Many parents hold ambivalent views about the Internet, being aware of its positive educational value but fearful of its "influence" on their children. In particular, parents are concerned that their children might become socially isolated due to excessive Internet use, might view sexually explicit images, and might divulge sensitive information to strangers.

The effects of "excessive" use of the Internet have not yet been clearly established. Some studies have looked at "computer" addiction and some at time spent playing video games. Both these activities have been linked to negative outcomes when done to excess. Excessive video game play, even when not of a violent nature, has been linked to aggression in numerous studies. Teens who use computers to excess have been found to report psychiatric symptoms, such as anxiety, hostility and obsessive-compulsivity. However, studies on the effects of excessive use of computers have not clearly shown the direction of the relationship and the negative outcomes reported may themselves be the cause of overuse.

Many teens are logging onto the Net both at school and at home but it is not yet known how many of them are using it to excess. Different criteria for Internet "addiction" are used by different researchers, making any valid assessment of how many individuals might be classified as addicted very difficult. Nonetheless, young people who spend inordinate amounts of time online, to the detriment of other activities, might be classified as "at-risk." Griffiths, in examining the impact of electronic technology on children and adolescents, suggested that when any activity is engaged in for such large amounts of time and other activities are displaced, it is likely that educational and social relationships will suffer.

The association between Internet use and psychological well-being in adults has been studied by Robert Kraut of the Carnegie Mellon University over the past few years. Kraut and colleagues have found greater Internet use to be associated with reduced psychological well-being, and reduced social support and increased depression. In a 1998 longitudinal study, undertaken with a relatively small but diverse US sample of 169 participants, including teenagers, greater Internet use was found to be associated with less family communication, greater loneliness and greater depression. In partial support of Kraut et al.'s findings, a study of high school seniors in the USA found that level of Internet use was not related to depression but was found to be related to poorer relationships with mothers and friends. However, it has also been suggested that it is people who are already lonely who spend time on the Internet.

In contrast, some research suggests that the Internet increases social connectedness and results in many positive face-to-face relationships. The anonymity of online relationships can increase intimate self-disclosure. For those who have difficulty with face-to-face relationships, the Internet may allow them to more easily express themselves and thereby experience social connectedness. Some people seem to feel that they are more their real selves on the Internet, which in turn leads to the formation of strong online attachments. For many teens, online communication may be just another way of keeping in touch with existing friends. Instead of being on the phone after school, teens are "talking" to their friends online.

Parents are also concerned about the amount of pornography children are exposed to online. Although some young people may deliberately seek out pornographic sites, others may be subjected to it unwittingly. Parents fears are not entirely unfounded, with 25% of youth aged 10 to 17 years indicating they had been exposed to unwanted pornography in a national survey conducted in the USA.

However, the biggest concern for parents is "stranger-danger." Parents have long been concerned about stranger-danger in the real world and this has now extended to the virtual world. Parents are fearful that children might divulge information that makes them vulnerable to potential predators who might be able to trace them through information disclosed on the Internet. Parents also fear that children might form a relationship with someone unsuitable online, possibly even a paedophile. Certainly, young people are the most vulnerable section of society when it comes to sexual assault and abduction. Crime statistics for Australia show that children aged 10 to 14 years and adolescents aged 15 to 19 years are three times more likely than the general population to have been recorded as a victim of sexual assault. Adolescents are also three times more likely to be the victims of robbery and kidnapping than the general population. Thus fears about safety in the real world are based in fact. To date, there is little but growing evidence that fears about safety as a result of contacts made online are also well-founded.

How Often Are Youth Online?

Children and young people are using the Internet in ever-increasing numbers. Research done in the USA has found that teenagers are much heavier users of the Internet than are adults. In one US study of 754 teens aged 12 to 17 years, it was found that 73% used the Internet and of these 42% went online daily.

In a national survey conducted by the Australian Broadcasting Authority in 2000, 58% of Australian children aged 5 to 12 years and 86% of teens aged 13 to 18 years were reported to have Internet access either at home or at school. The latest Australian Bureau of Statistics figures, using 2001 data, found that 28% of Australian children aged 0 to 17 years had accessed the Internet from home in the previous week. Given that this figure includes very young children and babies, the likelihood is that use by teens is substantially higher than indicated by these figures. Furthermore, many young people use the Internet at school and some of this use is undoubtedly for reasons other than schoolwork.

Why Do Young People Use the Internet?

Research into reasons for young people's use of the Internet is relatively scarce. However, research with adults suggests that the Internet is used for entertainment, education, information gathering and communication. In a sample of 236 American college students with a mean age of 20 years, the main reasons for using the World Wide Web were entertainment, passing time, social information, relaxation and information. In a survey of 684 adults, the main reasons reported for using the Internet were to find information, to relieve boredom, to get to know others and for entertainment.

Recently, some studies have begun to investigate the reasons for teens' use of the Internet. An American survey conducted by America Online of 6,700 teens aged 12 to 17 years, found that 81% used their computers for email; 70% for instant messaging; 70% to play online games; 58% for homework research; and 55% for listening to and downloading music. In a study of 625 American youth aged 10 to 17 years, 71% used the Internet to get news or information about current events; 68% used their computers to send and receive emails; 56% to get information about sports, entertainment and hobbies; 54% to talk in chat rooms; 17% to get health or medical information; and 17% to shop.

Younger children's reasons for using the Internet were examined in a study of 194 Dutch children aged 8 to 13 years. Children reported using the Internet because they had an affinity with computers; in order to gather information; for entertainment; to avoid boredom; for online social interaction; and for off-line social action, in that order. The last mentioned reason "off-line social interaction" referred to children's desire to talk about the Internet with friends because their friends were also using it.

Results of the Pew Internet and American Life Project showed that teens go online for entertainment and information. Some of the things teens specifically reported going online for were to send or receive email; to use instant messaging (IM); to visit web sites about movies, television shows, music groups and sports stars; to look for news; to look for hobby information; to play and download games; to research information on items they might like to buy; and to play and download music. Teens reported that IM messaging is very important to them, with 74% of online teens using IM. One-fifth of teenagers in the study reported using IM as the main means of contacting friends.

Cyberspace: Consequences for Children and Adolescents

The overwhelming concern of parents and the public alike is that young people will form cyber-relationships with predatory strangers, which in turn may lead to them being lured into a meeting with a paedophile. A growing body of evidence suggests that both adults and teens are forming relationships online, and in some cases turning online relationships into offline ones. However, American studies report that most teens and adults are taking appropriate precautions when meeting with online "friends." The news from Japan, however, is rather more worrying, with reports of a number of sexual assaults on teens as a result of meetings arranged via online dating sites. On the positive side, American research also suggests that most young people tend to form relationships with similar age peers rather than with older people, and that many of these online relationships are initiated through existing social networks. Similarly, there appears no evidence as yet that spending time online results in social isolation; on the contrary, research to date with adolescents suggests that Internet use increases social interaction.

Psychological Well-Being and Social Connectedness

Most of the time, young people online are interacting with friends from their existing social networks. In an American study of 130 children aged 11 to 13 years, participants' IM partners were usually friends from school. However, 12% of IM partners in this study had been met online. Most of the online communication was devoted to the usual topics discussed offline, such as friends and gossip, and was motivated by a desire of companionship. Of concern, however, is the finding that those young people who felt lonely and/or anxious were more likely to have online relationships with people with whom they did not have a close affiliation. This is consistent with research which suggests that not all teens are equally likely to form new online relationships. In one US study, boys who had poor communication with their parents or were highly troubled were more likely to form close online relationships than were other boys. Similarly, girls who had high levels of conflict with their parents or were highly troubled, were more likely to form close online relationships than were other girls.

Some teens, however, have reported that use of the Internet improves their relationships with friends. Results of the Pew Internet and American Life Project, in which 754 young people aged 12 to 17 and 754 of their parents were interviewed, showed that 73% of teens were online. Of these online youths, 48% said that use of the Internet improved their relationships with friends; and 32% reported that the Internet had helped them make new friends. Girls aged 12 to 14 years were the most enthusiastic about the Internet's ability to help them make new friends online. Teens in this study reported that the Internet allowed them to be more their true self, which is in line with research with adults.

Frequent Internet users have reported engaging in more social activities than less frequent users. In a study with 927 Israeli teenagers aged 13 to 18 years from a representative sample of Israeli households, it was reported that more than a third of the respondents were frequent Internet users, although the authors classified frequent use as anything more than once per week. Only 10% of respondents reported using the Internet daily. Importantly, however, frequent users reported having fewer friends and feeling more socially isolated than did light users.

Pornography and Sexual Harassment

Parents' concerns that their children will be subjected to online pornography are valid. Young people may visit pornographic sites by choice but also they may be subjected to pornographic material unwittingly. In a national survey of American youth aged 10 to 17 years who were regular Internet users, 25% had been exposed to unwanted sexual pictures in the previous year. Of these, the majority reported no negative effect of their exposure but 25% reported distress at being exposed. More boys than girls reported exposure and older youths reported substantially more exposure than did younger children.

With a younger sample of Dutch children aged 8 to 13 years, 4% reported experiencing violence on the net, 4% reported experiencing pornography, and 1.5% reported experiencing sexual harassment. Although these figures are small, they are nonetheless of concern.

As part of the Australia Broadcasting Authority's survey of Internet use in the home, a cyber-panel of Australian families was questioned regarding exposure to offensive material on the Net. A total of 192 of the cyber-panel members were teens aged 11 to 17 years and almost half (47%) of them reported having been exposed to offensive content such as violence, pornography and nudity. The overwhelming majority of offensive content cited by these teens was pornography.

Even more disturbing than viewing unwanted pornography is being sexually solicited online. A survey of American youth found that 19% of Internet users aged 10 to 17 years had received an unwanted sexual solicitation in the previous 12 months. Thankfully, none of these solicitations resulted in any sexual contact or assault.

Safety

Young people, for the most part, spend their time online with people they already know but nonetheless many do appear to form friendships with strangers. In a large US survey of 1,501 adolescents aged 10 to 17 years who regularly used the Internet, 55% had used chat rooms, IM and other forms of online communication in the previous year, to communicate with people they did not know face-to-face. For some of these youths, the online strangers were in fact friends-of-friends. Twenty-five percent of the participants reported forming a casual online friendship, while 14% reported forming a close online friendship, 7% had a face-to-face meeting, and 2% had established an online romantic relationship. In all, 17% of young people reported establishing some form of close online relationship. The majority of participants stated that mutual interests and activities were what initially drew them together. Of the 101 young people who had face-to-face encounters, 77% were accompanied to the meeting by a friend or relative, 1% were made to feel afraid at the meeting, and none of the youths were physically or sexually assaulted at the meeting.

Reassuringly, the majority of teens in the Wolak, Mitchell and Finkelhor study who met their online friends face-to-face, were accompanied to the meeting. This caution in face-to-face encounters is consistent with research conducted with a group of 30 undergraduates who regularly used the Internet. In this study, 80% of the undergraduates had formed online friendships and 33% met their online friends face-to-face. Most of the participants reported that they were careful to protect their anonymity and took precautions before meeting face-to-face. Nonetheless, not all teens are cautious, which raises serious concerns for parents.

In contrast to the relatively small number of face-to-face encounters reported in the Wolak, Mitchell & Finkelhor study, are findings from a survey conducted in Japan and reported by Yasumasa Kioka of the Japanese National Policy Agency at a conference earlier this year. Japan adopted the latest third-generation (3G) technologies early on, thus Japanese children were some of the first to use mobile-Internet services. In 2002, Japan had 3,401 "dating sites" available from Internet-mobiles and Kioka reported that a survey completed in 2002 showed that 22% of female high school students and 18% of male high school students had used one of these dating sites. Of these, 43% of females and 28% of males had met their date face-to-face. The arrest statistics for dating sites in Japan showed that 84% of a total of 1,517 crime victims were children under the age of 18 and that the majority of dating site crimes were related to mobile-Internet use.

Fears that children and teens may be tracked on the Internet to their home addresses are also not entirely without foundation. Although many web sites have privacy policies, they do not cover the advertising banners that pop up seemingly endlessly when accessing many web sites. Young people may be lulled into a false sense of security when on the Internet and may disclose sensitive information. In research conducted in the US with 304 youth aged 10 to 17 years, one-third of younger teens or "tweens" aged 10 to 12 years reported visiting chat rooms while half of those aged 13 to 17 years reported doing so. Of those going online, 73% said they "look to see if a web site has a privacy policy before answering any questions" and 79% agreed that teenagers should get consent from their parents before they give out information online. However, many of the youngsters in this study were prepared to give out sensitive information when a free gift was offered. Interestingly, gender differences were found, with girls less prepared than boys to provide information to web sites in return for a free gift; girls were also less prepared than boys to trust web sites not to share information with others. Girls were also significantly more likely than were boys to have talked to their parents about how to deal with giving out information on the web. While this study suggests that many teens are conscious of cyber-safety, a sizeable minority are not. Lack of caution was also shown by teens surveyed in the Pew Internet and American Life Project, with 22% of online teens who used IM reporting that they had shared their password with a friend.

Although many parents report closely supervising children's Internet use, there appears to be a gap between children's reporting of parental supervision and parents' reporting, with parents saying they keep a closer eye on children's Internet use than their children report. This inconsistency might be due to teens being unaware of their parents' supervision; alternatively, parents may be over-reporting their level of supervision.

For parents who are particularly concerned that their children may be accessing inappropriate material on the Net, there are various tools which can be used to block access, such as filters, labels and safe zones. A good Internet site, which provides information about these tools and other tips on safety for both children and parents, is the Australian Broadcasting Authority Cybersmart Kids site. . . .

Teens in Cyberspace: Finding Friend or Foe?

There appears to be strong agreement between parents and teens that the Internet is valuable tool that helps young people with their schoolwork. For many young people the Internet is also useful for entertainment, information and social communication. Although no definite figures exist for the numbers of teenagers that use the Internet to "excess," it is likely that those who are neglecting their schoolwork, their sports and their leisure activities in order to surf the Net, are in danger of becoming addicted.

It is likely that children and teens will be subject to occasional violent and pornographic images and parents need to be aware of this and discuss it with their children. Older teens are more vulnerable than younger teens to this type of exposure, probably because of the amount of time they spend on the Net and perhaps because they are more likely than younger children to explore more and varied sites. The consequences of young people's exposure to pornography are not yet known; however, research with adults suggests negative consequences. In particular, exposure to violent pornography has been found to be associated with violence against women and repeated exposure to non-violent pornography has been found to be associated with the promotion of more permissive sexual attitudes.

To date, research suggests that online relationships of some kind, whether casual or close, are formed by large numbers of teens. Reassuringly for parents, most of these relationships seem to be extensions of the young person's social circle. The early evidence from American studies suggests that cyber-safety is not a big problem as yet; however, evidence from Japan suggests otherwise. Japan is perhaps a few years ahead of most other countries in terms of ease of Internet accessibility. Nonetheless, it remains to be seen whether the problems with "dating sites" is one that is peculiar to Japanese culture, or whether the type of problem currently seen in Japan will emerge in Australia and other Western cultures in the near future.

For some children and young people, the anonymity of online relationships may be helpful as they go about practising their social communications. Teens with healthy, happy offline relationships are likely to continue to explore and expand those relationships further via online chat. Young people who are geographically remote, disabled or housebound due to illness, may find online chat an important form of communication. However, of concern, is the fact that a small minority of young people who are socially anxious or lonely may deliberately seek out relationships online.

Parents need to be aware that some children and teens will form close, intimate relationships online. Existing relationships that are extended and consolidated on the Internet, appear to be healthy ones although the jury is still out on the quality of relationships that are newly formed online. It is important that parents discuss issues of Internet safety with children and teens and try to discourage face-to-face meetings; however, if these do take place, children and even older teens should be accompanied to the meeting by a friend or family member and it should occur in a very public place. Girls appear to have taken the messages of privacy and safety to heart more than boys have. This may be due to parents talking more to their daughters about Internet safety than to their sons.

The Internet is a juggernaut which parents cannot stop. Even without home access, many teens have access to the Internet at school, at friends' houses or at Internet cafés. Rather than banning online communication, parents need to be aware of what children and adolescents are doing online by talking to them about their Internet use and showing an interest in what they are doing. Imposing some restrictions on the information that young people are allowed to disclose online and imposing restrictions on the amount of time spent online are first steps towards keeping kids safe. Even though many teens appear Net-savvy, they still need to be reminded of the potential dangers lurking online. There may be many friends in cyberspace but there are undoubtedly a number of foes.

Chang-Hoan Cho and
Hongsik John Cheon

Children's Exposure to Negative Internet Content: Effects of Family Content

The Internet has become an indispensable element of life for most people in the contemporary world, and children are not excluded. Because of the ubiquitous availability of Internet access, in schools and libraries, children are increasingly becoming involved in this new technology. As of December 2003, 23 million children in the United States ages 6 to 17 have Internet access at home, which is a threefold increase since 2000. According to a survey conducted by the Corporation for Public Broadcasting in July 2002, 78% of family households with children have Internet access at home. A survey by Yahoo and Carat showed that children ages 12 to 17 used the Internet an average of 16.7 hours per week in 2003. Given this extensive usage, the Internet has the potential to be a very powerful socialization agent.

The Internet has a double-edged sword characteristic for children: providing many opportunities for learning while exposing children to potentially negative content. The Internet not only provides significant benefits for children, such as research access, socialization, entertainment, and a communication tool with families, but it also connotes negative aspects such as violence, pornography, hate sites, isolation, predators, and commercialism. The Web sites considered detrimental include those dedicated to negative content such as pornography, violent online games, online gambling, and so forth. For example, many children can easily access pornographic content on the Internet. They can also be accidentally exposed to numerous obscene pop-up banner ads and extensive pornographic content when they type seemingly innocent key words into a search engine, for example, the name of a singer such as Britney Spears, Christina Aguilera, or Madonna. According to Finkelhor et al., 25% of the respondents ($n = 1,501$, ages 10–17) reported receiving unwanted exposure to sexual materials while online, and 19% received a sexual solicitation online.

Despite the potential negative effects on children using the Internet, more than 30% of surveyed parents had not discussed the downside of Internet use with their children, and 62% of parents of teenagers did not realize that their children had visited inappropriate Web sites. Recognizing the ever-serious

From *Journal of Broadcasting and Electronic Media*, vol. 49:4, December 2005, pp. 488–492, 502–505. Copyright © 2005 by Broadcast Education Association. Reprinted by permission of Broadcast Education Association (BEA).

negative aspects of children using the Internet and parents' possible underestimation of, or ignorance about, their children's Internet usage and its effects, this study explores the degree of children's exposure to negative Internet content and detects the possible discrepancy between what parents think their children are doing online and their children's actual activities. In doing so, this study carefully dissects the possible causes and consequences of perceived parental control over children's Internet usage. Concerned that inappropriate Internet content may jeopardize the health or safety of children, the present study is a crucial attempt that aims to address the following research inquires with regard to children's Internet usage: (a) to understand the degree to which children are exposed to negative Internet content, (b) to detect a possible discrepancy between parents' perception and children's actual exposure to negative Internet content, (c) to examine various antecedents explaining perceived parental control over children's Internet usage, and (d) to suggest various ways to decrease children's exposure to negative Internet content.

Literature Review

In fall 2002, 99% of public schools in the United States had access to the Internet and 64% of children ages 5 to 17 had Internet access at home (National Center for Education Statistics, 2002). Children ages 13 to 17 spent more time online than watching television—3.5 hours versus 3.1 hours per day, and used the Internet mostly for exploration (surfing and searching), followed by education (learning and homework), multimedia (music, video, etc.), communications (e-mail, chat, and instant messages), games, and e-commerce. The place children were most likely to use the Internet was in the home, rather than at a library or school: 20% of children ages 8 to 16 had a computer in their bedroom, of which 54% had Internet access.

Negative Effects of Using the Internet

There is an increasing concern from educators, psychologists, and parents about the negative effects of using the Internet on the physical (e.g., information fatigue syndrome), cognitive (e.g., inability to discriminate between the real and cyber world), and social development (e.g., identity confusion) of children, among which, detriment to social development (hurting children's skills and patience to conduct necessary social relations in the real world) is a paramount problem. One of the most serious concerns regarding children's social development involves the proliferation and easy accessibility of negative content on the Internet, such as pornography, violence, hate speech, gambling, sexual solicitation, and so forth. It is easy to see how these types of negative content harm children and destroy their development. Extant literature shows that children's exposure to inappropriate media content yields many negative outcomes such as increased aggression, fear, desensitization, poor school performance, prevalence of symptoms of psychological trauma, antisocial behavior, negative self-perception, low self-esteem, lack of reality, identity confusion, and more.

In particular, sexually explicit materials on the Internet can desensitize children to deviant sexual stimuli and encourage them to enact antisocial aggressive sexual behaviors. Furthermore, the anonymity of the Internet makes it easier for pedophiles to approach children through online chatting. Children who spend hours in chat rooms looking for friends or just passing time can be easily targeted and abused by unknown adult sexual offenders. Violent online games are another serious concern. It is known that violent computer games increase children's physical, verbal, relational, and antisocial aggressions. These negative effects of violent games on children are even more serious regarding the Internet because access to such violent games has become easier for unsupervised children due to free or fee-based online games. Online gambling has also been cited as a serious Internet problem affecting children. It can seriously disrupt children's social and psychological development, for example, addiction, being unable to repay debts, missing school, and so forth.

However, little is known about children's actual amount of exposure to such inappropriate content and activities on the Internet. Extant literature shows that a discrepancy exists between the reports of parents and children on children's media usage; for example, parents tend to underestimate time spent on television viewing and the amount of violence to which children are exposed. This discrepancy leads parents to underrate the impact of media messages on their children and to not exert much control over their children's media use. Surprisingly, 38% of surveyed children ages 8 to 18 said that their parents do not enforce any rules on watching television, 95% of older children watch television without their parents, and 81% of children ages 2 to 7 watch television unsupervised. This may be true for children's Internet usage, but we know little about the possible discrepancy between parental estimates and children's actual Internet usage. In this vein, the present study tries to detect the degree to which children are exposed to these sources of negative content and whether parents overestimate or underestimate their children's exposure to such content. In doing so, this study strives to examine how children's exposure to such negative Internet content relates to the social context of Internet usage, that is, the role of family communication and relationship on children's exposure to such content.

Social Context of Children's Internet Use

People use media within a social realm, and children are no exception. Social context of media usage, especially parental influence, is crucial in children's social development. However, many social aspects of children's Internet usage are still unknown. Therefore, this study focuses on the social context of children's Internet use, especially relative to family environment such as parental guidance, influence, and relationship with children.

Children live within a family boundary; therefore, parental influence on children's media usage and effect is very important. Extant research shows that family communication exerts the greatest influence on children's socialization and development. Stemming from political socialization research, family communication patterns have been widely applied to various socialization contexts such as consumption, political process, media usage, and so forth. In particular, in mass media research, it was found that family communication patterns mediate the extent and type of children's mass media use and effects, for example, watching public affairs television programs, interest in and knowledge about politics, imitating their parents' television usage, interpreting televised violence, attitude towards nontraditional sex roles, child consumer learning, and so forth.

More specifically, concerning children's Internet usage, Wartella et al. found that parental attitude and guidance significantly influence children's judgment of quality Internet materials. Recognizing the importance of family context on children's Internet usage, the present study tries to examine the role of family context (parent–child communication, relationship, and activity) on children's exposure to Internet content and parents' control over children's Internet use. In short, the research contributes to this area in the following three aspects: (a) understanding children's actual Internet usage in terms of content, not by Web sites or general activities; (b) examining the role of family environment on children's negative Internet exposure; and (c) providing a theoretical framework to explain children's exposure to negative Internet content and parents' perceived control over their children's Internet usage. . . .

Discussion

This study was an exploratory study to understand children's exposure to negative Internet content. The objective was to provide insight into family context factors that influence children's exposure to negative Internet content and to test their proposed interrelationships. In pursuing that goal, a theoretical model of children's negative Internet exposure was synthesized from the theoretical traditions of a representative body of diverse referent disciplines. Possible contributions of this study are threefold. First, it is the first attempt toward understanding children's negative Internet exposure in terms of content, rather than by Web sites or general activities. Second, this study builds a theoretical model explaining children's exposure to negative Internet content. Third, the study identifies the importance of family environment on children's negative Internet exposure and suggests two important family context variables that reduce children's exposure to negative content.

This study found that parents generally underestimate their children's exposure to negative Internet content. This finding suggests that children are more exposed to negative Internet content than what parents expect. It implies that the effect of negative Internet content on children can be more serious than what most parents estimate. Moreover, among various demographic variables such as family income, parents' education level, and age and gender of children, only the gender of children is related to children's exposure to negative content (male children are exposed to negative content more than female children). This finding suggests that demographic variables do little to explain children's negative Internet exposure, which amplifies the importance of identifying other significant factors that explain children's Internet exposure. This study proposed family relationship, interaction, and control as important antecedents of children's exposure to negative Internet content and built a theoretical model on the effect of family context on children's negative exposure.

The acceptable fit of the final model generally supports the stated hypotheses: Parents' perceived control is explained by shared Web activity and family cohesion, and perceived control results in more appropriate use of the Internet by their children (less exposure to negative Internet content). . . . There was a significant effect of family cohesion/intimacy on parents' perceived control over children's Internet usage. The result suggests that parents who perceive high family cohesion/intimacy tend to have high perceived control over their children's Internet usage. This finding implies that parents need to maintain intimate emotional bonding with their children to have better understanding of, and control over, their children's behaviors (negative Internet exposure). The result is consistent with previous studies on the role of family cohesion on the parent–child relationship, and this study substantiates the importance of family cohesion in the context of children's negative Internet exposure.

. . . Findings demonstrate a significant effect of shared Web activities on parents' perceived control over children's Internet usage. The result implies that parents who spend more time online with their children are more likely to have high perceived control over their children's Internet usage. The result is consistent with previous studies on the role of shared family activities on parent–child mutual understanding and children's media usage and learning. This study further confirms the importance of shared family activities in the context of children's negative Internet exposure. Although not initially hypothesized, a new causal relationship (family cohesion → shared Web activity) was discovered. This relationship seems conceptually sound because high emotional bonding among parents and children may lead to more shared activities and interactions between them. Actually, previous studies have demonstrated the positive relationship between family bonding and family interaction.

Unexpectedly, however, the effect of parents' Internet skill on perceived control over children's Internet usage was not confirmed. The hypothesized relationship was derived from "flow" research (more skill, higher cognitive control), but the result failed to show the importance of parents' Internet skill on the perceived control over their children's Internet usage. The finding suggests that parents' Internet knowledge and skill do not necessarily give high competency and control to parents; instead, emotional bonding and shared Web activities contribute to increase parents' perceived control over children's Internet usage. In terms of relative importance, shared Web activity exhibited the strongest predicting power of parents' perceived control ($\gamma = .43$), followed by family cohesion ($\gamma = .39$). The result suggests that the most important contributor of parents' perceived control over children's Internet usage is shared Web activities between parents and children. In addition, parents' perceived control led to decreased children's exposure to negative Internet content. This suggests that parents' perceived control through shared Web activities and family cohesion actually reduces children's exposure to negative Internet content.

The findings of the present research provide substantial implications for child education in school and at home. This study suggests possible home education strategies to parents, for example, locating the computer in a common area and having regular shared Internet sessions, encouraging children to evaluate Web sites and Internet ads and commenting on and explaining the subjects, teaching quality Web browsing and clicking choices, building and maintaining family love, affirmation and intimate relationship with children, and so forth. Parental oversight and interaction through these home education strategies can help reduce the temptation for children to use the computer to explore inappropriate content. The results of the study also can help educational organizations and governmental agencies develop various workshops or educational programs for children and parents to teach quality Internet use and importance of family context in children's negative Internet exposure. The study also provides implications for government regulations regarding Web sites that are potentially negative to children, for example, the need for developing a universal rating system for inappropriate Internet content (such as early childhood, everyone, teen, mature, and adults only) and requiring the Web sites to post the rating to better inform children and parents about the content of the Web sites before they observe the content.

Limitations and Future Research

This study has several noted limitations. The first concern relates to sampling issues. First, the sample was relatively more upscale in terms of reported family income and parent education level than reflected in the sample school's general student population. Second, the sample size of 178 was relatively small and was not a national sample. Third, the sample was limited to children ages 11 to 16. Therefore, it would be valuable to replicate the present study with a larger and more representative national sample including younger, more vulnerable children. Another concern is that the study employed self-reported measurement of children's Internet exposure without any actual observation of the children's behavior. Even though this study tried to address social desirability effects by assuring the anonymity of participants and employing accidental exposure, as well as intentional exposure, there is still a chance that social desirability may have factored into the responses. Hence, it would be fruitful to conduct an experiment that directly measures actual children's Internet exposure (e.g., log file analysis, surveillance software, etc.) by controlling social desirability effects. Similarly, for the measure of parents' control, it might be more valid to assess actual behavioral control, instead of perceived control, for example, how often parents intervene, monitor, filter, and/or supervise. In addition, the list of inappropriate Internet content could have been more exhaustive; for example, hate Web sites were not included. Hence, it would be useful to include a more exhaustive list of inappropriate content for future research. Last, Family communications patterns inventory could be another important indicator of parents' perceived control of their children's use of the Internet. Therefore, the relationship would be worthwhile for future study.

In conclusion, this study has provided a theoretical framework for understanding the role of family environment on children's negative Internet exposure, such as family cohesion, shared Web activity, and parents' perceived control. The proposed model is an initial step in understanding the relationship between family context and children's exposure to negative Internet content. Theoretical approaches to understanding children's Internet exposure have rarely been conducted in previous literature, and this study was undertaken to guide future empirical research and theoretical work. For example, the focus was on the family environment from the parents' perspective. It would be worthwhile to examine children's perspectives of family context, such as the role of children's Internet skill, children's perceived intimacy with their parents, children's perceived shared Web activities with their parents, and children's perceived control over Internet content. Second, this study only examined the role of family environment on children's negative Internet exposure. It should be noted that other social contexts might also be crucial in children's media usage. For example, children interact with other peer students outside family boundaries in school or other places. Children's exposure to negative content may be influenced by their interactions with other peer children. In addition, education in school on quality Internet usage may also significantly reduce children's negative Internet exposure. Therefore, as future research, it would be fruitful to examine the effects of peer interaction and school education on children's exposure to negative Internet content.

POSTSCRIPT

Is the Internet a Safe Place for Teens to Explore?

Chang-Hoan Cho and Hongsik John Cheon found that children are exposed to more negative Internet content such as pornography, gambling, violence, hate speech, and sexual solicitation than parents realized. Factors such as family cohesion and parents who spend time online with their children reduced the amount of negative Internet content children experienced. Michele Fleming and Debra Rickwood contend that teens are safe on the Internet. They state that studies, especially ones done in America, show that most teens are taking appropriate precautions when meeting online friends and are aware of the dangers of online predators. They contend that with the proper education, teens can be safe on the Internet.

Although both selections disagree on the degree to which the Internet is safe for teens, both promote the idea that children must be taught skills of navigating the Internet safely. Parents teach their children a variety of critical life skills such as how to drive, how to manage money, and how to understand their sexuality. The reality of the situation is that now parents have another life skill to teach: how to navigate and stay safe on the Internet.

Rules of Internet safety include never giving personal information (such as filling out questionnaires sent to you), knowing everyone personally who you are communicating with, and not downloading anything unless parents say it's OK. In addition, children are never to meet anyone they don't already know, never to post embarrassing pictures, or never to share passwords with anyone. Internet safety is not only a concern in the United States, but is a worldwide concern. As an example, The New Zealand Model for Internet (ICT) Safety Education can be found at www.netsafe.org.nz. Most important is to teach children how to evaluate an online source and to become media savvy. Does the Web site have reliable information? Is it secure? Does it do what it says it does? Parents can never protect children from every danger, including dangers on the Internet, but they can help arm their children with the necessary tools and skills to protect themselves.

Protecting children from Internet dangers is no different than protecting them from all the other dangers of childhood and adolescence such as underage drinking, drugs, and premature sexual relationships. In order to protect children, parents must first educate their children, and then spend a lot of time listening to them and accepting them for who they are. The development of a sincere and trusting relationship between parent and child is one of the most important protective factors parents can create.

Suggested Readings

Catney, N. P. (2003). Cyberproofed? How to promote Internet safety for children. *Police Chief, 70*, 428–434.

Eastin, Matthew S., Yang, Mong-Shan, & Nathanson, Amy I. (June 2006). Children of the net: An empirical exploration into the evaluation of Internet content. *Journal of Broadcasting & Electronic Media, 50*(2), 211–230.

Jackson, Linda A., Von Eye, Alexander, Biocca, Frank, Barbatsis, Gretchen, Zhao, Yong, & Fitzgerald, Hiram E. (2005). How low income children use the Internet at home. *Journal of Interactive Learning Research, 259*(14).

Radford, Benjamin. (2006). Predator panic: A closer look. *Skeptical Inquirer, 20*(3).

Whitehead, Barbara Dafoe. (2005). Online porn: How do we keep it from our kids? *Commonweal 6*(1).

Contributors to This Volume

EDITORS

DIANA S. DELCAMPO is the child development and family life specialist with the New Mexico Cooperative Extension Service at New Mexico State University in Las Cruces, New Mexico, and holds the rank of professor. She is a member of the National Council on Family Relations and the National Extension Family Life Specialists' Association. She received a BS from Concord College in West Virginia, an MS from Virginia Polytechnic Institute and State University, and a PhD in curriculum and instruction from the University of Michigan. She presently develops educational programs in child and family development, supervises grant projects, and coordinates projects with other state agencies in New Mexico. She has published educational guides, chapters in several books, symposium proceedings, and articles in various journals.

ROBERT L. DELCAMPO is a professor of family science at New Mexico State University in Las Cruces, New Mexico. He is a licensed marriage and family therapist, clinical member, and approved supervisor of the American Association for Marriage and Family Therapy. He also holds memberships in the International Family Therapy Association and the National Council on Family Relations, and he is a former president of the New Mexico Association for Marriage and Family Therapy. He received a BS from the State University of New York, an MS from Virginia Polytechnic Institute and State University, and a PhD in family relations and child development from Florida State University. His work has appeared in such journals as *Family Relations* and *Contemporary Family Therapy*.

AUTHORS

ADVOCATES FOR YOUTH is an organization in Washington, D.C., that helps youths make informed and responsible decisions about their reproductive and sexual health.

ELIZABETH BARTHOLET is the Morris Wasserstein Public Interest Professor of Law and faculty director of the Child Advocacy Program at the Harvard Law School.

DIANA BAUMRIND is a researcher at the Institute of Human Development, University of California at Berkley and is known nationally for her publications and research on parenting and spanking.

RACHEL L. BERGERON is an assistant clinical professor of psychiatry at Yale University, School of Medicine.

SANDRA BLAKESLEE is a science correspondent for *The New York Times*.

T. BERRY BRAZELTON is founder of the Child Development Unit at Children's Hospital Boston and has been a practicing pediatrician for 45 years. He has authored many books on children and families.

JEANNE BROOKS-GUNN is professor of child development and education at Teacher's College, Columbia University, and the author of numerous publications. Her specialty is policy-oriented research focusing on family and community influences on child and youth development.

PAUL CAMERON is the publisher of the Family Research Report, Colorado Springs, Colorado, which examines data on families, sexual social policy, drug addiction, and homosexuality.

MARK A. CARROZZA is the director of the Institute of Health Policy and Health Services Research at the University of Cincinnati. The Institute addresses local, state, and national health care issues from an interdisciplinary perspective.

CENTER FOR SCIENCE IN THE PUBLIC INTEREST is a consumer advocacy organization that conducts research in order to represent citizens' interests and provides information to consumers about health.

HONGSIK JOHN CHEON is an assistant professor in the department of marketing and finance, College of Business, at Frostburg State University. His research interests include interactive marketing, international marketing, and consumer information processing.

CHANG-HOAN CHO is an assistant professor of advertising, College of Journalism and Communications, University of Florida. His research interests include Internet advertising, new media technology, product placement, interactive television, multicultural advertising, and international advertising.

STEPHANIE COONTZ is cochair of the Council on Contemporary Families and teaches history and family studies at Evergreen State College in Olympia, Washington. She has written several books, including *The Way We Never Were: American Families and the Nostalgia Trap* (Basic Books, 1992).

PHILIP A. COWAN is a researcher at the Institute of Human Development, University of California at Berkley.

FRANCIS T. CULLEN is the Distinguished Research Professor of Criminal Justice at the University of Cincinnati and has interests in criminology and white collar crime. He has written four books in the area of crime and theory.

CYNTHIA DAILARD was a senior public policy associate for the Alan Guttmacher Institute, a nonprofit research and advocacy group on women's sexual and reproductive health issues. She wrote numerous articles and spoke prolifically on matters such as family planning and adolescent sexual behavior. She passed away on December 24, 2006, at the age of 38.

W. J. DOHERTY is both a professor and marriage and family therapy director at the University of Minnesota in St. Paul, Minnesota.

KYLA DUNN is a former biotech researcher and is now a reporter for PBS and CBS.

MARTHA F. ERICKSON is director of the University of Minnesota's Children, Youth and Family Consortium. She developed the Steps Toward Effective, Enjoyable Parenting (STEEP) and is the author of numerous journal articles and book chapters as well as a weekly parenting column.

LEONARD D. ERON is a researcher for the Research Center for Group Dynamics, Institute for Social Research at the University of Michigan.

MICHELE FLEMING is a lecturer in the Center for Applied Psychology at the University of Canberra, Australia. Her current research focuses on the effects of new media, such as video games and the Internet, on children's well-being.

NANCY FOLBRE is cochair of the National Network on the Family and the Economy and is professor of economics at the University of Massachusetts. Her interests include the interface between economics and feminist theory. She has written numerous books and papers.

JIB FOWLES is a professor of communication at the University of Houston–Clear Lake. He is the author of *The Case for Television Violence* (Sage Publications, 1999).

ELIZABETH THOMPSON GERSHOFF is a researcher with the National Center for Children in Poverty, Columbia University, Mailman School of Public Health.

STANLEY I. GREENSPAN is clinical professor of psychiatry and pediatrics at George Washington University Medical School.

EZRA E. H. GRIFFITH is deputy chair of clinical affairs and a professor of psychiatry and African American Studies at Yale University, School of Medicine.

WEN-JUI HAN is assistant professor of social work at the Columbia University School of Social Work. Her professional interests include effects of maternal employment and impact of welfare reform.

THE HENRY J. KAISER FAMILY FOUNDATION is a nonprofit, private operating foundation that focuses on providing unbiased information on major health care issues.

E. MAVIS HETHERINGTON is professor emeritus in the department of psychology at the University of Virginia.

WADE F. HORN is assistant secretary for children and families in the department of health and human services. He has been a clinical psychologist, president of the National Fatherhood Initiative, and a columnist for the *Washington Times*.

L. ROWELL HUESMANN is a researcher for the Research Center for Group Dynamics, Institute for Social Research at the University of Michigan.

JOHN KELLY is a writer in New York and co-author of numerous books on relationships.

LISA KOLB is a public information specialist for the Missouri Department of Social Services in Jefferson City, Missouri.

EDWARD F. KOUNESKI is currently completing his doctoral dissertation in family social science, with a specialization in marriage and family therapy, at the University of Minnesota.

STEPHEN KRASHEN is currently a professor of education at the University of Southern California and is the author of more than 250 articles and books in the fields of bilingual education, neurolinguistics, second language acquisition, and literacy.

LAWRENCE A. KURDEK is a psychologist at Wright State University in Dayton, Ohio.

ROBERT E. LARZELERE is a researcher with the department of psychology's Munroe-Myer Institute, Nebraska Medical Center in Omaha, Nebraska.

JULIA LEWIS is a professor of psychology at San Francisco State University, director of the Psychology Clinic, and coordinator of the Clinical Psychology Program.

SHANNAN MARTIN is a research assistant in welfare policy at the Heritage Foundation.

LORI A. McGRAW is the 4-H program coordinator for the Oregon State University Extension Service. Her responsibilities include involvement in the school-age child care programs and the 4-H Adventures Program.

JESSICA MOISE-TITUS is a researcher for the Research Center for Group Dynamics, Institute for Social Research at the University of Michigan.

NATIONAL ADOPTION INFORMATION CLEARINGHOUSE provides accurate information related to adoption and is a federal service of the Children's Bureau, Administration for Children Youth and Families, U.S. Department of Health and Human Services.

MELISSA G. PARDUE is a former policy analyst for the Heritage Foundation.

GREG PARKS is an intern program specialist in the Research and Program Development Division at the Office of Juvenile Justice and Delinquency Prevention, which is part of the United States Department of Justice.

CHERYL-LYNN PODOLSKI is a researcher for the Research Center for Group Dynamics, Institute for Social Research at the University of Michigan.

DAVID POPENOE is a professor of sociology and an associate dean for the social sciences at Rutgers–The State University in New Brunswick, New Jersey. He is the author of *Disturbing the Nest* (Aldine de Gruyter, 1988).

ROSALIE PEDALINO PORTER of Amherst, Massachusetts is an advisor to school districts across the United States on the education of immigrant children.

RONI RABIN is a columnist for *The New York Times* who writes extensively on women's health issues.

ROBERT RECTOR is a senior research fellow for the Heritage Foundation. He is an authority on poverty, marriage, and the U.S. welfare system.

DEBRA RICKWOOD is an associate professor in psychology at the University of Canberra, Australia. Her research interests include adolescent help-seeking behavior and the use of new media with regard to enhancing the well-being of young people in Australia.

DIANE SCHETKY is a forensic child and adolescent psychiatrist and clinical professor of psychiatry at the Maine Medical Center.

SEXUALITY INFORMATION AND EDUCATION COUNCIL OF THE UNITED STATES (SIECUS) is a national nonprofit organization in New York that promotes comprehensive education about sexuality and advocates individuals' rights to make responsible choices about sexual behavior.

THOMAS M. VANDER VEN is assistant professor in the department of sociology and anthropology at Ohio University in Athens, Ohio. His areas of specialization are crime and delinquency as well as linkages between work, family, and crime.

JANE WALDFOGEL is associate professor of social work and public affairs at Columbia School of Social Work. Her professional interests include social policy impact on child and family well-being as well as child protective services and child welfare policy.

ALEXIS J. WALKER is both a professor of human development and family sciences and director of the gerontology program at Oregon State University.

JUDITH WALLERSTEIN is the founder of the Judith Wallerstein Center for the Family in Transition. She is a senior lecturer emerita in the School of Social Welfare at the University of California at Berkeley.

ROBERT A. WEINBERG is a member of the Whitehead Institute for Biomedical Research and is a biology professor at MIT.

MARY-LOU WEISMAN is a freelance writer who has written about children, ethics, and social issues for the *New York Times* and *The New Republic.*

JOHN PAUL WRIGHT is an instructor in the division of criminal justice at the University of Cincinnati.